ACTS OF THE HEART

Also by Robert Sardello from Lindisfarne Books

Facing the World with Soul: The Reimagination of Modern Life

Love and the World: A Guide to Conscious Soul Practice

Acts
of the
Heart

Culture-Building • Soul-Researching

Introductions, Forewords, and Prefaces

Robert Sardello

With Contributions by
Christopher Bamford • John Lee • Lee Nichol
• Scott Scribner • Cheryl Sanders-Sardello •
Joanne Stroud • Gail Thomas

Lindisfarne Books | 2011

2011

Lindisfarne Books

An imprint of Anthroposophic Press/SteinerBooks

610 Main St., Great Barrington, MA

www.steinerbooks.org

Cover & book design: William Jens Jensen
Cover symbol from *Geheime Figuren der Rosenkreuzer aus
dem 16ten und 17ten Jahrhundert* (1785)

LIBRARY OF CONGRESS CATALOGING-IN-PUBLICATION DATA

Acts of the heart : culture-building, soul-researching / introductions by
Robert Sardello ; with contributions by Christopher Bamford ... [et al.].
   p. cm.
ISBN 978-1-58420-112-0
1. Anthroposophy. 2. Spirituality. 3. Psychology, Religious. I.
Sardello, Robert J., 1942– II. Bamford, Christopher, 1943–
BP595.A36 2011
204—dc23

                                                          2011039190

Print: 978-1-58420-112-0

eBook: 978-1-58420-113-7

CONTENTS

ACKNOWLEDGMENTS

This book was made possible by contributions from a few of the dearest friends of The School of Spiritual Psychology, including: Gayle Copeland, Robert and Louise Hill, Joanne Stroud, Gail Thomas, Scott Scribner, and Gene Copeland.

Valuable donations were also made by: Terry Blakely, Elizabeth Long, Tim and Judelon LaSalle.

We also received invaluable support from The Guild of Sacred Service, Denver, Colorado: namely, from David Bovard, Mary Jane McCormick, John Lee, Loretta Harvey, and Shirley Sullivan.

We also want to thank John Lee, Scott Scribner, Eva Casey and Lee Nichol, Tim and Judelon La Salle, and Gail Thomas and Joanne Stroud for holding and helping with the vision of creating this book. Scott and John both approached me separately, years apart, with the same idea. It's taken longer than we thought, Scott, but once it starting coming together, it all fell into place with amazing determination. Thank you, John, for re-lighting this project and really getting it moving! And, of course, it would not have come together without the magical capacity of the wonderful and wondrous Christopher Bamford. Thank you, dear one, most of all, for taking an idea and weaving a mantle of grace out of friendship.

With Love beyond Knowing,
Cheryl L. Sanders-Sardello

This book is for Robert, whose thoughts are all live things.

FOREWORD I

Gail Thomas

How is it that we can open a book and enter a realm yet unfamiliar to us? What guides us, leads us forward? What initiates the trust? For decades now, Robert Sardello has introduced us to unknown territory, virgin terrain, forbidden fruits.

Through his introductions, we open the door to heretofore unimaginable experiences. He shocks us, cajoles us, teases us, and lovingly beckons to us, until we say to ourselves, "We can go in now; the door is open."

I have worked with Robert Sardello for forty years: at the University of Dallas when he was Chairman of the Psychology Department and then Chair of the Institute of Philosophic Studies and Graduate Dean; and when we, together with Louise and Don Cowan, Joanne Stroud, and James Hillman, started the Dallas Institute of Humanities and Culture in 1980.

While Chair of the Psychology Department at the University of Dallas, Robert initiated a journal called *Dragonflies*. He introduced the journal this way:

> The work of this journal is imagination: the response of psychological imagination to experience....
> The breakdown of the world is the world seeking our attention; it is an action of love on the part of the world, which responds only to a similar action of love.

It was during this period that Robert wrote a small monograph, *Educating with Soul*, published by the University of Dallas Center for Civic Leadership that I was directing. In that monograph, he asks:

Who is making reading happen through us? If it is not I who reads, then who is animating the letters and words of a page, bringing them out of inert inky blackness where they can do the work of transformation? What is the myth of reading?

He describes reading as an action of love and suggests it is Eros, the winged god of Love, whose fiery passion ignites a flame in our hearts and compels us to unknown territory. There is a drama enacted between reader and text.

> Greek imagination pictured words as having wings, which enabled them to fly between the mouths of speakers.... Erotic speech hovers between psyche and life, transforming psyche into life and life into psyche. Eros carries imagination into life and life into imagination.... For Socrates, true teaching was possible only through the daimon of Eros.... In Hesiod's Theogony, Chaos is first, then came Eros. Then the rest of creation follows. Eros does not mean. He is the genesis of meaning, invisibly penetrating everything, provoking it into meaning—a book that feels important while we cannot say exactly what it means.

"Winged Words," set into motion by the fiery passion of Eros, the love god, entice us in.

At the Dallas Institute, Robert and I were, in the beginning, co-directors. The language in the brochures and the Newsletters were, for the most part, his words, and it was a most unusual language for Dallas ears. At the time we started the Institute, Dallas, a city that experiences boom and bust cycles seemingly every decade, was beginning in the 80's a cycle that was every developer's dream. Building cranes laced the Dallas skyline. Older buildings, even historic ones, were meeting the wrecking ball, some on Sunday morning while the community was in church. Dallas was at this time like a pioneer town, building as fast as it could to catch up with dreams as vast as the sky.

It seems now to have been a giant act of hubris to have initiated an institute in the very heart of this bustling mercantile town. My sense is that Robert's words spread out through the wings of Eros, and opened hearts to receive what we had to offer. These words appear as images in the book we coedited, *Stirrings of Culture*, and in many of the numerous books published by the Dallas Institute Press, paving the way for our work to imagine, to grasp, and to aspire to make a better culture and a good city.

Gail Thomas, Dallas 2011

FOREWORD 2

Joanne Stroud

To bear witness to the gifts that Robert Sardello has given to all who know him and his writings is quite a challenge. First, and foremost, his introduction of so many truths about the wisdom of the heart in combination with the life of the spirit must top the list.

Next, there is Robert's skill as an editor. While acting as codirector of the Dallas Institute of Humanities and Culture, his selections in compiling the Newsletter established our reputation as an institute of serious thought.

Finally, personally, and most totally life-reorienting for me was his introducing me (while I was in graduate school at the University of Dallas) to the twentieth-century French philosopher, Gaston Bachelard. What a difference this has made in the last thirty years! My academic life was greatly enlarged (if at times maddeningly complicated) with the task of translating Bachelard's books on the imagination of matter.

For his broad but deep understanding of essential values, for his originality in giving new slant to eternal verities, no amount of thanks to Robert fully suffices.

Joanne H. Stroud
Director of Publications
Dallas Institute of Humanities and Culture
2011

FOREWORD 3

John Lee

The Introductions collected in this volume are not the usual dry out-lines of some stranger's books. What you will discover is the soul of those books. More important, you will discover the imagination and vision of Robert Sardello. I purchase books simply because Sardello has written the Introduction. The pieces assembled for this book are a message of hope for the future of the world. This hope (not merely speculations on trends or revisions of ancient texts) is the outcome of an original research and practice of spiritual psychology (which will be revealed as you read ahead). The hope emerges through developing the inner capacity of an awakened heart.

If your heart and spirit long for a way to participate in the building of the Earth's future, you will find a guiding partner in the writings of this visionary man. In rereading this material, (much to my delight) I found the experience the highlight of my year. This is the one time you will not want to skip the Introductions!

John A. Lee, D.Min.
The Guild for Sacred Studies
Denver, Colorado

INTRODUCTION I

Christopher Bamford

It seems appropriate to begin by welcoming you, the readers, to this collection of introductions by Robert Sardello. Welcome! I say, "Welcome," because an introduction is itself an act of welcome, a "leading in" of one person to another, one soul to another; an infolding of souls, a world into a world. A soul is folded into another in an intimate deed of openness and generosity of heart. A true introduction is thus always an expression or communication of heart knowing—welcoming another into the sphere of what one loves. It is a gesture of friendship and of community; it builds a common culture. In that sense, it is "mediating." It "mediates" because we are two; and "I" introduce "you" to a "third," who is a friend of mine. I do so in the hope (and trust) that you, too, will become friends, and that out of the vessel formed by your new friendship something new will enter the world. Or, better put, I myself am the third and I know and love both of you individually and separately; and I introduce you to each other because I feel that you have much to offer one another, so that between you something can grow that is larger than all of us, a new cultural reality.

In these Introductions, Robert Sardello introduces us to many people, whom we may not otherwise have met, and introduces us to many ways of being and thinking, which we didn't know before. In fact, the range of those whom we meet in these pages is staggering. At the same time, there is a sweet harmony and ever-unfolding deepening of a single theme. Miraculously, it pervades and shapes the entire sequence of those whom he presents—even though he often wrote in response to a request, and not initially on his own initiative. This is so, because—and this is why I used the word *generosity*—in each instance, he writes out of what he has made a deep friendship with, and out of that friendship he has received and participated in a communion of ideas, which he communicates. He is able to do this because he has entered into the aspiration of whoever he is introducing at the deepest level, making their insights his own, and deepening them in his own way, so that reading them is like overhearing a conversation between two friends who know each other so well that, as their conversation unfolds, they no longer know who says what.

An introduction, then, bespeaks not only a complex phenomenon but also a particular soul capacity. In fact, for Robert, "soul capacities" are of the essence of what he calls "spiritual Psychology." Together with the worlds and beings to which they correspond, it is such capacities that make us human and enable us to fulfill our human tasks.

If our culture were different—if we recognized and gave a place of honor to our deepest thinkers, to those dedicated souls who out of their inner freedom, soul capacities, and creativity were able to articulate a new vision of humanity for us—then Robert Sardello might well be called a "national treasure" or, from anther point of view, what some spiritual traditions call a "hidden pillar." Certainly, Robert is an "American" presence—national in that sense. He is also a person who has followed his psychological-spiritual vocation unerringly, developing himself in manifold ways, never for himself or for any reward, material or spiritual, that he might gain, but always in service, that is, for its own sake and for the sake of the world that he loves.

This is to say that, the state of culture being what it is, he is still known largely only to a small circle of friends, students, and coworkers—a group comprised of readers of his books and of those who have studied with him in the School of Spiritual Psychology and in the many seminars he has conducted almost continuously over the last thirty years; and, equally importantly, of those archetypal psychologists, Jungians, and Anthroposophists, who have worked with him professionally and collegially over the same period. For all these, Robert is not just (or even primarily perhaps) a writer; he is also an example and a living source of true ideas, that is, *a teacher*—not in the sense of one who dispenses information, but rather in the exemplary Socratic style of a "midwife of souls." For many of these, he is a "spiritual friend" or *anamcara*. For what, as a friend, Robert teaches—which is also what he writes—is *a way or path of soul/spiritual research*, one that simultaneously and non-dualistically transforms both the worlds we live in and us.

It is this "non-duality" that makes what Robert does difficult to describe. At once "psychological-spiritual" and "cosmological," it is both "inner" and "outer," "imaginal" and "real." Moreover, it is so in a way such that, without our falling into mind-only idealism, we experience the "outer" as only the other face of the only reality, known also as "inner." What this means each person must discover as an individual. Robert himself, of course, is the primary source for this; working with him is perhaps the most direct way to discovering what he is about. Then, second, there are his books—which can be meditated, read, and reread and will continue to be so long after he is gone. Third, there are his "introductions."

Reading these Introductions is an astonishing experience. Within their short, individual compasses, they allow us to participate in Robert's own journey—to catch, as it were, the bird in flight and fly with it. That is, they map his journey, at least, that portion of it that began to unfold as his destiny began to crystallize.

Biographically, at least, that journey began on the eastern side of the Sangre de Christo Mountains, in high desert country in the small town of Trinidad, Colorado. Three seeds, we might say, at once psychological and religious-spiritual-mystical, were planted there—seeds that still continue to germinate and bear fruit—love of rocks and minerals (geology), born of his natal landscape; a love of solitude, silence, and interiority (the permission to develop soul capacities, born of a naturally introverted nature and a sense of otherness, of difference); and a love of, and gift for, thinking in all its senses—clear thinking, intuitive thinking, as well as thinking as thanking in Heidegger's sense—probably the fruit of an unusually excellent, even intellectually radical, Catholic education. Graduating High School, leaving Trinidad, Robert moved north to Denver, to Regis College, where for a year, until a summer job in the field persuaded him otherwise, he studied geology. His love of rocks and the Earth clearly went deep, but not in the direction of either academic or corporate geology—in fact, quite the opposite. Transferring after a year to St. Mary's University in San Antonio, Texas, he switched to psychology, and, graduating from there, moved on to St. Louis University in Saint Louis on a NASA scholarship, for graduate school and a doctorate.

For his first job, destiny took him to Duquesne University in Pittsburgh, Pennsylvania, then as now one of the centers of phenomenology and phenomenological research in the United States. Already, we may imagine, dissatisfied with the materialism and reductionism of existing approaches to psychology, and having a deep and abiding affinity for philosophy, Duquesne provided him with a perfect first site to raise the deepest issues—philosophical, epistemological, and ontological—of his chosen field. Serious study of philosophers like Husserl, Heidegger, and Merleau-Ponty as well as phenomenological psychologists like J. H. Van der Berg began the process of rethinking the whole nature of the psyche. It turned it toward the world, thereby showing the poverty and the essentially egotistic blinkers of individualist psychology. Phenomenology did this by opening the attention—the "empty" attention—to the phenomena of *experience*. Sticking close to experience, phenomenology sought to allow the gifts of experience as mediated by the mind and senses to unfold as naturally as possible according to intertwining of their and our own natures. Thereby the hard and fast boundaries between subject and object, us and the world, began to dissolve; the world, formerly opaque, became transparent; and, in the place of objects, the possibility of something like what Merleau-Ponty called "the flesh of the world," the chiasmic infolding of the world and experience, arose. Surrounded by this promise of phenomenology, Robert cannot have remained unaffected. Phenomenology had confirmed what he must already have understood—that psychology was a path of *soul research*, an experiential research of experience. Soon, he was ready for the next turn of destiny.

This came in 1970 when Dr. Donald Cowan, President of the University of Dallas, visiting Duquesne, met Robert and subsequently invited him to the University of Dallas to create the Department of Psychology.

Within a year, Robert had discovered the work of James Hillman and was deeply impressed by it. A new vision began to form, and not just theoretically; Robert and the Department of Psychology invited Hillman to Dallas. He came first in 1974 and again the following year with Pat Berry. During that visit, Robert Sardello, Gail Thomas, Joanne Stroud, James Hillman, and Pat Berry planned the First International Archetypal Psychology Conference, which took place in Dallas during January 1976. Soon thereafter, James Hillman was invited to join the Psychology Department—an invitation he accepted, lured by the possibility of working with Robert, despite the other "good" offers he had received. In this way, not just a friendship, but also a cultural movement was born and lives were set on a course of change.

Over the next four years, academic activity continued as this group increasingly turned away from the ivory towers of the university toward the city and the world—away from the solitary atomized individual soul toward its immersion in and relation to the soul of the world (though that language was not yet in full play.) In 1976, the university formed the Center for Civic Leadership, with Gail Thomas as its Director. The center drew students from active civic institutions throughout the city. Robert, in addition to heading the psychology department, helped in the planning and direction. Meanwhile, his own passion for breaking through to a new vision of psychology continued to motivate his studies, and his actions. Together, they began to bring such transformational thinkers as Mortimer Adler, Hans Georg Gadamer, and Marshall McLuhan to the University. Amid this intellectual ferment, in 1978, Robert initiated *Dragonflies*, a journal dedicated to soul and imagination—"the response of psychological imagination to experience"—in all its forms. That same year, he organized a conference with Raphael Lopez-Pedraza, the great Cuban-Venezuelan Jungian analyst, mythically linked with James Hillman in the formation of Archetypal Psychology. Here it should be noted that, while supporting and recognizing the "archetypalists" as fellow laborers in the vineyards of reimagining psychology, and valuing their sticking to the image phenomenologically, thereby overcoming "representation," as well as their turn toward the "soul of the world," Robert himself was never an archetypalist in the strict sense. He was seeking something else.

The great opportunity to look differently and elsewhere came in 1980, when, after an ugly break with the University—over the rejection of the great phenomenological psychologist J. H. van der Berg, invited to teach by the Psychology Department and turned down in the last minute by the University, Robert, Gail Thomas, Joanne Stroud, James Hillman, as well as Donald Cowan (president of the university) and Louise Cowan (head of The Institute of Philosophic Studies) and others walked away from the University to form the Dallas Institute for Humanities and Culture. It was an epochal moment.

At first, the Institute was seen—and thought of itself—as a "think tank," but it soon became clear that such a description was inappropriate and misleading. What the Dallas Institute sought to become was more like a "school of thought"—that is, the first seed of a movement dedicated to *the return of soul to the world*. In this sense, it saw itself more like the Florentine Academy under Marsilio Ficino or the early German Romantics gathered around Novalis and the Schlegel brothers:

> In reality, there never was a group quite like ours: we were a group of thinkers from different disciplines who shared a "piety" toward culture, considered certain aspects of it "sacred"—amazing that psychologists, a literary person, and a scientist could share views on the imagination and its redemptive power for a flagging culture. We were going back to the Greeks and finding

in their wholeness of thought a remedy for our modern-day shal-
lowness. (Louise Cowan)

From the very first, we were contrarian. We did not fall in with
current thinking. We wanted to be "on the edge of thought" and
pledged to "keep our bags packed" and to "pitch a tent for our conversations, in case we were asked to leave town." In fact, it seems
a miracle now that we were not only allowed to carry on, but were
embraced in our endeavors. Our conversations seemed courageous,
bold, and risky. And we loved it that way. Others supported this
bold enterprise, and we were launched. (Gail Thomas)

Robert remained at the Dallas Institute for about ten years and
would continue to give classes, courses, and seminars there for another
ten years, until 2000. During his time there, amid great excitement and
intellectual ferment, he finally enjoyed the freedom of being able to walk
his own path—to lay down his own path in walking it. When he left, he
had realized his true vocation; he was ready to develop—unfold, create,
research, deepen what he would later call "spiritual psychology."

Fundamental to this enterprise—transforming and radically refram-
ing all that he had already learned and digested of phenomenology,
Archetypal Psychology, and much else—was his discovery and profound
study of Rudolf Steiner, Anthroposophy, and related authors.

To understand Steiner's impact on the development of spiritual psychology two things need to be born in mind. Both the phenomenological
and the archetypal approaches had opened a profound and revolution-
ary new way of understanding "soul," but both had stopped just short
of "spirit," and were fearful of taking the next risky step—to encounter actual "spirit realities." Steiner's "spiritual science" made such a
step possible. It was risky only in the positive sense of allowing one to
step right out of the existing paradigm into the formation of a new one.
Robert's path to accomplishing such a move was made possible by the
genial insight of realizing that spiritual science could be read *spiritually* and *psychologically;* that what Rudolf Steiner had researched and
communicated could be read and practiced as a new kind of psychology,

one that opens naturally, by virtue of the meditative path it takes, to spiritual realities of the soul. Thus, discovering Steiner made clear for Robert, in a new way, where he had been heading all along. It articulated what, in fact, was a life mission from the start. In practice, it meant forging out of the understanding and practice of Steiner's insights and methods (meditative exercises), melded together with phenomenological and archetypal approaches, a new path of psyche-oriented psychological-spiritual practice and path of research.

But besides this broadened path of practice and research, encountering Steiner, Anthroposophy and the related fields and authors to which they led made possible something else; it allowed Robert to develop what we might call his inner or esoteric Christian side. From a certain point of view, Anthroposophy is "esoteric Christianity." This is a Christianity that has nothing to do with religion (with either a large or a small "r") but rather one that seeks to research and understand the breadth, depth, and height of the divine, cosmic, human, and earthly soul/spiritual meaning of "The Mystery of Golgotha," that is, the Incarnation. Robert, born into Catholicism, educated entirely in Catholic Schools, and for many years a practicing Catholic, then as now alienated from and deeply disappointed by the institutional Church, always remained Christian in his soul. He must have longed for an appropriate way to fulfill that part of himself; to create a truly "Christian" psychology. Here, too, Anthroposophy, understood from the logos of the psyche, provided an opening he was able to take.

The Dallas Institute years gave Robert the freedom to explore and test all these new approaches to psychology. It gave him friends and colleagues who, though they could not follow him and perhaps did not wholly understand where he was heading, nevertheless respected him deeply, trusted him, and honored his freedom. Thus, as he pursued his path, always pushing forward, he was able continuously to expand *the boundaries and capacities of the soul*—its frameworks, contexts, and milieus—exploring, as he did so, the "soul" of culture, of things, of the "world," and even beyond that into other and cosmic soul/spiritual realities.

I first met Robert while he was still in Dallas. It was the late 1980s. At the time, living in Western Massachusetts as I still do, I was working with Thomas Moore, who had recently left Dallas, where he had taught at SMU and been a Fellow of the Dallas Institute. Arriving in the Berkshires, he had opened a branch of what he and some friends had founded, called "The Institute for the Study of Imagination." I joined in this venture. We held seminars and sponsored speakers. We ourselves spoke and had visits by luminaries like James Hillman, Kathleen Raine, and others. Thus, one rainy, late autumn weekend (as I recall it) Robert Sardello, too, visited us. He came with his partner, Cheryl, now Cheryl Sanders-Sardello. She had met Robert in Texas, first at the University of Dallas as a more-or-less anonymous student, then, much later, during the Institute years. Already a long-time Anthroposophist, she had been working intensely with him now for a number of years on spiritual psychology and the task of reading Steiner from the perspective of the soul. That evening, Robert spoke on "Sophia." Next morning, we met for breakfast. It was a meeting of minds and hearts—of intuitions and aspirations. A friendship was formed, a first fruit of which was Robert's first book, *Facing the World with Soul* (Lindisfarne Press, 1992). By then, Robert had already left Dallas, and, after working for a short while as a faculty member with Therese Schroeder-Sheker at the Chalice of Repose School of Music-Thanatology at St. Patrick's Hospital in Missoula, Montana, had gone on to establish The School of Spiritual Psychology with Cheryl, located initially in Boulder, Colorado. The school later moved to Great Barrington, Massachusetts, and by 1999 to North Carolina.

The rest in a sense is history. The School unfolded, developed, and deepened, as Robert (and Cheryl) did. At first based in Great Barrington, Massachusetts, it moved after a time to Greensboro, North Carolina, and finally to a true home and "campus" in Benson, North Carolina. During the early years, Robert and Cheryl travelled ceaselessly crisscrossing the continent, giving seminars and workshops in which they were able to test their ongoing research. This history, besides being carried in their own ways by those who worked with him, is inscribed in Robert's subsequent books (*Love and the Soul; Freeing the Soul from Fear; The Power of Soul: Living the Twelve Virtues; Silence; Steps on the Stone Path: Working with Crystals and Minerals as Spiritual Practice*) and the Introductions contained in this book.

The Introductions speak for themselves; they are introductions. While the books, we may say, map one aspect of the development of spiritual psychology *as such*, the Introductions show this same spiritual psychology *in relation to* some "other." We witness it embodied, and enacted—interacting with a particular theme, topic, text, or approach. Through this "other," each introduction presents, as it were, a new opportunity for research, for a new step forward.

Reading through this volume is to be taken on a journey. It is to walk with Robert Sardello on *his* journey as he pushes forward toward new realities. In a sense, each step is not so easy. The thinking often appears dense, the ideas often new and therefore disconcerting. But each individual piece, as the whole, is bathed in an aura—in a way, we may say it is bathed in soul; in love, in generosity, and friendship. Attending to these, we find the ideas and the new possibilities begin to make sense. We are moved to change our lives.

The experience of reading through this book reminds me of two poems by Rainer Maria Rilke. In the first—the famous "Archaic Torso of Apollo")—Rilke is in the Louvre Museum in Paris contemplating an ancient statue of Apollo, now headless. In his poem he writes of how in the presence of this headless gaze, the eyes as it were having passed into the torso, the whole ancient sculpture became all eyes and burst toward him like a star, so that there was no place that did not see him. The message "You must change your life." Reading these introductions can have a similar effect.

In the second poem, called "After the Storm," Rilke, invoking Jacob wrestling with the Angel, writes:

How small what we wrestle with is,
what wrestles with us, how immense,
were we to let ourselves be conquered,
the way things do, by a great storm—
we would become wide and nameless.

What we triumph over is the small,
And our success itself makes us petty,
The eternal and uncommon
will not be bent by us.

. . . .

Those whom the Angel, who
so often declined to fight, overcomes,
walk upright and justified
and great out of that hard hand
which, as if sculpting, nestled around them.
Winning does not tempt them.
Their growth is: to be the deeply defeated
By ever greater things.

   In these introductions Robert shows us how, if we are not afraid to
plunge into the mystery, to encounter the unknowable in silence, we may
be blessed (as well as wounded) as Jacob was.

Christopher Bamford
Mount Washington, Massachusetts
2011

INTRODUCTION 2

By Scott Scribner

When I elected some years ago to excise a personal myopia by laser vision correction, I did not anticipate an inner perspective to fill the "absence." Asked afterward, I would answer, "I am pleased with the results. I could hunt rodents from a great height. But I do not do that." Imagining a traffic light a mile distant as a raptor's viewpoint seems eccentric in a world of meetings, computers, and smart phones, perhaps because our hunting heritage has receded into "anomalous awareness." In this volume of introductions by Robert Sardello, we can experience anew—in the intellectual and spiritual realms—a lofty sense of powers and perspective. He soars on thoughts of great variety, beauty, and complexity, highlighting, gleaning, and synthesizing disparate domains into a fresh perspective. The results are always enlightening and frequently breathtaking.

I have known Robert for sixteen years since synchronicities joined our parallel paths through experimental psychology, Jung, phenomenology, and Rudolf Steiner. Setting out four decades ago on a quest for a "Christian" psychology, I travelled many paths attempting to meld "the within" of perception and "the without" of intuition in an open, dynamic understanding. Robert's work lays the foundation for such a framework, while always reminding us that it is not a system or a theory but a living thing. Robert asks questions and addresses them and then asks them again.

What is a *spiritual psychology* and by implication any religious psychology, including a Christian psychology? The term has been appropriated in contexts too numerous to describe here. Has the idea of a *spiritual* psychology already suffered the fate of psychology itself, a study of the soul already reduced to "common sense," fit to the Procrustean bed of a trivializing materialistic worldview, or in Robert's words, has it been "taken for granted"? Can psychology be resurrected in a living form, or must it pass away to be replaced by some other characterization?

The twentieth century's models of personality—whether stimulus-response (behaviorism), stimulus-organism-response (cognitive psychology), or even the paranormally clever organism-response-stimulus—are all too limiting. Human actions are not more or less deducible (let alone predictable) from any *picture* of the psyche; instead, our so-called behaviors flow directly (and in that sense simply) out of a much larger cosmos. Simultaneously we behave (talk, write) *about* our contextualized observations among ourselves and devise ways and means of measuring them, until the talk, the writing, and the data precipitate out, creating our fixed contexts. In such a realm, much of our exploration has stopped, for we do not see that the keys "back" into the psyche—and what lie at its root—are just beyond where we choose to live.

Within our analytical realms, so-called facts are not all that they seem. We must learn to distinguish between the *mere facts*—already embedded in and dependent on fixed contexts—and the *working facts* that do their work between and among our contexts, breaking them down and rebuilding. One such working fact is the *asymptotic time horizon*, which bridges the findings of neuropsychological research and theological concepts of the afterlife to illuminate a physical-spiritual prospect that is productive as well as imaginatively real. In the interstices of our knowledge, imaginal fires burn as potent as ever, but these energies remain feared terribly outside the economic and political realms that seek to exploit them. And among our misunderstood modern mysteries, the resulting manifestations (such as Marian apparitions or UFOs) become reified unless held in tension to allow new forms to emerge.

Then and now, Robert's generosity, collegiality, and humility inspire my continuing support for the work of his School of Spiritual Psychology. As a computer engineer by profession, I find greatest satisfaction in the counterweight that Robert's work provides against the modern world's *engineering fallacy*: once we create a "detailed enough" picture, or can model an observed process "well enough," or design a machine that operates "just like" our observations; then the cosmic order is conquered and reversed, and we think we understand all that we "need to know" to stumble one more step. Little wonder that we are where we are. In Robert's words, "soul life cannot be controlled" in our favor.

The Readings

You can read the collection in its chronological sequence, or explore it in your own thematic groups. I offer an arrangement based on one person's pilgrimage in the spiritual imagination.

Soul Practice Cycle (4 essays)

Introductions to the following works can be read as a *soul practice cycle* in the realm of ψυχη (*psyche*). The practices employed include creative writing, imaginative observation, food preparation, and others to center the "I" in the heart. In this way, we learn to bring conscious awareness into contact with incarnated (body) awareness—without fleeing the attendant anxiety into defenses.

> Introduction to Paul Matthews, *Sing Me the Creation* (1994)
> Foreword to Dennis Klocek, *Seeking Spirit Vision: Essays on Developing Imagination* (1998)
> Foreword to Anne-Marie Fryer Wiboltt, *Cooking for the Love of the World: Awakening Our Spirituality through Cooking* (2008)
> Foreword to Kristina Kaine, *I Connecting: The Soul's Quest* (2008)

Community Cycle (3 essays)

A second set of essays can be read as a *community cycle* in the realm of πολισ (*polis*). Practice meditative awareness within the artistic imagination of a thoughtful community. Step back from mind, step down into body, step through into soul, but soul *as* ourselves in the social world. The result is a new spirituality of society and geography.

> Rober Sardello, *Educating with Soul* (1979)
> Introduction to *Stirrings of Culture* (1986)

Introduction to Gail Thomas, *Healing Pandora: The Restoration of Hope and Abundance* (2009)

Steiner Cycle (5 essays)

Introductions to Rudolf Steiner's works and also Steiner commentators can be read as a *philosophical cycle* (realm φιλοσοφια). What is psychology; how is it "taken for granted"; and how can it once again—in Hippocrates' words—"do no harm"? This cycle illustrates how Sardello's spiritual psychology is the Christian psychology that he states must exist. What stands in the way of the path is mass consciousness, a abstract mental consciousness without bodily connection. Here Robert reads Steiner as one with a true understanding of Incarnation—and reincarnation—as imaginations.

Introduction to Rudolf Steiner, *Psychoanalysis and Spiritual Psychology* (1990)

Foreword to Gerhard Wehr, *Jung & Steiner: Toward a New Psychology* (1990)

Foreword to Rudolf Steiner, *Anthroposophy (A Fragment)* (1996)

Introduction to Rudolf Steiner, *A Psychology of Body, Soul, & Spirit: Anthroposophy, Psychosophy, Pneumatosophy* (1999)

Introduction to Michael Gruber, *An Unknown Destiny: Terror, Psychotherapy, and Modern Initiation—Readings in Nietzsche, Heidegger, and Steiner* (2008)

Spirit Cycle (5 essays)

After exercising in the mental worlds of different Steiner perspectives, the following essays can be read as a *spirit cycle* in the realm of θεοι (the gods). These reflections reimagine prayer and art as conscious engagement with soul life. Here also Robert identifies the "current from the future"; an accessible dimension *outside of time*, that is, unconditioned by the psychological and cultural times in which we are embedded.

Robert Sardello (ed.), *The Angels* (1990)

Introduction to Linda Sussman, *The Speech of the Grail: A Journey toward Speaking that Heals and Transforms* (1995)

Essay in *So That You May Be One: The Visions of Joa Bolendas* (1997)

Introduction to Rufus Goodwin, *Give Us This Day: The Story of Prayer* (1999)

Introduction to Kurt Falk, *The Unknown Hieronymus Bosch* (2008)

Mineral Cycle (3 essays)

In a *mineral cycle* (realm πετροι, *petroi*) from 2007 to the present, Robert reads different imaginations of matter. These essays constitute his published responses to spiritual working with stones, and the imaginations of stones and gems as living artists, a channeled spiritual testament under conditions of sensory deprivation as a metaphor of modern society under the growing hegemony of material and virtual realities.

Robert Simmons and Naisha Ahsia, *The Book of Stones: Who They Are and What They Teach* (2007)

Robert Simmons, *Stones of the New Consciousness: Healing, Awakening & Co-creating with Crystals, Mineral & Gems* (2009)

Anonymous, *The Mysterious Story of X7: Exploring the Spiritual Nature of Matter* (2011)

Body Cycle (2 essays)

In these essays, Sardello explores and critiques the neurophysiological concept of resonance or "mirroring," and also penetrates the ways by which Medicine and Psychology operate as cultural forms among "closed systems" of power and manipulation, hailing back to the lure of Parmenides' *that which is, cannot not be.* In that phrase of mental consciousness, a mental construct becomes an entire worldview.

Foreword to Joseph Chilton Pearce, *Strange Loops and Gestures of Creation* (2010)

Joaquin Tan, *Healing Ourselves from Medicine: How Anthroposophy Can Save Your Life* (2011)

Robert Sardello's insights navigate many hazardous abstractions from the so-called New Age through the perennial philosophies. With Sophia as his muse, the "current from the future" calls him, carrying its many imaginations as energy, the always-immediate now, and the truly new. Across these authors' writings, his visionary perspective deepens in dialogue with the different works as authored beings. For writings possess their own spirit, or how otherwise do they engender a unique spirit when reborn within our own imagination?

Listen and savor.

Scott R. Scribner
Society for Spiritual Psychology
Los Alamitos, California, 2011

ABOUT THE CONTRIBUTORS

Christopher Bamford is, among other things, editor in chief of SteinerBooks and Lindisfarne Books, the author of numerous introductions, the editor of many books, and the author of *The Voice of the Eagle: The Heart of Celtic Christianity*; *An Endless Trace: The Passionate Pursuit of Wisdom in the West*; and (with Peter Lamborn Wilson and Kevin Townley) *Green Hermeticism: Alchemy and Ecology*.

John A. Lee, D.Min., is a graduate of the Theological School, Drew University, Madison, New Jersey and San Francisco Theological Seminary, San Anselmo, California, where, for his dissertation, he developed a model of how the imagination develops images. The imagination and fly-fishing have been his lifelong passions. Now a retired Methodist minister, having served pastorates in Wyoming, Montana, and Colorado, John Lee has been in private practice as a pastoral psychotherapist since 1985. He is a founding member and leader for thirty years of the Guild for Sacred Studies, a group devoted to researching the visionary imagination of Jesus of Nazareth.

Lee Nichol is the editor of several books by David Bohm, including *The Essential David Bohm*, *On Dialogue*, and *On Creativity*; he also wrote the foreword to David Bohm's *Thought as a System*. He helped with the editing of the two books he comments upon here.

Cheryl Sanders-Sardello is cofounder, codirector, and administrative director of the School of Spiritual Psychology and coeditor of Goldenstone Press. Her focus is on teaching and writing on the spiritual psychology of embodiment and sensing, the spiritual psychology of aging, and our spiritual connection with those who have died and its implications for the health of the social world. She has contributed chapters to numerous books, including *Silence* and *Love and the Soul*. An independent teacher and scholar, she has taught all over the U.S., Canada, and the U.K., as well as the Philippines and Australia.

Scott Scribner has known Robert Sardello since 1995 and is a member of the International Advisory Board of the School of Spiritual Psychology in Benson, North Carolina. He studied astronomy and cultural anthropology at Harvard University's Mount Hermon Liberal Studies Program; physics and sociology at Rensselaer Polytechnic Institute (where he joined NASA's Mars Survey Vehicle Development Group); philosophy and cognition at the University of New Hampshire; and the relationship between religion and psychology at Fuller Theological Seminary and Fuller Graduate School of Psychology. His doctoral research—chaired by Robert Sardello—examined phenomenological descriptions of fear in alien abduction narratives. Scott works in the computer software industry and lives in Southern California with his wife Michele and several cats.

Dr. Joanne Stroud is a founding fellow of the Dallas Institute, Director of Institute Publications, and Editor of the Gaston Bachelard Translation Series, which consists of seven works on elemental imagination written by the twentieth-century philosopher of science, and which Joanne is on the verge of completing after two decades. The 2002 Bachelard Symposium she chaired in Dallas, "Matter, Dream, and Thought," attracted international attention. She received her M.A. and Ph.D in Psychology and Literature from the University of Dallas and lectures in Dallas, New York City, and Connecticut. She has taught literature and psychology and is author of *The Bonding of Will and Desire*, the four-volume series *Choose Your Element*, and *Time Doesn't Tick Anymore*.

Dr. Gail Thomas is a Founding Fellow of the Dallas Institute and creator of its Center for the City. She served as the Institute's Founding Director for seventeen years and has throughout her career been a strong advocate for the active presence of the humanities in the life of the city. Dr. Thomas has taught at The Dallas Institute, Schumacher College in the United Kingdom, and The University of Dallas, where she directed the Center for Civic Leadership. She was instrumental in the creation of Pegasus Plaza in downtown Dallas and also led the successful effort to recreate the Flying Red Horse landmark sign in downtown Dallas. A recipient of the Kessler Award, she currently serves as President and Executive Officer of the Trinity Trust Foundation, whose mission is to raise private funds to implement the "Balanced Vision Plan" for the Trinity River Corridor and coordinates with the City of Dallas and the Trinity Commons Foundation in the effort to build public support, secure public funding and build the project.

EDUCATING WITH SOUL

A PHENOMENOLOGICAL/ARCHETYPAL
REFLECTION ON HIGHER EDUCATION

The following monograph was prepared for the Institute of Philosophic Studies at the University of Dallas by its director, Dr. Robert J. Sardello. During his tenure the past two years as Graduate Dean, Dr. Sardello has helped shape and guide the academic programs of the Center for Civic Leadership and has taught several courses in the degree program. The Center is grateful to Dr. Sardello for his imaginative leadership and is honored to have the opportunity to publish his provocative paper on education.
Gail Thomas, Director, The Center for Civic Leadership,
University of Dallas, 1979

Our field of depth psychology originates in the consulting room. Because of this origin, we are often reluctant to consider other places in which the field of depth psychology has application. While events such as language, behavior, memory, dream, fantasy, and mood are brought to psychological reflection, the psychologizing of such events is valued for its relation to the situation of psychotherapy. If the field is to avoid becoming a "cult" of therapy, however, it must risk entry into other domains. Where is there to be found a depth psychology of money, of food, of cities, of architecture, of culture, of medicine, of law, of science? A beginning was made to release psychology from the confines of the consulting room in the first International Conference in Archetypal Psychology held at the University of Dallas in January 1977.[1] The con-

---

1   This conference was sponsored by the Rockefeller Brothers Fund and the University of Dallas. The participants included Charles Boer, Edward Casey, C. West Churchman, Stephanie De Voogd, Adolf Guggenbuhl-Craig, Stanley Hopper, James Hillman, Patricia Berry-Hillman, Robert Romanyshyn, Neil Micklem,

versations during the conference focused on many of these neglected areas. The work of education is one such neglected area that was also bypassed in that conference. While Jung wrote several critical essays on education, higher education has received no attention whatsoever from depth psychology.[2] The metaphors "high" and "deep" seem to have nothing to do with one another. Perhaps they are antithetical to each other, for outside of the University of Dallas, is there any place where depth psychology appears in the classroom? Academic psychology goes on in the universities while depth psychology goes on in the training institutes. The situation will persist until the depth of higher learning can be remembered; the breakdown of higher education will persist as long as the academy is valued for scholarship, acquisition of information or skills, professional training, research, and specialization, to the exclusion of the transformation of the person.[3]

Education as Transformation

Educational rhetoric is filled with the language of goals: the pursuit of excellence, the search for truth, the concern with knowledge for its own sake, and wisdom. But these goals obscure the psychological resonance of the events of the classroom. The actual situation of the

---

Charles Scott, Gordon Tappan, David Miller, Rafael Lopez-Pedraza, Tom Kapacinskas, and others. Diverse fields such as philosophy, literature, religious studies, city planning, art, and psychotherapy were discussed.

2   These essays by Jung on education are collected in the volume, C. G. Jung, *Psychology and Education* (Princeton, N.J.: Princeton Univ. Press, 1954).

3   It is no accident that phenomenological/archetypal psychology is emphasized at the University of Dallas. Donald Cowan, president of the University of Dallas for eighteen years, has formulated a coherent philosophy of liberal arts education which places imagination at the center of learning. In a recent article in *Vision Magazine*, he states:

> The imagination is the realm of experience, where phenomena become events and events take on meaning. It is the realm of learning. What is called liberal education instructs the imagination rather than programs the memory. The effect of a liberal education is never wholly preconceived. It is internal in the student; he is transformed, made different but more fully what he is. It is the nature of a liberal education to people the imagination with presences that, in mysterious and ambiguous ways, manifest the virtues.

classroom is filled with mistakes, with blunders, with humor, with the twisting, nonsensical juxtapositions of words, with gaps in reasoning, with a multiplicity and duplicity of speech, with the inability of words to be logically precise, and with constant misunderstandings. These constant deviations which constitute the actual situation of learning are of value because they are reminders that the goals of education are an elaborate, necessary fiction[4] which motivate the work of higher education. But when the goals are taken literally, then the work of education becomes that of getting a degree, getting credentials, becoming a specialist, receiving training, or believing that one has the truth. Lacking the awareness of its inferiorities, education confuses its work with its goals. A psychology of education begins with the realization that the classroom is the place where the work is to speak as if truth can be attained. Truth and knowledge are unattainable goals. The words "I have the truth," or "I have knowledge," then signal the death of both. Without an "as if" quality, learning would cease because the goal attained kills desire. The "as if" quality which motivates education is retained when, coupled with the love of learning, there is the realization that the only thing that we know is that we don't know. The desire for learning may be the desire for truth, but the depth psychology of education is more interested in exploring the truth of desire. What keeps the desire for learning alive?

The Oxford English Dictionary lets the word *education* speak in the following ways:

1. The process of nourishing or rearing a child, or young person, animal.
2. The rearing of silkworms.
3. The process of 'bringing up'; the manner in which a person has been 'brought up.'
4. The systematic instruction, schooling, or training given to the young in preparation for the work of life.

---

4   The relation between soul and goal in the psychology of Alfred Adler is worked out in James Hillman's 1977 Eranos lecture, "Psychotherapy's Inferiority Complex."

5. Drawing out; culture or development of powers, formation of character, as contrasted with the imparting of mere knowledge or skill.

When these definitions are heard as image—that is, when all parts of this word *education* are heard as going on together, each part necessary to every other part, each part implicating every other part—then the part of the image that comes as a surprise is that event in the word that says that education is also "the rearing of silkworms."[5] The other events in this word speak in terms of education's goal quality. Rearing and bringing up the young, systematic instruction, preparation for life, development of abilities—these are the things that education sets out to do, what education hopes to accomplish, and what gets literalized into systems, theories, and practices of education. An image resounds through all these events, but that event in the word *education,* which is "the rearing of silkworms," has a special imaginational value because of its surprise appearance. This event within the word leads us into the word on its own terms, and it can release the word to speak anew, as if for the first time. The deviation in the definition is its depth, where knowledge yields to imagination.[6]

The silkworm is the larvae of a moth called *Bombyx mori,* a moth that feeds on the mulberry tree. The *Bombyx mori* is a rather large white moth with black-lined wings, measuring a little more than two inches from wingtip to wingtip. As an image, it thus presents itself as a simultaneity of black and white, of light and dark, of illumination and darkness. The appearance of this moth within the word *education* suggests the co-presence of knowledge and ignorance—education's black and white necessarily belong together.

---

5   This understanding of the character of the image is developed in detail by Patricia Berry-Hillman. See especially her article "An Approach to the Dream," in *Spring* 1974 (Zurich and Dallas: Spring Publ., 1974).

6   The importance of an imaginal approach to language is the theme of the Fall 1978 issue of *Dragonflies* (Dallas: Dept. of Psychology, 1978). See in particular, R. Kugelman, "Etymology as a Psychological Operation" in that issue.

The raising of silkworms requires a great deal of care. Silk farmers treat the *Bombyx mori* as carefully as they would treat a newborn baby. They raise it under controlled temperatures. They protect it from mosquitoes, flies, and other insects. They carefully protect it from disease. If this rearing is their learning, what is being stated here is that for learning to occur, attention must be paid to the pathology of what is occurring.

In early summer, a female *Bombyx mori* lays from 300 to 500 eggs, and dies soon afterward. The silkworms which hatch from the eggs have an enormous appetite. They eat mulberry leaves almost continually, grow to about seventy times their original size and shed their skin four times. When fully grown, the silkworm stops eating and begins to spin a cocoon. As the worm moves its jaws in a figure eight pattern, two glands near the lower jaw give forth a fluid that hardens into fine silk thread as it hits the air.

When finished with the cocoon, the worm changes into a pupa and, if left alone, would be transformed into a moth in about three weeks. Before this happens, however, the silk farmer kills the pupa by placing the cocoons into a hot oven. The cocoons are then soaked in basins of hot water to dissolve the gummy substance that holds the threads together. The loose threads are then pulled by pulleys through a tiny porcelain guide, much like the eye of a needle. The thread is wound on a reel, boiled in water, and is then ready for weaving.

Such is the education of the silkworm. An elemental imagination may immediately hear this as a mystery story. The moth, whose element is air, is bound to the Earth through the seduction of the mulberry tree. It undergoes a death of fire, is purified in water, and emerges as silk. We are in the middle of a transformation mystery, for, instead of renewing the cycle of nature, the moth offers itself in death so that silk can be made. Silk is the strongest and most elastic of all fibers and because of its beauty is called "the queen of fibers." The silkworm forgoes nature for culture. The mystery within the word *education* is the mystery of transformation, and is its secret work. It is a transformation of consequence.

This transformation, as evidenced in China where silk was first made, is necessary to the making of culture. According to Chinese legend, silk was discovered about 2700 B.C. in the garden of Emperor Huang-Ti. The emperor ordered his wife Si-Ling-Shi to find out what was damaging the mulberry trees. She found white worms eating the mulberry leaves and spinning shiny cocoons. As she was looking at a cocoon, it slipped from her hands into a cup of hot water, and as she played with the cocoon in the water, a delicate, cobwebby tangle separated itself from the cocoon. Si-Ling-Shi then persuaded her husband to give her a grove of mulberry trees where she could tend thousands of worms that spun such beauty. She is said also to have discovered the silk reel and the silk loom.

The Chinese guarded carefully the secret of the silkworm, and in so doing guarded their culture. Disgrace and death faced anyone who attempted to reveal the secret. Only the Chinese knew how to make silk for 3000 years. Around the year 550, the Byzantine emperor Justinian sent two monks to China as spies, and they smuggled out silkworm eggs and mulberry seeds in hollow bamboo canes.

Locating this image within the word *education* makes of education a transformation mystery. The work of education is the making of culture from nature. What is natural to us, that which has its own beauty, undergoes a death for a different kind of beauty, a beauty that enters the world, enters life. The natural beauty of the moth is transformed into the garment of civilization—preserving it, extending it, giving it strength and flexibility.

Education is transformation and transformation is mystery. Seen in this way, much of the work of education cannot be made into programs, made visible. Any attempt to do so would be to take that way of knowing which is capable of seeing the invisible, what Henry Corbin indicates as *batin* in the Sufi tradition and reveal it to the literal mind, which in this tradition is called *zahir*. The result, Corbin says, can be psychosis.[7]

---

7   H. Corbin, *Creative Imagination in the Sufism of Ibn 'Arabi*, trans. R. Manheim (London: Routledge and Kegan Paul, 1970).

Two consequences follow from this warning. The first is that the education with the highest goals can contain the most mystery. Liberal education, speaking through the goals of knowledge and wisdom, can contain more transformative mystery than can career education with its immediate goals. That is, to the extent that a goal can be attained, the work of transformation is reduced and to the extent that a goal is unattainable, the work of transformation is increased.

The second consequence relates to the actual activities of education. I want to examine these concrete activities of the classroom—the work of language, the work of the lecture, the psychology of reading, and the issue of evaluation—as *rituals* of transformation. But the uselessness of such an endeavor is to be recognized at the outset. None of what is said can be put into practice. This is not a warning that it should not be put into practice. It is the recognition that it cannot be put into practice any more than myth can, for it is impossible to put into action something that is already always happening. It can only be given attention. Education is a mystery, the uniting of individual souls of teacher and learner with those who have taught and learned before. The rituals of its transformation include an initiation into reading, listening, writing, and speaking. Let us take each of these rituals in turn.

The Sexuality of Reading

The first matter I wish to give attention is the fact that higher education places considerable value on learning through books. What is transformative about a book? A book is a mark of culture which seems to show forth the visibility of a goal attained. It pretends to be clear, without error, without fumbling, without hesitation. This is so even when a book is written as an exploration of a problem, a meditation, or as a pondering of some reality. Though errors may be discovered, a book never presents itself as in need of help; it shows itself forth as an achievement. Even a book of aphorisms which is meant to puzzle and to open imagination presents those aphorisms clearly. Books are approached in a similar manner; namely, as if they were completed, finished, having only a certain amount of information. When that information is mastered, it is time to move on to a new challenge. Approaching a book in this manner is the result of what Paul Ricoeur calls *distantiation*, a movement that occurs when writing takes the place of speaking and reading takes the place of listening. A book is not the work of a speaker but an author and does not address a listener but a reader. No movement is possible in the abstract relation between author and reader.[8]

But let us start all over again, this time staying closer to the actual situation of reading, and giving attention to that activity. Books are objects. But they are peculiar objects, unlike, for example, a chair, or a vase, or a table. A book on a table, on a shelf, in a store window, sits there obviously hoping for someone to pick it up, hoping to be delivered from the fate of being only an object.

When we take up a book and begin to read, the book as object disappears. In fact, everything surrounding the reader disappears. A transmutation takes place in which the world of things is transformed into the world of language; the durable world of things is transformed into the elastic world of language. In this world of language there is no longer a separation or an opposition between the reader and the world, and yet the world has not been reduced to the realm of subjectivity, for we are surely involved in an objective world when reading a book. This world of language that is reading is a world that is simultaneously mine and not mine at all. It is not possible, while reading, to distinguish where my thoughts end and those of another begin. While reading, the language that speaks is mine at the same time that it is foreign to me, though this unfamiliarity goes almost without recognition. It becomes apparent only when some disruption occurs in the reading, as for example, when I stop reading and ask, now what did I just read? In reading, then, is a dissolution of the division between the familiar and the unfamiliar. Language reads itself through the reader just as though the I did not

8   P. Ricoeur, "What is a Text? Explanation and Interpretation" in D. Rasmussen, *Mythic- Symbolic Language and Philosophical Anth*ropology (The Hague: Martinus Nijhoff, 1971), pp. 135–150.

exist. While reading, the ego is "on loan" to someone else, to an imaginal ego who thinks, feels, suffers, and acts. Only when reading ceases does being gripped, excited or caught by the language speaking, bring the realization that we are being read by someone else.

Is this figure that takes us over while reading the one who writes the book?[9] While reading, what matters is not the author but the work. What matters is the way an individual life has been radically transformed and now speaks in a new way, and it is this new speaking that makes a claim on us. Reading is a mode of active imagination in which language reads through us, a speaking which is not abstract if heard as speaking rather than seen as writing. If it is speaking, then someone is speaking. It is far too limiting, however, to claim that when we listen to a text we hear the writer.

As soon as a book is opened it becomes a voice and a world. Archetypal psychology is concerned not with why this happens, or how this happens, but with who is making reading happen through us. If it is not I who reads, then who is animating the letters and words of a page, bringing them out of inert inky blackness where they can do the work of transformation? What is the myth of reading?[10]

Whether we are reading aloud or silently, there is always the rhythm of voice and silence, a sexual rhythm of the masculinity of the word in sensuous love-making with the depth of silence. When the pause between the voice of language and its silence is attended to carefully, the silence is filled with image. Silence filled with image in this way is the connotation

---

9   The hermeneutics of Wilhelm Dilthey is based upon the assumption that the reader knows the author better than the author knew himself. The limitations of this view of interpretation are discussed in R. Palmer, *Hermeneutics: Interpretation Theory in Schleiermacher, Dilthey, Heidegger, and Gadamer* (Evanston: Northwestern Univ. Press, 1969).

10   In addition to the mythology of reading presented here, see R. Severson, "Freud and the Alchemy of Dreamwork," *Dragonflies*, Spring 1979, Vol. 1, No. 2 (Dallas: Dept. of Psychology, 1979). Also, R. Sardello, "Imagination and the Happening of a Psychological Tradition," unpublished lecture, Lecture Series in Foundational Issues of Phenomenological Psychology, University of Dallas, March 26, 1976. These additional reflections show that it is never possible to place a phenomenon in relation to a single myth.

of language, bringing fantasy to the word, inseparable from the word. *Imagination* stirs in the silence of language. Sometimes this silence is extended enough so that it is possible to attend to this stirring of imagination; as for example, when attention drifts away from the words and we find ourselves in a world of fantasy. Such flights of fantasy revive a kind of egocentricity, but usually the masculinity of the word, its life as Eros, calls attention back to the text, condensing the misty vapors of the anima stirrings of fantasy. The images stirred in the silence of the language of reading bring beauty to the word, which by itself stands there dark, naked, and literal. The voice of language responds to the touch of image, bringing solidity to connotation, the solidity of voice uniting with the silence of tradition, saying that this love-making of reading is not isolated but takes place in the midst of remembering that language relies on those who have spoken before. It is possible to get close to this shaping of the image in reading when a pause in reading accentuates a movement into memories. Often, reading touches or ignites a memory, a stirring of past happenings as primordial values that continue to surge within our blood. The voice in language shapes and forms image by bringing image into connection with memory, lifting the image from isolated privacy into the community of communication.

The psychology of reading has its pathology. Reading often seems to have nothing to give, no connection seems to come. Imagination is needed to read; going back to a book that was a source of torment and hearing it speak for the first time is an indication of psychic movement. When attention persistently drifts from the text into fantasy or memory while the words seem to remain literal, it is as if the image in silence will not allow herself to be penetrated by Eros, wants to remain virginal and asleep, or does not trust that Eros will treat her with love. She needs time to differentiate her moods and her feelings, and most of all her word fantasies. During that time reading is depressive and suicidal: "I'll never understand this; it makes no sense at all. This is all just words." The voice in language has its pathology, too. The rush of fiery words, monstrous energy, the compulsion to read more and more, faster and faster. Without image, language is hostile, a liar and a deceiver; hot, dry and airy.

These pathologies are necessary to reading, reminders that reading needs time and ritualization. Then reading is transformation, felt through the body as the birth of pleasure. Reading as pleasure destroys the book as a mere thing, a container of information. In the destruction of the book is the birth of a world, a world not only seen and known, but one that is bodily felt, touched, heard and smelled. Books then are simultaneously of no value at all and are of the deepest significance. They are of no value because they offer themselves in order to be forgotten as books. They are deeply significant because without books, the world is reduced to the oppressiveness of personal and immediate experience.

Lectures as Lies

My interest in the depth psychology of higher learning began with the realization that the myth of the consulting room places emphasis on the transformation of something within the person that comes about through a particular kind of relationship. A major portion of this relationship occurs in the space of one hour per week. University classes meet three hours per week, and that ought to be the setting for some kind of transformation. But the consulting room cannot be applied to the classroom without a terrible confusion resulting in something like the work of Carl Rogers applied to education. When the consulting room is brought into the classroom the result is group therapy. Higher learning must see through the activities of its own tradition rather than borrowing from other traditions. The lecture is a tradition in education, and there is a story to be told of the lecture.

The *Oxford English Dictionary* lists two ways that the word *lecture* speaks. Taken together, these senses of the word surprise the imagination:

1. A discourse or reading presented before an audience.
2. To read out tales to an audience.

The first way this word speaks is familiar. A lecture presents information to an audience. When executed well, a lecture is quick, without fumbling, hesitation, or doubt. The lecturer is in command of the material, and the speaking is brilliant. Connections come for the audience. The material lights up things in a new way. There is enthusiasm and insight. Truth is spoken.

The second way this word speaks is unfamiliar. The direct image contained in the first way of speaking seems unrelated to the speaking of a tale as a story with complications, with erroneous paths, deviations, maybe even false, certainly not to be taken literally. In fact, the second sense of this word *lecture* is that it is fiction, not to be taken as fact. The lecture's extraordinary quality lies in its duplicity of clarifying confusion, straight crookedness, discourse and tale. A phenomenon of immense complication, of united opposites, it is backed by the most complicated imagery of psychic life: the union of male and female, spirit and body, animus and anima, love and soul—Hermaphroditus.[11]

The lecture is an opus that at first glance belongs to the personality of the teacher. Provided the lecturer is engaged in more than presenting information or someone else's thought, the speaking appears to be the position of the lecturer. The single-mindedness of the lecture, its effort to stand as an achievement of clarity and insight, is supported by an appreciative audience. At the same time, what is said is constantly undergoing a necessary deformation through the relationship between lecturer and audience.

The lecture must be disengaged from the lecturer if it is to be of psychological value. This separation is implied in the language—someone gives a lecture or presents a lecture, or a lecture is delivered—indicating that it does not belong to the speaker as a possession. To do its transformative work, the lecture must be transferred. Transference

---

11 The hermaphroditic character of the lecture image presented in this section is based upon the examination of the importance of the hermaphrodite image in psychotherapy. This image is developed by R. Lopez-Pedraza in *Hermes and His Children* (Dallas and Zurich: Spring Publ., 1977).

presumes an intense human connection that means something to the soul. Disengagement is something quite different than attending to the information presented in a purely intellectual fashion. In this way, there is nothing to be disengaged because there was no engagement in the first place. The psychologically effective lecture depends upon Eros as educator making associative connection between speaker and listeners. He is at play in the classroom; he is at one and the same time the hindrance and the indispensible element in the event of transformation. Here in the lecture he makes for engagement and also makes for the difficulty in freeing Lecture to do his work.

The quick clarity of the lecture must be slowed down if it is to deeply affect both teacher and student. It becomes entangled in order to be contained as substance for psychological reflection. The "inner questioner" that enters into the movement of a lecture provides a kind of deflection. The "inner questioner" emerges from the reflective instinct. By reflective instinct I am referring to the way in which questions seem to come on their own, spontaneously. They are not "thought up." They simply come and intrude. The "inner questioner" wrestles with the personality of the lecturer, like the nymph Salmacis jumping in the pool where Hermaphroditus was bathing to entangle him. The ensuing struggle is duplicitous. Although it looks like a purely intellectual battle to see who can come out on top, the struggle is as well a personal response to the images of the lecture as they stir and move the listener. The moment of the question is an exceedingly delicate psychological moment in which duplicity is essential. The duplicity is more vivid in its pathology. For when questions are posed and answered single-mindedly, a defensive, ego-involved struggle ensues. Real answers are sought, as if the issue could be resolved once and for all. But the spontaneous question emerges from psyche's desire to complicate the issue by locating the issue in a different place, in relation to the historical context of one's own psychic life. Duplicitous, hermaphroditic consciousness realizes the unity of clarity and confusion. When they are split apart the lecture gets stuck in either ego defense or in personal meaning. The duplicity is reflected by the lecturer also, who answers questions as if there were a real answer. At the same time, the dark side of the lecture which is realized as a question indicates that something was heard that was not intended in the speaking. The duplicity of the lecture is located neither with lecturer or questioner alone, but with the figure of Lecture who complicates their relationship. We must ask, then, what kind of imaginal creature is Lecture?

A psychological lecture is not something that is *brought into* the classroom. It is created *in* the classroom, through the psychological relationship that occurs there. The Lecture is a duplicitous character who simultaneously speaks discourse and tale, who both knows and clouds knowing. In some stories the parents of Hermaphroditus are Hermes and Aphrodite. Hermes is the god of hermeneutics, or interpretation, and Aphrodite is the goddess of persuasion. The Hermes aspect of the lecture calls out questions, makes for deviations, and slows the material down by making translation necessary. Hermes moves the lecture into the realm of soul, where things must be said indirectly. And the Aphrodite aspect of the material makes it *matter* by taking it out of the realm of abstraction and bringing it into the world of sensuality and substance. As a hermaphroditic style of consciousness, the lecture is on the one hand an accomplishment, a product, a presentation of some subject matter in clear discourse. And it is simultaneously something that speaks another language, tells strange tales that do not ask for interpretation but engagement through persuasion. These two languages of the lecture are not put together out of separate parts. The meaning of the material is its substance; its substance is its meaning. What the lecture *means* and what the lecture *wants* are paired and inseparable. The work of learning drags on so long because this duplicity is the only way insight and psychic relevance can deepen ideas into experience. The psychological lecture, in the image of Hermaphroditus, produces conflict while it encourages psychological movement.

The psychology of the lecture brings another angle of insight to education as transformation. When learning involves an identification with goals, and lectures are faithfully received in order to be able to master those goals—to know someone else's position literally—then a single-mindedness of meaning occurs. The result is not a community of learners, but rather an ideological following. The psychological lecture refuses to be tied to lecture notes, and remains as image, unique in memory. Its transformation occurs in the "gap" of duplicity—the disruption between what is intended and the deflection of that intention into a tradition which belongs neither to the lecturer nor to the listener.

Testing and the Valuing of Tradition

Higher learning is a place where reading and listening transform the soul. These rituals, like all rituals, demand that initiates be "put to the test." An essential part of education's transformative mystery concerns evaluation, a much more conscious process than teaching or lecturing or reading. Evaluation is a process going on through a certain period of time requiring a conscious organization of consciousness, the performance of what Jung speaks of as a *function*. In *Psychological Types*, Jung speaks of four functions: Thinking-Feeling-Intuition-Sensation.[12] Here I would like to explore feeling as the depth psychology of evaluation.[13] Because the visible side of evaluation depends so much on thinking and a concern for what is right or wrong, feeling is certainly the "inferior function" in evaluation. For both teacher and student alike, the extraction of feeling from evaluation is held to be most desirable because feeling seems to be a subjective response. If I openly state that my grading of class work is founded in feeling, I seem to be standing in the realm of personal emotion and revealing what I want rather than what is objectively "right" or "correct." But that is a very narrow view of feeling, taking time and depth away from feeling. Whenever learning is expressed through time—in a written examination or an essay, or a

---

12 C. G. Jung, *Psychological Types* (Princeton, N.J.: Princeton Univ. Press, 1954).

13 For an excellent presentation of the feeling function, see J. Hillman, "The Feeling Function" in M. Louise Von Franz and J. Hillman, *Jung's Typology* (Zurich: Spring Publ., 1971), pp. 75–149.

term paper, things that "take" time—grading must also be a process which occurs through time, as the slow differentiation of feeling. When learning is expressed as if time were not a factor—in an objective test with instantaneous answers which cover or elude the time process—then feeling does not seem to enter into evaluation. The material is instantly evaluated as right or wrong. But *psychological* comprehension of someone's classwork means as well feeling comprehension. The psychology of evaluation begins with a question analogous to the opening question of the therapeutic hour: how does it feel? The feeling function is that psychological process in us that evaluates. Through the feeling function we appreciate a situation, a person, a work, in terms of value. *E*-valuation, then, is the calculation of value. "Objective" evaluation in terms of right or wrong emphasizes the calculation and suppresses the value. The psychology of evaluation recognizes the value and realizes that the calculation is concerned with the conscious expression of the value in an unambiguous manner.

Because the feeling function is a conscious organization of consciousness, ego is deeply and inseparably involved in evaluation; hence evaluation is inevitably personal if not subjective. Recognizing this inevitability, why would anyone allow themselves to be evaluated? First, the recognition that feeling can be a manifestation of Eros in education gives evaluation a necessary impersonal background. The discrimination of feeling is related to a connection, not to the teacher, but to the material. Not to the material as fact but as something which needs loving attention. There is enormous risk in such foolishness, however, because the basis of grading may be power and not Eros. There are, after all, psychopathic teachers, just as there are psychopathic learners.

The oppressiveness of evaluation's attachment to ego is relieved by the fact that evaluation is a temporal organization of feeling. There is always a tentativeness to grading, a tentativeness felt by the student when he feels that the value of the work was or was not appreciated, a tentativeness felt by the teacher when he realizes that the mark may miss the mark, but that the mark must be made to embody the feeling.

The value of a written work, or of speaking in the classroom, reaches beneath personal likes and dislikes when that writing or speaking resounds the tradition within which the work occurs. Value has to do with duration, as when we speak of the tonal value of a musical note. The more differentiated and rich the work resounds, the deeper the value. Work has value when it animates a tradition; the depth of its involvement with those who have spoken before is an estimate of the heart.

In evaluation, a conscious connection is made with the values resounding through a work, and at the same time there is a tentative closing of that connection, a closing which prevents the work from being too precious. Surprisingly, then, evaluation as feeling is warm and cold at the same time. A warm "A" affirms the value of a work as it coldly sits there saying that it is not an "A" in life. The grade says that the work of resounding a tradition must begin again with all the same tentativeness.

Especially important to the psychology of evaluation is negative feeling. Without its negative dimension, feeling disintegrates into affect and lacks discrimination. Is there not disappointment and suspicion when a paper is returned with only praise and appreciation? One suspects that it was really not appreciated at all because the evaluation lacks psychological honesty and psychological courage. Signs of struggle indicate deep connection. Without the signs of this struggle the work lacks importance, for the value of the work has not been sorted out. The negative dimension of feeling indicates that the relationship with the work and with the tradition must begin again in another work—that the work is never finished.

Feeling begins by trusting first impressions. Included, then, is a willingness to allow feeling its errors. A work presented by a student feels clever or trite or heavy or ethereal or deep or insightful. These are first impressions, feelings to be held in consciousness so that the feeling function can feel the feelings. First feelings need time and containment. If immediately acted upon, the judgment is *affected*. Similarly, for those being evaluated, the first impression of a grade and of comments on a paper is a feeling which needs containment. First impressions—anger, confusion, hatred, disappointment, elation, admiration—are strong ones, but when consciously admitted and held, are followed by value discrimination. Evaluation in this sense is always also a self-evaluation in which the soul encounters itself in an act of psychological courage emanating from the reason of the heart. The feeling function's feeling of feelings is not an analyzing of feeling, trying to figure out what we feel and what it means, but is the heartfelt discrimination of value.

Evaluation itself is transformative when the value of a work resounds the tradition of a discipline, when the heart feels and judges that Plato continues to speak here in this small class paper in philosophy. Then this is not just another paper about Plato. Or that here, in this moment of class conversation, Jung is present. More deeply, whoever inspires Plato and animates Jung is still here in this college classroom. We are trans-formed through such connections with tradition.

The transformation from affect to the discrimination of value requires that there be a vessel to contain first feelings. Marriage is, for example, an impersonal vessel for the containment of feelings of every sort and thus for the differentiation of the feeling function. Similarly, the impersonal vessel in education is the course. Through this vessel the values of a tradition of a discipline can be felt. Courses are never *just* courses. They are good courses or bad courses, depending on their value for the soul. A course is a much more delicate vessel than marriage (although these days it is as easy to drop a marriage as it is to drop a course). Yet the course is an impersonal structure which surrounds the relationship between teacher and student, and a wide range of feelings can occur in that vessel. Unless feelings do emerge no transformation can occur.

The psychology of evaluation is such a tenuous affair that one won-ders why do it at all. Many universities have given it up altogether or grade in broad categories as pass/fail so that no fine discrimination can occur. Most universities are experiencing grade inflation, indicating a loss of discrimination. Evaluation gives body to the work by valuing the immediate situation. Evaluation as feeling creates an awareness of where I am right now in relation to a tradition. It is not possible to evaluate potential or background. Evaluation does not speak of what could go on or what should go on, but how the soul is with the tradition right now, at this moment, in this particular situation.

Eros as Educator

I have been staying close to the actual activities of the work of higher education, trying to see through those situations for their psychological value. There are two threads woven into this discussion which still require elaboration. This psychologizing of education has suggested that error and speech are both essential for transformation. Reading, lecturing, and testing each seem to have knowledge as their goal. We read and go to class with knowledge as our goal, and are tested in order to know whether we know. But the transformational quality of these activities is found in the secret life of error working invisibly through the actions of education. When reading is pervaded with connotations, then there is soul in reading. When lectures are valued for their confusion along with their clarity, the lecture can transform. Evaluation is valuable when tentative, filled with the ambiguity of feeling.

But it is not error alone which makes for transformation. The visibility of the word pervades the activities of reading, lecturing, and evaluation, i.e., these actions are actions of language; language as word, as presentation, as conversation. Now not all language is educative, nor is all error transformative. When language, though, is connotative, confusing, tentative, it is transforming. Said in another way, when speaking is suggestive, moving, and metaphorical, it is educative. So, I want to attend now more closely to the connection between error and speech in the situation of education.

The experimental psychology of learning seems to have little to do with depth psychology. But they in fact share a common and central interest: a concern for error. While the experimental psychology of learning focuses on the elimination of error, depth psychology values error as a path into the language of psychological experience. This interest in error, though moving in opposite directions, employs a common investigative mode of inquiry, that of association studies. Edward L. Thorndike's three-volume work, *Educational Psychology*, written in 1913, established associationism as a principle of learning that has since influenced all theories of learning.[14] Connections are made by association, and the goal of learning is to strengthen "right" associations through confirmation and to weaken "wrong" associations through neglect. Jung's experimental researches in word-association in 1909 need to be viewed in relation to the associationist theory of learning.

Through the experimental studies on word association, Jung discovered the complex, the relatively autonomous character of imaginal life that seems to pull the accomplishments of conscious tasks into error and deviation.[15] The word-association studies employ a series of stimulus words to which a subject is asked to respond. The reactions do not come with equal smoothness, but vary irregularly in terms of the length of response intervals. Or other disturbances intrude, such as the repetition of stimulus words, slips of the tongue, or several reaction words instead of one. In a recent article, Paul Kugler reflects upon the importance of these word association studies for language.[16] As the subject's attention deviates from the task of association, the associations are influenced less by the semantic aspect of words and more by their phonetic aspect. An example of a semantic association would be the response flower given to the stimulus word *bloom*. An example of a phonetic association would be a response like *bloomers* or *blood* to the stimulus word *bloom*. Kugler states: "the semantic association is governed by the meaning of the word, while a phonetic association is according to *sound pattern*."[17] Kugler then arrives at an amazing insight:

---

14 For a presentation and evaluation of the work of E. L. Thorndike, see E. Hilgard and G. Bower, *Theories of Learning* (New York: Appleton-Century-Crofts, 1966), pp. 15–48.

15 C. G. Jung, *Experimental Researches*, trans. L. Stein (Princeton: Princeton Univ. Press, 1973).

16 P. Kugler, "Image and Sound: An Archetypal Approach to Language," *Spring*, 1978 (Dallas: Spring Publ., 1978), pp. 136–151.

17 Ibid., p. 138.

Jung's association work, which took place seventy years ago, offers insight for the most contemporary thinking in linguistics, because it suggests a fundamental law of imagination; that its mode of operation is sonorous, acoustic, phonetic, that there is an innate connection between logos and image, between word and fantasy, that words are fantasies in sound.[18]

Seen through the experimental psychology of association learning, making association through sound rather than meaning is an error, an imperfection because a goal is not attained. But seen through Jung's psychology, what constitutes errors in meaning at the same time constitutes psychological connection. "Failures" take us into the complex, get us close to what fantasies soul is in. "Failures" take us into psychic image where it is possible to experience psyche's spontaneous imaginings. We seem to have gotten ourselves into a difficult situation here. The psychology of learning seems to say that learning cannot be psychological, and depth psychology seems to say that "the complex is unteachable." Language, as we see from Kugler's work, is the crux of this complexity. But if we return again to the actual situation of language in the classroom, we see there that every speaking is at the same time meaningful and nonsensical. We have yet to differentiate what kind of speaking can be psychological and meaningful at the same time.

Erotic language brings together in union realms that are otherwise apart, separate, disconnected, unrelated. The mythology of Eros tells us that this god embodies the spirit of relatedness. He is the god of relationship.[19] Language is erotic whenever it is spoken as a *relating* or a *telling*. Education, too, is a ritual of telling. Greek imagination pictured words as having wings which enabled them to fly between the mouths of speakers. Language is the connection between "inner"

---

18 Ibid., p. 139.

19 The relevance of Eros mythology for the discipline of psychology is developed by J. Hillman, *The Myth of Analysis* (New York: Harper Colophon Books, 1978). The implications of Eros as educator are alluded to in Part One: "On Psychological Creativity."

and "outer." Taken as an image this winged Eros does not take what is "inner" and move it to the "outer" realm, but is between "inner" and "outer." Erotic speech hovers between psyche and life, transforming psyche into life and life into psyche. Eros carries imagination into life and life into imagination. Recall that for Socrates true teaching was possible only through the daimon of Eros. The word is educative when Erotic, and Erotic when connecting soul with world. Hear how he speaks in the classroom. In the Orphic story of the beginning of things, Night conceived of the Wind and laid a Silver Egg in the lap of Darkness. From that Egg sprang Eros. This Eros was named Phanes: to "show forth." As Protagonos, Eros provokes a world into appearance. That is, Eros shows forth, or provokes, the appearance of everything in the Cosmic Egg—the whole world. Eros is seen in what he provokes while he himself remains unseen, like the erotic word which shows forth a world while itself remaining invisible.

Eros is invisible. He is the invisibility of language, and he is the potency of speech, of gesture, of movement, of communication. He cannot be defined because he is shifting in shape and elusive. When he speaks in the classroom, there is a genesis of meaning. What is spoken cannot be pinned down or defined, but it is profound, penetrating, and provoking. The language that connects image and world is not itself meaning; it provokes meaning.

In Hesiod's *Theogony*, Chaos is first. Then came Eros. Then the rest of creation follows. Eros does not mean. He is the genesis of meaning, invisibly penetrating everything, provoking it into meaning. A book that feels important while we cannot say exactly what it means; a lecture that provokes but cannot be explained to someone else; a test paper that "feels" right though it may be objectively wrong—these are the ways of erotic language.

In Plato's *Symposium*, Diotima says of the powers of Eros:

> He interprets and conveys exchanges between gods and men, prayers and sacrifices from men to gods, and orders and gifts in

return from gods to men; being intermediate he fills in for both and serves as the bond uniting the two worlds into a whole entity.

Erotic language is this kind of intermediate realm between archetypal imagination and human meaning. The classroom is such a realm, where what happens is half-crazy, an erotic madness. Walk by a classroom and stand outside listening. Imagine the teacher saying what he is saying in the classroom outside on the street. There he would be considered completely mad. Universities must sanction this half-madness; they must stand in and for the realm of Eros. Every time a skills course or a "relevant" course is introduced in the college curriculum, Eros dies. Every time the *only-human* realm tries to take over the classroom—in the shape of teaching machines, programmed learning, audio visual aids, competency based evaluation, pedantic scholarship—then divine madness dies.

In Orphic mythology, Eros is regarded as the creation god. He is Protagonos, the first-born, born from the Silver Egg. As first-born he is the eldest of the gods and as first-born he is also always new-born. Erotic speech is old and new at the same time. Old words are spoken in new ways. There is no need for specialized terminology or jargon which are opposed to the character of Eros as eldest and youngest. Worn words bear new connections when erotically spoken.

Similarly, in Plato's *Symposium*, Diotima instructs Socrates concerning the character of Eros. Eros is the son of Resourcefulness and Poverty, conceived at the birthday party of Aphrodite. As the son of Poverty, he is continually poor and in want. As the son of Resourcefulness he is vehement and energetic, full of resource, has a passion for knowledge, and is a lover of wisdom. The erotic language of learning is this state between ignorance and wisdom, between unending want and flourishing success. We return again and again to the tasks of learning—another book to read, another lecture to attend, another test to take. Success alternates with want. The work continues because it is beautiful. Eros is the lover of the beautiful, the servant of Aphrodite.

Perhaps learning is not the pursuit of wisdom or the expulsion of ignorance. At least, the depth psychology of learning and education does not locate psychological transformation in the transition from ignorance to knowledge. For we are forever between ignorance and knowledge. Education seeks the beautiful, the unattainable. The Beautiful Lady guides education. Constantly out of reach, she is the transformation figure that keeps us between ignorance and knowledge. We are satisfied with neither because that is not what is being sought. Celestial Aphrodite, the world soul, *Anima Mundi*, keeps our language a language of seeking. She keeps the wound of love open; she keeps language open and moving, poetic and sublime. Erotic speech, then, is Aphrodite's beautiful, persuasive speech. The psychological object of education is beauty, made visible through persuasive speech. It is enacted in the soul as *sophrosyne*, the beautiful, harmonious, rightful ordering of all the elements of psychic life. This ordering receives from Plato the name *katharsis*.[20] *Katharsis* is a reordering of the life of the soul, and does not come to mean a purging of passions until Aristotle's use of the word. Katharsis is therapeutic, but it is not a therapy of the individual soul. It is a therapy of soul in community—of soul in the world.

The way through the individualism that can too often be narcissistic in a "cult" of therapy, and the way into the life of the world, is through the soul of education. Jung found the gods in our diseases. Our diseases are no longer confined to "my" depression or "my" compulsion, or "my" phobia. Our diseases are our schools, our buildings, our money, our food, our energy, our entertainment, our art, our transportation, our medicine. These places are the new materials of soul-making. We live in a neurotic and a psychotic world because we have lost imaginal connection with the things of the world. The heroic ego would want to build better schools, solve the problem of inflation, discover new energy sources, make higher buildings. Depth psychology, however, finds the gods in the world and Eros is the connection

---

20 P. Lain Entralgo, *The Therapy of the Word in Classical Antiquity* (New Haven and London: Yale Univ. Press, 1970), pp. 108–13.9.

between the gods and the world. And the way to Eros is through a re-visioning of education.

This paper was prepared for the Institute of Philosophic Studies at the University of Dallas. A version of the paper was presented at the 1979 C. G. Jung Conference, "Psychology: With/Without Soul," at Notre Dame University. Special thanks are due Tom Kapacinskas for his critical comments.

2

DRAGONFLIES: STUDIES
IN IMAGINAL PSYCHOLOGY

FROM THE EDITOR

With this, our third effort, I wish to reflect some sense of what *Dragonflies* is all about. The work of this journal is imagination: the response of psychological imagination to experience. The individual presented himself in the therapy room of the nineteenth century, and during the twentieth, the patient suffering breakdown is the world itself. Medicine, education, money, food, energy, media, technology, religion, buildings, law, literature, transportation, leadership, business, drama— all of those activities that bring a people together are suffering a massive breakdown. The new symptoms are fragmentation, specialization, expertise, depression, inflation, loss of energy, jargoneze, and violence. Our buildings are anorectic, our business paranoid, our technology manic.

Dragonflies seeks neither to moralize, categorize, nor prescribe treatment. The aim is not to rehabilitate, cure, overcome, romanticize, or transcend the situation. The themes of each issue situate themselves within the culture of the Western imagination, widening and deepening that positivistic approach that seeks to analyze, plan, and restore "normality." Psychological imagination looks upon the breakdown of culture as the breakdown of what the collective ego thinks culture ought to be, and thus allows the appearance of psychological experience in the world.

The work of imaginal psychology is to be true to what is happening: to see that what is happening in the world is happening to us and that the movements of the world are the movements of the soul. As such, culture cannot be looked upon naturalistically as if the world goes on independent of our experience. Culture needs reevaluation in terms of metaphor, image, fantasy, and dream. The true work of imaginal psychology is to become conscious of the stories being enacted in the things of the world. The true work of imaginal psychology is to retell and to relate these stories in a more profound style, taking the fragmentations of culture as analogous to dream fragments through which the depth of the world is seeking to be remembered.

Our approach derives from a phenomenology that restores the sense of the experienced world, and from an archetypal psychology that restores the autonomy of imagination as the place between the empirics of the material world and the literalisms of the world of spirit. The events of the world are regarded as they present themselves and as metaphorical expressions. Imaginal psychology works on culture as if it were a dream to be approached as descriptive of a psychic condition. The stories told through the events of culture are given the respect due independent beings, and the task in hearing them is the education of the imagination: learning to live in the company of events taken imagistically. When the events of the world are recognized as imagistic, then it is possible to face the world in a more psychological manner. Learning to live in a more continually imaginative mode is finally an act of love. The breakdown of the world is the world seeking our attention; it is an action of love on the part of the world that responds only to a similar action of love.

Winter, 1980

3

STIRRINGS OF CULTURE

Essays from the Dallas Institute

INTRODUCTION

Sometimes you can know a book by its cover.... A book jacket, most often, serves as an illustration designed to attract a potential reader by first exciting the visual imagination. Usually, one cannot know a book by its cover. The work of art that is the cover of this book is not usual. It needs to be addressed. Entitled "Echo," it is the work of Dallas artist Joe Guy. Unquestionably beautiful, breathlessly so, it seems to me to be a perfect presentation, not an illustration, of "Stirrings of Culture."

Art critics have said the following about the work of Joe Guy: some technical details—he stretches paper over wood frames and coats it with graphite and wax; the mixture of graphite and wax can cause the black undercoating to become almost a reflective surface, while at the same time it is an absorbing absence; some influences—critics locate Guy's painting within the modernist tradition, liken it to that of Ad Reinhardt or Mark Rothko, with an infusion of Oriental aesthetics; what his paintings present—it is a return of the spiritual to art. His paintings are objects of contemplation rather than objects of perception. To see them, people must enter into their own spirit or soul.

In addition to "Echo," some of the titles of Guy's paintings include "Waiting...Listening," "Concealing," "Shelf," and "Homage." Each series of wall reliefs takes on a particular shape, such as a folding screen, a diptych, an altarpiece, or a fan. These shapes are not representations but minimal structures through which the subtleties of spirit and soul resound.

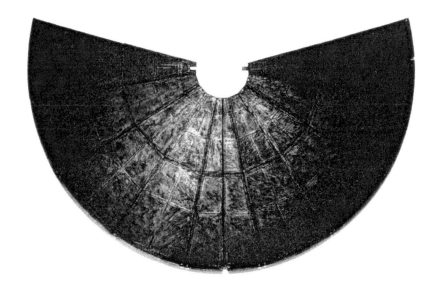

What of the particular painting, "Echo?" The critic can help us to see, but finally it is up to us to see. The fan shape of the painting places us in the presences of the wind of the spirit, its breath. To indicate the character of this breath as it actively creates the actual world, the Chinese call it "the breath of nature." The breath of nature, in its inhalation, is the change from nothing into being, and in its exhalation, the change from existence to nonexistence. At the top of the fan, at the center-point, rests, with great energy, a fan-shaped void. From this void radiates the fan that we see, backed by the energy of the void. The substantial fan, at the top, inclines upward; and if the point of view of the space above is taken, it inclines downward. The fan that we see actively engages with an invisible other half impressing itself downward, embraced by and creating that which we see.

The strength and power of what lies invisibly above must be tremendous, for two small details, in the vicinity of the void have the purpose of providing a right relationship with what presses from above, utilizing the energy in a manner that makes rather than destroys. At the left of the void is a small notch, and at the right of the void, a small key. The notch receives what comes from above; the key returns what is given back to its source. Between the notch and the key stirs the tension of the whole work. To the far right, at the edge of the top section of the fan, lies another notch, which does not receive energy, but gives it back, allows the key to penetrate the void. A third notch lies at the very bottom center of the painting, and has more to do with the dark radiating lines, particularly the centerline, which is the deepest. All the energy of the tension above gathers at this place, and the fan that we see is equivalent to the small key above.

The vertical direction of the painting, if left at that, would indeed give the impression of a purely spiritual work. Moreover, the texture of the painting would be ignored. The shape of the void repeats in the shape of the fan; as well, we could say the void receives the shape of the fan. But, it is the texture of the tension between that counts most. The fan is sectioned, vertical sections, projections of the notch below, producing the beauty of the material world, full of subtle sensuousness, where light is simultaneously reflected and absorbed, where the deepest density of matter shines with the sparks of vitality. While the work may be spiritual, or a presentation of meditation and contemplation, it nevertheless belongs completely to this world, not so much an object in the world, an entity to be perceived, as the perpetually nascent state of physical things.

A significant detail, one difficult to see in the photograph of the painting, concerns the manner in which the nine sections of the work hold together. Thirteen hundred paper hinges link the sections. Many other techniques, far easier, can be imagined, so this method must be considered essential to the presentation. It produces the sense of great strength, the body of the painting, and the signature of labor... both in the sense of work and in the sense of birth.

"Echo" does indeed echo the character of this book, *Stirrings of Culture*. Over the past five years—in conferences, seminars, lectures, The Dallas Institute of Humanities and Culture has worked in the vortices between prevailing institutions and guiding ideas of society such as education, medicine, city planning, economics—and the primary originating imagination from which society draws its vitality. Culture stirs between the imagination and the enactment.

Critics sometimes view the process of culture as occurring in three phases—the visionary, the aesthetic, and the technological. Certainly, the stages are not progressive; as in the painting, "Echo," all three go on simultaneously. The Dallas Institute gathers together people with the capacity of incorporating all three phases in a unified vision to address the major concerns of society. In many instances conversation is promoted among those who, on their own, may be restricted in imagination to one of these planes, but who, nevertheless, have courage and desire to go beyond known boundaries. Such conversations intend to stir culture—not to produce it or affect it in any immediate fashion. Combining vision, imagination, and know-how, the work has been to prevent any one mode of thought fragmenting from the rest. The Dallas Institute has sided, for example, neither with occult or alternative medicine on the one hand, nor with current technological medicine on the other; and in education it has prompted thought as diverse as art and classics; it has heard proposals in economics from the benefits of establishing local currency to the necessity of global economy; it has considered design in the city all the way from movable chairs in public places to skyscraper architecture.

Diversity is not equivalent to eclectic; imagination determines the difference, and this difference reveals itself in language. Eclectic language is specialist, self-serving, the promotion of a singular view patronizingly presented along with other views. Imaginative language is symbolic, metaphoric, encompassing, and suggestive. This language is determined by and centers on the thing itself and requires submission to something larger than oneself. In order to shelter the centrality of real things and their language, The Dallas Institute refrains from addressing causes, engaging in political stances, and resolving disputes; it abdicates both power and control. Such a modest endeavor may thus seem to be of no practical value. The value lies in value itself. An institute concerned with culture—not as culture refers either to individual or group development, but to the wellbeing of society as a whole—can do very little to direct it. It can draw attention to culture, serve it, remember it, and engage in those modes of knowing which illuminate the necessities of the human condition and have the power of restoring human reality to human life. The Dallas Institute exists for the purpose of stirring culture.

The articles in this volume have all been previously published in *The Institute Newsletter*. They represent five years work of the Institute and condense a lifetime of labor of the authors. Each article has been carefully excerpted from a more lengthy writing in order to provide a core thought for consideration. The intention has been to produce, in each case, a memorable image to be contemplated, to be returned to and reread with ease. Most certainly, the reader will be motived to search out more extensive writing of some or all of the authors. This volume, though, presents a community of thought.

Robert J. Sardello, Dallas, Texas, 1986

THE CANCEROUS BODY OF THE WORLD

We must confront the fact that cancer is not only a medical problem and the possibility that cancer will not find its cure in medicine as currently practiced. Cancerophobia, the fear that death resides in the everyday things of the world, calls for a world-centered cultural psycho-therapy seeking to understand the predicament of cancerous things. There is almost complete agreement in the view of cancer as an environmental disease, a silent affirmation of a chronic illness of the world....

Two peculiarities characterize substances determined as cancerous, primarily things made from synthetic organic chemicals: they do not belong to nature and they make possible the proliferation of mass-made objects on a scale unheard of before. The first of these qualities, a radical suspension from nature, is met by a bodily desire to return to Earth, to feel rooted, grounded, sheltered, nurtured—to dwell again in a simplicity that never was. This sentimentality, the body's nostalgia, tears the present from the past, making it impossible to value things of the present world on their own terms, letting them determine what relation to the past they bear rather than dictating what that ought to look like....

The second characteristic of cancerous things, a proliferation of synthetic, mass-made objects, produces a catastrophe of organic form. The instantaneous production of cancerous things hastens or replaces the slow course of organic generation. These things are not rooted in the soil of natural ways—hand-crafted, skilled transformation of Earth into art, but are stamped out by computer-directed machinery, understood from inception as commodities made for profit. They appear and disappear almost instantly, more like dream things than natural objects. When approached only as commodities, they appeal to the herd instinct, making cancer a disease sweeping one along with the herd....

In the tradition of homeopathic medicine, disease consists of the materialization in the body of imagination belonging to worldly things. Oswald Croll, Paracelsus's student, states it in this way: "Man is a hidden world, because visible things in him are invisible, and when they are made visible, then they are diseases, as truly as he is the little world and not the great one." The object of therapeutic treatment is to return imagination to the things that have become only physical. It we look at such treatment psychologically, not literally, it suggests a change in cultural attitude toward the world. The homeopathic therapy of cancer employs an extract of mistletoe, administered to the patient because mistletoe resembles the disease, is equivalent to the imagination. Why mistletoe? It is a peculiar plant form because it appears unaffected by either solar or terrestrial forces. Plants satisfy both earth and sky, creating from the tension and balance of that relationship multifarious organic forms. Mistletoe belies those forces: it grows perpendicularly to the branch that bears it, belonging to no vertical direction—neither nature or spirit. It remains green the whole year long, independent of exposure to light.

The berries of the mistletoe ripen in winter, without warmth. The leaves are indifferent to their orientation to light. If we feel the imagination of the cancerous world in this unnatural plant, it is a world detached from both earth and sky. Beneficent nature is gone and so is the celestial god. Everything seems barren and abstract. Cancer wants our body. Cancer cells are qualitatively no different from normal cells, so it is as if this disease has the purpose of taking over the flesh; that is to say, the abstract world needs flesh, it needs the imagination of body.

The things of the abstract world, mass-made, unnatural things, need the individuality of imagination's body. The fear of cancer is like the fear of being caught in a mob, where particularity no longer has any part to play. Cancer, then, appears in the body as the uprising of undifferentiated cells destroying the individual structure of the body. Upon close examination, however, a malignant mass shows form. A "ripe" cancer of the ovaries, for example, is not a formless growth, but often shows fully formed teeth. Other cancerous cavities exhibit the growth of hair, or of brain tissue—a body is trying to materialize in cancer, for that is what the world is in need of....

For the human body, uninitiated into psychological perception, living according to the wish of natural, organic life, daily existence is a constant threat and trauma, producing the modern malady of stress.... The possibility of body—along with its organic, physiological, and anatomical life—realizing its psychological life, through which the world takes on imagination, occurs with the onset of precancerous symptoms. Medicine gives little attention to such symptoms since they seem like minor psychological difficulties, unrelated to disease. An understanding of these symptoms may be important because any cancer that shows itself as a bodily condition is already an old cancer; in fact, the appearance of a tumor indicates the terminal phase of the disease. Approaching cancer after it already materializes in the body may be looking in the wrong place in the wrong way.

Victor Bott finds two invariable pre-indicators of cancer. The first is the onset of fatigue that will not go away, a particular kind of fatigue, unlike exhaustion from work and also unlike depression. The fatigue can be described as more like a lack of animation, an inability to feel engaged with the world. The second symptom is insomnia. Bott says, "One could even say that any insomnia beginning without evident cause must make one suspect latent cancer." These symptoms appear as signs of the body under attack by a deadly enemy, some unknown virus, only to the materialist eye. The fatigue of the natural body, its apparent loss of animation, calls for a different kind of engagement with the world, one sensing everything in the world as alive, as image, as autonomously animated. Only in our fatigue can the world's animation begin to show. The symptom of insomnia points in a similar direction. The inability to sleep, to enter into the dream world, suggests that the dream world has changed its location from the invisibilities of the night to the appearance of things-as-image. . . .

I do not intend in any way to suggest that realizing the psychological character of the body is equivalent to a cure for cancer. The body of medicine makes us forgetful of the world as suffering things. The organic natural body makes us wish we did not live in the world of abstractions. The psychological body makes a home for the suffering things of the world, allows them to show themselves. . . .

When psychological body is given to the world, will we see a world of freaks—things as crippled, deformed, misshapen, idiotic? There may be a particular kind of intelligence to this monstrous world, for it can show us something of ourselves that has been repressed. In the midst of the urban world, the city of constructions that are supposed to function perfectly, efficiently, we are still village idiots.

CITY BEASTS

Universities have writers-in-residence, museums, artists-in-residence, as well as symphonies and composers-in-residence. I speak as the fool-in-residence at The Dallas Institute. The city needs its jesters, particularly the successful city; and The Dallas Institute is the abode of the foolhardy. That is why it is an institute and not a civic institution. Its sole purpose lies in instituting ideas of the city. Since our work concerns ideas, we need to distinguish ideas from other kinds of realities. I would like to spend a few moments doing exactly that. The ancient philosophers exerted much effort separating ideas from opinions, belief, faith, and knowledge. They knew this was an important task, a guide to whatever they needed to develop. I am no philosopher, merely a psychologist of imagination, and thus will attempt to imagine what ideas are like.

Ideas are very strange creatures indeed. In order to be able to listen to them, we first need to tell them apart from other urban creatures with whom they are most often confused. Certainly, ideas are not the same as opinions. Opinions are tenacious beasts with large saber-edged teeth; they seldom smile, are generally unapproachable, almost impossible to tame. I have heard stories of people who have been attacked by these beasts; they are really quite terrible because upon sinking their teeth into you they contract the disease of lockjaw. Release from them requires a most painful operation. The operation is in fact so painful that, when bitten by a small opinion, most of us prefer to let it hang on to us for the duration of our life, provided of course that it is not too noticeable. This beast roams the city; reportedly, the whole population has been affected to one degree or another.

Another urban creature often confused with ideas is the fact. Several species of this animal exists in the urban environment, the two most notable being *factus informatius* and *factus knowledgeius*.

Factus imformatius, a very flat, grey creature, lacks any vivid coloration. Its behavior is quite uninteresting, and only collectors become intrigued with it. It does not appear to be dangerous or aggressive except in large groups. It may be related to rabbits, for its favorite pastime is self-reproduction. The favorite habitat of the fact in the city is the computer, where it seems quite content to rest undisturbed. Facts feed mainly on paper, often using reams at a time.

The more aggressive of the species is *factus knowledgeius.* While flat and grey like its closest relative, the *factus knowledgeius* appears more attractive because it is able to camouflage itself so that it looks exactly as we think an idea would look if we could see one. This species likes to act like it knows something, imitating a form of life that it itself does not possess. This beast is related to the vampire for it is a creature that looks substantial but actually casts no reflection. It pierces the neck of the unsuspecting victims, secretly draining away the lifeblood of the city.

The next animal we must consider is the plan. It is not certain whether the plan actually qualifies as an animal. Its name in fact comes from the word *plant* (there, you see; I was just attacked by a *factus knowledgeius,* a fact acting like it knows something). It lies always close to the ground and consequently sometimes goes by the name of ground plan. It too is thin and flat; it moves by spreading itself like a thin membrane over the city. While slower, it is related to the centipede. When it walks over the city it leaves the imprint of the grid. Once caught by a plan, it is almost impossible to get out of its grip. It produces the chronic disease of conformity. The plan can be very colorful. Just last week, at the planning session for the urban neighborhood of the near east side, I saw a large picture of one that was red and green and blue and yellow with black stripes.

Finally, let me describe the creature known as the goal. It is a speedy little creature; reminds me somewhat of a roadrunner. It is always on the move, going somewhere, traveling only in straight lines. And it always travels upward, never downward. Very few people can catch a goal, though it makes for great sport. Whenever you get close, it jumps a little higher. I know of many people in the city who spend their life trying to attain a goal for their trophy case. A few people have large collections of interesting varieties. Goals themselves, however, are not very interesting creatures; the pleasure comes from chasing them.

Now, ideas are the most difficult of all to describe. They are nearly extinct within the city. Almost everyone considers them dangerous, though in all of the sources that I have consulted there is not a single report of anyone ever having been harmed by an idea. We fear them; sometimes they act wild or crazy, and when they attach themselves to you they will not let go. Sometimes they bounce off walls. Everyone likes big ideas, and few are interested in small ideas. I myself prefer the little ones because you can hold them in your hand, and they are absolutely delightful. One of the few places you can find them in the city is over on Routh Street, often on a Wednesday evening, where they love to gather. What is most amazing about these creatures is that they are able to talk, and love to have conversations with each other.

Now, I have not provided a very good description of ideas, and I really would like to do so in order that you will have no trouble recognizing one when you see it. Well, from what I have already said, you know that it does not have sharp teeth, is neither flat nor grey, that it does not reproduce by itself, is not flashy in color, does not spread itself over a large area, does not move in straight lines, and does not soar to great heights. You would think that the best place to get a good look at them would be in the university. When they were thought to be dangerous to the city they were all gathered up and placed in the idea sanctuary because no one wanted to be accused of ideacide. I went out to several of our local universities to see if I could observe them carefully because I really did want to provide you with a clear description of this creature. When I asked about them at our local campuses everyone remembered them and spoke very fondly, almost reverently of them. They recalled how you could play with them and contemplate them and delight in their curious ways. But, alas, I was told that ideas have not done well in the university because almost no one knows how to care for and feed them.

Some thought it best that they be kept locked in cages called books, and whoever got the most into books and journals would be rewarded by being appointed professor of ideas. Others thought that they ought to be put into computers in order to make instruction in ideas more efficient. This was an example of *factus knowledgeius* killing off ideas. Still others thought the best place to keep students safe from ideas was to imbed them in film and tape—audio-visual aids, I believe they were called.

Well, I am sorry to report, I did not get a look at an idea in the university. I did hear them though. In just a couple of classrooms—where students were not pounding away on computers or looking at film-strips—as I stood outside the door, I heard the most wonderful conversations. I do not know what the creature inside looked like, but they simply could not have been opinions, facts, plans, or goals. I could only hear scattered words through the heavy doors, but I am quite sure it was the voices of ideas. I heard words like truth, imagination, city, love, care, evil, goodness, soul, holocaust, leadership, war, peace, death, hope, psyche, thought, memory, poetry, mystery, history, dwelling, god, myth, human, life, birth, sky, polis, suffering, wisdom, eternity, understanding, time, celebration, ritual. I don't know why, but just hearing such words made me cry with joy. And there were long moments of silence in that room, as if ideas need lots of time and quiet. But there was also laughing and arguing coming from within the room. And absolutely no one in that room said anything like "what do you do with all this talk," or "how do you implement these ideas," or "what is the practical value of this conversation."

So, I come before you now to plead a case for the reintroduction of the species idea into the city. And I have to do so lacking the clear description I had hoped to gather. Even if we cannot see them, why don't we try to reintroduce them into the city on a trial basis. Let's close off a small space, call it The Forum, keep out all the beasts—opinions, facts, plans, and goals—and see if the kind of language heard outside the classroom visits us. Ideas seem to be very closely connected with conversation, so we will have to talk with one another in these Forums, and when we find that this talk takes on a life of its own, then we will know that ideas have entered.

Now, I don't think that we can talk directly about ideas—they are probably too shy and self-conscious. But we can talk about the city—maybe the crisis of public education or leadership, or the imagination of the city, or criticism in the city. If they don't think that we are talking about them, maybe ideas will join in, and we might get a glimpse of them.

THE LEARNING INSTINCT

I want to begin with a claim which counters present theories of learning, but nevertheless carries enough force to be cultivated into insight. The claim reads: of all the instincts—reproduction, hunger, aggression, survival—the most characteristically human instinct is learning. While much of education has as its goal the preparation for earning a living, if one starts with the premise of learning as instinct, the goal of education transforms into "learning a living," for the instinct continues to awaken all through life....

Who can deny experiencing an impulse for learning, a force welling up from within, a powerful, autonomous urge, satisfied only through release, and when released producing an intense form of pleasure that can only be called joy? My purpose, then, consists of serving the forgotten soul of learning, beginning with a description of its impulsive vitality....

The impulse for learning originates in an alluring display of the things of the world, evoking desire for union with them—an urge toward intimacy with the spirit, soul, vitality, the particular beauty marking each thing as standing forth from an abyss of holiness. Things draw us to intimate knowledge as if they need us, though in an entirely impersonal manner, for their own completion. The forceful allure of the world to be known draws the soul out of a self-enclosing illusion of mastery through detachment into soul engagement with reality. This innate desire to experience the world pulsing through the body constitutes a drive toward transformation initiating care for all things. Learning compels us to have regard for what is outside and beyond ourselves, and in knowing this to become like them. Thus, the basis of the learning instinct lies in mimesis, an imitation of the action of the things of the world, knowing as entering the manifest mystery of things. In climactic moments of history the inner life of the world bursts forth initiating a flowering of culture. Renaissance begins, though, in the soul, through release of its most natural activity, learning.

The repression of instinctual life prompted the creation of psycho-analysis. Freud uncovered two primary instincts, eros and thanatos—the urge toward life and the urge toward death. The contribution of Jung lay in the rediscovery of the psyche, which, he showed, does not belong singularly to human experience, but to physical things as well. A third instinct, learning, drives us between life and death; it has as its purpose a union with the psyche of the world. An understanding of this instinct requires mythical modes of thought reminiscent of the pre-Socratic philosophers and early storytellers. One such myth, central to learning, concerns genius.

Ancient psychology spoke of genius as mythical beings, daemons of a particular sort, whose work consists of guardianship of the world. The genius within things gives them vitality, continuity between generations, and attractiveness. The spirits of things at the same time, though in a slightly different manner, are guardians of individual human beings; individuals are also accompanied through life by a genius. The relation between individual genius and those of the world, the push and pull between them, seems to me to lie at the heart of the learning instinct. In the act of knowing, to become united with the thing known, is predisposed by the presence of the personal genius attracted to its similars in the world—which may be physical things, ideas, books, art, language, music—all have their guardians....

Today we equate genius with extraordinary ability, as if it were a possession of a gifted few, a mistake perpetuated in schools through programs for the talented and gifted. The word *genius,* however, comes from Roman mythology, equivalent to the daemons of Greek myth. The word derives from *gignere*—to engender, or engenderer; *genius* names those guardians who engender, give gender, generate life and vitality in our surroundings, assuring that things will be cared for because they are animated by spiritual presences. When things are approached with care, their genius shines forth. Genius also inspires the potency of individual life. In those times when the world was perceived as living, individual genius was honored on the day of one's birth. At the birthday celebration certain foods appropriate to the nature of the genius were offered. Those who indulged their genius were called *"genialis,"* from which we receive the word *genial.* The person who refused indulgence was called *"aridus,"* dry.

The coordination between world-centered and individual-centered genius has its own specific mythological rendering in astrology; one's astrological chart depicts the attractions between individual and world. The latin word *natale* means "companion," and from this word comes the term *natal chart.* The chart gives images of the particular sectors of the world with which one's genius is congenial. We now call this attraction talent or ability and try to measure it with intelligence tests; and in so doing, the necessary contribution of the genius of the world is obscured....

The central task of learning consists of learning to learn, a yielding to one's genius, allowing the instinct to be released. Those who more fully allow themselves to be inhabited by their daemon, who no longer seek to control and keep it repressed are true teachers. They are teachers because they cannot stop learning themselves. When education recognizes this force, the spiritual/cultural necessity of learning will take its rightful precedence over practical and social concerns. The purpose of learning, its goal, is to be a means without an end. Indulging the appetites of one's genius leads to voracious seeking after the pleasures of knowledge. Learning is to the soul what food is to the body. Bad soul food consists of undigested facts, raw information, half-baked ideas, cafeteria curricula. Good soul food is prepared with imagination, warmed with the heart, served as a feast of ideas. Then learning can get into the blood, circulate, enter the materiality of the body, transform it, and be released into the body of the world.

While the specific effects of learning thus understood are unpredictable, the locus of those effects can be specified. If learning were free to work in the world it would produce a ferment of conversation, writing, performance, speculation, investigation, and the making of images—in art, music, poetry, drama, music. I am not suggesting that the arts would flourish, for the arts would no longer be separated, specialized realms. Culture would flourish, bringing about a synthesis of imagination such as we have not seen since the Renaissance. The manic world of economics, production, consumption, would cease, replaced by the living materiality of world-filled imagination....

In a recent film, *Teachers,* a call is put in for a substitute teacher for a high school history class. Unknown to the recruiter, the man who answers the phone is not the substitute but an inmate of a mental institution, who happily responds to the opportunity for early release by walking out of the asylum and entering the teaching profession. He takes well to the task of the classroom by costuming himself as the historical figures who are the subject of the lessons—as Lincoln, as Washington, as Custer—and enacting scenes of importance, engaging the students in the lessons. This teacher was not utilizing a ploy, a trick, a kind of audio-visual aid to illustrate history. He became inhabited by those figures. When he is finally discovered as a lunatic, the men with the white coats are called in and he is hauled away, rather brutally. As the attendants drag him down the corridor, the teacher exhorts them to take their hands off him and treat him with respect, for, he says, "I am a Teacher." Now, in the whole high school, it seems to me, this person was in fact the only teacher. The hero of the film is supposed to be the real teacher because he is so involved in the lives of the students; actually, he is more of a social worker, concerned with making school "relevant." Others are involved in school politics, or concerned with how to keep discipline, or lobbying for a union for pay increases, or satisfying the superintendent. But only this one madman is hospitable to the spirits; the madman is a genius.

The qualities of learning I have been attempting to evoke cannot be institutionalized. But the educational institution might be revisioned, seen as the structure whose task is to protect the inviolate space of the classroom, whose duty is to arrange a situation in which teachers are allowed to teach. With such protection, teachers could follow the demands of their genius, awakening the genius of their students. The genius of teaching makes the following demands: to at all times engage in living thinking—the recognition that ideas are living entities; to be devoted to the pleasures of truth and knowledge; to teach out of a deeply rooted feeling that there is something higher than ourselves; to take "outer" things and allow them to re-echo in the soul by exercising the faculties of imagination, inspiration and intuition.

PSYCHOLOGICAL BENEFITS OF CAPITALISM

I speak as a psychotherapist, as one engaged, with care, in the disease of economics; as one who adheres to the therapy of the word, taking things as they are, working to sense more fully the value that lies within symptoms. My technical knowledge of economics may be off. My nose for the inner workings of the disease is not.

Methodical, systematic, continuous pursuit of gain with avoidance of all pleasure characterizes the original spirit of capitalism, born
of the Protestant Reformation. The relation between capitalism and
psychology, as far as I know, has never been explored, an apparent
oversight, since the two begin at the very same moment. The great
Philipp Melanchthon, friend of Martin Luther, fellow theologian, supported and gave clear formulation to the respectability of restrained
accumulation of capital. He also introduced the word *psychology* into
the modern vocabulary. I hope to show that because of Melanchthon,
modern economics consists of a single, simple psychology of individual
subjectivity projected onto society, and that the final benefit of such
economics lies in the breakdown of human subjectivity, leading to the
discovery of reality....

Psychological sensibility has been around in the Western world since
Heraclitus, 500 BC. Psyche, or soul, permeated everything and was not
limited to human beings. The world was ensouled, and economics simply meant the care of the household of the world. Heraclitus put it this
way: "You could not discover the limits of the psyche, even if you traveled every road to do so; such is the depth of its meaning." The care
of the household was not simple, nor automatically given as some primordial contact with the beauty of nature. It took place through ritual
oriented toward conforming human life to the life within the cosmos;
it took place through disciplines such as astrology recognizing human
reality as a microcosm of the macrocosm; it took place through including care of all objects of the household as part of the familia, the family,
and thus all objects as alive.

Melanchthon, by naming a field psychology, by limiting psyche to
what goes on in individuals, stopped soul from appearing in any place
but individual subjectivity; and economics changes from care of the
household of the world to the pursuit of personal gain....

Capitalism has come a long way—from the pursuit of limited gain
with the avoidance of pleasure to the pursuit of unlimited gain in order
to produce pleasure. Melanchthon's psychology lies behind it all. The

first part of his *Loci Communes Theologici* presents a simple model of individual psychology. He says:

> We divide man into only two parts. For there is in him a cognitive faculty, and there is also a faculty by which he either follows or flees the things he has come to know. The cognitive faculty is that by which we discern through the senses, understand, think, compare, and deduce. The faculty from which the affections arise is that by which we either turn away from or pursue the things known, and this faculty is sometimes called "will," sometimes "affection," and sometimes "appetite."

This definition of what constitutes the human soul founds the capitalistic spirit. Knowledge of what is to be done comes from cognition. Will, which contains the appetites, cannot be trusted and is therefore turned over to the guidance of God. People may know what to do to acquire gain. That greed may enter, cannot be controlled, but they may proceed as long as they have turned their will over to God, pursuing gain without seeking their own pleasure.

Adam Smith's classical economics wrote the divine out of individual psychology and thus out of economics altogether, replacing the element with propositions concerning human nature, claiming acquisition as an innate human trait. He says: "The desire of bettering our condition comes with us from the womb and never leaves us until we go to the grave." This version of Melanchthon's psychology serves as base for his primary economic proposition: "Every individual is continuously exerting himself to find out the most advantageous employment for whatever capital he can command."

Unlimited acquisition becomes respectable and acceptable by interpreting it as rooted in human nature. Such an interpretation represents the elevation of a culture-bound historical orientation to a universal principal.

The psychology of self-interest puts a severe strain on restraint, a central element of capitalism. The utilitarian psychology of Jeremy Bentham and John Stuart Mill heightens self-interest even more, for they say the basic individual propensity is to seek pleasure and avoid pain, though pleasure is defined as long-run pleasure, not immediate satisfaction. The direction of economics, in keeping with this view of human subjectivity, turns from valuing labor to valuing the production of goods, the crack in the door that will change the word *goods* into the word *commodities*.

Neoclassical economics, whose founder was the British economist Alfred Marshall, the originator of microeconomics, introduced efficiency as the center of a psychology needed to accommodate pleasure. Once pleasure is introduced as the purpose of economics, the danger arises that behavior incompatible with economy will surface—the disinclination to work, art, the senses, meaningful work—for these are all pleasures. The new variation of Melanchthon's psychology says that it is natural for human beings to maximize monetary or consumptive gains. Opposing forces, values, and interests are balanced in such a fashion that they maximize advantages—this is the definition of efficiency. Marshall states:

> And in a money economy, good management is shown by so adjusting the margins of suspense on each line of expenditure that the marginal utility of a shilling's worth of goods on each line shall be the same. And this result each one will attain by constantly watching to see whether there is anything on it which he is spending so much that he would gain by taking a little away from that line of expenditure and putting it on some other line.

This is of course the budget, and the budget is a way to manage satisfaction of pleasure efficiently. Economics becomes the management of pleasure. The new psychology states it is natural to seek more and more satisfaction by consciously, deliberately maximizing all gains at a given moment.

This new psychology shifts the whole sense of economics. The classical economic individual was supposed to maximize something concrete: income, wealth, savings, investments, capital, durable goods, durable possessions. Efficiency is based on manipulative maximizing of pleasure, of inner psychological states, the efficient management of desire. It is entirely relative what one chooses to maximize. It could be the pleasure of cocaine or the pleasure of giving to the poor; it makes no difference. . . .

This position, where we are now, opens the way for consumer economics, the manipulation of goods and services through attaching them to pleasurable states which have nothing to do with said goods and services, through advertising. Economics turns into public relations and promoting the satisfaction of subjective states.

I read the history of economics since the sixteenth century as the history of human subjectivity separated from the world we inhabit; economics is the psychology of an uninhabited world. The new emerging economics, so aptly under creation by Hazel Henderson, an economics of the household of the planet, is the first sign that we just might be able to forego the glorification of subjectivity. But, one more hidden element of Melanchthon's psychology must be exposed. All economic theories begin with the proposition that it is natural for man to be greedy, and that the best way to make society consists in harnessing greed. It is impossible, however, to base economics in a psychology of greed without greed becoming the single creative factor in the world. Restraint only proves the necessity of the proposition. Greed produces restrained greed which accumulates in the world. A second factor also enters. Since all economic theories are based in speculation about individual psychology, we must also say that subjective psychology is the same thing as the psychology of greed. Basing psychology on the nature of persons rather than on the nature of the psyche, which includes far more than greed, makes greed into the primary virtue; since greed, according to economic psychology, is the basis of human nature, greed must express itself for us to be true to our nature. Economy, from this point of view, is nothing more than human nature, greed, expressing itself in the world, creating a world, without the burden of guilt. If greed could be felt with its attendant affliction of guilt, there would be spontaneous movement out of subjectivity into care for the world. The third factor in all economic psychology which makes this movement impossible is that all such psychologies include rationality as basic to human nature, along with greed. But since, like greed, rationality is defined in such a manner as to be content-less, without a world, the content of rationality has to be greed, as the content of greed is that greed becomes harnessed to rationality. That is all there is to work with in economic psychology—greed and rationality playing off each other. The primary way greed plays off rationality is by rationalizing greed so that guilt does not accompany the affliction of greed. The result when all this is leashed onto the world over a period of two hundred years is one gigantic psychopathic world; we do not live in a world of anxiety or hysteria, or depression, or a schizophrenic world, but a psychopathic world—very successful, very adapted, very clever, but there is no feeling of affliction. That is the psychological benefit of capitalism. All possible fantasies can be enacted in the world without inhibition because nothing hurts, nothing feels wrong, nothing feels off the mark. It can all be rationally justified as being good if individual gain is involved.

Now, to the real psychological benefit of capitalism. Economic psychology, bringing about individual gain, has made the world sick. Well, now there is something real to care for. And since psychology made her sick, psychology must be central to her healing. But the whole paradigm must be shifted. It is we who are dead and the world is alive and in pain. We can no longer trust our humanity, no matter how much we sugarcoat it with the psychology of peak experiences, the return to feelings, and more body; it's all psychopathic. All you have to do is spend one evening watching television to see that every human emotion possible is now under the domain of manipulation for gain. But the world does not lie about its afflictions, and it does not cover them, for it has no ego to protect. The terrible misery of the world has nothing to hide behind. And I mean the world in a concrete, particular sense. The room with its false, water-stained ceilings, hollow doors, skyscrapers forced to act like neon signs, the most atrocious, nasty images polluting the room, emanating from the television eight hours a night, fabricated foods, cancerous plastics, ugly computers. These things I trust. A new economics must be based in a psychotherapy of the things of the world, a care for the psyche within things, a care for their afflictions. Now that may be the psychological benefit of capitalism—there is so much sickness to care for—it forces us to forget ourselves and return to the world to recover its soul, its mana. We cannot help ourselves anymore or rely on ourselves to make a decent world. We are failed, and now we must care. We are totally anesthetized to human suffering. But the afflictions of the things of the world still have power to move us.

The approach to caring for the world I have in mind can best be carried forth in daily life in the city. Think of it as saving $80 an hour for visiting a psychologist in an office who treats your illness and sends you back out into a sick world. First, there must be the felt recognition that the city, in spite of its glitter and flash and self-promotion, is dying. Once we get through the process of denial, a response of rage follows. We all feel it at moments. It is an important feeling; it scares us because it is not subjective. It is a feeling that breaks through the numbness of anesthesia. If it is acted out, however, rage would meet with powerlessness, and isolated subjectivity would return. Rage, felt, held, not shut off nor denied, leads then to compassion. It is the point it dawns on us that the loss of sensibility we suffer is also suffered by the things, the material things of the city.

Compassion is the capacity to be with the suffering of another; but this capacity is not limited to human relationships. It can be developed to the point of suffering with things. Let me assure you, this is not foolish, merely an unusual way of understanding. Thinking that the world is dead is a relatively recent historical development—since the sixteenth century, the time modern economics took hold. It is a development that has allowed us to gain power over the material world by declaring it dead; and it is the stance that makes us live with the fear of holocaust, the final result of taking the world as dead. So, imagine caring for the things of the world, giving them time and attention, sensing what they need, as an act of anti-nuclearism, as psychological activism against the literal bomb. As the viewpoint of subjectivity breaks down, as it is now doing in this great age of transition, we are provided with an opportunity to enter a new age, a new economy of care for the world. I think it can be the age of life—not utopian and spectacular, but simple attention to reality, a simple recognition that human beings are nothing more than emanations of the world; her first, us second. If Dallas is really the city of the future, then it ought not to rely on a dead worldview. This new age can be ushered in right here in Dallas. All that is needed is a recession; a recession of human subjectivity.

4

Freud, Jung,
and Spiritual Psychology

Lectures by Rudolf Steiner

We live in an age when psychotherapy in its myriad forms is taken for granted. Imagine, just for a moment, how many people in the world practice psychotherapy, how many patients of one therapy or another are now involved in the growing numbers of therapeutic groups focused on various addictions. One might think that a great deal of "soul work" goes on here. However, owing to fundamental errors at the very founding of the discipline, it may well be that psychotherapy is oriented toward conquering soul rather than entering into soul wisdom. By "soul wisdom" I mean the capacity of self-knowledge based on the development of the practice of a fully conscious meditative awareness leading to a picture-consciousness that "sees through" experience of both inner and outer worlds to the activity of spiritual beings. These lectures on psychoanalysis and spiritual psychology, given by Rudolf Steiner in the years 1912, 1917, and 1921, at the very time when the "talking cure" was in its beginnings, force us to confront the inadequate knowledge used in founding psychoanalysis and psychotherapy as a method of soul work. Now, some eighty years later, this method has multiplied endlessly, and without questioning the kind of knowing involved. Arguments can be found pitting one school of therapy against another, but I can think of only one contemporary analyst, James Hillman, who questions the whole enterprise. Hillman bases his critique on the astute observation that, by sequestering it in a private room, therapy removes soul from the world and thereby degrades its intricacies. The result, he says, is a world lacking the sense of soul. Now, exactly how psychotherapy got into this situation and how it contributes to a culture lacking in soul can be learned by following Steiner's exploration of the development of psychoanalysis.

Step one: The nature of a wound of the soul, of inner life, was misread very early on in the history of psychoanalysis. Consequently, instead of learning how to pay attention to soul, psychoanalysis was diverted to the supposed circumstances in which the wounding occurred—circumstances that were said to take place during the historical life of the person. Thereby, with a brilliant move of ordinary intelligence, Freud sidestepped the opportunity to develop a kind of knowledge suitable for the soul. That is to say, he did not see that the appearance of psychological symptoms, a new phenomenon of the age, points to the need for the development of new capacities of perception. Psychological symptoms indicate that the boundary between consciousness and subconsciousness has become unreliable, that the lower soul forces have begun to penetrate into ordinary consciousness, producing disruption because there are no forms for this new experience. New capacities of perception would mean the development of moral, aesthetic, and intellectual qualities—qualities that would broaden and deepen the middle realm of the soul, and could then enter into culture for further development. Instead, Freud contended that a person's suffering is not due to the wounding but to the inability to understand what is happening within what Steiner would call sense-perceptible knowledge. Psychoanalysis helps the suffering patient to achieve this form of understanding by associating the wounds of the soul with historical events in the person's life; once the wounding "makes sense," relief occurs. Psychoanalysis in this sense is training in making the soul conform to the scientific analysis of cause and effect, an education into materialist logic that undoubtedly goes hand in hand with learning to view the events of the outer world with this same kind of logic.

Step two: Once a theory of causation is established the psychoanalytic researcher, in good scientific fashion, must look for a principle that accounts for all cases of the phenomenon. Freud found this in the principle of sexuality—that behind all neuroses lies a wounding brought about by a trauma of love. This step is one further departure from the soul because it is an abstraction separated from the life of the person as a whole. Interestingly, the current popularity of addiction and code-pendency groups even more strongly reinforces this departure from the nature of the soul that culminates with Alice Miller's work, *The Drama of the Gifted Child*. Here Freud's starting point, which is the present experience of a wound of the soul, is completely disregarded, and the original wound is now taken to be an actual wound in the historical life of the person. The difference is crucial. While Freud avoided investigating soul directly through developing a means of perception that would give such knowledge, he nevertheless never took the stories told by patients to be actual accounts of the past; he took them to be memories, and, as such, filled with fictional elaboration. In the new version, soul is taken out of the picture altogether, and now literally thousands and thousands of persons come together weekly in groups to discuss the historical events of their wounding at the hands of abusive parents. From there they are led into the Twelve-Step recovery program, into a dependency on one's self-selected version of a "higher power," as if one could get to the spirit by completely bypassing soul. The vessel is now completely broken. The eruption of soul experiences, a cultural phenomenon of the age, is again suppressed, and the possibility of developing a true knowledge of the inner life is thereby decreased.

Now what is the inner life? Talking about one's feelings, recovering early childhood memories, delving into emotions, describing personal experiences—none of this concerns the inner life. There is a story told concerning the writer Balzac that when he was on his deathbed, many of his associates and friends came to see him, as if to get a last word from the master. Balzac would ask these people about certain other people— how they were doing in life, how their marriages were faring, whether a certain person ever got out of his trouble with the law. Balzac, however, was not talking about actual people. He was talking about the characters in his novels. This is the true inner life, when the goings-on of the inner world become as real as any outer event. True wisdom of the soul would seek to develop this kind of strength of inner perception, not to cure it.

Psychoanalysis and all its offshoots have a further, more far-reaching effect than simple ineffectiveness in encouraging a genuine inner life. Once a theory of the unconscious is established, an iatrogenic disease of the psyche ensues. That is, the cure of the illness becomes the source of illness. The theories themselves, Steiner points out, agitate the subconscious, and in this manner, what begins as a limited field of inquiry spreads into a cultural phenomenon. That is to say, psychotherapy is a self-perpetuating phenomenon; the more it is done the more illness is created.

The student of psychological systems might think that the difficulties pointed out thus far may be true for Freud and those psychotherapeutic approaches that can be linked back to him, but that with Jung a real breakthrough into the realm of the soul proper occurs. Not only does Jung break with Freud's sexual foundation, but he also sees the limitation of personal memory, realizing that symptoms cannot be accounted for by simply following the events of early childhood, and that there exists a whole other realm of memory, the collective unconscious, which seems to be the image presentation of the soul world. Mythic memory, not personal memory, becomes with Jung the source of psychological illness. The gods, Jung says, have become our diseases. The difficulty, according to him, is that the mythic content stirring within the soul, when it is not conscious, causes illness. Relief comes when conscious connection is made with these mythic stirrings. The gods are necessary to human beings, but simply as a psychological function. The psychology of Jung, therefore, does not open perception to spiritual reality; it stops short. The cultural result here is more complex than in the case of Freud. The legacy of Jung has led to a psychology of abstractions—anima, animus, projection, shadow, and introversion, extraversion—that do their share of creating illness, but in a different way than with Freud. Rather than focusing on the historicity of the soul wound, the legacy of Jung produces instead a wholly subjective psychology in which the gods are reduced to the familiarity of ordinary cognition, set into dramatic interplay by abstract concepts acting as if they were real. Furthermore, patients in this kind of psychoanalysis become students of those amateur mythologists, the analysts themselves, who set about convincing their patients that they are walking texts upon whom are written the stories of the gods, which they do not know they are enacting in their lives. Once they become willing carriers of these gods and goddesses, symptoms are relieved. An important exception to this tendency is to be found in the work of James Hillman, whose work is indebted to Jung, but who refuses to engage in such tomfoolery. The archetypal psychology of Hillman takes the imaginal world to be fully objective and real. But, as I have already indicated, this leads him to reject the notion of therapy.

I see the influence of Jung working in two directions in our culture. On the one hand, it has fostered an imitation religion, the conception of Jung as a mystic, and the elevation of subjectivity to the status of religious experience. That is to say, inadequate cognition becomes honored as religion. It produces bad art and a form of ritual in which individuals worship themselves thinking they are honoring some deity, and dreams are treated as sacred texts. On the other hand, Jung's cultural influence has brought about a peculiar interest in myth, exemplified most clearly by Joseph Campbell, in which myth is reduced to the terms of ordinary consciousness. Campbell, I propose, is not a mythologist but a demythologizer, faithfully explaining to millions of television viewers the workings of myth in terms that require nothing of the viewer, coupled with the sentimentality of the wonders of lost worlds. Interpreting myth, as Campbell does, differs considerably from mythological thinking. The former stands outside the myth while the latter appreciates and practices it by moral investigation; that is, it recognizes that myth demands a response in the present. It approaches myth as the symbolic expression of correspondences between prototypes above and their manifestations below. Campbell, conversely, approaches myth as the symbolic expression of archetypes in the past, with the result that one only learns what has been lost and is not directed toward seeing these expressions in new forms occurring in present circumstances. Jung mixed and confused prototype and archetype without knowing he was doing so.

In the middle of the second of this series of lectures, Steiner makes a statement that is not a mere observation but a report of something he saw by way of suprasensory faculties concerning the life of Nietzsche. It is quite astounding, Steiner says—and we also know this from other places in his writings—that Wagner, after his death, was the spiritual guide of Nietzsche. Then, however, Steiner says that Wagner allowed Nietzsche to become mentally deranged to protect him from entering consciously into dangerous regions of spirit. What might have occurred, we must consider, had Nietzsche had the benefit of psychotherapy? What forces would have been loosed on the world? Does not psychotherapy sanction a truly terrible hubris when it treats the situation of the soul as if it were diseased? Is it not hubris when the analyst determines that what the patient is given to confront in life is the wrong thing for that person to confront, or is being confronted in the wrong way? One cannot, however, even consider such a possibility without the benefit of true spiritual perception. In truth, the psychotherapist has not the faintest notion of what he is dealing with or of how very simplistic even the most complex of psychological theories really are because of the failure to recognize the reality of the spiritual worlds. For instance, even when a transpersonal dimension seems to be taken into account, as with Jung, the individual soul is never considered beyond the life between birth and death. Spiritual cognition, on the other hand, sees feelings as carried over from the soul life of the period of an individual's last death to this birth, while will is seen as the soul life of the previous incarnation. Current psychology is capable of seeing these qualities of soul only as limited to individual life between birth and death.

The real dangers of psychotherapy are exposed when the full spiritual nature of the human being is brought to light. The key to the full cognition of individual human reality lies in reincarnation, which for Steiner is not an idea but a matter of spiritual perception. I hope that the reader who is encountering Anthroposophy for the first time will be led to study Steiner's researches concerning reincarnation. With respect to the question of psychotherapy, it is most important to gain an understanding concerning what I would call the porosity of the soul between death and rebirth. By porosity, I mean that the soul life during the period between death and birth, as well as the soul life of previous incarnations, permeate and are permeated with the whole spirit world. Soul is not isolated within itself: it extends into the whole spirit world. In the life between birth and death this means that feeling and will are not isolated within the individual soul, are not a purely individual matter. Symptoms, then—and this is what is so hard for us to accept because of the all-pervasive acceptance of psychology as concerning the subjectivity of soul—do not belong to the individual but to the culture as a whole; they are individually lived aspects of the milieu in which one lives. Furthermore, symptoms indicate the needed direction for knowledge of the spiritual world that must be taken by the culture as a whole. Symptoms do not simply call for the effort to ameliorate individual suffering, as if the world in which such suffering occurs does not matter. Let me provide an example, that of addictions.

Within our addictions lies the expectation of magical, ritual, and spiritual transformation. One gives oneself over to a substance that comes from afar and is supposed to carry one far away. The exotic drug is a metaphor for wisdom and psychic/spiritual experience, a metaphor indicating a longing for spirit. The process of addiction involves three components, only two of which are presently recognized. First, a physical, organic habit is formed. Then a more subtle habit develops which forms itself into a kind of conditioning. The silent, unrecognized component is a striving, an unfruitful quest for spiritual experience. Drug addictions, moreover, point to a much larger field of addictions to virtually anything—substances, other people, position, knowledge, pleasure, money, power, possessions, sex, recognition. Addictions indicate a taking-in of the materialistic worldview, as if possessing the world would produce completeness of spirit. As a spiritual symptom of the age, however, addictions indicate that today's spiritual task is to develop the capacities to experience the world in a more spiritual way, to actually find spirit in the world through a relation to the world that develops the perception of spiritual activities occurring there. Working with addiction as an individual problem or enacting laws and legislation misses seeing the spiritual task of the time. The task does not direct us to some abstract idea of spirit or equally abstract idea of learning to ask for guidance from a higher power, but directs us to develop a spiritual cognition of the world that does not depart from the particularity of every individual thing of the world.

Anthroposophy leads to a wisdom of the soul and is thus never content to stop with the act of careful examination of limited systems of knowledge. While Steiner agrees that the phenomena originating psychoanalysis are of critical importance, he says that because Freud did not recognize spirit, soul became identified with individual history, which led to a view of history without soul. This development of the psychoanalytic model indicates that the soul is not sufficient unto itself. It is part of spirit and therefore can be investigated by the means of spiritual research. Now I want to show how such investigation differs from psychoanalysis. This difference is actually more subtle than one might think, for there seem to be close similarities. In order to perceive the difference, therefore, it is necessary to avoid all abstraction.

First, the spiritual investigator must learn that there is a difference between one's own inner life and the experience of the objective spiritual world. Avoiding this crucial difference leads on the one hand to the confused mysticism of Jung, and on the other to modern psychologists such as R.D. Laing, who approach schizophrenia as if it were spiritual experience. The first reduces spiritual experience to subjective psychology; the second enlarges subjective experience beyond its proper domain. Only the spiritual cognition of the life of the soul can produce the kind of knowledge that avoids such confusions—a knowledge of the difference between soul that is self-enclosed and soul that is permeated with and radiates into the objective spiritual world, the difference between subconsciousness and supraconsciousness. One might think that Jung made this distinction, that he recognized the supraconscious realm with his more mystical investigations of the archetype of the Self. But the

Self may be no more than mystical megalomania, whereby one sees the divine only within oneself or identifies the ordinary, empirical self with the higher Self and then the higher Self with God. True, Jung fully recognized this danger and called it inflation. He gave warnings, but no way of distinguishing. Further, the explorations of the archetype of the Self, and along with it the process of so-called individuation, never lead to the multiplicity and particularity of the spiritual worlds, but only to abstractions such as oneness and wholeness—terms we are now endlessly subjected to in popular spirituality.

The work of distinguishing sub- and supraconsciousness must occur before—not after—their fusion, and the distinction is not one of ideas, but of a feeling for what is real. Steiner tells us how to go about this task. This is something that must be actually done, not just read about. You will find in the text, for example, the procedure of picturing a double of yourself arranging all the circumstances that brought about in your life what you did not wish to happen but which happened nonetheless. The result of this crucial experiment—this careful attention to experience—gives a very solid feeling of how soul brings about what needs to happen to us. By experiencing all we do not desire as what we do desire, we prepare ground for releasing the soul from its imprisonment in itself. Now we find this theme to be also quite popular in new age spirituality; in a certain sense it is also present in the Twelve-Step programs of the addiction and codependency movements, where it is called being "responsible." Surely, however, such language fosters further imprisonment in the self. In addition, the addiction program says that nothing within me was responsible for what happened to me as a child in the past. Once I clear away the rage at what was done to me by others, only from this point on can I take responsibility for what happens to me. All egotism and no soul. And yet we see within this modern procedure a longing for something for which we have no tools, no language. One must develop a real feeling for the enclosure of the soul within itself during the period after death when the soul's life experience is displayed before itself as if it were an objective world. In addition, one must develop a real feeling for the soul's full engagement in the spiritual worlds—which are not of the soul's making—that occurs after this first period following death. One does not have to be clairvoyant to do so; we have intimations of these experiences even in daily life. Then karma becomes no longer a spiritual buzzword but an actual experience of the soul's suffering and of how this suffering can be endured in time as the universal solvent and taken up as a spiritual task—a task that is not for personal benefit but has the aim of collaborating with the forces of the spiritual worlds.

Anthroposophy not only takes us out of the limited domain of psychology as concerned with subjective states and into the broader realm of culture, it also takes us into an understanding of the body as the necessary organ through which spiritual perception must find its orientation. Psychology still suffers from the legacy of its official namer, Philipp Melanchthon, who narrowed psyche to subjectivity. From the point of view of this legacy, it matters not whether that subjectivity is conscious or unconscious; the body is not considered except insofar as it is affected by the psyche, as if psyche were not of the body. Steiner's comprehension of the historical development of consciousness, however, places what is now called psyche in the realm of the sentient soul and thus it belongs to the body and the organs of the body. Great confusion arises due to the fact that matters of the sentient soul are treated as if they were matters of the intellectual soul. Compare, for example, Heraclitus, who said, "You could not discover the limits of the psyche, even if you traveled every road to do so," with Melanchthon: "We divide man into only two parts. For there is in him a cognitive faculty, and there is also a faculty by which he either follows or flees the things he has come to know. The cognitive faculty is that by which we discern through the senses, understand, think, compare, and deduce. The faculty from which the affections arise is that by which we either turn away from or pursue the things known, and this faculty is sometimes called 'will,' sometimes 'affection,' and sometimes 'appetite.'" Now take Melanchthon and start talking about the gods and goddesses, and you have the kind of intellectual gossip about the gods characteristic of much current popular psychology that speaks about the gods and goddesses within—a very peculiar, confused mixture of fabulous tales and pop subjectivity with spiritual overtones. When this kind of fare becomes commonplace, spiritual wisdom sounds incomprehensible, whereas in fact the reverse is true: nonsense has taken the place of accurate perception. Thus a first encounter with the latter essays of this collection may be met with difficulty at first because it is necessary to counter a great deal of cultural conditioning. The key lies in realizing that Steiner speaks meditatively; consequently one is required to work with what is presented by first reading the essays as a whole, suspending what one thinks one already knows, and then thinking through the particularities of the whole in an attitude of meditation.

When the body is not divided from the psyche, an account must be given first of everyday consciousness, and then of those perceptions that are not available to everyday consciousness, not only dreams, but also all those phenomena that form the field of so-called abnormal psychology. What makes consciousness possible is not the brain as a producer of consciousness, but the processes of the body as a whole. These serve as a mirror reflecting the activity of the soul. You can never arrive at the spiritual dimension by starting with material processes; a dualism will always result. But it is possible, when the starting place is soul and spirit, to show the necessity of the body in relation to soul and spirit; it is not a matter of concocting an idea, but of paying attention to what is actually given to experience. Goethe's theory of colors, for example, is such an instance of careful attention to experience that shows the activity of the soul. When one stares at a blue spot for a few moments and then closes one's eyes, a yellow afterimage of the spot is seen. Physiology cannot adequately account for the phenomenon that whenever an outer color is seen, an afterimage of the complementary color is seen simultaneously. (When one looks at the blue spot for a time, a pulsating yellow emanates around the spot.) The soul activity of the blood (see Ernst Lehrs, *Man or Matter*) creates the complementary, and thus makes color perception possible. This exemplary instance gives a feeling for what happens in all of ordinary everyday consciousness. That is to say, consciousness is a phenomenon of soul requiring body. It is not a result of a stimulation of the bodily nerves being transmitted to the brain, which then produces the experience.

In addition to being the reflector for everyday consciousness, the body is also the reflector for all that arises from the depths of the soul unrelated to outer experience. Spiritual training is oriented toward entering these depths with proper discrimination. With Steiner's approach to these matters we have the foundation for an entirely new direction for abnormal psychology, one based on the reality of spiritual worlds and the soul's progress from one incarnation to another. Abnormal psychology, then, becomes a primary mode for researching the processes of reincarnation. Furthermore, care of soul changes radically when one's vision is expanded to include not only past lives but also, more importantly, future lives. Indeed, Steiner's perception of the relation of the bodily organs as expressions of the soul to psychological irregularities is particularly oriented toward care of the soul, with a view toward future lives. He sees that psychological difficulties arise when something that is to be lived in a future incarnation is, so to speak, squeezed out of a bodily organ in this life, producing disruption. To state the matter in this way sounds fantastic, but that is so only if such a proposition is heard without knowledge of the higher worlds. Thus an adequate training in spiritual science is required to follow this line of research, and the aim of sketching out the approach of Anthroposophy is to stimulate the impulse to take up this direction of work.

Steiner considers in these essays the following organs in relation to psychological irregularities. Remember, however, that he is not proposing a cause–effect relationship, as if when there is physical organ damage this causes a particular form of abnormality—he is not putting forth a psychosomatic theory, for all such theories are dualistic. Rather it is the case that the bodily organs as living body processes act as reflectors of psychic activity. The lung surface serves as reflector of abstract concepts, and also of thoughts concerned with perception of the outer world. The lungs—and this is immediately available to experience—have to do with the ongoing exchange between the outer world and inner life. When the forces of the lungs are too strongly stimulated, the result is coercive thoughts or illusions; what should be the head-forming forces of the next incarnation are expressed as overpowering thought. The liver surface reflects thoughts colored by feelings; indeed, the liver is the organ that, even in its name, means "life." What should form the inner forces of the brain in the next life, if pressed out in this life, they are lived as hallucinations and visions. The forces of the kidneys, concerned with excretion, when forced to pour these out in this life, instead of preparing the emotional organization of the following life, express themselves as hypochondria and depression. The heart as a spiritual organ concerns the spiritualization of life processes and conscience, our deeds. Our deeds carry our karma into the next life, and if the forces of the heart are activated in the wrong manner a kind of frenzy results. What Steiner speaks of as frenzy, I suspect, is what modern psychology would call obsession. Obsession is a malady of our age, a cultural phenomenon characterized by the idealized thought of relationship enacted as deed without the restraint that would produce hesitation of action.

The nuances of Steiner's development of these forms of illness are well worth study and contemplation. This way of approaching psychological phenomena completely shifts the perception of psychology, and indeed are the foundation for a true spiritual psychology. Now within this context, what of psychotherapy—does it have a place at all? Probably not, for this way of seeing soul work does not in any way diminish the difficulty previously pointed to—that what should occur in life, psychotherapy places in the interaction between two or more individuals in an artificial situation, which is an incursion into the karma of an individual. Care for the soul, however, is something that can be practiced by the individual. The fundamental reason psychotherapy is such a dubious practice is that karma is moral, and thus feeling and willing are moral activities of the soul. They are the way soul works on itself, producing exactly what is to be experienced in exactly the right way and time in life. If one proceeds abstractly, then it could be said, well, when one gets to real stumbling blocks in life and is in a really impossible situation that leads to the door of the psychotherapist, this, too, is to be considered karma. Such a point of view, however, is a naive abstraction because it takes a cultural invention, psychotherapy, and treats this idea as if it were something belonging to life; but it does not belong to life; rather, it is an artificially arranged situation that places people together in a form that imitates the most intimate aspects of life.

What then could be put forward as a true alternative? After all, psychological suffering is undeniable, and to ignore it would be like saying that when thousands of people undergo the devastation of an earthquake, that is their karma. It would be ludicrous not to help these people, even though it is quite true that those who find themselves in the exact time and place of an earthquake are confronting karma. First, it is necessary to locate psychological suffering as a cultural phenomenon and to bring about knowledge of the spirit suitable to present cultural circumstances. Such knowledge of the spirit must not be abstract, but capable of addressing the actual situation of our times. Anthroposophy forms such a method of knowledge; however, it is not yet psychology, though it implicitly carries a psychological dimension. Knowledge of the spirit becomes psychological knowledge when the focus is on the body—not only the individual human body, but also equally the body of things and the body of the world, what in the ancient world was called the anima mundi, or "soul of the world." The focus, of course, is not only on the physical body—training in spiritual science awakens the sense of the living body (physical, etheric, astral, ego) and of the relation between the living macrocosm and the living microcosm. The critical point, however, is this: the endeavor to bring about a true spiritual psychology belongs to the realm of education rather than psychotherapy. Why is this so? There is nothing whatsoever within the human being that would call forth from the processes of life such a particular cultivation of life as what is called psychotherapy.

Friendship and the intimacy of a love relationship may come to mind, but neither of these forms of being human takes place in an isolated chamber, and even friends and lovers do not know what a therapist knows because he knows what he should not. Self-knowledge is an unbreachable intimacy one has with one's soul. Certain cultural expressions, which I shall speak of in a moment, can awaken an awareness of the necessity of self-knowledge and the path toward this knowledge, but even these expressions cannot substitute for the complete individuality of self-knowledge. Psychotherapy is an abstraction, culturally sanctioned in a world of materialistic abstractions. Learning, however, does belong to the very nature of living. Let me give an indication concerning how learning belongs to living; then it will be possible to propose the particular kind of education required for spiritual psychology.

The impulse for learning originates in an alluring display of the beauty of the world, evoking desire for intimate connection with the world—an urge toward the spirit, soul, vitality, the particular beauty marking each thing as standing forth from a holy abyss. Things draw us to intimate knowledge as if they need us for their completion. The beauty of the world draws the soul out of a self-enclosing illusion of mastery through disengagement into an engagement with reality. This living desire to experience the world pulsing through the body constitutes a drive toward transformation, initiating a care for all things. When things are approached with the care of the soul, their spiritual reality shines forth. The central task of learning is not the accumulation of information, but is learning to learn, that is, coming to realize the individual body in conjunction with the body of the world as the container and reflector of soul processes. Now this process of learning cannot be divided into those who learn and those who teach. Teachers are simply those whose vocation is learning, those who have learned that life is learning. When educators recognize this force, the spiritual/cultural necessity of learning will take its rightful precedence over technical and social concerns.

The phenomena of abnormal psychology, when seen within this context of learning as essential to life, lead not to psychotherapy but to adult education: spiritual psychology as the field of adult learning. That is to say, the missing element in contemporary culture is an education into the life of spirit. This form of learning does not really belong to the young. Education in the seven liberal arts is the field of learning for the young; in ancient times, the study of the liberal arts—grammar, dialectic, rhetoric, geometry, arithmetic, astronomy, and music—was the preparation needed for spiritual knowledge. I propose that what Freud and Jung observed as the manifestation of psychological symptoms was simply the disappearance from the world of a culture of soul and spirit. Cultural forms are needed for the cure; psychotherapy cannot do the job and seems to me a deviation contributing to the destruction of culture.

Spiritual psychology as the field of adult education certainly does not mean adult education in the current sense of the practice; presently, adult education is oriented either toward furtherance of technical skills or toward personal enrichment. Where then is an education of the soul to be found today? There isn't one, because the imitation, the double, of such a task occurs as psychotherapy. That is to say, self-knowledge has no culture. Adult education, then, would restore to culture knowledge of the soul. Its method would be quite different from education of the young, for the task of cultural learning in this sense lies much more in the hands of the learners and with the community of learners. The teacher is not as important in a certain sense. He or she must be skilled enough to recede into the background while nonetheless serving as a guide who can help shape the vessel and restrain the learning from wandering into personal subjectivity. Adult education is community learning, but is in no sense group psychotherapy. And it is learning to care for soul, explicitly. The method of such learning is meditative rather than intellectual, for soul learning is an education into subtlety. In reading these lectures by Steiner I think it is imperative to have this form of education in mind; otherwise, when he touches upon certain exercises that are needed to come to living knowledge of the soul, it is easy to think, "Well, that can be imported into the work of psychotherapy?" and what Steiner is really pointing toward is a different approach to psychotherapy. Not at all, for then all that he works to bring to light in the early lectures in this series is for naught. Nor, however, do I think Steiner is suggesting that in place of psychotherapy one find a spiritual master who will be one's individual spiritual guide.

Adult education into soul wisdom must also be distinguished from reading or study groups. Such groups tend to be oriented toward detailed understanding of a particular work or text and foster a strengthening of the intellectual soul rather than the consciousness soul. What the teacher of soul wisdom must first gain and then sacrifice is the development of the intellectual soul; this is necessary in order that a spirit of meditative consciousness pervade this new situation of learning. The way such teaching occurs in practice is that the teacher actually has much knowledge and information, but cannot give it forth. He does not withhold it, but brings it into the learning situation to be given up, in order to, as it were, provide the context for the meditative learning pursued by the community of learners. Reading is approached in a similarly meditative manner. Meditative reading is encouraged that takes place through picture-consciousness rather than through the grasping of concepts. That is, the aim of reading and study is not oriented toward what one can take away from the text but toward going into it in a living way. Needless to say, this form of learning is noncompetitive. No evaluation takes place and no examinations are given, and no grading. These devices stimulate the wrong forces for soul wisdom.

Is there a curriculum for the soul? A crucial question: Yes, there is material, but there is not a sequentially arranged form of studies that progresses from the simple to the more complex. Secondary texts are avoided, and as well the use of excerpts from works because the aim is to become immersed not in what is said about some topic but in the reality itself. The curriculum then is formed not out of the personal interests of the teacher, but out of a considered intuition of the teacher in relation to the community of learners concerning the soul development of all involved.

Art is of particular importance for an education into spiritual psychology—myth, fairy tale, story, symbolic image, mandala, poetry, drama, painting, music, and film. Furthermore, art forms that are explicitly made as revelations and expression of spirit, carrying the intention of awakening and initiating the conscious life of spirit, are important. Because the focus is on works of imagination, the middle realm of soul is engaged which thereby affects both body and spirit. Since the works are of a spiritual nature, the lower regions of the soul are educated and what otherwise would be disruptive chaos is given cultural form. Examples of such works include: J. W. von Goethe, *Fairy Tale of the Green Snake and the Beautiful Lily*; *The Chymical Wedding* of Christian Rosenkreutz; Wolfram von Eschenbach's *Parzival*; Verdi's operas; the major arcana of the tarot; alchemical engravings; Rudolf Steiner, *The Four Mystery Plays*; the paintings of Hieronymus Bosch; the poetry of Novalis; the films of Andrei Tarkovsky; Greek mythology.

Psychological irregularities, in spite of a cultural form of education into soul are, of course, still bound to exist. These instances are to be cared for within the field of medicine: not medicine or psychiatry as currently practiced, not drugs and incarceration and therapy, but medicine with soul. This does not violate culture because medicine is a communal expression of culture. Once the knowledge that intense psychological difficulties are expressions of the forces of the bodily organs is brought forth, then the need for a medicine capable of working with body as soul is apparent. Psychoanalysis originated in a confusion of soul work with medicine, and all current forms of psychotherapy are knowingly or unknowingly pervaded with a medical attitude. One might be led to think that what needs to be brought about is a clearing away of all medical suppositions in psychotherapy, the main one being a diagnostic attitude that begins therapy with the question "What is wrong with you?" Then, it would be possible to have a new form of therapy. When this diagnostic attitude is relinquished, however, what presents itself as psychological disruption is the invasion of unfamiliar images, feelings, thoughts, and actions. Such phenomena make even more apparent the need for cultural forms that can shape disruptive forces into coherent images. In spite of the popular appeal of the romantic attitude that everyone is or can be an artist, only those who have devoted their lives to such tasks are really capable, and, fortunately, they have made cultural artifacts through which we can be led where we cannot go on our own.

The careful reader of these lectures is led into vital considerations of the forming of a more spiritual culture. The conclusions are not easy to confront. They have led me, a practicing psychotherapist, to the necessity of relinquishing this practice. But following through Steiner's wisdom has also led to the founding of an initiative, which I have called adult education into soul wisdom, and that produces a great sense of relief, as well as hope that possibilities will also be released in the reader.

5

JUNG AND STEINER
THE BIRTH OF A NEW PSYCHOLOGY

GERHARD WEHR

For the past fifteen years, I have worked to institute a new orientation in psychology. This effort has centered on bringing the soul psychology of C. G. Jung into a relation with the spiritual science of Rudolf Steiner. This creative synthesis would, I believe, give birth to a new psychology—one that is fully cognizant of the spiritual and soul worlds and how human consciousness forms in association with them.

Imagine, then, my excitement in learning of this book by Gerhard Wehr, the author of an important biography of Jung, and an anthroposophist. Reading and rereading his book, I felt assured that these years had not been wasted, for here at last was a linking work, one that would be appreciated by anthroposophists and depth psychologists alike. Even more, the concerns addressed in this remarkable book were living questions that applied to everyone, not just to the practitioners of each of these movements: How can we live and be open and receptive to the spiritual realms? How can we know what is going on in the depths of our soul? How can we approach others and our work and the world soulfully and with spiritual intent?

Psychology is vastly misunderstood in our time. It is regarded either as a therapeutic endeavor or as a rather meaningless scientific discipline that tries, mostly unsuccessfully, to model itself after the physical sciences. Thanks to Jung, the field has been ennobled, and the word *psychology* has been somewhat restored as the discipline of the soul. A true discipline is far more than an academic area of interest. One takes up a discipline, enters it—one becomes it. It then becomes a way of knowing oneself and knowing the world. Thanks to Steiner, the possibility exists of taking this discipline of the soul and placing it within the context of understanding the place and work of the human being in the whole cosmos. The kind of psychology that could come from working through the whole of Jung and Steiner in an inner, experiential way is a practical psychology. It is not confined to the therapy office but is rather the work of living a conscious soul life.

If one goes even a little way into the labor of self-knowledge, it soon becomes necessary to reimagine one's place within the whole world and, indeed, the whole of existence. Most of us do not have the capacities to do this on our own. Thus many of us find ourselves in a liminal place. No longer dominated by mass consciousness, we are left on our own, without ground or the capacity to steer a course for ourselves. Then we find we no longer belong to the guiding myth of the time—the technological myth, the myth of materialism. Where do we go? We need a new myth, a large imagination within which understanding of who we are makes sense. In medieval times, Dante offered a whole soul cosmology of this kind. He couched it in Christian tradition, language, and practice, because that satisfied his need for a means to convey a large picture within which we can find our place. Such a cosmology interprets us; it tells us who we are, what we are doing, where we came from, where we are going.

Both Jung and Steiner have given us a cosmology within which we can see ourselves soulfully. That is why both are worth lifetimes of study. We should not make our task easy by considering these two individuals as only providing systems that agree in certain ways and diverge in others. Nor should we try simply to determine which one to follow. Both decried followers, but hoped to see independent workers inspired by their efforts.

Jung and Steiner does not merely offer a comparison of two creative individuals, each of whom has brought something decidedly new to the world. That approach might be interesting, but it would create nothing more than another academic study. This book goes much further, and its reach has to do with the method employed, which Wehr calls the "synoptic" method. Rather than setting the externals of two systems side by side and looking at each for similarities and differences, Wehr sets the core meaning of each beside the other. Out of the tension something new comes into being. Jung himself knew that this method belongs to the very nature of the psyche. He employed it many times. It requires developing the capacity to hold two irreconcilable positions together without seeking resolution. Something new will then emerge. Steiner advocated something similar when he advised developing the capacity to hold twelve different views on the same issue. Moreover Steiner's lectures are full of contradictions, demanding that one enter into his work with an awakened imagination in which these contradictions become pregnant with new meanings.

Jung and Steiner, for all its merits, does not push this method as far as it could. In this introduction, I want to push it even further to begin to show the outlines of a new psychology, a spiritual psychology that emerges from holding the tension of the opposites of depth psychology and Anthroposophy without seeking resolution.

The opposites involved here are extreme. They consist of bringing the greatest possible development of waking consciousness into relation with the deepest level of unconsciousness. The tension is exacerbated by the fact that these two ways of viewing the human being are separated by no more than a thin veneer. When we go into that seemingly thin separation, we find two sides of the same thing. That is to say, there is a central element that unknowingly joins depth psychology and Anthroposophy. This union is the image of the Grail as the central myth of each of these cultural creations.

In *An Outline of Esoteric Science*, Steiner spoke explicitly of Anthroposophy as a Grail science. He meant that if Anthroposophy is a science of the cosmos working into the earthly and the earthly working into the cosmos, then the human being is at the very center of this relation. Jung for his part was a Westerner through and through, and his central myth was the Grail. He had a very dear dream of the Grail, which is described in chapter eleven of Wehr's book. He had this dream when he was on a long journey in India and when everything in this environment seemed to verify all he had to say about culture, symbolism, and myth.

The new psychology that begins to emerge from the flying sparks of a path founded in the reality of soul and a path founded in the reality of spirit will be one that is symbolized by the Grail cup. Among its many other aspects, this symbol gives us a picture of the spiritual soul. The vessel itself symbolizes the soul, open and receptive, receiving whatever it needs from the spiritual worlds. This image perfectly represents the spiritual psychology of which I speak. It also represents the current of psychology that comes about by holding in tension a love for the soul and a love for the spirit. I define that psychology as follows:

> Spiritual psychology is an active practice that develops embodied, conscious, soul life to make that life open and receptive to the spiritual realms. This is done as an act of love toward others, the world, and ourselves.

Steiner followed the spirit side of the Grail myth; Jung, the soul side. The great appeal of both is the quest. We cannot undervalue the tremendous motivating power of an image of questing. Thus in both Jung and Steiner, we find a continual criticism of the way things are in the world, an urging to throw off the immediate past and to seek to establish both a soul and a spirit perspective for the future of humanity. However, unless their endeavors are seen as quests, each of these two very strong conceptions of the human future is bound to gather dogmatic disciples.

The content of the Grail cup must be taken into account as well. It is blood, which is an image of the very essence of desire. Desire is essential. So if the desire of soul or the desire of spirit is not addressed, then it gets at you from behind. It is mistaken for what we think the founders wanted, which will be confused with our own unexamined desires. But the blood of the Grail is also the blood of Christ. Thus it represents purified desire, which can be wholly oriented toward the divine rather than becoming confused with personal desires.

Both Jung and Steiner went through personal transformations that ensured as much as possible that the desires they followed were free of personal taints. There is no doubt that both individuals were also tremendously ambitious, wanting to see their views adopted in the world. But their followers tend to foolishly ignore the factor of desire in themselves, and the necessity of working with this before all else. They think they are being good anthroposophists or good Jungians if they adopt the master's content, oblivious of how their own desires figure in. In Anthroposophy, the follower's desire tends to be falsely purified. Anthroposophists often act as if they had no bodies and were already pure spirits, bringing the world exactly what it needed. In depth psychology, there is often a reveling in the experience of following soul down into the depths, completely unaware of anything like a need for purifying desire. There is a temptation to allow the content of those depths to take hold in the foolish belief that because it is soul, it has to be good.

Working with desire requires holding irresolvable tensions without seeking resolution. Our main cultural model for working with the desire of the blood, placing that desire within the Grail cup, may be neither Steiner nor Jung but Dante. The whole of the *Purgatorio* is explicitly concerned with holding opposites together without resolving them. Remorse is held in tension with joy, pride with humility, contemplation with action—responsibility toward the timeless with responsibility toward timely need. This play of opposites finally opens the soul to the spiritual realms. So perhaps we have a greater psychology in Dante than can be found in either Jung or Steiner. Or perhaps we can follow the lead of Dante, whom Steiner quite seriously called "the greatest man." This would mean holding Steiner and Jung in a tension of opposites, noticing that the inherent reason for such tension is that, as Dante shows, this is the one and only way that love enters, a love that is greater than any of our desires. We do not do love, in spite of our glorification of the possibility of loving. Our desire is too confused for us to love otherwise than out of our own self-oriented desires. The purifying power of love enters through the opening, the soul space created by holding impossible contradictions.

Love enters the discussion here because it is the central dimension of the spiritual psychology that emerges from holding Jung and Steiner in tension. Love is not mere feeling, but the very essence of the action of the spiritual soul. It is what the spiritual soul does. Love is not desire already purified; it is desire in process of being purified.

Jung had little to do with the world beyond his circle and his soul interests. Steiner had a great deal to do with the world. He created new systems of education, medicine, and agriculture and new forms of painting, dance, architecture, and drama. He inspired a religious movement known as the Christian Community, thought through a new social order, and engaged in many other cultural endeavors. Jung is characterized by an innerness without which dedication to soul life is impossible. His whole autobiography is written as an inner biography, an entirely new form of biography, a memoir of the soul. Steiner's biography, on the other hand, is completely external, so objective that it is downright dull. It belongs to the genre of esoteric spiritual biographies where it is not uncommon for the writer to speak of his own life in the third person. So here is one tension to hold: soul as inwardness, spirit as being out in the world. Soul as where we have been, the depth of memory, and memory as imagination. Spirit as where we are going, the not-yet, the yet-to-be-established in the world.

When read closely, Wehr's chapter comparing the biographies of Jung and Steiner reveals something amazing about the inner origins of spiritual science and depth psychology. Both Steiner and Jung had a particular and profound relationship with the dead. When he was only four years old, Steiner was visited by a woman who had died—an experience that made a lasting impression. He later gave numerous lectures on the importance of remaining in connection with those who have died, even providing methods for doing so. Jung also had experiences with the dead. Wehr points to Jung's experience (also at age four) of seeing a funeral over which his father presided and the strange impression it made on

Jung. His depth psychology began with association experiments he carried out with his cousin, who had contact with the dead as well.

The mysteries of death impress themselves on both of these figures, but in different ways. In Steiner's vision, the dead woman asks for help. The experience originates a scientific interest in him: what are the methods for remaining in connection with the dead? Jung leaves the impression of having a simultaneous fear and attraction to the realm of the dead. For him, there is more of a sense of a struggle against the mysteries of death, characteristic of one who is fully aware of the tragedy of death, the leaving of life.

The death experiences of these two individuals, when held in inner tension, open the way of spiritual psychology. It is the way of a double consciousness that characterizes both Steiner and Jung. They both lived an ongoing relation with the dead, a relation of actual presence, but one that must be understood as an act of the active imagination, not of ordinary consciousness. And they both lived an ongoing connection with the world (albeit Steiner seemed to do this more effectively). In both we observe two forms of consciousness side by side: for Jung, personality 1 and personality 2: for Steiner, ordinary consciousness and clairvoyant consciousness: This dual consciousness is the consciousness of the future. It belongs to the Grail myth, and is what we are all being asked to develop. We are asked to be consciously open, in soul, to the spiritual realms and to work effectively in the world.

If we look at these two individuals as initiates, forerunners for the rest of humanity, this is what they introduce as a human possibility. We can work for the world and work for the soul and spirit at the same time. That is the kind of consciousness spiritual psychology encourages. Jung and Steiner were born into this consciousness and lived with it in different ways. The next step is to develop this consciousness in full awareness. This is now possible because of the initiation experiences of these two individuals. We can say that double consciousness was initiated in both of these individuals by the dead. The real founders of spiritual psychology are those who have died and have a continuing interest and love for the world; they are tremendously interested in what happens here. They concern themselves with whether we can meet the challenge of living as soul and spirit beings housed in earthly garments.

The way of double consciousness is well known in the mystery traditions. We see it, for example, in the *Bacchae* of Euripides. When Pentheus, who is one-sidedly rational, is overtaken by Dionysus, the god of embodied imagination, he looks up into the sky and suddenly sees two suns. The two suns signify a consciousness of Earth alongside a consciousness of death. While this doesn't do much good for Pentheus (who ends up torn to pieces by Maenads), it does renew the community. We need Jung's psychology in order to remain imaginal. We need Seiner's spiritual science in order to apply this imagination to the forming of the world. These two together make possible a conscious, imaginal sun alongside the sun of our usual earthly consciousness.

In the past the experience of two suns signified extreme danger. Like Pentheus, one might go off the deep end. The right capacities must be formed. We cannot jump into this kind of consciousness. We need to undergo the throes of transformation, and the way to go about radical change of capacities is found in the written work of Jung and Steiner. Their writing is completely unlike other writing. You can't go through it and come out the same. However, they need to be read together or in tandem, and read with the whole of one's being, not just through the intellect.

Spiritual psychology is a result of working this tandem approach. It is founded in the consciousness of death, and signifies the importance—and even the method—of working toward something without doing so for our own benefit. We know, of course, that even when we seem to be generously working for the benefit of others, our own self-interests are involved; usually they are at the forefront. The spiritual-psychological perspective, a mode of consciousness rather than a theory, operates within a continual undoing of itself—dying as a way of living. This is the only way to allow soul to be genuinely open to the spiritual worlds and serving those worlds truthfully.

Closely related to the presence of the dead as a central factor of human consciousness is the problem of the term *the unconscious*. For Steiner, there are many kinds of consciousness—waking, dreaming, sleep, trance, to name but a few. There is no unconscious: that is only the way waking consciousness speaks of other forms of consciousness. Furthermore these different consciousnesses are not states but beings. Psychological symptoms that appear seemingly out of nowhere, for example, are sometimes due to the living presence of the dead who have not been remembered. That is to say, one of the worlds of consciousness is the spirits of the dead. This is a much more forceful way of speaking than Jung's references to a psychic structure that has a certain content much of which remains under the surface. The right and proper field of psychology includes not only the dead, but also all sorts of other beings who are not in the unconscious, but are different worlds of conscious-ness—spirits, angels, or gods.

If we try to speak of these different worlds of beings without developing the capacity of the spiritual soul, we run the risk either of completely literalizing them (when approaching them in terms of Anthroposophy) or of regarding them as mere images (when working from a depth-psychological perspective). The spiritual soul, the goal of spiritual psychology, does not make a sharp division between what is literal and what is imaginal. Are these beings real? Yes. Are they physical, affecting us in terms of the laws of cause and effect? No. When the beings of a certain world of consciousness affect us, we are that consciousness. It is not a matter of something external impinging on us like rocks hitting the flesh; nor is it a matter of their imaginal presence acting as content of the soul. Soul is not a container of contents but the inherent capacity for perceiving spiritual realities. We are soul and spiritual beings, not beings with a soul and with a spirit. We are also embodied, but even so soul and spirit do not hover around phantomlike within our physical being. Rather than being caught by the laws of cause and effect, as Jung still was to a greater or lesser extent, we have to grow accustomed to working within the laws of sympathetic and antipathetic currents. The presence of such currents creates a resonance within us. We are like harps, sounding when the beings of the soul and spiritual worlds sound. And this resounding is possible only because we are of the substance of those beings.

There is a differentiation in understanding the structure and functioning of the body in Anthroposophy that makes it clear how something completely immaterial, such as the dead, or other spirit-beings affect us in such a way that physical symptoms would arise. The living body consists of matter, but also of subtle, etheric forces, which provide a link with the immaterial. There is nothing theoretical about the etheric body. It is recognized by all spiritual and esoteric traditions; moreover it can be quite easily experienced through the life-forming processes of the physical body. When Steiner criticizes psychoanalysis, saying that it lacks the proper tools to address the kind of reality that it is trying to investigate, he is, among other things, referring to the absence of an understanding of the etheric body.

The concept of the etheric body makes for completely different understandings of psychological symptoms in Jung and in Steiner. Jung always traces a symptom back to an archetypal image, looks for the gods or spirits or dead in the disease, and speaks always of such figures as images in the soul. Steiner looks at the same symptoms and also traces the symptom back to the gods, the spirits, or the dead, but he takes these spirits as directly acting on the human being. Without Jung's perspective, these acts by spiritual beings would be taken literally, as if they were just like earthly beings, except perhaps a little more shadowy. Without Steiner's perspective, on the other hand, the truth of the actual presence of spiritual beings is sidestepped.

Another expression of the irresolvable tensions of opposites between Steiner and Jung concerns soul and spirit. Everywhere I have taught for the past fifteen years, someone inevitably asks me to define soul and spirit and tell how they differ. Such a question goes nowhere because it shifts something known and felt to the level of the ordinary intellect, where it cannot be answered. The question assumes that there is some way out of the confusion other than finding deeper ways into the questions substance.

This book takes us further and deeper into the tension between soul and spirit. Here also the two are sometimes interchanged. This confusion persists, for example, in the essays by Hans Erhard Lauer in the second part of this book. Nevertheless, holding the tension begins to bring some clarity. For example, we find that both soul and spirit reveal themselves as inner experiences, even though the "inner" of soul is different from the "inner" of spirit. Jung speaks of how, at an early age, he was initiated into the Earth mysteries. Steiner speaks of being taken into the cosmic mysteries. Both speak of archetypal realities. However, Jung is always concerned with the archetypal patterns and figures that reveal themselves as contents of soul life. Steiner is always concerned with the archetypal beings that shape the human being and the Earth.

Another difference: for Jung, psyche is image, and image is understood as a particular content, whether dream content or mythic content. Jung, of course, is more sophisticated concerning image than this, and we have the distinct feeling in his work that image, more than picture content, is that through which content appears. In Steiner, image is activity, the pure activity of forming or coming into form of the actual presence of spiritual beings. Image is the first way in which we can be present to the activity of spiritual beings. Image, in Steiner, is a decidedly spiritual notion, while in Jung it is the very heart of soul.

We can focus on the fruitfulness of keeping these two orientations in relation rather than on the divisiveness that arises by separating soul and spirit too sharply. Taken alone, the soul perspective leads to a forgetfulness of the human being in the context of the world. Jung seals soul off from the world and unwittingly promotes self-absorption. Taken alone, Steiner's perspective leads to a literalizing, unimaginative, sometimes manic working to bring practical endeavors of a spiritual nature into the world, expecting that artistic endeavors, rather than conscious soul work, will answer the soul's needs. When we hold both the spirit and the soul perspectives together, we have spiritual psychology. This new psychology, which has its precursors in Jung and Steiner, places the spiritual soul at the heart of its endeavors. Holding the tension between soul and spirit is the attempt to provide the practical way of working in the world that is the forming of a spiritual culture. Our task concerns developing the capacities of allowing the spiritual realms to work through us into the world, and keeping this conscious. How this work happens remains open to inspiration; it is not a work of applying what Steiner said to the world.

The two perspectives of soul and spirit show up in another way—Jung's notion of the goal of inner development as the awakening to the Self and Steiner's call for the development of the "I." Are these two goals the same? Wehr puts them together, but I think it might be better to avoid collapsing them and keep the inherent tension between the two. The Self can be imagined as soul at the border of spirit. The "I" can be imagined as spirit at the border of the soul. The "I" is the Self from the spirit's point of view. The Self is the "I" from the soul's point of view. The Self is the collective soul raised to the level of individuality. The "I" is individuality in connection with the whole. Holding this tension between Self and "I" can help anthroposophists, who are forever confusing Steiner's understanding of the "I" with their own egotism because they often lack a sense of soul. (Steiner also uses the word *ego* in multiple ways. Sometimes he is speaking of the "I" when using the term *ego*. Sometimes he is speaking of ego in the ordinary sense.) Similarly, this tension can help those in the Jungian stream because the notion of the "I," while somewhat linguistically awkward, has a solidity about it that prevents the misconception that adhering to soul life leads to mysticism.

The knot holding together "I," "Self," "self," and "ego" still persists. Neither "I" and "Self," nor "self" and "ego," it seems, should be collapsed. Nor should we try to untie the knot with definitions. The value of seeing these notions collide in Jung and Steiner is precisely so that they collide in us. We have to find the way into the problem, which is a living problem for each of us. For example, in light of the spiritual individuality that is described as "I," a specific relation to ego has to be worked through. Ego is not quite the same in Jung and Steiner. For Steiner, ego would be the reflection of the spirit individuality within us, a kind of a shadow of our true spirit being. It takes conscious inner development to come to the "I"; it takes a long process of the purification of desire, developing a presence to creative thinking, a conscious awakening to imagination, inspiration, and intuition. For Jung, ego is a part of the whole of soul life that takes itself to be the whole. Consciously entering the whole process of individuation, something that is never complete, is required for coming to the point of a presence of the Self. It is of vast importance, both personally and culturally, to know when we are in ego and when in Self. It is vital to have a clear sense of the kind of experience characterizing the "I" and the kind characterizing the Self.

The relation between the "inner worlds" and the "outer world" is another tension to be worked through. Steiner belongs more to the Aristotelian line, Jung to the Platonic. Thus in setting the work of Jung and Steiner side by side, as Wehr has done, we have to hold this tension and try to see into it as clearly as we can. For Steiner there are three domains to research with respect to the human being: the realm of the senses; how sense experience lives on in soul life; and how the human being knows. This approach seems decidedly different from Jung's. Jung is far more interested in preexisting patterns, traced back to the acts of archetypal beings, which still live on as contents in the soul. The contrast between the Aristotelian and Platonic points of view could not be greater, except that Steiner's approach to working through his three domains of research is wholly and entirely internal: It is not subjective, but inner. He may, for example, start by describing the senses and their functions from an external point of view. But he never stops with the external. He goes on to explore sensing from an inner point of view, skillfully taking us further and further into an inner view of the human being and of the whole of the cosmos from within. He is no simple Aristotelian. As he moves us gradually inward, it is done with impeccable logic. Mysticism is not an option.

The inner way of working that characterizes Anthroposophy is completely free of dualism. Approaching the human being's physical innerness does not mean "inside" versus "outside:' the "outside;' too, can be approached in an inner way. For example, among the most important researches of Steiner into the inner physical being are his studies of human physiology. He avoids dualism by seeing that the whole human being participates in three worlds—the physical, soul, and spirit worlds. Each of these worlds can be explored with equal precision, but only through the development of the capacity of nondualistic perception and thought, the "I." Dualism is founded on the mistake that there is only one world. Thus it separates mind from body, locating the body as part of the physical world. It also separates soul and spirit from body and from world, and then searches for peculiar connections, such as parallelism or reductionism.

Jung is also completely faithful to the inner world. Strictly speaking, he is not Platonic but Kantian (the archetypal psychologist James Hillman emphasizes Jung's Platonic side, minimizing his Kantian side). His emphasis on soul is somewhat misleading because he does not and cannot reach the cosmological level of soul with his psychology. He is always concerned with the contents of the soul and steers completely away from saying anything about whether the contents reflect the actions of "real" spiritual beings. This is important because, with the help of Steiner, it is possible to reset Jung into more of a Platonic imagination. It is simply a matter of taking the archetypal figures as real, as existing in themselves. But it takes Steiner to make that move because it is not sufficient to simply state that this is so. Capacities of consciousness have to be developed that reveal the nature of spiritual beings. Steiner developed such capacities and wrote extensively concerning how others can develop them as well.

Kant stated that the object, the transcendent, the thing-in-itself is absolutely inaccessible, so that you have to confine yourself to the empirical world, to the finite, to appearances. Jung adopted as his own unshakable foundation for psychology the restriction of Kant's phenomenal world and the dosing of the door to the noumenon. This is why Jung posited the existence of the archetypes but would never say anything of their reality beyond what could be said "psychologically." Thus, for Jung, the question of truth is dosed, or at best we have a special notion of truth, easily susceptible to being completely misused— "the truth within."

Once we have exposed Jung's decision to remain completely empirical, confining his work to inner soul images, it may seem that the comparison between Jung and Steiner must cease. Steiner says a lot about the reality of spiritual beings; they are, in his view, completely autonomous, and we are required to develop the soul as the organ for the perception of these realities. The tension, though, needs to be maintained because of the phenomenological acumen Jung brings to the inner life.

Steiner does have a clear notion of the transcendent and goes after it with incredible descriptive capacities along with an accuracy of observation equal to that of any scientist. In addition, he develops the capacities for making observations of the invisible spiritual realms. He goes about this in such a way, however, that he reports what he has seen, not as interior conversations with the spirits, but as ideas—the closest we can come with our consciousness to the realities he experienced. We have no direct reports of Steiner's immediate experiences of the spiritual worlds. We have the ideas he gives as descriptive of those realms. However, because the spiritual realms remain dosed for most people, there is an extremely strong tendency to take Steiner's ideas at face value, even though he himself says over and over again to test them. However, to test them requires the capacity to enter into the interior of those ideas. Rather than merely examining them with our ordinary consciousness, we must experience them within; we must enter into the soul of the ideas. This is where Jung comes in as absolutely necessary. He shows how to find the way into and inhabit the interior of things. Without Jung, I propose, Anthroposophy becomes the dogmatic application of the ideas of a remarkable individual without inner understanding. The application of these ideas, without the capacity to discover their soul nature, becomes the imposition of those ideas onto others. In the long run, such imposition can fare no better than, say, the imposition of the technological worldview on us because it will supposedly make life better.

A number of years ago I spoke to a large gathering of anthroposophists, introducing a basic view of spiritual psychology as being founded in Jung and Steiner. The address was met with little enthusiasm; in fact, I could hear a number of stomachs turning over. One person forcefully stood up and said something to the effect that because of Steiner we have absolutely no need for psychology. Many of those gathered agreed with this naive view. Nevertheless the fact that Steiner explored soul does not acquit us of the need to be present to soul realities from within rather than accepting Steiner's findings. Steiner shows us much concerning the ways of soul, but then there is the problem of living them. This can only be done by finding the way into the interior of soul, which is Jung's forte.

A significant question arises at this point. If Jung's reliance on Kant confines him to immediate appearances, why go to Steiner for the way through to the reality of spiritual beings rather than someone like Hegel, as the very astute Jungian Wolfgang Geigerich has done? (See his book *The Logical Life of the Soul*.) The answer is that while Hegel perhaps provides a better philosophical basis for Jung than Kant, his approach would be devastating to soul. Image-consciousness would be lost to abstract thinking. Only Steiner provides the needed basis capable of comprising both soul and spirit, and as such is a basis within psychology itself. The very fact that Wehr can put the work of these two individuals side by side and make a meaningful comparison of them is due to their shared basis of soul and spirit.

The problem of seeing soul in terms of the picture content of myths, memories, and stories is unfortunately perpetuated somewhat by Wehr, who often uses content-oriented language in his text. Speaking of the soul as having contents gives the impression of some kind of container filled with images. Yet soul, at least in part, concerns the act of picturing, not the picture contents. Myths too are not picture contents, but worlds of picturing; that is, if you take myths as still living. If myth are now completed and dead, then indeed all we have left are the corpses, the picture contents.

Learning to imagine in terms of picturing rather than pictures is one of the most important things I have learned from Steiner. In his most profound work on the soul, *A Psychology of Body, Soul, and Spirit,* he describes how soul functions. Among the most significant aspects is the soul's apprehension of a time current from the future. This is the picturing act I am talking about. It does not concern content, because the future coming toward us has no content. The moment it does have content, it is necessarily from the past; this is a reflection occurring in the etheric body, where there is something like pictures from the past, both personal and archetypal. But this time current from the future is something real and actual. The future here concerns the possibilities of our being. While the notion sounds remote, it is not. We experience this time current with every movement we make. I get up and go to the door. Within the deep will, what is to come is already happening before it happens. I could not get to the door if it were only a mental idea. Getting to the door is already in my movement as I approach the door. This little example is but a shortened version of how our whole life approaches us from out of the future.

Each act that we do is internally connected with the whole of our life and expresses itself as belonging to the whole. But much of that whole has not yet happened. This is the time current from the future, and in *A Psychology of Body, Soul, and Spirit,* Steiner calls this current the astral body of the soul. It is picturing in the process of coming-to-be. The life of the soul is being formed out of the whole of the cosmos: "astral" comes from a root meaning "star." This world is whole, but it is open, unfinished. The pictures as content—memories, but also archetypal images—are from the past, from what has already happened. Steiner speaks of this current as the etheric body of the soul. The pictures of the etheric body are completed, done. They are not necessarily dead and gone; they still live on but are closed to new meanings. I thus make a distinction between the soul's immersion in fate—how we are shaped by the past—and the soul's immersion in destiny—how we are shaped from the future. Jung's psychology belongs more to the former, Anthroposophy more to the latter. Spiritual psychology works with both at once, but tries to be conscious of the difference.

For example, when in our lives we encounter a real deviation from our usual experience, is this fate or is it destiny? The words are often used interchangeably, but they are definitely distinct experiences; if you know how to be present to each, the difference is very clear. Here depth psychology has a lot to learn from Anthroposophy. It is as if half of psychology has been neglected because of the discipline's bias toward explanations in terms of the past. It is a matter of looking at images, even archetypal and mythic images, in terms of what they intimate about what is coming rather than looking backward to their past.

Methods of individual inner development reveal another area where it is fruitful to hold both Jung and Steiner together without seeking resolution. Jung speaks of analysis as the only initiatory path available in the modern Western world. He either was unfamiliar with Steiner or scornfully chose not to acknowledge that Steiner's work is above all a path of individual inner development. The methods of Jung and Steiner seem at first unrelated. For Jung, the method is analysis of others (though one must have gone through analysis oneself). Then, within analysis, it is constant inner work with dreams, trying to get close to the images, feeling their living presence, amplifying the images through myths, and, most of all, engaging in the transference, where the real transformation occurs. For a few, there is the work of active imagination, which is the work of those initiated into the process of individuation.

Steiner's method is meditation, which focuses on developing the capacity of remaining in full control of consciousness, not allowing anything to enter consciousness that is not put there deliberately by the meditator. Moreover, what is supposed to be put there is a thought or an image of something unrelated to the sense world. One might, for example meditate on the Rose Cross, which does not exist in the sensory world. After holding this in consciousness for a while, letting nothing else enter, the content focused on is erased, creating an empty consciousness. Then one waits, as the consciousness does not remain empty. An image, a thought, an insight enters, a response from the spiritual worlds.

Steiner recommends a host of other exercises, such as the backward review of the day; exercises for controlling thought, feeling, and will; and special meditative practices for developing the capacity to experience karma. Steiner's recommendations for each area he worked in—such as medicine, agriculture, and education—also include particular meditative exercises.

A primary difference between these two methods is that Jung's meditative work takes place primarily in the presence of another person, the therapist, while Steiner's takes place in private. In Anthroposophy, group meditative work has been discouraged and even disparaged.

In looking at the methods of Jung and Steiner, what is most important is to look at the capacities that are being developed, not the way the meditations are structured. Steiner is actually very clear about this. For example, in such practices as the Rose Cross meditation described above, it is the force of building up the thought and the force it takes to erase it that is central. Here it is as if the soul is a muscle that is being exercised to build up its strength. This makes it possible for the practitioner to be in soul in a conscious way.

For Jung, if we look at his methods closely, what is most essential is the relation between the individual and the therapist. This is where the strength to go on with analysis, dream work, and active imagination is centered. Much, of course, comes from working the material, but the soul transformation has to do with the transference. Transference is a name for the capacity to feel the autonomous presence of love without acting it out, without reducing it to something personal.

There is actually an element of something like transference in the methods of Steiner. This element is Steiner's insistence that all meditations be done with a strong sense of reverence. Here a relationship of love is established with an as-yet-unknown other. It is, I think, going in the wrong direction to say that Steiner's mediations are solitary while Jung's are communal, though that is what strikes one most at first. If we hold both of these methods together, we come to the method of spiritual psychology. Spiritual psychology values group meditative work, recognizing, mainly from Jung, that the element of feeling is as important as the element of thought in meditative work. At the same time, following Steiner's lead, spiritual psychology refuses to literalize therapy but sees individual meditative work as inherently therapeutic. It is perfectly possible to do individual meditative work in a group context. Here the exercises are like those proposed by Steiner, so that building up inner strength of soul is what is most important. The results of the exercises are discussed in the group, which develops the feeling dimension of the soul, and also serves as a way of doing soul research together. The method of spiritual psychology is a new form of therapeutic work that takes therapy away from concentration on the personal, which easily becomes ego-centered, and yet strengthens the soul and spirit forces that are, in any case, central to any therapeutic healing.

The valuable lectures by Hans Erhard Lauer, printed here as an appendix, look at the relation between Jung and Steiner from a slightly different point of view. I want to mine this material, too, for what it contributes to spiritual psychology with depth psychology and Anthroposophy as a base.

The first essay gives a good picture of how an anthroposophist who is sympathetic to depth psychology interprets the vision, meaning, and methods of the latter. At first the essay may seem to resemble what one might find in a textbook about depth psychology. Notice, however, the inner clarity of the thinking and how Lauer slowly builds his theme.

Lauer first finds within the stream of depth psychology the play between individuality and collective forces. The polarity of that play is represented by Freud at the collective end—with his emphasis on the collective force known as sex—and by Adler on the end of individuality. Jung lands right in between. For Jung, illness manifests when these polarities conflict. His depth psychology explores the collective forces of the soul and the archetypes, as well as how autonomous symbolic forms seep into consciousness, producing illness when there is no capacity to receive these forms consciously. Lauer sees Jung as helping to prevent a total split between collective inner forces and individuality.

Steiner also wishes to heal this split, but from an entirely different angle than Jung. His work consists of developing the capacities of individuality to the point that the ego becomes the conscious "I," the spirit individuality that can make spiritual sense of what comes from the depths while doing practical spiritual work in the world. This is a very large order indeed. When these capacities are not developed spiritually, the split widens. For the many anthroposophists who work to develop the practical cultural forms Steiner initiated—education, medicine, agriculture, painting, science, drama, movement, and so on—there is the inherent possibility of developing severe disturbances that go unnoticed. The content of the various areas of Steiner's work is taken up, but often not the meditative work. Even those who do practice the meditative work do not reckon with the size and degree of the split in the culture between the individual and the collective, or perhaps they somehow feel exempt from this split. In actual fact, the split has proceeded so far that it is highly dangerous, I think, to do spiritual practices without accompanying soul work.

There is a notion in Anthroposophy that the content of what Steiner created can be beneficial in the world on its own. But taken alone, without conscious connection to soul life, and without inner connection to the activity of conscious life, not just its contents, Anthroposophy is just another content, operating out of the same sleepy consciousness as the world at large. Furthermore, evoking spiritual authority that has no actual basis in oneself is deadly when accompanied by upsurging forces that leak into consciousness. This stance of authority can lead to abuse, cruelty, dogmatism, false superiority, and a self-isolation of anthroposophic communities from the rest of the world.

According to Lauer, depth psychology works out of the same kind of consciousness as modern science: it makes theories and hypotheses concerning the human soul that are then investigated through therapy.

Lauer here misses Jung's phenomenological basis as well as the central significance of the transference. On the other hand, according to Lauer, those who take up Anthroposophy can, through meditative work, come to experience the soul inwardly, independently of the body. This meditative work potentially leads to a fully conscious "I." It is the fully conscious "I" that is supposed to be able to meet whatever rises from the collective forces of the soul.

Much of ego life is not conscious. This is the real discovery of Anthroposophy, but one that goes unnoticed, even in Anthroposophy. There is always an inner collusion going on between the unconscious aspects of the ego and the collective realms of the soul. Our ordinary ego is filled with pride, self-aggrandizement, anger, envy, and much besides. Most of all, the ego is the structure of fear. Freud's wonderful list of some fifty ego-defense mechanisms is very descriptive of the unconscious aspects of ego life. Ego defends itself, but in wholly unconscious ways, such as denial, projection, introjection, and so on. For the very few people who do follow through with the meditative regimen recommended by Steiner, there is the possibility of doing conscious spiritual work of a practical nature in the world, with the capacity of meeting whatever comes from the depths. However, anthroposophic training goes on without any guidance in inner soul work, with no recognition of the importance of depth psychology, and almost no guidance in the meditative work recommended by Steiner. In these matters the student is left to fend alone. The ego is thus left isolated from the usual forms of ego gratification and development. It is cut off from help in finding a healthy connection with the collective forces of the soul; it is also cut off from guidance in coming to the "I."

The anthroposophic path, taken alone, requires one, through meditative exercises, to experience the soul as independent of the body. It requires one to be able to enter into the activity, rather than the content, of thinking. This development opens imaginative consciousness. This path then requires one to go through exercises that make it possible to enter into the activity, rather than the content, of feeling life, where inspiration is experienced as the activity of actual spiritual beings. Then one goes through exercises that make it possible to enter into the activity, rather than the content, of the will, where intuition is experienced as direct participation with spiritual beings. All this, it is expected, can happen in a culture in which the most severe split has occurred in soul life, a split in which individualism reigns and there is no connection to the collective forces of the soul.

Spiritual psychology, a creative synthesis of depth psychology and Anthroposophy, sees inner soul work as a necessary preliminary to any kind of spiritual work. "Preliminary" here is meant as something akin to doing warm-up exercises, as, for example, done by a musician. You can be a very advanced musician, but you cannot do away with finger exercises. In our time, it is utter foolishness to try to take on meditative exercises without coming into healthy connection with one's soul life and doing a lot of work to keep that connection. How to keep open and keep these connections, and how to do so specifically within the kind of work one does in the world, is the work of spiritual psychology. Spiritual psychology as a practice, a doing, needs to be a part of every Waldorf training program, every anthroposophic medical training program, and all other anthroposophic endeavors.

In contemplating Lauer's essays, it might occur to the reader that the body must be gotten away from in order to work within the spiritual soul. Lauer strongly implies this. Lauer does not mention (nor does Wehr) that there is a whole dimension of Steiner's work that concerns developing the capacities to enter into imagination of the organs of the body and, through these, to enter into the soul and spirit worlds underlying them. Anthroposophy mostly touts body-free meditation, but this is not the direction that is necessarily required. It would be extremely fruitful to develop a synoptic comparison of Jung and Steiner by going to Steiner's meditative exercises and the results of those exercises reported in his book *Occult Physiology*.

I do not want to avoid contemplating the most difficult issue of all in this synoptic comparison of Jung and Steiner and the forming of spiritual psychology. This is the placement of Christ at the center of Anthroposophy and the importance of Christ in Jung.

Unfortunately, in Anthroposophy this focus is almost always sentimentalized, although Steiner does not sentimentalize it. He underwent a profound spiritual experience that showed him something of the true mysteries of Christ, reorienting the direction of Anthroposophy. But when the meditative side of Steiner's work is not practiced, the central freedom of the human being slides into a veiled religion, justified by Steiner's esoteric Christian viewpoint. Anthroposophy is practiced as a Christian religion (although this is vehemently denied). Many anthroposophists want to have it both ways. They want to experience themselves as completely free "I"-beings, but they also want to believe that Christ is working in them—without working through all the baggage of Christian belief that each and every one lives, whether Christian or not.

Neither Jung nor Steiner asks for Christian belief. But both realize the utter foolishness of speaking of a psychology of the dead, the gods, and the spiritual worlds without coming up against the status of Christ. Jung clearly emphasizes the religious character of the psyche, but wants to hold that soul is influenced by many archetypal myths besides the Christian myth. He does, however, see the Christian myth as the future of the psyche, that is, individuation as realization of the Self and Christ as the archetype of the Self.

If one does not just accept Jung's view, but meditates on it deeply as well as on Jung's writings concerning Christ, then what he says makes good sense and provides a way through the barrier encountered by anthroposophists. This barrier is simply that there is no other way to apprehend Christ from the consciousness of the ordinary ego than through what we are given from outside, by others. In Anthroposophy, the risk is that of forming a relationship to the religious notions of Christ, thinking that it is an immediate experience of developed spiritual consciousness. The development of the true capacity of the "I" would be needed, and if that takes place, we might well have Christian spiritual psychology. Steiner's writings have disseminated concepts of

Christ that are more powerful and astute than religions that either completely humanize Christ or completely deify him. But to simply accept what Steiner has to say would be falling into religion. (Actually, there is nothing wrong with falling into religion. Far worse is doing so without knowing that has happened.)

The concern here is whether there is or can be such a thing as a Christian spiritual psychology that is something other than imposing a certain belief structure onto a discipline. Here Steiner is more helpful than Jung, but the whole of Steiner has to be worked through. This means coming to see that the very structure and meaning of consciousness, of the natural world, of culture and civilization, of the Earth, of the human being in body, soul, and spirit, is permeated with the forces that are Christ. Thus it is impossible not to have a Christian spiritual psychology. It is only possible to deny the fact that spiritual psychology is completely the same as Christian psychology. Speaking in this way, at the end of this introduction, is not intended to be a pronouncement. It is deliberately provocative, a call for the working through the details of Christian spiritual psychology without falling into institutional religion, actual or veiled.

6

THE ANGELS

ROBERT J. SARDELLO, EDITOR

When we began to think about presenting a conference on angels at the Dallas Institute, the idea was whispered around quite softly at first. For here at the Institute, where really important issues such as public education, the teaching of teachers, and designing a master plan for the city of Dallas in the year 2000 occupy a good deal of time and effort and have a high profile, would there be any interest in something as intangible and seemingly impractical as angels? Well, around that time, the German film *Wings of Desire* was showing, and it aroused a good deal of discussion among the Fellows of the Institute. This interest made it possible to speak a little louder about getting together and talking about angels. None of the Fellows thought this strange or odd; to the contrary, everyone I talked to had a secret or not so secret interest in angels and was delighted about the prospect of an angel conference. In the ten years I have been putting together various programs, this one by far had the most enthusiastic reception. Something quite mysterious, I began to feel, was going on.

A sign of the times, perhaps: Ramtha, Lazaris, Kevin Ryerson, and many other channels have made contacting spiritual entities both popular and profitable. However, the willingness to pay attention to these channels indicates a growing cultural realization that we are in need of help. Furthermore, we might be ready to ask for help. And that readiness to ask for help connects us again to a much longer and deeper tradition, which offers a different kind of help than channeling. An angel never interferes with nor takes over one's consciousness or in any way counters the freedom of the human. Thus, angels are far subtler than, if I may say, the denser entities, who are the source of channeling.

Rather than introduce these papers by saying why we should give attention to angels, I want to indicate what will occur if we do not learn how to establish relationships with the angels.

On October 9, 1918, Rudolf Steiner presented a lecture in Zurich called "The Work of the Angels in Man's Astral Body." Steiner, as you may know, was the originator of Anthroposophy, the study of the wisdom of the human spirit. He says in this lecture that the present age—up until around the third millennium, that is up until about the year 2000— is given the task of consciously becoming awake and aware of the angels. During this time, the angels are seeking to come into connection with our conscious, waking lives. The angels are inclined toward us, but we must consciously, freely, be inclined toward them. They have a work to do for humanity; this work will take place regardless, says Steiner. However, if we are not consciously and freely working to establish a relationship with them, angel work will show up as symptom and pathology.

In Zurich, home of C. G. Jung, Steiner repeats for the spirit what Jung had stated for the soul. Jung says that in the symptoms of the soul are the gods. Steiner says that in the symptoms of the spirit are the angels. What symptoms in particular? First, Steiner indicates, and not out of speculation but out of a conscious clairvoyance, there will occur in culture a prevalence of certain kinds of sexual difficulties. Remember, this is Steiner talking in 1918. His exact words are:

> Certain instinctive knowledge that will arise in human nature, instinctive knowledge connected with the mystery of birth and conception, with sexual life as a whole, threatens to become baleful if the danger of which I have spoken takes effect [i.e., if we do not become consciously aware of the angels]. Certain angels would then themselves undergo a change—a change of which I cannot speak, because this is a subject belonging to the higher secrets of initiation—science which may not yet be disclosed. But this much can certainly be said: The effect in the evolution of humanity would be that certain instincts connected with the sexual life would arise in a pernicious form instead of wholesomely, in clear waking consciousness.

These instincts would not be mere aberrations but would pass over into and configure the social life, would above all prevent men—through what would then enter their blood as the effect of the sexual life—from unfolding brotherhood in any form whatever on the Earth, and would rather induce them to rebel against it.

What could he be talking about? That is something to let the imagination work on.

Then, Steiner goes on to speak of a second symptom. Everything connected with medicine, he says, will make a great advance in the materialistic sense. We will acquire knowledge of certain substances and certain treatments—and thereby do terrible harm. But the harm will be called useful. The harm will be called health-giving.

And then, Steiner speaks of a third symptom. Man will get to know of definite forces, which, by means of certain manipulations, will enable him to unleash tremendous mechanical forces into the world—and the whole of technical science will sail into desolate waters. But, he says, human egoism will find these desolate waters of tremendous use and benefit.

We need only to reflect for a moment on the very large difficulties culture now faces within the three areas of sexuality, medicine, and technology to know that Steiner saw in 1918 the possibility of our refusal of the angels.

I introduce these concerns here, at the start of these papers, to indicate something all of the essayists feel: the concern for angels at this particular time is serious business. We live in a time of great change, a period in which it is possible to make preparations for the forming of a new culture. This culture will either be dominated by fear and the task of survival or recognize spiritual reality actually present in the world as active force. If the latter is chosen, new capacities of perception, knowing, and action need to be developed, capacities enabling everyone to participate in the subtle dimensions of reality. The following essays contribute to the development of that larger sense of reality and point toward the creation of a spiritual culture that does not abandon the material world.

Perhaps I can assist your reading of the papers by offering an Ariadne's thread to hold on to as you go through the labyrinthine worlds of psychology, science, literature, and art in search of the angels. What most characterizes the following, I believe, is the attempt to work out of the present circumstances of consciousness so as to seek break-through points indicating the presence of the angels. That is to say, none of these writings works within esoteric traditions nor asks or requires the reader to be an "initiate." Rather, all of the contributors begin with the world as we now know it, with ordinary consciousness, and seek the mystery, which lies right in front of us. The careful reader will find, here and there, statements concerning the kinds of disciplines needed to begin feeling the nearness of angels—the importance of silence and stillness, emptying out, giving attention to words and language, appreciating rhythm as a world phenomenon, healthy terror, the capacity of "almost seeing." But nowhere will be found a doctrine or a set of established practices to follow because the aim does not consist of taking up a religious or spiritual practice other than the practice of daily approaching the temple of the world in a spiritual manner.

One of the intricate passages in the labyrinth leading to the angels concerns the role of science. On the one hand, a number of the authors show that the angels withdrew or were banished from the world with the development of natural science as a mode of consciousness. Robert Romanyshyn, in particular, has pursued this development in a most astute manner, showing how science reduces multiple planes of reality to a single, material plane. On the other hand, those very same papers that point out the difficulties of science also look to science as now crossing the threshold and finding again the spiritual worlds. I believe it is necessary to distinguish the prevalent materialism of science from the historical and cultural development of consciousness that is signaled by the onset of science. As a mode of materialism, the angels will never be rediscovered through the procedures or findings of physics, biology, or astronomy; one must be a little bit aware of the possibility that the angels are being reduced to natural phenomena. However, science as an indication that the human spirit is in the process of development from a kind of dream-like state which existed from pre-history up until about the fifteenth century, characterized by the capacity to have direct perception of the spiritual worlds, to the point where an objective view of the world excludes spiritual presences, shows the task now necessary. When spiritual presences accompanied a dreamlike perception of the world, there was no choice involved on the part of humanity concerning participation with spiritual beings. Nice, but naive commingling. Scientific consciousness, taken as a development of the human spirit, brings loss of spiritual worlds but also makes possible the choice to seek connection with clear and fully awake consciousness. Thus, in some of the papers you will find some rather astounding recent scientific findings. However, it is not the findings in themselves that are the breakthrough but, it seems to me, the choice to look upon these phenomena in a truly spiritual manner.

An additional aspect of this collection is the felt importance of tradition. None of the authors, it seems, cares much for "new age" language. I am afraid my own contribution comes dangerously close to that, and I am grateful to be surrounded by those steeped in the sense of tradition. Tradition simply recognizes that the work lies in adhering to the wisdom of the ages, of re-creating this wisdom in forms suitable for present times. Tradition does not imply rigid repetition of the past; it does require a real feeling for the past as not past but continuing into the present and shaping the future. Not the least aspect of this sense of tradition involves never forgetting the world. As Gail Thomas so beautifully develops it, if we forget the seasons, we forget the angels. Seasonal consciousness, too, belongs to tradition. Then, also, there is plenty of room within tradition for differences. For example, Larry Dossey adheres quite strongly to the tradition of angelic hierarchies, while Donald Cowan makes room for equality; both views are within tradition.

The contributions in this volume also present wonderful contradictions that assure that you are not being told what or how to think about angels but to go and find out for yourselves. An extraordinary feature of a community such as the Fellows of the Institute is that major differences in each other's work are appreciated. Thus, in one paper, that of Fred Turner, a view that angels will perhaps be created through genetic engineering is juxtaposed with Louise Cowan's view of an absolute division between the realm of the angels and the realm of the human, a view she supports with her reading of Dante. These contradictions spark the imagination and prevent "angelology" from being confined to one sector of the world, thus thwarting a kind of consciousness eager to judge one side as evil and the other as good.

Finally, I wish to point out one more dimension of this work on angels, and that is the force of the angels. You will find very little sweet talk here about the angels and instead a wonderful absence of sentimentalism. Plenty of mystery, yes. But at the same time, most clearly presented in Robert Trammell's paper, real strength and healthy terror are instilled, which makes clear that adequate preparation of the vessel of the soul is required to face the angels. As Dona Gower wisely warns, there is a tendency in the tradition of angels toward disembodiment and abstraction. That kind of angelic imagination will not be found in these papers; indeed, it is even suggested by Eileen Gregory, in her skillful reading of the poet H.D., that terrible events such as war, rather than a retribution for cultural wrongdoing, is an apocalyptic uncovering of the angels.

You can perhaps begin to see why we felt that it would be of service to have the presentations of this conference on angels made available in published form. There are a number of works around that give accounts of the history of angels and of the classical classification of angels. There are some "new age" publications that present sweet views of the angels and how to contact them for personal help. And there are esoteric approaches to angels that approach them from the magical traditions. However, a cultural view of angels—that, to my knowledge, has not been available until now. Making such an approach available, we hope, constitutes a service to the angels.

7

The Speech of the Grail

A Journey toward Speaking that Heals and Transforms

Linda Sussman

The Grail story forming the substance of this wonderful interpretive study by Linda Sussman was set down in writing around A.D.1208. *Parzival* differs considerably from other epics because it is a story, not about what happened in humanity's past, but about what can happen in its future. Moreover, this great work does not belong as much to literary tradition as to the body of initiation practices; that is to say, it forms a practical guide by which any individual can find the way to the spiritual worlds. Linda Sussman's book helps us along this way by suggesting a healthy approach to spiritual practice. This begins by developing the capacity of attention and a strong, reproductive imagination. Her close, descriptive approach to the text of *Parzival* also provides a basis for developing further capacities.

The value of what this author contributes cannot be overestimated. It is a beginning, which nonetheless is carried through to the deepest and highest levels to which one might aspire. Until one can make, hold, and sustain inner pictures in consciousness, further inner work falls apart into abstractions or self-constructed egoistic fantasies. An additional merit of Sussman's approach is its indication that strengthening imagination does not have the purpose of merely expanding consciousness beyond ordinary perception and thought. Rather, such strengthening is always intimately concerned with our earthly world, with becoming ever more vividly alive, which for our author shows forth most clearly in human speaking.

Sussman's detailed recounting of each of the sixteen books of *Parzival* is far more than a summary intended to simplify the work of encountering a complex text. In retelling the story, she is demonstrating the necessity of developing the ability to reproduce inner pictures of something given first through the senses. Practicing the art of the storyteller, she is, at the same time, practicing the art of transforming a text that is read into a story that is heard. Her readers will immediately recognize an inner experience that is quite revealing. When we read something that is in the nature of an explanation, it makes us tired; it is as if our life forces were expended in giving body to something that, by its nature, is abstract. Abstractions suck the life out of us. Sometimes such a sacrifice is well worthwhile. But, if it is carried out prematurely, that is, without a living imagination, the result is that we feel we have been depleted to provide life for a sclerotic world that left on its own would run its rightful course of withering away and dying. Hearing the story of Parzival, on the other hand, and recreating it in the inner word, does something quite different. We are refreshed rather than exhausted. A work of the imagination gives life rather than sucks it away. We know that Sussman is a storyteller rather than a summarizer because, hearing the story as she tells it, we feel more alive, more awake, more vital.

An alchemical picture may help us to understand the artistry involved. Alchemy is concerned with transforming soul life in such a way that one gradually comes to perceive the world not as a collection of objects but as a living, metamorphosing, creating activity. Such alchemical work begins with the process known as putrefaction. A well-known alchemical emblem of the twelfth century, for example, was the alchemical Tree of Knowledge. This tree had twelve branches, each containing a picture to be contemplated. The first picture—the first branch—depicted a black bird, with wings outstretched, standing on the earth. Beneath this, under the earth, lay a human skull.

This bird, flexing its wings, is an image of our ordinary consciousness, ready to take flight and take in whatever the world offers for perception and thinking. It is an image of the way we take in the contents of the manifest world, while the skull beneath the earth depicts the dying away of immediate perception into the dark recesses of the skull.

The whole tableau thus indicates what typically happens in our ordinary way of being receptive to the world. We take in the world and it recedes into the tomb of the skull. An immediate presence to something living is deadened when we try to know about things by separating them from us rather than by finding the way to let them live within us, which would lead to a new kind of thinking, a thinking with the world rather than about it. Putrefaction takes place because what we take in recedes into us and lies there rotting, like stinking refuse. This refuse becomes the habits of our soul life—all the opinions, half-formed ideas taken from others, prejudices, reactions—with which we navigate in the world. The alchemists recognized that putrefaction must be met with the development of inner forces, primarily the force of imagination. The first step toward true imagination involves developing the capacity to make accurate inner pictures that mirror what we encounter from outside. This first step develops the ability to concentrate the soul. Linda Sussman's retelling the story of Parzival teaches this art of concentration. Nevertheless, it is up to the reader to form the inner images of the story, gradually building them up to the point that he or she can live within the story as a whole, and not seek quick results.

One can work a very long time with the tale of Parzival, the first thread composing the tapestry of this book. However, the retelling of each episode of the story is followed by two commentaries. The first addresses the reader as a person working with the process of initiation. The second addresses the reader's gradual development toward a deepened experience and practice of the mystery of the word, of speech. The first commentaries can be seen as a way of intensifying the images of the story. They are not so much interpretations of the story as aids in hearing the story more vividly. It is extremely helpful, following a reading of a commentary, to go back and reread the episode of the story that it deals with. Sussman's work, I believe, is best approached as a process to work with, rather than a text to read through from beginning to end.

The second commentary following the retelling of each part of the story is more on the order of interpretation. This interpretive work constitutes one of the ways of approaching the question of the meaning of *Parzival*. Linda Sussman, who has a particular interest in the act of human speech, has discovered that Parzival's path of development corresponds to what is involved in working to transform our use of words from a mere utilitarian mode of communication into an imaginative language that simultaneously embodies thinking, feeling, and action. This interpretation of *Parzival*, of course, is only one of the many possible ways of understanding this work. Other interpretations include cultural, psychological, spiritual, literary, historical, and even educational ones. That Wolfram's text can simultaneously make itself available to such a variety of approaches verifies its worth as a true worldview. As a further orientation toward Ms. Sussman's work, therefore, I would now like to say something more about the worldview inherent in the Grail quest. This will perhaps show why her truly new understanding of this quest as having to do with living speech perhaps comes closer to its essence than previous interpretations.

The Grail is said to be the chalice of the Last Supper, which Joseph of Arimathea used to receive Christ's blood on the cross at the moment the spear of Longinus pierced His side. Such a legendary origin has led to many quests for the literal object, the chalice, known as the Grail. A broader, more comprehensive view, however, shows that we have to do not with a literal object, but with the mysteries surrounding the possible connection between the earthly world and the spiritual worlds. Stories of a mysterious concave object surround this connection.

Over six thousand years ago, at a particular time of the year, shamans would go into a dark cave or carefully constructed mound built at a geomantically-selected site aligned with particular star movements and the yearly course of the Sun. This cavernous hollow was completely dark except for the light admitted by a single slit. At a particular moment, a beam of light from the starry world would enter the opening and fall upon two cups carved into a rock receptacle. A polished rock crystal was placed in each cup and, at the moment the beam of light entered, it was split by the crystals, striking the shaman who was in deep meditation and transforming him or her into the light beam itself. At that moment, the shaman experienced a vision of his or her own creation. This vision consisted of seeing that the human being was the microcosmic form of the whole of the macrocosm. The macrocosm, in this vision, was seen to be the working of angelic beings, and the forming of the cosmos was seen to be at the same time the forming of the Cosmic Human. The shaman then carried this vision of the birth of the Human to the community by carrying some of the water from the hollowed stone in a cup and distributing it. For the community, this ritual was a constant reminder of the necessity of harmonizing the human being with the cosmos, of maintaining the ongoing relationship of the human and the spiritual worlds as an actual reality. The site of the ritual I have described still exists at Newgrange, in Ireland, and its use for this purpose has been carefully verified.[1] The content of the vision, of course, is not available as physical evidence, but was given to us through the clairvoyant research of Rudolf Steiner, who also spoke of the work of Anthroposophy, the investigation of the human being as a being of the cosmos, as a Grail science.[2]

The shaman saw an intimate correlation between the dome of the heavens and the inverted dome of the receptacle that received the light; that is to say, all of earthly creation is in the image of the divine spiritual worlds. Further, the spiritual worlds need the earthly world to complete their purpose, and the earthly world needs the spiritual worlds to complete its purpose. Virtually all sacred traditions acknowledge this relationship by giving special significance to a sacred vessel. The Buddhist focuses on the rice bowl as a sacred object of meditation; the Taoist sees the three-legged bronze cauldron; the I-Ching, as reflecting the divine world; the Jew passes the Seder cup, which contains knowledge of the Cabala; the Christian takes communion from the chalice, uniting the recipient with Christ.

---

1   See, for example, H. Harrison, *The Cauldron and the Grail* (San Francisco, The Archives Press, 1992).

2   R. Steiner, *An Outline of Occult Science* (Hudson, NY: Anthroposophic Press, 1950).

In many myths, the ongoing relation between the spiritual worlds and this world is depicted as a miraculous vessel that gives abundant life. Irish legend tells of Dagda's Cauldron, which could feed an entire army without becoming empty. Nordic myth speaks of the vessel of Sinnreger containing a beverage of wisdom and inspiration. Welsh legend speaks of the basket of Gwyddno Gahanhir. Although food for only one person was placed in this basket, it was found on opening to contain sustenance for a hundred. Similarly, Joseph of Arimathea, who was imprisoned for forty years without food, was sustained by the chalice in which he had caught Christ's blood.

This Grail chalice, the chalice of the blood of Christ, which became the focus of the thirteenth-century stories of Parzival, is of particular importance, because it has to do with the transformation of the individual human being into a chalice. The responsibility for maintaining the connection with the spiritual worlds now falls upon each and every individual and must be carried out in completely individual ways. The many stories, myths, and sacred practices surrounding a holy vessel all prefigure and prepare the way for transferring cosmic responsibility to the individual. Further, the mystery of true individuality lies in the fact that the Christ lives within each of us, making the way to the Grail a Christ initiation. Wolfram von Eschenbach's *Parzival* is the story of such an initiation.

As Linda Sussman points out in the very beginning of her work, Parzival's quest is a path not to perfection, but rather to forming a right relationship to our imperfections. Parzival makes all kinds of errors and mistakes, and, indeed, commits murderous deeds. This path through the middle, through the veil of the world, requires learning through earthly misery and guilt, rather than trying to maintain innocence and purity of soul. Further, it requires moving beyond the self-absorption that can come about through suffering. It demands sensing a possible future, rather than feeling endlessly trapped by the past. The spiritual path of the middle is the path through the world. This means coming into a right relationship with evil, neither rejecting it, trying to stay away from it, projecting it onto others, or fighting it only from the outside; rather one must become conscious of it, which is a gradual process. Because it directly confronts the mystery of evil, a mystery that we are just now entering into in ways never encountered before, *Parzival* is a picturing of the future rather than of the past.

In the far distant past, evil was imagined primarily in cosmological images and myths as a cosmic struggle between the creating angels and the fallen angels. Thus, evil was imagined as a struggle that was of concern mainly to the gods, the results of this concern filtering down into the human world. Later, among the Greeks, evil was felt to be closer to this world; but its resolution was primarily an aesthetic work. Then, in the Middle Ages, evil became a soul problem, and the task was to maintain purity of soul in the face of clear temptations. Today, however, and this has been coming for a long time, evil is pervasive in the human world; and it is no longer possible to delineate clearly where good and evil separate. Here, the importance of speech comes to the center. In the future, as is already clear in the way that cold, institutional evil now permeates the world, it will be impossible to tell in any outer way what is good and what is evil. Good and evil will use the same language—as is already happening. Navigating through this mixture will require an inner sense of truth for how one speaks rather than for the content spoken. Now, this inner sense of truth in speaking concerns a living connection with the Christ as Logos—the divine Word made human—living within the heart of each individual.

The path of initiation into the Christ as Logos has nothing to do with institutionalized religion. The Church, as an institution, can no longer serve as an adequate outer guide into the inner mysteries of human evolution because it too, of necessity, is pervaded by evil. This is not to say that the Church is evil. It is no longer possible to say that some things are evil and others are good. Evil is like death; everyone takes part; it is unavoidable. But that does not give everything over to it. However, it does mean that navigation becomes infinitely more difficult, primarily because everything on the outside that looks evil must be located by each one of us within, as part of who we are. We must find the forces within to transform evil gradually through a self-transformation that never takes its eye off the wider world. Such transformation, as shown in *Parzival,* begins with the steps toward self-knowledge, beginning in Soul Wisdom, whose intricacies in *Parzival* revolve around the women of the Grail.

Linda Sussman works in a wonderful way to bring to the fore of our imaginations the central importance of the women of the Grail. She carefully avoids casting this epic into a male initiation experience or falling into the traps that could cast the whole story into an antifeminist tale, of interest only as new fodder for the Men's movement. She also avoids quick categorization of the figures of this story into the now standard Jungian abstractions of Anima and Animus. Indeed, all of the actions of Parzival can be said to originate from, be sustained by, and revolve around the feminine characters. The women of the Grail are representatives of the soul qualities necessary for transforming the self, for realizing that true individuality lies in coming to know ourselves as human spiritual beings. None, absolutely none, of the women figures of the Grail are passive; they are all receptive, and a totally new, active sense of the quality of radical receptivity slowly dawns on the attentive reader.

Attention to the women figures in this story leads to the great temptation of interpreting the story in terms of depth psychology. A new and enlarged sense of soul is needed not to commit another reductionist psychological explanation. Soul is first and foremost the Wisdom of the Cosmos, known in the Egyptian Mysteries as Isis and, later in Earth evolution, as the Sophia. There is Soul, and then again, there is soul. Soul as Sophia, as described in the Gnostic myths, refers to the Intelligence of the Cosmos, She through whom everything in the Cosmos works with the right rhythm, the right timing, and in the right relationship. At the same time, Sophia is the Intelligence of the Earth, She through whom everything of the natural world reflects Cosmic Wisdom. But, Sophia, again as told in the Gnostic myths, is also fallen. In Her desire to be united with the Creator, she becomes disoriented and is cast into the realm of Chaos at the center of the Earth. Here She suffers torments

ACTS OF THE HEART

instigated by other fallen beings—the demiurge and a lion-faced being filled with pride. Her torments are grief, fear, bewilderment, and ignorance, from which the elements of earth, air, fire, and water are formed, condensing into fallen nature. In *Parzival*, we must gain a feeling for the women or Soul figures as depicting Sophia intertwined with individual soul life. Sussman does not make this distinction, but it is crucial. Four of the Sophia representatives—Herzeloyde, Belacane, Jeschute, and Sigune—express the quality of grieving. Only when there is redemption of the Sophia, which occurs in various ways for each of these Sophia representatives, does a harmonious individual soul life become possible.

The difference between Isis and the Sophia concerns the fact, made available to us through the spiritual research of Rudolf Steiner, that Sophia has united herself completely with the human being in such a manner that the whole of the Cosmos exists within each individual; every individual human is an expression of the whole of the spiritual Cosmos, the macrocosm in the microcosm of individuality. But, because Sophia is fallen, soul life is pervaded with an intractable ground of grieving, fear, ignorance, and bewilderment. Individual soul life is separate from, but not independent of, these passions. Individual soul life consists of all our sympathies and antipathies; it is filled with all our desires, needs, wants, and, most importantly, with all that needs to be worked through from past lives, namely karma. What modern depth psychology has yet to see, but what is already contained in *Parzival*, is that soul work must be simultaneously oriented both toward becoming free in the individual soul realm—which does not mean clearing all desire, but rather becoming fully conscious of desire—and toward a soul conversion, a turning around of soul life in the larger sense of Soul that is fully receptive to the world and reaches toward the spirit. This is necessary to bring about the restoration of Nature from the effects of the fall. If modern psychologies of soul were completely successful in finally getting every person in the world to care for individual soul life, the primary passions of fallen Sophia would still exist; in fact, we would be more present than ever to grieving, fear, ignorance, and bewilderment. Until it becomes apparent that soul work is not for our benefit alone, but for the sake of the world, care of soul is doomed to becoming trapped forever in one egotism after another. Now, the nexus uniting individual soul with World Soul lies in the realm of the heart, which involves the adventures surrounding Gawan.

Some of the best work done by Ms. Sussman is to be found in the chapters relating to Gawan. As she points out, many literary critics over the years have been unable to make sense of the Gawan books, and thus leave them out of consideration, feeling they are not a part of the original text and must have been added later. Building on the work of Walter Johannes Stein, Sussman sees that Gawan concerns the heart aspect of Parzival. The conversion of soul life from individual matters alone to a concern for the Soul of the World takes place through uniting cognitive capacities that are spiritually oriented with the life of feeling, centered in the heart. The heart is also the center of the commingling of the individual soul with the Soul of the World. From Gawan's first appearance, we learn that he is a healer. The capacity of healing depends on the ability, demonstrated by Gawan, of individual soul perception coupled with perception of the soul qualities of the world. Gawan heals a wounded knight with herbs and is also instrumental in the subtler healing of his beloved, Orgeluse. He loves her from the moment he sees her, and in spite of her constant and vociferous rejections, he never wavers from his love. He sees deeply into her soul, sees that something is blocked, but does not seek to make her reveal it so he can gain power over her; rather he acts in the world on her behalf in such a way that healing follows. Psychotherapists and counselors would do well to study these books carefully for insights into the way soul healing comes about and, in particular, into the delicate balance needed between individual soul and World Soul.

Through Gawans actions, we are also led to insight into how evil may be healed through soul. Here, even Gawan has much to learn. The marvelous scene of Gawan's trials in the Castle of Wonders, the domain of the black magician, Klingsor—his encounter with the Wonder Bed, being tossed to and fro, warding off the arrows from all sides, fighting to the death with the lion—are all pictures of coming face to face with the interior of the heart, the center able to work in the right way with evil.

First, we have a picture of evil in the very construction of the Castle of Wonders. Upon entering the castle, Gawan sees a great domed entrance hall painted the colors of a peacock. The peacock signifies a level of spiritual initiation. In alchemy, this stage of initiation has to do with attaining a first level of connection with the spiritual worlds. But what is attained at this level must be sacrificed. That is, one must give up what one learns of the spiritual worlds at this stage. If it is not given up, and instead, the knowledge is used to bring about effects in the physical world, the result is destructive to the world, even though it might initially look helpful. For example, contemporary scientists, the truly creative ones, sometimes come to this level of consciousness, mostly without knowing it. Discoveries are made and then immediately put into practical use, without an understanding of the whole picture. Thus, some invention, some technology, some scientific discovery is put into use prematurely. Only much later, often generations later, do we see that what looked helpful is actually harmful. The Castle of Wonders is a citadel for this kind of bringing of evil into the world, which, remember, is not to be fought against, but balanced with soul capacities.

In a way, the Castle of Wonders is a technological marvel. The centerpiece of this technology is the magical pillar in the tower. Looking into this pillar, one is able to see what is happening for a distance of six miles. Such a marvel is somewhat analogous to the present electronic technology, which allows us to make phone calls anywhere in the world, but works also to make us forgetful of far more important connections to be made—connections with the spiritual worlds—that can never come about through materialistic technology.

Another most important aspect of the magical powers of the Castle is connected with the fact that four hundred women are imprisoned here. Moreover, while there are men in the castle, no relationship takes place between the men and the women. Coupled with this, Klingsor's magical powers stem from the damming up of his desires because of his being castrated. Clinschor, master of the Castle of Wonders, apprenticed himself to black magic, transforming sexual energy into power. Here, we have another, most helpful image related to the present technological world. The kind of technology now promoted is not only excessively masculine, it is also a deviated masculine, lacking a healthy relationship to the feminine or soul element, which it nevertheless relies upon, and indeed feeds upon. It is as if a great deal of modern technology replaces what is supposed to be going on in healthy relationships between men and women with materialistic comfort. As soul activity is in the process of being replaced by comfort, it requires deliberate, attentive work to make and keep it conscious.

Gawan shows the way through the imprisonment of the feminine soul element. The way through is to enter into the realm of the heart, which, as the story shows, is no easy matter. Gawan's turbulent, dizzying, disorienting, life-threatening encounters in the room containing the Wonder Bed, the attacks of arrows from unknown sources, his fight with the pure instinctual passion of the lion, all picture what is involved in coming to be conscious of desire rather than simply acting out of desire. The closest we come to such an experience in ordinary life are obsessions of the heart. Obsessions take us into the heart of desire, but usually we think that we are obsessed, in love, with another person; the intensity is such that all other capacities are totally disrupted. As obsession, however, the object of such a symptom is an opening of the heart. This demands not that we kill or control desire but that we come into a right relationship with it: that we recognize desire as the living movement of soul life itself and accept the attendant responsibility of coming to experience the inner and outer worlds through the heart in a fully conscious way. Through initiation into the realm of the heart as the nexus of soul life, love is enlarged in such manner that love for another is never separated from love for the world.

This introduction would be incomplete without giving attention to the third aspect of Parzival, pictured in the mysterious figure of Feirefiz, the offspring of Gahmuret and Belacane. We do not hear anything of this half-brother of Parzival until the closing books. If Parzival has to do with the quest for spiritual knowledge through development of soul capacities, and Gawan has to do with the quest of soul to find heart through the right relationship with the feeling life, then Feirefiz has to do with the quest for a right relationship with the will. In this regard, note well Ms. Sussman's careful attention to Feirefiz's appearance. He is truly a magnificent sight. His armor is bedecked with every imaginable precious jewel. His shield is made of asbestos, which can neither burn nor decay. On top of his helmet, he wears the strange emblem of a being known as the Ecidemon. Feirefiz is a picture of pure human nobility, of all that a human being can develop into solely out of purely human, earthly forces. That he belongs to the earthly element is shown by the jewels he proudly displays; it is as if he has reached down into the Earth, finding there precious material to be shaped, formed, forged into works of beauty. He leads vast armies consisting of every race, an image indicating that his work concerns the earthly world and the transformations of that world possible through the forces of the will. Feirefiz is a representative of humanity, of all of those individuals who strive and work in the world with great nobility, carrying out what they have to do, making important contributions—but having little inkling of the spiritual worlds.

The Ecidemon, a dragonlike being, is the source of Feirefiz's inspiration and action for noble work. The Grail scholar Walter J. Stein says that the Ecidemon is one's angel united with the human being. The description we are given certainly does not look like an angel, but is a description of what others see. When we first get a glimpse of another person's true being, we do not see the individual spirit in the other person. Instead, what is felt is hostility. That is the real paradox; when we see the true individuality of another person, it is as if we fear that we will be robbed of our own strength. When we see someone accomplish something in the world, we feel as if we have been robbed of what we might have done. Moreover, and even more paradoxically, the further one develops spiritually, the more hostility toward others becomes a possibility. After all that

Parzival has been through, after all he has suffered and learned, when he sees Feirefiz, he does not see the guiding star of this individual, but rather the Ecidemon, and he meets Feireifz with hostility.

When Feirefiz and Parzival meet in a duel, Feirefiz wins. Parzival's sword breaks. However, the noble brother will not kill an unarmed person, and instead they sit down and talk, discovering that they are brothers. Here, again, we find a hint intimating why Ms. Sussman pursues the importance of speech in her interpretation. But, what is most important in this picture is that it is Feirefiz who stops short at the moment when he could have destroyed his brother. What an amazing picture! It is a picture that says no matter how far one goes in spiritual development, no matter how far one develops the interior life of the heart, what must not be forgotten is the central fact of being an earthly human being. In the image given earlier of the alchemical Tree of Knowledge, the final stage of spiritual work, of concentration, contemplation, and meditation, is the picture of the sparrow. The final aim of spiritual initiation is to be able to see ourselves as a sparrow, an ordinary bird, out in the world, the beautiful earthly world, making our way just like everyone else.

Of course, the speaking encounter between Parzival and Feirefiz changes them both. After Parzival discovers his human brother, a self-discovery of his own humanity, and Feirefiz discovers his brother, his own aspects of spirit and soul being, significant events follow. Parzival is now able to return to the wounded Anfortas and speak in an entirely new way—as a human being, from the heart, with spiritual knowledge. He is also able to lead his brother to the place of the Grail; that is to say, initiation into the path of love is not for one's own sake, for one's own salvation, but for the sake of others.

The question that Parzival is now able to speak to Anfortas, which previously he was unable to speak because of ignorance, is "What ails thee?" Other legends of the Grail indicate that there are two further questions: "How can I help?" and "Whom does the Grail serve?" By this time, in working carefully, meditatively, with the text, there can be no doubt whatsoever that these questions are not spoken merely out of curiosity, but from the very depth and core of Parzival's full being. The first question expresses the capacity of true compassion. Only because Parzival has suffered all he has, only because he knows error and guilt, and has come to know love, is he able to ask this question. There is no need for Anfortas to answer the question, to describe the nature of his ailment. The questioning itself suffices because it is the speaking, the true soul gesture of an act of compassion, that heals.

The second question, "How can I help?" speaks the action of love. Often, asking "How can I help?" means "How can I help myself in helping you?" Here, the questioning issues from a transformed heart. Again, this is not a question seeking an answer, a sure sign of egotism, but contains its own answer; love is not for one's own sake, but for the sake of others, for the sake of the world. These first two questions are asked not out of duty, not out of obligation, not out of the stance of a professional helper of others, but out of true freedom, fully respectful of the freedom of the other. These questions are not general, abstract questions; we must not look at their content but rather at the way they are spoken from an individual who has come, through an initiation experience, into the mystery of love. Indeed, we have to say that when Parzival asks these questions the whole of the spiritual worlds are focused, through the individual, in compassion and love.

Then there is the third question, "Whom does the Grail serve?" The Grail serves the servers of the Grail. Still, we have not satisfactorily answered the question of what the Grail is in the first place. On the one hand, the Grail is the Christ at the center of the whole vessel of the Cosmos, the Christ at the center of the spiritual worlds, the spiritual Sun. On the other hand, the Grail is the Grail server, the individual as vessel with Christ as the center and light of spirit, body, and soul life. And the Grail is also the whole Earth, the Earth as vessel containing Christ's blood, open to the streaming spiritual forces of the Cosmos. However, this is no definitive answer to the question. Each reader, in taking up this marvelous book is brought into the region where it becomes possible to live with the question and mystery of the Grail.

I am aware that still more esoteric understandings of *Parzival* are possible. The aim of this introduction has been to try to orient the reader toward the importance of what Linda Sussman has created. I am also aware of much that I have bypassed in order to say something briefly. Readers of this book will be led into the contemplation of many more things than I have addressed. For example, one may contemplate how entering into this quest involves leaving behind all that we have been given from the past. Here we find a basis for truly encountering what comes to meet the soul, rather than endlessly analyzing how we are formed out of influences from the past. One may meditate, too, on the peculiar, important figure of Cundrie, the sorceress. Doing so, we experience that what is most vile and uncomfortable is actually our most precious source of guidance and our protection from trying to meet our destiny too hastily. One may reflect, further, on the full Significance of a path through the middle between longing, which if followed leads to literalizing the forces of spirit, and sorrow, which if followed leads not only into the depths of the soul, but also to self-absorption. Finally, one may also meditate on the Significance and the true reality of community—for, after all, the Grail also refers to the Grail kingdom, to the renewal of the whole Earth through the renewal of community.

A great deal of praise is due Linda Sussman for what she offers in this book. While she draws adeptly from many sources, we are never led into a single view, a reductionistic way of looking. Rather, the reader is taken into a complete, if unfamiliar world, the world of the possible future. Praise be, that we are not given yet another interpretation, either from psychology or from the results of someone else's spiritual investigations! We are left free to enter into Parzival's world—aided to be sure, by a great deal of study and inner work carried out by the author, but none of this is imposed. Nor do we find in this book an abstract, removed, intellectual, scholarly approach to the subject. The reader is able to be fully engaged because the author was fully engaged, not only in the text of Parzival, but in the deepest questions of her life, which are also the deepest questions of everyone's life. The result is a book that is alive and can be worked with again and again. One is led from reading into meditation and then from meditation back again to this book. And one is led from this book back to the original, and from that text itself again into further meditation. And most important, all of this inner activity does not take us away from the world, but rather much deeper into a capacity to see the world anew, to begin to act differently, from a different center, from love.

8

SING ME THE CREATION

PAUL MATTHEWS

Paul Matthews' *Sing Me the Creation* stands as probably the most unusual guidebook for creative writing in the world. Some eighteen years ago, when I was a university professor teaching in a program in depth psychology and literature, I had the privilege of working with Caroline Gordon. She was an accomplished novelist, in the tradition of the great writers of the American South, such as William Faulkner and Eudora Welty, and was also intimately involved in the movement known as the New Criticism, with significant writers such as John Crowe Ransom. Miss Gordon taught creative writing. Through her I learned that it was not possible to get very far by approaching writing through the kinds of technical manuals in vogue. Her approach was to immerse students in the great literature of the world. Her notion was that it was more important to develop imagination than to work at writing skills. She was astute enough to know that imagination was not a subjective reality and that great literature changes the world and could therefore change potential writers as well. I always felt that she had solved half of the problem of learning to write. Now, after eighteen years of waiting, I think that Paul Matthews has solved the other half.

In this book, Paul Matthews provides an effective guide into the imagination of the word. Further, his approach to the word is somewhat akin to that of Owen Barfield; he has found a way to enter into the word that is at the same time a gateway into an imagination of the soul of the world.

Technical approaches to writing do not work because they are infected with the great disease of language, nominalism. Nominalism sees the word as no more than an instrument, empty of any substance of its own, language as a mere device for bringing the mind out into the open. To understand what constitutes a paragraph, a sentence, a metaphor, a simile, preposition, synonym, antonym can be seen as nothing more than a technology of nominalism. This approach to the word has been with us since the seventeenth century and can be traced to Marin Mersenne. Mersenne carried on a thirty-year intellectual war, taking the side of rationalism against imagination. He took metaphorical statements at their literal level and tried to show that imagination-imbued language was nonsense. For example, he posed questions such as "How high is Jacob's ladder?" Such a question cannot be answered, for "Jacob's ladder" is imaginative rather than scientific language. Through the centuries this scientific view of language has taken hold; we are all infected with it. In the domain of the literary arts, the final result of nominalism is that the world of fiction is reduced to entertainment, reading a form of self-indulgence, words a vehicle for conveying untruth, writing only a means of expressing subjective imagination that has nothing to do with the "real" world.

In the past decade or so, another approach to creative writing has sprung up. Instead of the deadly approach to the technology of language, aspiring writers are now doing inner visualization work, paying attention to dream images, shifting attention to the inner world. The intention here is to learn how to stay close to the image, and to write directly out of the inner experience of image. Such psychological approaches to creative writing put the emphasis on creative rather than the act of writing. No doubt this shift is due to a popularizing of Jung's psychology. I suspect that writers enjoy these kinds of workshops, not recognizing that subjective approaches to imagination cannot heal the illness of the word; it is a little like seeking a cure for cancer by going to the movies.

My friend and colleague, James Hillman, had written as early as the 1970s that in the field of language what is needed is a new angelology of words so that we may once again have faith in them. Angel means "emissary," "message-bearer," and that is exactly the kind of renewal of the word we find here in this wonderful book. Hillman is not suggesting that words bring to us the messages of the angelic world, but that words themselves are angel worlds. Seeing words as angels, as independent carriers of soul, and soul as referring to the inner quality of all things, not simply to subjective experience, saves us from the suffocating thought that speech is no more than the utterance of personal opinions. Hillman's proposal has the capacity to alter completely our now unconscious habit of using words thoughtlessly. But, how to go about inhabiting words as holy messengers, the actual task of doing the necessary work, that is found here in *Sing Me The Creation*.

Because the word as angel of the soul has atrophied to an alarming extent, the sclerotic body of language has to be taken out of five centuries of imprisonment and given healthy exercise. This book is filled with exercises that can be seen as homeopathic remedies. If the word is ill then it is the word that can heal; that is a homeopathic principle. Technical exercises, which are something completely different from what is found in this *materia medica* of the word, exercise only the physical, literal body of language. Such exercise may build muscle, but leave the soul untouched and sick. Exercises of the inner imaginary life may enrich fantasy, but do not strengthen the speech organs, and soul is set adrift without a body. Another aspect of approaching healing homeopathically is that the forces of healing are not brought in from the outside but come through the development of one's own inner forces. Mr. Matthews does not do the work for us; he only indicates a healthy way of working.

The exercises recommended herein have an additional dimension that goes even further than homeopathic remedies. The healing of the word is not only based on the principle that like cures like. The truly great contribution of this book is to be found in its putting forth the basic truth that the word is the whole of the universe, the Logos. Here homeopathy, which is a strictly empirical approach to healing, is taken up and fulfilled by anthroposophic remedies. The remedies of anthroposophic medicine, while also homeopathic, are based on knowledge of the correspondences between the body, soul, and spirit of the individual with the rhythms of the creating powers of the universe. Thus, the exercises in this book are more than empirically based experiments that have been found to work based upon other than mechanistic assumptions. Each set of exercises also embodies one of the qualities of the creating elements of the world—Earth, Water, Air, and Fire. The elements are not material substances as we have now come to think of them but are pure qualities of creative activity unifying both inner soul and outer reality. Further, this arrangement is far more than a scheme oriented toward bringing order to the way one goes about working anew with language. The work Mr. Matthews invites the reader to participate in is none less than renewing the universe through reenlivening the word.

The scope of this book really takes it altogether out of the realm of a self-help instruction manual for writers. As it begins to dawn on the reader that the approach of this work concerns healing the world through healing the word, what first was perhaps seen as an innovative way of teaching creative writing now appears as an essential discipline of world renewal. This discipline fosters interiority of word and world, the co-penetration of one with the other. Thus, this is a book of spiritual practices, taken out of the realm of pious religiosity that has nothing to do with the actual world within which we live and properly placed within the practical dimensions of everyday life.

Anyone serious about the craft of writing is bound to feel sheer joy and delight that someone has finally acknowledged that writing is not a lonely, private endeavor that some few people seem to have to do, not knowing exactly why. In effect, Paul Matthews is saying that writing is world work, and those engaged in such work are an invisible community doing the most practical work imaginable. Anyone serious about spiritual practice will be equally delighted to find that they are part of this same invisible community, silently working toward world renewal. It is not at all accidental, then, that most of the exercises in this book are best carried out in a communal setting. Further, *communal* here means more than a group of people who are all doing the same thing. These exercises, like the creating powers of the universe itself, do not take place by each individual privately following instruction while happening to be in the same room with others. The exercises are based on the principle that the part is equal to the whole. Thus, the individuality of those doing these exercises together is not annihilated for the benefit of the whole, as often happens when activities are put forth as communal. Rather, true individuality is to be found in the fact that we are each the whole of the universe, but at the same time, this wholeness needs the equal wholeness of other individualities in order to be rightly expressed.

I do not want, by trying to point out the tremendous significance of this book, to imply that this work is destined to be of interest primarily to the serious-minded, the esotericists, the occultists, the metaphysicians of the world. Quite the contrary; while I do want to emphasize that learning the skills of writing as put forth here is in fact learning the skills of living in a new way that is desperately needed, perhaps the ultimate value of this book is that it is great fun. The exercises are humorous, delightful, surprising. The vision of this work is comic, which does not mean just funny, but rather corresponds to the creative genre of the universe in terms of its destiny rather than its origins. My most significant teacher, Dr. Louise Cowan, a noted literary critic, has a wonderful view of the world as epic, tragic, lyric, and comic. All of the great literature of the world, it seems, falls into one of these domains, with a few transitional forms that bridge between. The epic has to do with the forming of the earthly world in conjunction with the powers of the gods. The tragic vision has to do with the necessary creative mistake of the individual hero trying to make a single view stand in for the whole. The lyric vision is a recovery of the whole, but as existing within the individual soul. The comic vision is the restoration of the whole, and is characterized as a marriage between the human and the divine. The restoration is, of course, always accompanied with laughter and mirth because this union is inexplicable to the rational mind. Great effort may be put into trying to find wholeness, but in the end, it is a matter of grace as much as human effort. The exercises in this book are certainly hard work. But, in doing them, there is always the moment in which laughter intrudes, an indication that the angels of words have indeed been invited back to inhabit language. The perceptible movement of their wings, I suspect, tickles us.

When a rare book such as this is published, one always wonders where it will be put on the shelves of bookstores. It belongs in the self-help section. It also belongs in the section on theology and religion, psychology, spirituality, hermeticism, literature, poetry, art, and humor. The pedantics who have to classify and catalogue are bound to find this work disturbing. In truth, it does not matter where this book is shelved, as it is one of those works that will locate its readers rather than readers locating it. This book, I predict, will more or less find its own way into the world, for after all, it has wings.

9

ANTHROPOSOPHY (A FRAGMENT)

RUDOLF STEINER

This remarkable work by Rudolf Steiner concerns the human senses, the life processes, and the forming of the human body; and it provides a basis for an anthroposophic understanding of the human being. It is also an indispensable foundation for the development of a spiritual psychology that adheres to an anthroposophic mode of thought. Rudolf Steiner himself indicated that the study of the human soul follows from an examination of the senses, and from there it is necessary to move to a study of the human spirit. These three areas constitute Anthroposophy in a restricted sense—for the field encompasses much more—and all that is needed to form spiritual psychology can be found in them.

Knowledge gained by careful observation alone is the basis for research in a spiritual psychology founded on an understanding of the human being as a revelation of the spiritual worlds. It does not require crossing into spiritual worlds with clairvoyance, though it benefits greatly from the observations of those who have developed such capacities. Such a psychology does require a heightening of observational capacities to understand correctly what can be known about the human soul through observation alone, and the only provision is that the observer be included in what is observed. One must become aware of the act of cognizing as an essential part of what is known. Spiritual psychology needs to develop to the very edges of observational capacities, where the presence of the spiritual worlds can be detected. However, spiritual psychology always reaches toward those worlds, while not crossing over into them. The other side of spiritual psychology is concerned with how soul enters every moment into physical life, and this makes it necessary to have a living understanding of the senses and the life processes. This aspect of the foundation of spiritual psychology is the subject of *Anthroposophy (A Fragment)*.

In this work, we not only learn about the human senses and life processes in an entirely different way than through physiology and contemporary sensory psychology, but we also learn how to meditate actively on these processes. New capacities of observation can thus be formed. The intensely compact character of the writing presents itself hieroglyphically. The aim is not to interpret what is said, but to enter into it, simultaneously to enter the activity of the senses and life processes themselves. By entering into this text meditatively we are not only being informed, but also being formed into beings who can make observations within the activity of what we are observing. It is as though the senses and life processes themselves are doing the speaking. What better training could there be for developing the style of thinking needed for accurate and descriptive presence to the mobile activity of soul and spirit life? If observations concerning our sensory life are handled as if sensing were a mechanical process, subject to description in terms of causes and effects, it is certain that our understanding of soul and spirit life would be falsely portrayed. The inner life would either be taken up and spoken of in the language of cause and effect, or it would be presented as a confusion of mystical, sentimental and religious speculation passing as science. Thus, a study of this work can be a source of extreme discomfort, as if losing one's mooring in the world of fixity. However, staying with this discomfort will gradually open up the world in entirely new ways and prepare us for even more mobile considerations as steps are taken into the inner life.

Those familiar with Anthroposophy have probably encountered Steiner's enumeration of twelve senses rather than the usual five to eight described by sensory physiology. In this text, however, only ten senses are described; both the sense for the "I" of another—the capacity to actually sense something of the true individuality of another person—and the sense of touch are not considered here to be senses in their own right.

In the last appendix, however, the capacity of the "I" to experience another, separate "I" while listening empathetically to what manifests through the tone of another human being is described as the archetype of an organ of perception.

To ordinary experience, touch undoubtedly seems to be a sense, the cause of which sensory physiology attributes to nerve endings at the surface of the skin. According to Steiner, the experience of touch can be accounted for solely by the combined effects of the sense of life, the sense of self-movement, and the sense of balance. What we call an experience of the sense of touch is actually a judgment based upon the immediate experience of these other three senses. The sense of touch, conveying nothing but "pure otherness," is devoid of sense experience in its own right.

The "I"-experience and the sense of touch form the two boundaries of the realm of sense experience.

The enumeration of the senses and what they do is quite revealing, but they are so clearly presented by Steiner that comment here is unnecessary. More revealing and significant for spiritual psychology is how different clusters of senses operate in relation to each other to bring about definite experiences.

The life sense, the sense of self-movement, and the sense of balance operate together to give us awareness of ourselves as physical beings. We know we are physical beings because this is first felt internally. The feeling of bodilyness is the soul's perception of the external world that comes nearest to the soul. This observation is important because the combined activity of these three senses then also provide the border, going the other way, into soul life proper. These three senses comprise a sort of boundary condition between soul life and external physical existence, which for the soul is the experience of an inner bodily state. For example, when we feel "out of sorts"—fatigued, stressed, ill, and so on—such states are experienced due to the life sense. But, at the same time, these states touch upon purely psychological qualities. In such a state we also feel out of balance, which is truly related to the sense of balance, and we also feel acutely uncomfortable with our physical position in the world, which is related to the sense of self-movement.

Owing to the combined qualities of these three senses and their close-ness to soul life, such psychological states of discomfort have a distinctly bodily character to them and can only be described as an overall condi-tion without much specificity. Therefore, it can be suggested that these states are likely to improve by giving attention to conditions of bodily health. On the other hand, if there is not an awareness of this bound-ary between these senses and soul life, and complaints are handled as if they were solely psychological, it is quite possible that imbalance will be driven into the soul. Spiritual psychology would thus be very interested in investigating the subtleties of these senses.

The senses of smell, taste, sight, warmth, and hearing form a kind of progression in which we are taken increasingly into not just the physical world, but even into the interior of physical things. We not only sense what is "out there," we also sense what is inside what is "out there." Through these senses, then, we can actually apprehend something of the soul of the world. The visual appearance of a thing in its color, for example, not only reveals its outer aspect, but already expresses some-thing of its inner nature. Speaking in the second chapter about hearing, Steiner stated: "It is more than merely metaphorical to say that a body's soul comes to manifestation through sound." A reflection such as this, if taken up in the forming of a spiritual psychology, vastly increases the range of the usual concerns of psychology. We need a psychology of the outer world in order to balance the possibilities of self-absorption and egotism, which are bound to occur when care of the soul is taken only to mean one's own soul, as if the outer world was not also included in the sphere of soul life.

The speech, or tone, sense is not concerned with understanding the meaning of what another person says, but rather with the immediate bodily sensation caused by phonetic tones, and through this sense we gain the ability to recognize the tremendously important difference between soul located in the world of physical things and the human soul. We discover through the speech sense that the soul of a body is alive, and further, that the soul reveals itself as freed from the bodily aspect.

We speak by means of the body, but speech itself can be sensed as free of the body. Sensing speech not only involves sounds, but also gestures and facial expressions, which also utilize the body, yet go beyond it. The speech sense is so important because it verifies the existence of human soul life. Soul is not a matter of speculation, nor is it at first a matter of religious sentiment or metaphysical argument; it is directly sensed, preceding any thinking or judgment. It can be suggested, therefore, that any attempts to work with the soul life of another, such as in psychotherapy, would do well indeed to concentrate on a training oriented toward the speech sense. This would avoid falsely attributing qualities to the soul that actually arise from thinking and judgment rather than from actual observation. Here, we might point to the extremely valuable work of current psychoanalysts, such as W. R. Bion and especially Christopher Bollas, who have developed a highly sophisticated inner discipline of deliberately forgetting what occurs with a patient from session to session, in order to be present in the mode of sensation. These analysts pay particular attention to the whole sensory array within which a session takes place, not seeking to analyze it, but sensing the immediate soul qualities unfolding before their eyes. In particular, they give attention to the speech of the patient, rather than to the meaning of what is spoken.

The same is true of what Steiner describes as the sense of concept. This sense does not reveal the meaning of what another person is thinking but is a direct apprehension of the activity of thinking of another person. Sensitive observation through this sense is imperative for soul work and involves learning to pay attention to the fact that we understand immediately, without judgment or evaluation. Therapeutic psychology has always taken the stance that another person must be understood without judgment. Usually, however, this stance is taken in a negative sense—stay away from judging. For the most part, what has actually come about in therapeutic psychology is that one should understand whatever is heard in a positive light, which is no less a judgment. Instead, approaching the soul life of another person should mean developing the capacity to be more present to another person through the sense of concept.

An essential and most important difference between an anthropo-sophically based spiritual psychology and the only other specifically soul-oriented psychology—the analytical psychology of C. G. Jung—can be found in the third chapter of *Anthroposophy (A Fragment)*. While Steiner does not mention Jung, it is important to mention Jung at this point, because analytic psychology lacks an appreciation for the sensory basis of soul life.[1] On the other hand, Steiner recognized that the dynamics of soul life—desire, sympathy, antipathy, urges, wishes, willing—stem from the way in which sensing is taken up by the soul. Jung and Steiner do wholeheartedly agree, however, that soul life itself is constituted by the activity of images. For Jung, the ultimate source of soul images is the archetypes, and that is the way he accounted for the very organization of soul life. Steiner saw that the organization of soul life is not due to archetypes, but rather to what we each call our own "I." At the beginning of the third chapter Steiner says, "A sensory perception becomes a soul experience when it is taken up out of the senses' domain and into the realm of the "I." In Jung's psychology, the "I" is at first a complex of the soul, before conscious work toward individuation takes place. This means that our ego—the ordinary sense of the "I"—is but a small part of soul life with which we identify, and takes itself to be all there is. Through the individuation process, the ego sense of the "I" enlarges into the experience of the Self, which bears some resemblance to the "I" as described by Steiner.

Steiner, out of his careful observation connected with the world, saw that the "I" is actually more comprehensive than the soul. We could say that the soul exists within the "I," which is the exact reverse of Jung's view. As interest in a spiritual psychology grows within Anthroposophy, it is apparent that this difference is not often fully appreciated. Currently, numerous writings in Anthroposophy speak quite loosely about arche-types, and do not sufficiently distinguish between their use of archetypes

---

1   Rudolf Steiner addressed the problems of analytical psychology and the need for a spiritual psychology in five lectures collected under the title *Psychoanalysis & Spiritual Psychology*, Anthroposophic Press, Hudson, NY, 1990.

and the way they were spoken of by Jung. Once the difference is established, a truly meaningful dialogue can be established between Jung's psychology and spiritual psychology, one which can prove to be most fruitful. For example, archetypes do not change for Jung, but are permanent patterns, experienced within the soul as archetypal images—such as the wise old man, the mother, or the divine child archetype. Anthroposophy recognizes that the "I," the very center of soul life, does change due to life experiences and that archetypal images evolve and change with the evolution of consciousness. The current popularization of Jung's psychology perpetuates an atavistic belief that the way to soul experience is through obliterating the ego. Even Jung did not hold this view, but such a misunderstanding shows the great need for a phenomenology of the "I." The "I"—such a small and overly commonplace word—is in fact tremendously complex. The "I" cannot be understood without moving toward it through an investigation of the senses.

Steiner followed the description of the senses with an investigation into the origin of the senses. Again, from chapter three, here is a sentence requiring much meditation: "Before the world can present itself to human beings as sense perception, the senses themselves must be born out of it." Because we ordinarily take ourselves, in our bodily existence, to be simply inserted into the world that spreads before our senses, we are not able to see the almost seamless mobile connection between sensing and what is sensed, and we do not consider what must be behind what is sensed. A whole different kind of thinking is required to bring this to reflection. At this point in Steiner's text, the mode of reflection has moved to a different level, and this is where you can begin to feel like you are swimming without any land in sight. At the same time, it would be a grave mistake to think that Steiner has become abstract; it is quite the opposite case. Our usual way of thinking is highly abstract, and thus when confronted with a careful description of experience from within the experience itself, a major adjustment of consciousness is required.

The world that forms the senses—senses that in turn give us access to the world from which they were formed, now in a physical manner—is a world beyond perception, a suprasensory world. How do we know this? If there were not a world of warmth beyond the senses and beyond the physical world, it would not be possible for there to be organs for the perception of warmth. If there were not a world of sound, the organs would not be possible for the sensing of sound; and so it is for all the senses. Is Steiner speaking here of the embryological development of the senses, or the act of sensing as it occurs each moment? Both. More can be said of this suprasensory world. It is at one and the same time varied and unified. The world beyond the senses forms the sense organs as well as what is sensed by the sense organs, and is as varied as the number of senses. But, insofar as we are able to say "I see a tree," "I hear a bell," and "I experience the world immediately without the intervention of thought," we are also able to say that the suprasensory world is unified as the "I" is unified.

The "I" is not a subjective or merely personal experience; it is the whole, unified suprasensory world condensed to a point, experienced now from within. Neither the "I," nor the suprasensory world, which is necessary for there to be a sense world and senses, belong to sensory life as such. Furthermore, we are not merely physical bodies with various sense organs inserted at various points, unrelated to the body as a whole. Certain of the senses—life, self-movement, balance—work also as forces from within the whole body, while shaping individual sense organs in accordance with the wholeness of the body. Other senses—smell, taste, sight, warmth, hearing—work as forces that meet these inner forces and shape sense organs at the surface of the body. With the sense of tone (or word), and the sense of concept, the direction of the suprasensory forces that form sense organs is wholly from without. Having pointed to these facts, we can now say something more about the nature of the "I": The "I" is the inner expression of the suprasensory forces forming the sense world and the sense organs.

The "I" was referred to above as a point-like condensation within the suprasensory world that forms the sense organs and the world to be sensed. This description, while accurate, might convey an impression of the "I" as static. However, it is far from static. In chapter 6, we are given a marvelous phenomenology of the "I" in relation to sensing. For example, the "I" functions in relation to the sense of smell by sending out its own being toward the world, but not quite reaching an outer object. Instead, the outer object sends its own being toward the body, and the "I" is thrown back before it meets the object, as if the outer world invades the "I." This activity constitutes smell. Steiner's descriptions of the activities of the "I" in relation to each of the senses are truly magnificent and worthy of contemplation. We can conclude from such contemplation that the "I" is not static and, in fact, constantly undergoes changes due to its encounters with sense experiences. And, if this is so, then a further conclusion follows: If the "I" changes, then the suprasensory world—which is the "I" expanded out to a world beyond the senses—also changes due to individual experiences of the world.

Notice where we have come to in this rather complex exposition. We have gone from a simple, everyday notion of the senses to an understanding of how the body is formed. We have also come to the point of having to say that there must indeed be a spiritual world, but solely on the basis of observing what can be known through description alone. No theory is involved, and clairvoyant perception is not relied upon. Further, we have moved into a dynamic mode of thinking in which the act of thinking, and what is thought about, play against each other like waves in relation to the ocean. We have also come to see the "I" as basic to the formation of a spiritual psychology. The validity of the term *spiritual psychology* also becomes apparent. The "I" is a purely spiritual experience, a condensation within of the suprasensory world. Soul experiences occur within the "I." A psychology that fully recognizes the reflection of the suprasensory, spiritual world within, and is concerned with the soul—as the word, psychology, or logos of the soul, implies—is rightly named spiritual psychology. Let us now turn to the life processes and their relation to the senses.

Steiner describes seven life processes: breathing, warming, nourishing, secreting, maintaining, growing, and generating. All of these processes are described as we actually experience them in bodily life. A wonderful exercise consists of meditation on these descriptions as a way of coming to a healthy connection with our body. Such exercises are also of vital importance for developing spiritual psychology; a picture can be built up showing the configuring of the human body from the inside out and taking place through these processes. More importantly, we can see the intimate link between the forming of the human body from within through these life processes, and the emotional experiences as the sense organs are linked to the "I."

Emotional experience is usually felt as a disturbance in one or more of the life processes. For example, a disturbance in breathing is felt as anxiety; a disturbance of nourishing is felt as an uncomfortable gnawing within, and the judgment of such gnawing is experienced as hunger. When the life processes are balanced, an emotional wellbeing is felt. Note that the "I" does not penetrate the life processes. Thus, what we often speak of as emotional experiences are actually judgments made concerning emotional life. For example, to say, "I feel anxious," is not an emotional experience but a conclusion arrived at through thinking about what one directly feels, but we do not have this clarity of consciousness within the emotion itself. Emotional experiences do not need the "I" to conclude that they are happening. The conclusion is revealed instinctively.

The life processes and their accompanying emotional states cannot be lumped together as if they were the same thing. On the other hand, the kind of thinking Steiner engaged in did not conceive of the life processes as belonging only to physiology and the emotions as belonging only in the domain of psychological experience. Since there is a suprasensory world that forms the sense organs and the sense world—revealed within the person as the "I"—so there must also be a world that forms the organs of the life processes, as well as what is experienced through the life processes, as an ongoing emotional life. The world that forms the organs of the life processes, Steiner called the world of life; and the inner point of this world of life that instinctively reveals an experience of the life processes, he called the astral human being. The organs of the life processes include the lungs, the heart, the circulation of the blood—and probably the other major organs of the body, such as the liver and the kidneys, though here they are not named. The organs of the life processes approach a flowing into one another; they are not as separate as the sense organs. Thus, different kinds of emotional experiences are easily confused with one another, and we also experience this directly— it is possible to be flooded with emotion and not be clear whether an emotional experience such as anxiety is related to breathing alone, or is perhaps centered more in another organ, which in turn affects breathing. Emotional life is far more mobile than sensory life, and this tells us that the life world must be imagined quite differently than the higher spiritual world, which forms the sense organs. The life world can be imagined as one in which different currents do not interpenetrate, but run into each other—or as Steiner puts it, overrun each other.

In addition to the instinctive experiences of the life processes mentioned above, there are feeling-like experiences that do not occur as a result of the life processes. These experiences are also not activities of the "I." Three such experiences are: impulses to movement that are apparently free of the life processes; desires; and images that arise from sensory experience. These experiences are not connected with particular bodily organs, but rather to organs of the astral human being. Of particular importance for psychological reflection is the relationship between images and desires.

Sensory experience lasts only as long as a sense organ is focused on an object, but we can turn away from the object and hold it in an inner way. What remains after the sense experience is an experience of the astral being. Images do not involve sensory organs or the organs of the life processes. The organs involved with images are not sense-perceptible but are the organs of the astral body. Images can penetrate the force of desire and, becoming desires, live on in movement. Images arise first, then desires, which finally become movement. Thus, we have a sensory experience which lives on as an image, the image lives on as desire, and desire lives on as movement. Impulses, desires, and sensory images thus do not belong to sensory life directly, nor can they properly be called soul experiences. Current psychology lacks an understanding of the astral realm and thus wrongly interprets these experiences as physiological conditions or as psychological experiences.

Let us further compare the anthroposophic understanding of emotional experience with what is typically offered by current psychology. First, current psychology has no way to relate organ processes to emotions other than in terms of cause and effect. It is, of course, well established in psychology that organ states are somehow related to emotions, but the connection is most often made by way of the brain. For example, a recent medical study reported that emotional support of heart attack victims by those close to them resulted in a significantly increased rate of recovery. The researchers reported that emotional support resulted in increased levels of norepinephrine and cortisol in the brain. The study further said that the exact role of those chemicals on the heart is unclear, but that they are believed to affect blood pressure and the heart's response to stress. The organs are taken to be no more than physiological processes, and emotions are described without reference to the body in a specific way. Psychologists who work with emotional life fare no better, and simply say that emotional stress can be physically debilitating.

There are many complex theories concerning emotions, both ancient and modern, but complexity does not necessarily constitute an adequate explanation. These theories almost always seek to coordinate physiological, chemical, neurological, visceral, sensorial, and the conscious and unconscious processes. All of the pieces are there, but they never result in a truly comprehensive view such as Steiner offered. By far the best investigation of emotions within current psychology is James Hillman's work.[2] After a thorough consideration of existent theories, he came to see the therapeutic significance of emotion in terms of the development of courage to face the emotions consciously. To be able to face emotion in this way, he proposed that the concept of psyche must be returned to psychology. Psyche has long been abandoned in favor of cognitive pro-

---

2   James Hillman, *Emotion: A Comprehensive Phenomenology of Theories and their Meanings for Therapy*, Routledge & Kegan Paul, London, 1960.

cess, behavior, neurology, physiology, and so on. He pointed out that we cannot face emotion from the viewpoint of ego consciousness, from which it always escapes. Hillman uses the word *psyche* to mean an organizing function that brings together the outer and inner worlds, and emotion is the energetic activity of the psyche. However, by establishing the psyche as a viewpoint, the specificity of bodily processes begins to disappear and is replaced by images that do not arise from observation of emotional phenomena themselves, but are imported from myths, art, and literature as a means of amplifying and clarifying emotional life. For example, he utilizes the image of a charioteer and his horses as an image of the way in which we are driven by emotional life—how we are connected to emotions by means of the reins, with which we drive the horses, and yet, are also being driven by them.

Modern psychology either tries to reduce emotional experience to physiological and neural processes, or it creates a concept of parallelism between physiology and psychological states, linking them together causally. Or it may depart altogether from the specificity of bodily life as essential to emotion. Modern psychology does not have the tools to give an adequate account of emotional life; its concepts are either too small or too general. Rudolf Steiner shows us that emotional experiences are neither just physiological processes, nor soul experiences alone—nor a combination of these. Psychology needs the concept of the life world, which forms the organs of the life processes. Moreover, psychology needs the concept of the astral human being—to begin with, the inner reflection of the life world—which is necessary for an understanding of how emotions are lived through the inner life organs of the body, but are, at the same time, experiences almost beyond the body. Finally, psychology needs an imagination of the astral human being, the being that has organs for experiencing impulses, desires, and sensory images. These concepts are not inserted as a theory, but can be seen as facts through careful observation.

The final chapters of *Anthroposophy (A Fragment)*—beginning with chapter seven—are extremely complex, and Steiner was not satisfied with them. He pointed out that he did not have adequate language to express ideas in writing as he could in lectures, where he formed pictures through repetition and emphasis. Nonetheless, these chapters are well worth struggling with.

Before the close of the nineteenth century, Rudolf Steiner wrote in the section on the primal phenomenon in chapter sixteen of *Goethean Science*:[3] "The picture of the world presented to the senses is the sum of metamorphosing contents of perception, without matter underlying it." This theme was worked out by Steiner in these later chapters. Substance is imagined here, not as consisting of atoms and molecules, but as imaginations formed out of the different sense experiences themselves. Different "inversions" of sense organs play a key role. Underlying the sense organs and life organs are different worlds that interplay in various ways, from which both space itself and the human form unfold.

These latter chapters are of particular importance to spiritual psychology for several reasons. Developing an imagination of the forming of the various organs, life organs, and the form of the human body can result in a new spiritual psychology of development. Research is needed that relates what Steiner has written here and what psychology usually presents as developmental phases. Some of this work has been done by Bernard Lievegoed from an anthroposophic point of view, but it is only a beginning.[4] It is also possible to imagine new approaches to cognitive and language development, approaches that explicitly take into account the human being as a revelation of the spiritual worlds.[5] But, more basically, these chapters form the foundation for meditative work that can result in doing the work of psychology with a living imagination of the human being. Psychology does not currently have such an imagination

---

3   *Goethean Science*, Mercury Press, Spring Valley, NY, 1988. (The above quote was retranslated.)

4   Bernard Lievegoed, *Phases: The Spiritual Rhythms of Adult Life*, Rudolf Steiner Press, Bristol, UK, 1993.

5   Linda Sussman, *Speech of the Grail: A Journey toward Speaking that Heals and Transforms*, Lindisfarne Press, Hudson, NY, 1995.

and is particularly deficient in understanding the living body. Its concepts of the body come wholly from biology and physiology; and, consequently, the mode of thinking in psychology is divided between causal thinking dependent on empirical natural scientific concepts that natural science itself has outgrown, as well as imagistic and mythological modes of thought that ignore the human body altogether.

These last chapters also impress upon us the conclusion that spiritual psychology needs to be a completely new psychology. We do not yet have such a psychology. It is a new field. Pieces taken from other psychologies here and there—parts that seem compatible with Anthroposophy—will only produce untold confusion without a clear understanding of the human being as a revelation of the spiritual worlds. This view provides the basis for evaluating what is of importance from other psychologies and what we need to leave behind. The possibilities of a fruitful, therapeutic psychology based on the spiritual psychology imagined here is even further away. In this work by Steiner, we can see that it will require meditative training that starts with extended concentration on bodily life as spirit-revelation. It will then need to incorporate a second level of meditative training that focuses on what can be known of the human soul by observation alone. Finally, a third level of meditation will be required, focusing on the edges of soul life, where it meets with spirit life. Only on such foundation will it then be possible to begin developing a therapeutic, spiritual psychology. It is my hope that this work by Steiner becomes a sort of handbook for the first phase of this work.

10

So that You May Be One
From the Visions of Joa Bolendas

Joa Bolendas

This work is a remarkable collection of very unusual records of
conversations and a journal of visions, telling of the connections
between an individual, here called Joa Bolendas, and spirit beings who
have been appearing to her since 1957. These beings range from angels
to Mary, Joseph of Arimathea, Jesus, unnamed saints, Matthew, Mark,
Luke, and John, and several individuals that Joa Bolendas has known
who have died. I know practically nothing about this woman; I have
never met her, nor have I corresponded with her. I first heard about
her from my friend and colleague, Therese Schroeder-Sheker, who does
know her, has visited her several times in Switzerland, and first told me
about this remarkable woman in 1990. What most impressed me—and
the reason I am involved at all—is that Joa had told Therese that it was
most important that these records be published in America. Therese
conveyed this appeal to me with such intensity and urgency that I immediately said I would be more than happy to do whatever I could to help.
This brief introduction constitutes a continuation of my promise.

First, let us try to clarify the genre of these writings. They do not
belong to what these days is known as channeled information. There are
indications in the writings themselves that Joa is in a completely awake
state during the visions and conversations. Her body is not taken over
by spirit beings. She retains her own voice, and the voices of those with
whom she communicates are apparently experienced as quite independent
of her own psychic being. These spirit beings cannot be heard by anyone
around Joa when they manifest, and others also cannot see what she

sees. Nor do these conversations belong to the related realm of medium-ism. A medium, or a seer, reports only what takes place within her or his own inner psychic being, even though this is more than mere subjective reporting and usually involves a capacity to sense in more subtle ranges of perception than are available to most people. Mediums report what they see. What is seen, however, does not in turn operate as an interactive partner, adding, modifying, or correcting the medium's experience.

These conversations and visions are also different from initiation experiences, in which the initiate goes through a long physical, psychic, spiritual, and moral training that makes it possible to enter other realms and modes of experience completely unfamiliar to ordinary experience. Contact with spiritual realms and beings achieved through initiatory experience must then be translated into ordinary human terms and ideas. The boundaries among these types of experience are not fixed; neither, however, should they be confused and considered basically the same. The experiences reported here most clearly belong to the realm of visionary experiences, which differs in important respects from any of the above-mentioned forms of spirit communication.

The visionary mode of experiencing other realms is quite unusual in the modern age. The figures that appear and speak do so in a way that is similar, or analogous, to ordinary perceptual experience. In several places, Joa Bolendas begins, for example, with brief descriptions of what one of these beings looks like, is wearing, or how tall it is. On the other hand, the visions are not at all limited by the laws of physical reality as we know them; she sometimes describes a mist or a veil that covers the entire inner space of a church, or sees the extension of a being ranging from one continent to another. The main question is whether these appearances are visions or hallucinations, and this is the same as asking whether what is seen originates from within or from without. The difference between hallucinations and visions is that in the former the subject involved is a distorted sensation of physical reality, whereas in the latter the subject exists in a world other than physical reality. The difference cannot be comprehended by saying that in visions something "real" is experienced, whereas in hallucinations something not "real" is perceived. If I were there with Joa in a church in Switzerland, and she was experiencing a vision, and I could not see nor hear what was going on, it would not be justifiable to say that she was hallucinating and that what she saw was not real. Perhaps she sees things that I am not capable of seeing. Further, the visions recorded in these writings lack characteristics that typically accompany hallucinations—namely, a severe change in the experience of one's own body, a confusion of subject-object boundaries in which the subject fuses with the environment, a destabilizing of everything being sensed, the stoppage of time, a boundlessness of space, and the disintegration of the order of experiential connections. In the auditory realm, in hallucinations one hears voices, but not the voices of people speaking. Even when the hallucinating person can identify the voices in a general way as male or female, loud or soft, clear or scarcely distinguishable, it is the voice that presses in, as if from all sides. Hallucinatory voices also typically deride, persecute, and command. There is no indication of any sort in the body of the text that the freedom of the person receiving these visions has been interfered with in any way. A great deal of care and discipline is displayed in the writing and in the ongoing records kept by this individual for nearly forty years.

Finally, we may consider if this writing is in the genre of imaginal dialogues—that is to say, the conversations have been created solely out of imagination. Perhaps the conversations are a variation of what Jung spoke of as active imagination, a procedure of either taking an image from a dream or fantasy life or of conjuring up an image and then initiating a conversation with an imaginal figure as if it were real. The primary reason that this is probably not the case here is that in such imaginal conversations the images do not cross the boundaries of their own world and intermingle with outer reality; their reality remains clearly psychic. Visions are not so clearly a part of an inner world. Some of the visions here, for example, take the form of Joa Bolendas seeing a halo of light around a priest saying mass or around a minister preaching a sermon; and such appearances, as described in the text, seem to occur spontaneously.

Still, searching through all of the possibilities, it must be stated that there is no way to prove conclusively or even to say very much about the reality of the beings who form the content of these visions. The intention of going through these possibilities, in fact, is not to attempt such proof. Rather, the aim is to make some positive suggestions concerning how to approach such a text. First, I suggest that the organ that perceived these visions is not the physical eye, but rather the heart. Such a suggestion is made, not to evoke a sympathetic response, but to indicate that this body of work is best read by engaging the heart, in order to see what is actually present. Moreover, the text itself can serve to educate one into the reality of the heart as an organ of perception; it resists a purely mental engagement, and remains forever closed to that point of view.

The suggestion that one approach this text through the heart and that by doing so one also develops the capacities of the heart, is not a call to sentimentality. The heart evoked here is the thinking heart, not emotional response. The first page of the text tells us something about what is needed for a proper relation to this kind of writing. Joa Bolendas is being spoken to, according to the text, by one who has risen from the dead; Joa is being instructed about the reception of visions, as are we who read the visions:

> Revelations have another wavelength.
> The words, images, sounds (the hymns) come over an extended
>   period or time—with great intervals—which demand a lot or
>   energy from those who receive them.
> Devotion and concentration are needed.
> Whenever someone receives revelations, the brain works more
>   quickly and the heart beats more slowly.

The particular form of visions recorded in this work are referred to as revelations. This designation indicates, I believe, that nothing was done on the part of the recipient to make these visions occur. They began spontaneously, and are not the result of any particular inner training or practice beyond a devout practice of prayer and a sincere belief in God and the revelations of the Old and New Testaments. That these visions are termed revelations does not imply that they have the same status as the revealed word of God, or biblical texts; it does mean that the initiation of the experiences was on the side of the spiritual worlds and that these experiences are evidently intended to increase and renew the connections between human beings and the spiritual worlds. The significant aspect of the above statement, however, concerns the conditions under which the visions occur—that is, devotion and extended concentration.

The attitude of devotion belongs to the capacities of the heart. Devotion means constant and fully engaged attention, such as, for example, the physical organ of the heart itself constantly gives to the circulation of the blood through the body. The heart, unlike any other muscle of the body, never ceases its work, even for a brief moment. We are thus led to conclude that these visions did not occur outside of the important context of a life lived in a constant attitude of love. It is farfetched, I am sure, to imagine that these visions occurred to one who lives a life forgetful of the divine order of all of creation, needing to be reminded periodically by jolts from the heavens. These visions are more like momentary episodes in an ongoing life of dedication to communion with the spiritual worlds. Thus, the indication that concentration is a condition for the reception of the visions is not limited to the actual moments of the visions, but also signifies a life orientation. From the text alone, we do not learn much concerning this extremely important context, but it seems crucial to be able to imagine the kind of life that must go along with these experiences, to be able to visualize that they are not episodic intrusions, but episodic concentrations within a life dedicated to bridging the seen and the unseen.

The passage quoted also hints at the specific alteration of attention needed for the reception of visions. More important, for the reader of these documents, this same passage indicates something of what is required for a right understanding of the work. The reader must recognize that reception becomes possible when "the brain works more quickly and the heart beats more slowly." If the text is read primarily by means of the brain—that is, through mental capacities alone—very little will be gained. A speeding up of the brain implies that another level of mental work is going on, a level that is bypassed entirely when the text is read in the ordinary way. In practice, if the text is read in that manner, extraordinary nuances are read as ordinary words, and their deeper significance goes unnoticed. To properly understand this sort of text, we are effectively told that the heart must beat more slowly. Reading must occur at a different pace, or different rhythm, than is usually asked for in reading. In fact, the key to benefiting spiritually from spending time with the text is found in the way the words are savored and felt, in the way readers allow themselves to be touched by what is said. If we approach revelation as new information, frustration follows. If we, on the other hand, approach the text with the possibility that untouched levels of our being can be moved and new capacities awakened, then something entirely different results. I want to explore this difference in detail.

The Difference between Information and Transformation

In this age of information there is a very great danger that abstraction will effectively seal off the possibility of learning anything truly new. Such a statement sounds strange indeed, for it would seem that the whole idea of the information revolution is to make it possible to know, in a broader sphere, what was previously known only by a very few. The inherent deception, however, is that knowing new information has little to do with learning. Learning is the transformation of our body and soul and the vivifying of our spirit through the development of otherwise dormant capacities. Knowing more and more information only adds, in a cumulative fashion, to the stock of available facts at our disposal. Information allows us to become more clever, perhaps more inventive, even more practical in certain realms, but it does not help us to become more human, or to realize what it means to be human. The intent of information is power, and power has become coupled with speed.

One might argue that I have just conveyed information. Information certainly is involved, but here information does not do business on its own. Information serves as a medium through which other, more subtle qualities can find a habitation and expression in the world. And, in the visions of Joa Bolendas, the informational content is further reduced while subtle qualities of soul and spirit are increased. I am not suggesting here that information is of no value; it is a necessary medium, but the problem arises when, as Marshall McLuhan said, the medium becomes the message. For example, the corporate head of Microsoft, the principal maker of computer software in the world, has tried to buy the rights to photograph all of the great art of the world in order to create a software program to display these paintings and other works of art on home computer screens. Such an achievement would make "information" available to vast numbers of people, but would this make art more available in the world? Would not these high-quality digital graphics increase the distribution of art that would remain otherwise largely unavailable? A most difficult question indeed. Answering in the affirmative neglects the fact that a work of art is not just a thing, even a beautiful thing; it neglects the reality of a work of art as having body, soul, and spirit. A work of art is a living being—not a human being, but more than a picture. A picture is the informational part of a work of art. I am not suggesting that the project of making digital reproductions of art is of no value; it has value as long as the makers of the product are clear that they are making only a certain version of art available—not the experience of viewing the paintings themselves. But, if this is not clearly stated, the result may be that art will become an abstraction; we may all know a great deal more about art, but it is likely that its transformative capacity will be curtailed. We are already in the habit of living with secondhand versions of things, which unfortunately leads to a basic incapacity to deal with the original. We want information about the spirit, but do not know what to do with its actual presence. What I feel urged to do, in a first gesture toward Joa Bolendas's visions, is to struggle against the likelihood of their being approached as information, attempting to open up a space where they may be considered with a fresh attitude instead of our habitual mind-set.

Information has become so widespread that there is a strong tendency to approach things that are not so easily codified as if they should be mere data. If a reader takes up these writings of Joa Bolendas infected with an attitude of seeking information, there is nothing much to be learned. In a certain sense, these writings are not about the reality of spirit; they are rather living manifestations of spirit, and thus must be read through presence of soul and spirit. The informational content is minimal; the transformational value is enormous. But, if they are to become available for their transformative value, it is necessary to dwell with them and not approach them as simply ideas or facts.

The reader is advised to refrain from coming to this book with the same attitude with which one approaches other books. A reader ordinarily believes that a book is already finished, completed, and self-contained. Such technical reading assumes that through reading one can possess the content of a writing. In general today, writing has taken the place of speaking, and reading has taken the place of listening. This book, however, has to be heard, even though the hearing comes through the process of reading; and, further, one hears not just his or her own inner voice, but also the voice of the ineffable. The noisiness of the knowing mind, with all of its curiosity and questions, has to be stilled; the will to hear must supersede the will to know. In an attitude that wills to hear rather than to master, the reader manifests a willingness to be modified by what is heard. The understanding that the reader brings to the text, which enables one to read at all, is placed at risk; suddenly we are placed in a space of unknowing receptivity. This kind of reading takes place between the familiar and the strange, the known and the unknown. One opens to the possibility of being transformed rather than informed.

What does it mean to dwell in the presence of these words, these visions? Whereas the aim of gathering information is to increase a sense of our own power, the aim of reading something communicated as a vision is to yield to its power. Here we become more by becoming less;

we are required to grow beyond our own egotism in order to learn. We have to give up the expectation of gaining something for ourselves from the text, entering its being as much as possible, and what may then happen is an increase, a development, of our own inner being, which is far greater than mere ego. Having done so, we may well be unable to say very much about what we have learned, but we experience in a most immediate way that we are different as a result of having relinquished, for a while, our own special interests. We are more open, more present to the moment, less self-involved, closer to a true impression of the spiritual worlds; new, inner capacities can be felt, in which we sense ourselves as more than we ever imagined we could be. Of course, these newfound capacities can also be used in an egotistical manner. We can begin to feel special, gifted, and spiritually astute. Thus, to allow ourselves to be formed by an original document of the sort presented in this series of visions also carries an attendant responsibility. The responsibility involves—in perhaps small and imperceptible ways, as far as the rest of the world is concerned—continuing in life with the ever-present challenge of gradually releasing the acquisitive act of wanting to add to our store of information. To relinquish this form of greed is not the end of learning, but rather its true beginning.

Observations Concerning the Manner of the Visions

The journal of Joa Bolendas contains entries from 1957 through 1990, and continues this journal writing into the present. The conversations with spiritual beings concerning the creation of the universe and the Old and New Testaments are not dated. Visions are presented without interpretation.

I would like to draw attention to the particular quality of the relationship between Joa and the spiritual beings who come to her. On her part, there is a deep attitude of reverence and respect, but she does not abdicate her own personality. In the conversations there is a remarkable air of what can only be called an equality of relationship. For example, as a member of the Reformed church, Joa at first has a difficult time handling the many appearances of Mary. These appearances often take place in a Catholic church, and Joa comes to a point when she tells Mary that she will no longer visit this church as it causes her to struggle with her own beliefs. Mary then accuses Joa of betrayal. Joa answers: "Mary, I will not betray you! I will write down everything, about your love, your light and your greatness. I will not betray my church. I will betray no one. I only want to serve. Understand me—forgive me. Do not withdraw from us. Give me and all the others time. I beg you—forgive me!" Notice the strength in the conversation. Mary does not coddle this woman. On the other hand, Joa does not simply prostrate herself in submission either. She says she will not betray Mary, nor will she betray her church, and in fact will betray no one. This response indicates a truly free person, or, even better, a moment of becoming truly free. She discovers her freedom in speaking what she really wants—to serve—and this is possible without betraying either Mary or the Protestant Church.

Could the essence of such interactions between Joa and these many spiritual beings have to do with discovering that the spiritual worlds do not want anything from us beyond a free and completely open relationship with them, one in which we are exactly who we are, which requires putting aside all that we think we are? Joa at first thinks of herself as a member of the Protestant Church, a church that says, "Christ must increase, Mary must decrease." She discovers that she can love and honor Mary and still belong to this church, but now, for her, this has become a free association; this is not a matter of her thinking whatever she wants, in spite of what the church might hold. Something far deeper is involved, a deeper sense of what constitutes church. But, such an understanding of church cannot be arrived at by logical thought; rather, this comprehension is encompassed in the vision itself. Mary does not say that Joa betrays her by choosing the Protestant Church instead of devotion to her. The one word spoken by Mary, "Betrayal!" does not even indicate that it is Mary who feels betrayed. She could as well be indicating to Joa that to choose one, the church, over the other, Mary, is a self-betrayal of Joa herself; or it could indicate a betrayal of both Mary and the church.

Mary speaks in a wonderfully objective manner; it is, I think, this objective way of speaking that makes possible Joa's discovery of freedom; it is not given to her, for no one, not even a spiritual being of the highest rank, can give one freedom. Rather, Mary here speaks in a way that opens a space for the possibility of discovering true freedom. Further, as we read this section of the text, it becomes clear that this moment of discovery emerged from a larger context, a context of struggle, of trying to find words for experiences that do not yield easily to words, of discarding more and more of what one could say, and of finally speaking when one does not want to speak at all—a long process of distillation of the heart: "I tore out page after page from my notebooks and rewrote them again. It is simply so difficult to put into words one's experiences with God. If only I could paint, maybe then I could pass on the visions in a better way—but that would be a never-ending task. I have taken so much out of the books about Mary and Holy Communion, but I can't leave out everything, when God wants me to write it."

The single instance described above shows the direct, frank, open form of the conversations between Joa Bolendas and spiritual beings, which is multiplied in many places throughout the text; it creates a tenor for the whole of the text. Joa, for the most part, says little, but her questions are direct, and sometimes a little argumentative. The spiritual beings always speak very directly, without elaboration or any rhetoric that could excite the personal imagination of the listener. The statements are almost oracular, so clearly stated and lacking in ambiguity that there is no need for any analysis. Nothing is presented in a convoluted manner; this is true even when quite esoteric notions are discussed. For example, in one conversation with an unnamed saint, the saint explains what is meant by Holy Communion. This figure instructs Joa to open her eyes, to see what is really before us when we are with another human being. At that moment, Joa sees the life energy of the person she was with the previous day: "And I 'saw' the same Hannes as yesterday, except that his body—his arms, legs, and head—was full of small rays of light, like small lines of light. The trunk of his body was darker than the other parts. I 'saw' an aura around his body consisting of thin, short, intensive rays of silver. And Hannes spoke, all this light was in movement—like active energy." The saint is then able to go on and say that Holy Communion is the life of Christ. Here, there is no elaborate explanation of etheric bodies, astral bodies, and such. The most esoteric of topics is discussed with such immediacy that one does not even stop to think that what is being presented is out of the ordinary. The effect of this mode, this tenor, is that the spiritual worlds are experienced as being right here, united and one with one's own world.

Whereas the effect of the tone of these visions is to unite us with the spiritual worlds, I do not intend to imply that this result is brought about by a deliberate use of a particular form of address. One never feels manipulated reading these visions. It must then be concluded that, if we only had eyes to see and ears to hear, we would, indeed, experience the spiritual worlds as all around us. By means of these visions recorded by Joa Bolendas, we may at least have an inkling of what this would be like. The journal and conversations have transformative power because of this immediacy of the reality of a spiritual universe, which is right here. Through a meditative reading of this work, it seems that sacred stories, angels, saints, and divine beings—realms that have, for some at least, been a matter of belief, even intense belief—suddenly come near—almost near enough to touch. This transformation comes about almost imperceptibly; what was previously more or less remote becomes close. On the one hand, a more vivid insight into the nature of belief becomes apparent. Belief is like seeing something very far in the distance, knowing that it is indeed there, but not being able to get to it, as if an impenetrable veil spreads out in front of us and blocks our way to the objects believed in. As the reading of this text proceeds, it is as if this veil is gently lifted, and what we may have known as true all along in our heart is clarified, despite the confusions brought about through our mind. On the other hand, as belief is transformed, we must look carefully into the precise nature of this transformation. I do not think of it as a transformation into immediate perception, but rather as a transformation into a new way of knowing, a knowing that may best be called faith.

For those who approach these writings in an attitude of radical receptivity, belief can be transformed into faith. Belief and faith are often thought of as virtually the same, but whereas belief gives an indication of something beyond the veil, faith is a way of knowing; with belief we do not yet know, but with faith there is certainty. This certainty is, however, of a different type than that given when we apprehend something in the physical world through the senses, or when we grasp something in an inner way with our reason.

Faith is a much more intimate way of knowing; it is as if the senses and reason are circumvented in favor of a more direct connection with the heart and spirit. To circumvent means either to go around or to encompass; it is the latter that I think applies here. We are not asked to close our senses or to stop thinking while reading this material. Rather, faith is opened, which also produces an alteration of sensing and thinking; they become more capable, as if augmented by a new inner capacity.

Faith is something like a first level of higher ways of knowing. Joa Bolendas, it seems, was born with a high potential for this capacity, and it seems to have awakened through a dream that occurred when she was sixteen. In the introduction, we are told this dream: "In the middle of the night, men came walking on a stone path. They carried wooden poles, upon which were stone plates. On the plates was written: 'Wake up, keep watch, and pray.'" She did not understand the dream but simply put it into action. To "wake up" is to enter into faith as a mode of knowing, and the principle way of strengthening this capacity is through prayer. The intermediary act between faith and prayer is keeping watch. Faith can go back to sleep, and usually does so in the particularly devastating sense that we do not even know we have fallen asleep. Joa is quite aware of this possibility, for there are times in the conversations when she is praying but realizes there is for her no living force in her words. This plight causes her severe agitation.

What do we learn concerning the character of prayer from these visions? Many times in the text we observe that a vision begins while Joa prays. But we can also feel, from the whole tone of the visions, that Joa is always praying; prayer is a state of the soul, not merely an external act. When she sometimes finds herself praying as an external act, she is merely talking to herself. Prayer, it seems, is the soul's mode of conversation with the spirit. It is not performed primarily with the lips nor with the mind, but is more like an action of the soul's breathing. As such, prayer has its own particular quality of rhythm. At one point, in a conversation with Mary about the Hail Mary prayer, Joa says to Mary that she finds this prayer decidedly uninteresting. Mary's reply is that the rhythm of the prayer is exactly right; and she says to Joa that her questioning of the prayer in this manner hurt God. Thus, to pray, it seems, involves establishing a rhythm in the life of the soul so that it becomes capable of spirit consciousness. Prayer is a way of exercising the capacities of the soul. And prayer is a completely free human act.

What could Mary be referring to when she says that the rhythm of the Hail Mary prayer is exactly right? First, it seems to mean that we are taken out of our established life rhythms, which have accumulated as habits over the years. We freely allow ourselves to be set within a different kind of movement and a different kind of space, which follows laws that are different from the laws of the physical world. For example, the rhythm of prayer decidedly partakes of a much slower movement than the events, experiences, and occurrences of ordinary waking life. If, for example, these visions are not approached in a prayerful attitude, then we will find our reading advancing too quickly. The rhythm of prayer thus refers first to its own particular time, which is very different than linear or clock time. Then, a second aspect of rhythm requires that every word is in its right place. When Mary says that the rhythm of the Hail Mary is exactly right, she is also referring to the particular placement of the words, which is to say that time is also a place; get the right timing and you find yourself in a different place. If we always pray by making up our own prayers, seeking for something from the spiritual worlds, it is likely that our timing will be off, and we will find ourselves exactly where we started. Formulated prayer thus has the important aspect of learning to become accustomed to a different mode of time. One can then go on from there and improvise according to one's own idiom, but the soul has to be strengthened first, or else we constantly fall back into ordinary consciousness.

The matter of prayer is relevant because this whole text of Joa Bolendas can be considered prayer. We could say, in fact, that vision is just another term for prayer. Prayer launches the visions, which are more intense modes of praying. This central characteristic of this text and the years of effort represented in this work, more than anything else did, separate these visions from channeling and mediumism. If we imagine a progression of human connections with the spiritual worlds, it might well be channeling, mediumism, active imagination, prayer, vision, and initiation.

Working toward Unity

We may now explore the purpose of these visions. The title itself gives us our starting place—*So That You May Be One*. This title is brilliantly ambiguous; it can refer to the individual, to all the peoples of the Earth, or to the church; it can also be something told to Joa Bolendas, having to do primarily with her, or suggesting that any greater unity begins with her. What we feel through the visions is the gradual unification of all of these spheres, and that unification in one sphere alone is illusory. Let us start, however, with the one sphere that is perhaps the most problematic—the unity of the churches.

In 1993, I attended the Parliament of World Religions in Chicago. The apparent aim of this huge weeklong gathering was to open lines of conversation that might eventually bring about a sense of unity. I was more than surprised, as I am sure many others were, to see the attitudes displayed among the many sects as each attended the showing of its wares to the others. In some sessions, bitter fighting erupted; I vividly recall one confrontation between Native Americans and an

Islamic sect. At the same time, once I got over being overwhelmed by the multifarious costumes and displays of incredibly strong tendencies to hold onto the past, and began to meet individuals, I found that conversations were possible and fruitful. We are, however, apparently light-years away from achieving anything resembling a unity among religions. And yet, for nearly forty years, the visions of Joa Bolendas have concentrated on this one theme.

One might wonder what one individual could possibly contribute to the unity of the churches. A meditative reader of these visions would conclude, I believe, that any possible unity will not come from the churches as organizations. By church, Joa does not seem to mean an organization. Over half of this text concentrates on the Old and New Testaments, and we are presented with nothing about the sacred texts other than those of the Christian religion; this does not necessarily imply that unity ultimately means that all religions will be absorbed by Christianity as we now know it. Joa works toward the question of unity from this background because it is her background. Much of what occurs in the visions of the Old and New Testaments consists of an angel or a saint saying to Joa that one thing or another is unimportant, that it belongs to the times when the Bible was written. The purpose of the communications does not center on doctrinal concerns. Rather, one of the central purposes of the biblical visions seems to be to help develop a symbolic imagination, particularly a capacity to sense the symbolic as true. Thus, purely historical matters are not excluded, but the focus is on how such matters are presented symbolically. A saint, for example, says, "The story of Adam and Eve—is not a legend. It is symbolic! A story that was told over and over again—from tribe to tribe: they, the tribes, eventually turning it into their own Hebraic history. Therefore it is both true and symbolic." Repeatedly, in these conversations, history and symbol are seen to be intertwined. But, apparently some things are only history, and have changed in the course of evolution; other things—those that are symbolic—are still meant to be observed today and contribute to the unification of the churches. Concerning Passover, a saint tells Joa, "Celebrate it—the Passover—in the language of today, with the Jews! (It is to be part of the one unifying church.)"

So That You May be One thus seems to be a title that conveys the possibility of developing the capacity to distinguish the essential from the nonessential; first, it is an individual capacity, one not easy to acquire. If we look at these visions in a certain way, seeing a unity between the visions and the questions Joa brings to those who appear to her, we see that two capacities combine to form a new capacity. On the one hand, there is the questioning—the quest—which must issue from a desire of the heart. On the other hand, there is the capacity of vision, of coming into connection with the spiritual beings, the reality that one quests to know and to understand. There is guidance that stems from a life of concentrated prayer, the inbreathing and outbreathing of the soul in communication with the spiritual worlds. In order to become One, we first need to establish a unity of mind, soul, and spirit. Prayer and questioning indicate the method. The new capacity that can develop out of such a practice is symbolic vision—not argument, logic, discussion, or philosophy. If individuals are disposed to be one within themselves and then to come together, a similar unity of quest and vision can take place in community. What has happened to this one person, Joa Bolendas, could happen for everyone; that, I suggest, is the purpose of these visions.

SEEKING SPIRIT VISION
ESSAYS ON DEVELOPING IMAGINATION

DENNIS KLOCEK

A good book is very much like a person. You have to establish a relationship with it, be open to what it reveals of itself, be willing to enter into its complexity, honor its inner life, have a sense of its inexhaustibility, and gradually develop an intimate friendship that lasts for years. An introduction to a book, I believe, ought to be much like introducing a person, making a space, an opening, a clearing that makes the meeting between reader and book a joyful experience. A very large clearing is needed for this book you hold in your hands, for this little volume, if you are willing to take it up and work with it, will change your life, as much perhaps as the most significant person you have ever met did. While most books these days qualify only as commodities, this one, if you wish, can become a lifetime friend—a very wise friend.

If a book is at all like a person, then you ought to be prepared in this text to encounter a very complex individual, but one that hides nothing from you, one that shows you from page one what you are in for, and one that demands the engagement of your deepest and highest capacities. *Seeking Spirit Vision* begins by telling us that it is a work concerned with our soul life and how to develop the capacities of soul in a balanced way, in conjunction with the particular phenomena of the sensory world of nature. As this development takes place, the soul becomes more and more able to reach toward a knowing participation with the spiritual worlds.

While the background and approach of this text are those of Anthroposophy, Dennis Klocek gives an entirely new and fresh approach to this endeavor. He thinks anthroposophically, rather than following what has already developed in Anthroposophy and simply adding an insight here and there. Further, current writers in Anthroposophy do not, I have to say, typically work out of the realm of the soul toward spirit with any kind of careful attention to the qualities of soul. This author does; he moves from soul toward spirit rather than jumping from soul into spirit. This care makes his anthroposophic work unique, work that answers the very real need in our time to hold together the depths of the soul with the heights of the spirit. Because such care is taken to give soul its proper attention, you will find that working through the intricacies of this book, taking it slowly, which is to say soulfully, results in a healing as well as a strengthening of your soul forces.

Anthroposophy as Jazz

The meditative nature of this book can be characterized as one in which ideas are fully united with the actuality of phenomena in the world. Klocek is a most astute Goethean phenomenologist. In this tradition of scientific observation, one does not make hypotheses and then devise experiments to support these conjectures. Through a discipline of inner training of the soul, the researcher becomes capable of observing and describing the archetypal ideas forming the natural phenomena under observation. Indeed, this book can be read as a kind of instruction manual on how to become this kind of participating observer of the natural world, and, more deeply, of the intimacy of the natural world with the creative forces of the spiritual world, and of the intimacy of both with the human soul.

The kind of observational thinking involved here is what Klocek rightly calls improvisation. In this creative mode of observation and thinking, one has to learn how to step across the boundary of ordinary thought and perception which rests secure in moving toward the future based only and completely on what is already known, and thus cannot discover anything truly new. Our ordinary thought and perception, and even the enhancement of them by the methods of natural science, can give us only innovative variations of what is already known. Improvising means willing thinking into being, creating thinking rather than just using thoughts. If you really take up and work with this book, you will go a long way toward being able to engage in this mode of active thinking, which is absolutely necessary to be present to the ongoing creative forces of the natural world.

A word needs to be said about the structure of this volume because it seems to me that its structure reflects the act of cognitive improvisation. The book takes the form of a series of essays. Sometimes you will find things said in an early essay elaborated upon in a later one. But, as in musical improvisation, when you come across such an elaboration, it is more in the nature of a creative variation than a repetition. After a number of these variations you not only know more clearly what is being developed, but you also find that this knowing has a deep feeling component. For example, anthroposophists often speak of the sentient soul, the intellectual soul, and the consciousness soul. Klocek not only introduces these terms but also carefully uncovers the relationships among these modes of soul life. He provides examples of how one's development can be sidetracked with each mode, shows how movement from one mode to another takes place, and presents numerous pictures of how these modes actually function in many different realms, from everyday meetings with people to quantum physics.

A great deal can be learned from this book, then, not only from what is said, but from how it is said. Much more goes on in this series of essays than one might expect from a compilation of thoughts that have been brought together in a single volume. A major aspect of the delight and wonder of reading this book derives from finding what was said earlier approached in a new way later, which amplifies, changes, deepens, and clarifies earlier resonance. Perhaps only a jazz musician could match the improvisational ability shown in this writing. To improvise in this fashion, one must know a great deal, and then give up what is known and step out into the unknown, discovering what is there rather than imposing knowledge based upon previous information.

Improvisation must be clearly distinguished from innovation. The former requires objective perception while the latter rests content taking imagination in tow and using it to create a simulated world, a double of the fullness of creation. As a way of demonstrating the difference between these two widely divergent ways of taking up imagination, Klocek takes us on a wonderful excursion into the realms of the relationships among art, shamanism, technology, and consumerism. There is no doubt that innovation now rules in the world, that consumerism has won out, and that the moments of possibility for developing toward a spirit culture, characterized by what might be called objective improvisation, requires deliberate and focused meditative practices. The remarkable contribution Klocek makes, taking us toward the realization of a true alternative to ultimately destructive innovation, centers on techniques of image-based meditation practices. What makes these techniques of extreme value is that they seek to unite inner image with outer world, a meditational way that must be accompanied with proper development of cognition.

The balance between image and cognition also forms part of the improvisational structure of this volume. Essays concerned with showing how soul life develops are interspersed with essays focused on matters such as art, myth, alchemy, brain physiology, and even Goethe's *Fairy Tale of the Green Snake and the Beautiful Lily*. The interweaving of such diverse topics is masterfully executed so that the essays are all of one piece, as if to form a unity of science, art, and religion. For example, the essay on the Black Madonna and Dionysos develops an elaborate but meaningful analogy between this mythic theme and artistic and scientific creation. Thus, through entering into the mythic imagination, what in some essays is developed in a manner that satisfies the intellect, in others is found stated in language that the soul understands—image, story, tale.

World Imagination and Alchemical Transformation

While this writing is rich in imagery, images here never stand alone, but are always woven together with concepts. Soul images, by themselves, can no longer be valid guides, either to the life of the soul or to the qualities of the world. Klocek astutely develops an exploration of the spiritual being of the Sophia, or the Soul of the World, showing that through the evolution of intellect, her presence in the objective realm of Imagination became obscured and distorted. Thus, today imagination is thought of as being an inner activity of the individual soul and virtually no one considers that imagination could be present in the phenomena of nature. Further, once this obscuring of the full nature of imagination occurred, what we speak of now as imagination as an inner activity, while it may be filled with fascinating material, is considered a hindrance to coming to valid knowledge.

The kind of soul development Klocek guides us toward concerns finding a new way to bridge inner and outer imagination or, said in another way, it concerns how the individual soul can again approach Sophia, the Imagination who creates the inner form of all things. This soul development requires going through the discipline of cognitive meditative practices. Such practices, some of which are gone into in great detail in the book, gradually reduce the illusion that knowing is centered in the capacities of intellectual abstraction; instead, they consciously bring cognition into the act of perception, uniting the inner and outer worlds. These practices actively involve the soul in the act of sensing the world and make a connection with World Imagination possible.

Another significant theme intimately related to coming to World Imagination concerns alchemy and the alchemical imagination. I dare say, Dennis Klocek may be one of a very few living human beings who understand the mysteries that lie behind the strange and peculiar emblems, formulas, and writings of the alchemical tradition. I do not intend to embarrass our author by such an exclamation, so let me qualify it a bit. Certainly, there are many scholars who understand something about what alchemy was. There are also many individuals who have become interested in alchemy as a result of the work of C. G. Jung, who, while he resurrected interest in this tradition, did so in a rather one-sided manner. Jung incorrectly felt that alchemy had nothing to do with the outer world and presented the view that the imagery of alchemy came wholly from the inner soul life of the alchemists, who projected their own soul images back into the world. Then, a third group currently tries to penetrate the mysteries of alchemy by attempting to engage in its practices as they were done in earlier times. The approach to alchemy taken in this writing does not correspond to that of any of these groups.

In contrast to these approaches, Klocek's ground in Anthroposophy on the one hand, and in Goethean science on the other, makes it possible for him not just to know about alchemy, nor to try to repeat the past, nor to psychologize it, but rather to see, not what the alchemists saw, but as the alchemists saw. In other words, alchemy must be updated, seen through the eyes of the consciousness soul. Then, much of what alchemy was getting at can be retrieved, but in forms suitable for present circumstances. Klocek carries out this project in a truly astounding manner. He does so not just as someone curious about this tradition, but as someone who finds it to be central to the project of developing meditative, cognitive, perceptual soul consciousness of the natural world.

In one of the essays toward the end of the book, some specific connections are made between alchemy and the thinking of Rudolf Steiner. Also, in the essay on *The Fairy Tale of the Green Snake and the Beautiful Lily*, the fact that Goethe had a very deep understanding of alchemy and that this tale can be read alchemically is firmly established. However, in the past, alchemy worked with substances from the physical world and put these substances through operations. These operations brought about transformations of the substances, and also, due to the perceptual abilities needed to execute correctly these operations, transformations of the soul life of the alchemist. The substance to be worked on now is our own body, soul, and spirit. Goethe understood this needed shift of focus, and so does the author of this present volume. And while it may seem that Jung made a similar shift, he did not go far enough, for he saw alchemical imagery as involving only the soul/spirit and not the body.

The series of essays presenting meditation practices based on the emblem of the "Great Tree" in the alchemical tradition may well be the heart of this book. Here the actual practice of developing the kind of soul/spirit consciousness able to know and perceive the natural world as an ongoing act of creative Imagination is developed. The processes of developing capacities for creating and stabilizing inner images, coming to experience image activity rather than a pictorial content, and of making the soul receptive to creative currents of the spiritual worlds are all carefully described.

At the point at which receptivity to spiritual currents opens up, a most important meditative work is required—giving back whatever was received from the spiritual worlds. The strong temptation at this point of soul and spirit development is to take what is received and use it for one's own purposes or to develop something of scientific or technical use. If this opening is utilized in this manner, ultimately destructive results follow. Giving back what is received prepares the possibility of developing intuition, a participation with creative spirit beings.

While you may recognize this meditative orientation as belonging to the anthroposophic path of spiritual development, it might be better described as a creative variation that provides several benefits. We gain a certain appreciation of what the alchemists were doing. Nonetheless, as you will see, it is not going back to what they were doing, as they were doing it. Because alchemy was concerned with the Soul of the World, this approach to meditative practice also keeps this intent close to the heart. Further, rather than simply going from one stage of soul and spirit development to the next, the precise relationship between one stage and the next becomes clarified, a continuity of states established. Klocek additionally elaborates a number of exceedingly useful analogies that help meditative practitioners not only to understand but also to have clear images of what they are doing. The alchemical conditions of salt, sulfur, and mercury are described as particular states of soul and spirit, of cognition, willing, and feeling. The earlier stages of meditative practice are pictured using chemical analogies, the mid-stages using the analogy of a capacitor, and the later stages are compared to the preparation of homeopathic remedies. The details of the alchemical emblem of the "Great Tree" itself serve as a pictorial geography of the worlds of meditation. All these analogies help to assure that the life of the soul is not abandoned as one develops toward the spiritual worlds.

The traditions Klocek draws upon and derives helpful analogies from are streams not addressed by most anthroposophists except in rather disparaging ways. At the same time, these traditions are of great interest to people seeking spiritual experiences these days. Does not Anthroposophy need to do more than to warn of the dangers of atavism involved in the practice of these traditions? Not only alchemy, but also shamanism, Native American spiritual practices, and dowsing, are given serious consideration in this book. Exactly what these traditions are about, seen from the point of view of someone who has evidently meditated long and deeply on them, brings us entirely new insights compared to those currently provided by the popular literature on these topics.

The service to seekers of spirit vision in the modern world provided by the honorable way these traditions are worked with in this writing is immeasurable. These spiritual traditions honor the Earth as well as the Cosmos, and what they potentially have to offer, what they can bring to Anthroposophy, is really enormous. At the same time, as Klocek so clearly understands, these traditions cannot be taken up now as they were once practiced. He clearly points out exactly why these traditions can cause difficulties if practiced exactly as they were in the past. He is not, however, satisfied with labeling them "atavistic" and therefore dangerous. Rather, he shows that these practices contain deep wisdom concerning the instinctive body, but now this wisdom must take into account the element of cognition.

Imagination's Physiology

A number of the essays take us into another rather unusual domain for a work concerned with soul and spiritual development—the anatomy and physiology of the brain and nervous system. Klocek presents many details concerning brain function during meditative states, as well as descriptions of how certain functions change as a result of meditative practices. These essays need to be approached with a high degree of acumen.

The introduction of these apparently physical concerns does not in any way indicate that soul and spiritual processes are being reduced to brain states. Nor do I think that the implication can be drawn that spiritual currents cause certain changes in brain states, or vice versa, at least not if causality is here understood in the usual way that scientists understand it. Science restricts the notion of causality almost exclusively to that of efficient causality, one material force affecting another material force, with both forces existing on the same plane. If the essays on physiology and neural anatomy are read from this perspective, that of material science, they would result in serious misunderstanding.

When a Goethean phenomenologist observes the physical world of nature, we would certainly never understand these observations, which engage in soul/spiritual perception, as reducing the spiritual world to physical processes. In fact, what happens in such observations is just the reverse; the spiritual activity forming, not causing, physical appearances is elaborated. The careful and detailed matters concerning brain structure and functioning presented in this work have to be seen from this point of view. I believe this point is absolutely crucial and when one is reading this material it must be kept clearly in mind. The intricacies of brain anatomy and function can make us feel a little bit as though we are reading portions of *Gray's Anatomy*. It is thus easy to fall back into a materialistic attitude, and that must be resisted, for the writing does not take that stance.

If the observations concerning the brain are followed through very closely, not only do we become filled with wonder concerning the wisdom of the body, we also learn a great deal about why remaining with the instinctual body in various methods of esoteric practice can be harmful. We also learn that we could not reach for the higher realms if our body did not incorporate such a possibility in its structure and function. For example, the essay on dowsing and divining goes into a detailed description of the functioning of the pituitary gland in relation to these kinds of practices. Our author gives a remarkable picture: "The pituitary gland and its surrounding tissues provide a picture of the wall between the upper world of the stars, the source of spiritual existence, and the lower world of the body, its metabolism, growth, and reproduction (p. 106)." This gland has an upper, neurological function and a lower, metabolic function, with a thin layer of cells coated with melanin dividing the two portions of this gland. In a later essay, this image takes on even more significance as the story of Cain and Abel is imagined in relation to this gland. If we take this picture of the pituitary gland into meditation, we become acutely aware that the dividing line between spiritual work oriented toward the spiritual beings of the cosmos and the instinctual body, where we can become caught by various elemental Earth beings, is gossamer.

The discussion concerning dowsing is important because it is connected not only with a whole field of alternative medical treatment, radionics, but also because the bodily processes involved in dowsing are also integral to other forms of spiritual healing, and even implicated in the process of meditation. The importance of being able to distinguish subtle instinctual experiences from higher forms of spiritual experiences is crucial. We may be aware of the importance of these differences, but the knowledge comes home in quite a different way when understood from the point of view of the organ functions involved.

The other gland specifically related to visionary states is the pineal gland. Klocek explores this gland through a series of images, so that anatomy here becomes imagination, the imagination of the heart center of the brain. Thus, terminology utilized, for example, by anthroposophists, such as heart thinking, may be an analogy that has substance.

In this book it is an imagination that prompts a consideration of the relationship between the pineal gland and the heart.

Earlier on, I remarked that following through these observations concerning anatomy and visionary states might seem as though we had entered into a medical textbook. A way in which you can know if you are reading this book as intended is by paying very close, ongoing attention to the activity of thinking that runs through this text. We do not have here a presentation of facts, flat and dead, but rather one thought-form flowing organically into another. The images employed in relation to bodily organs and functions are thus more than suggestive; they are more like inner pictures of the outer form of particular organs. Further, while at one moment we may be in the brain, the next in the heart, and the next in the midst of an image taken from Jacob Boehme, these movements are quite organic; they also can help us toward the development of a flexibility of soul that ranges between the physical and the spiritual, refusing all hard-lined divisions that bespeak one kind of dualism or another. Perhaps the height of this flexibility is demonstrated in the essay concerned with a reading of the story of Cain and Abel in connection with the pituitary gland, where we can see that an anatomical analogy of this story continues to live on within the body.

If the kind of thinking demonstrated here seems unusual, it is for the modern world, where knowledge has been cut up and divided, the pieces parceled out to various specialists. If we happened to be interested in spiritual matters, then we have certainly come across the bit of knowledge that indicates the esoteric doctrine of correspondences. We have also perhaps been intrigued with the exotic character of the saying: "As above, so below." Here, in this writing, we see actual demonstrations of these laws in operation, something that has seldom come to the light of day since the time of Paracelsus.

A reader who is a student of Anthroposophy and someone who engages in the kinds of meditation practices suggested by Steiner may well be somewhat disoriented by the emphasis placed on the body in this work. One of the essays specifically addresses this question, for Rudolf

Steiner spoke both of exercises to learn to live consciously outside the body and exercises concentrating on currents within the body. This essay is nothing short of a masterpiece of investigative work into the writing of Steiner and some of his students which aids us in seeing that methods leading to out-of-body cognition and methods leading into body currents have to be held in a paradoxical tension. More importantly, until you come to this essay, the material on physiology may leave you somewhat puzzled. Are we being presented with speculation, or with the results of a great deal of inner meditative work? This question you will find answered. Incidentally, the quotation from Rudolf Steiner beginning on pages 274 should be read and studied very thoroughly. You will, I think, find it quite astounding, and I suspect it also reveals something of the meditative technique of our author.

At the very end of the essay concerning in-body and out-of-body meditation practices, a comment is made that warrants a good deal of pondering: "It is hoped that these contributions are seen as a modest beginning for the destiny of Anthroposophy in America, which has as its task the transformation of materialistic thinking into imaginative cognition." All during my reading and studying of this book, the impression kept coming that indeed what we have here is a particularly American approach to Anthroposophy. Here in America, where people are so concerned with the body, with science, with electronic technology, with consumerism, and with practicality and efficiency, spiritual work must take these things into account and not simply try to turn away from them. Klocek approaches these concerns, by first taking quite seriously what they have to offer, seeing the imagination that forms them, and then lifting those imaginations to the spiritual realm.

The great and marvelous complexity of this book can perhaps result in the reader's losing sight, from time to time, that this work, through and through, is a text of practices. The specific essays concerned with technique are at the center of the book. Work with these mediations can, I am convinced, lead to capacities of sustained concentration on and receptivity to the spiritual worlds. The essays surrounding those concerned with meditation per se are themselves meditations, which if worked with will strengthen the practices themselves. Very little speculation exists in this work. The reader, however, is not invited to take up these practices unquestioningly. To do so would be opposed to the whole tenor of what has here been so carefully developed. Rather, we are shown new ways of doing spiritual scientific research, grounded in Anthroposophy, capable of restoring both our imagination and World Imagination.

12

Conversation Amoureuse

Jacques Lusseyran

Biographical Notes

As you begin reading this remarkable book, it may be helpful to know that Jacques Lusseyran, born in Paris in 1924, became blind at eight years of age, the result of a piercing of one eye and the tearing of the retina of the other eye in an accident. He nevertheless developed unparalleled capacities of "inner seeing," which he described as an inner light that allowed him to see things in the outer world, though in a manner quite different from the rest of us. He was, under certain explicit circumstances, able to experience inner images revelatory of the outer world. These images did not replicate the visual picture of the things and persons in his presence but were nonetheless distinctive colors and forms. For example, he describes meeting a girl when he was around eight years old, seeing her inwardly as a "bright and red" form. For these images to be present, and to convey aspects of the outer world and not just his own subjective images, two conditions were necessary: first, he had to be free of fear, anger, jealousy, impatience, and all disruptive emotions; and second, he had to cease living as if things and people were displayed in front of him, and begin to live within them—a condition of living the reality of love fully consciously. The acuity of his senses of touch, hearing, and smell also intensified, subject to the same conditions. The development of this discipline of love allowed him to come to understand that the way we typically divide the world into an inner world and an outer world is but a preconceived idea; things outside do not exist unless you go to meet them, and things inside cannot be clearly seen unless those outside are allowed to enter. There is only one world.

A second fact of some importance in approaching the present book is that in 1941, at the age of seventeen, Jacques Lusseyran organized an important student resistance group during the Nazi occupation of Paris, a group that eventually numbered over 2000. In 1943 this resistance group was betrayed by one of its members, and Lusseyran, along with many others, was captured and imprisoned at Buchenwald. The whole of this individual's life, it seems, was lived under the signature of courage. He wrote exquisitely of his love of life in a previous book, *And There Was Light*. Another significant work of his that has been translated from the French is *Against the Pollution of the I*, a paper he was on the way to present at a conference on July 27, 1971, when he and his wife were killed in an automobile accident.

LOVE IN THE AGE OF THE CONSCIOUSNESS SOUL

Conversation Amoureuse may well prove to be among this century's most consequential writing concerning the mysteries of love. For here, we have something entirely new, something completely unspoken of before. Certainly Jacques Lusseyran, with his highly developed sensitivities, has plunged into the depths of love as few before have done, but there is even more. He recognizes that the very possibility of love is in danger of being lost due to the kind of consciousness now experienced by most human beings. We are able to separate ourselves from the world and from others, and even from ourselves and become mere spectators to all that happens. This mode of consciousness came into ascendance in the fifteenth century, with the dawning of what Rudolf Steiner describes as the age of the consciousness soul. This "separated" mode of consciousness brings us the gifts of scientific understanding and technical control, but it also produces the risk that we human beings will also approach one another as objects and will increasingly think, feel and act out of such a degraded comprehension. There is no deliverance from this kind of consciousness, but there are healthy ways of living within it. The capacity to observe objectively finds its easiest route when it comes to penetrating the physical world. This capacity runs amok only when it stops short there, producing an exclusively materialistic outlook. We must go even deeper into this mode of consciousness and discover how to observe the invisible along with the visible, the soul and spirit along with the physical. And this way of looking needs to be done without falsely dividing body, soul, and spirit. Can this challenge be met? In the arena of love, Jacques Lusseyran has gone far indeed in meeting this charge.

Living in the consciousness soul, as humanity for the most part now does, additionally means that we are aware of not only outer things but also inner experiences as if they existed independently of any source from which they arise. There is a certain naivete to this kind of consciousness, but one that cannot be helped. We see the trees, the mountains, the plants, the animals, and other human beings. Perceived through the senses, all this reality seems simply to exist, to be there before us and around us, but it is not possible, through ordinary sensory experience, to see that this reality is connected to a source, an origin, an ongoing creative wellspring. We can imagine that behind all this reality we perceive through the senses there does exist a source. But we cannot perceive what is bringing reality into its visibility. Our perceptions of inner states are subjected to the same estrangement. With respect to the topic of this book, love, it too simply seems to be there, and we are unable to have an experience of its origin. We develop psychological, physiological, or neurological theories to explain its beginnings, but have no actual experience, no connection with its source. Lusseyran has gone a long way, however, toward showing us how to go through the limitations of spectator consciousness and begin the great restoration of love.

Lusseyran enters his meditations on love through the door of the particular mystery of the love of a man for a woman. He speaks intensely and deeply of his own experiences of love, not of love in general. This delineation does not count as a limitation, for where else is one to begin except with who one is? Of course, it is possible to imagine someone entering the great mystery in other ways, but for Lusseyran, his manner of approaching the question of love came out of a kind of necessity; he tells us that from at least age five he felt a deep attraction, a wonderment, in the presence of girls. His attraction consisted of far more than precocious sexuality, and is better described as an intense interest in that half of the world that remains closed to each of us, the world-experience of one's countergender; if a bridge cannot be found to this other half, then one is fated to remain forever incomplete. The whole of this book can be read as a search, an adventure to discover the half of the world that remains closed to us by virtue of being either man or woman.

Love can certainly cross the boundary to the unknown half of the world; but, in this age of the consciousness soul, we are left completely to ourselves to find out what love may be. And we find that it shows many faces. We may encounter the love that is infatuation, a kind of love that is not so much an encounter with another person as it is a meeting with love itself. The early pages of this book describe the beauty and confusions of such an experience, met by Lusseyran when he was sixteen years old. For a man, this experience is a meeting of the feminine within oneself for the first time, and for a woman it is a meeting of the masculine within herself. But we need the other for this meeting with ourselves. A peculiar familiarity characterizes this meeting, and in it we learn something of the frailty, not only of love, but of our own soul. If one attempts to close the distance of the whole of one's future by testing to see whether this infatuation is returned, the future of love can be prematurely short-circuited, the adventure ended too quickly. One lives with infatuation the only way possible—unanswered, and with great and deep pain.

At age twenty-five, Jacques touches a second kind of love. This time it does have more to do with the other person. Now he meets the stranger, the woman, who lives an entirely different soul-body connection than perhaps a man is capable of truly understanding. He finds it rather impossible to determine when the woman whom he loves is present in body, when in soul, when in desire, or in reasoning. His descriptions reveal how paltry, how shadowy are our thoughts, our theories, our psychologies of the feminine, of the masculine, and of relationships. He gives a much more vivid sense of relating with an actual person, in all her complexity, and shows us that we really can know very little of another person except through constant effort. Our ideas of how she should act, or how one should act toward her—all such notions bear little resemblance and relevance to the actual acts of relating. The great lesson of this experience of love: to guard oneself against the hell of trying to change another.

Now, suppose one becomes at last so fortunate as to find someone who wants you to be exactly who you are, who wishes you to change not in the least, who loves you for who you are. Ah, that would seem to be true happiness! And it is, but happiness, as Lusseyran discovered, is not the same as love. Remaining exactly what your partner wants, even when done with the noblest of intentions, constitutes a form of egoism, of self-centeredness that also blocks the other person from changing. Life itself, to be vital and exuberant, requires, demands, that one change, and thus life dictates that we can never remain the person our partner found to be exactly what she wished for.

Is love, no matter how one approaches it, doomed to failure? None of these intense instances, so poignantly described by Lusseyran in a far more living way than my reflections could ever hope to convey, can be considered failures. I do not think that Lusseyran ever, not once in his whole life, experienced failure in love. One experiences failure only if one knows what is supposed to happen. In the region of love, as it now exists, no one knows what is supposed to happen, how it is supposed to take place; no universal way exists that can be canonized as the right way of love. Certainly, human love does not exist as already formed, as if it were something to be found, whole and complete, just waiting for us to stumble upon it when the right person arrives.

Central to the effort of creating rather than seeking to find love fully formed is to be able to make room for the soul and the body to cohere in the same earthly dimensions. The awakening of sexuality in adolescence signals the arousal of the soul-body, an awakening that so frightens us that a kind of split immediately occurs, separating our form into two separate components—a soul component (dreams), and a body component (desires). A man *dreams,* not so much of the perfect woman, but of the luminous feminine, a dream that, for the most part exists only partly consciously. He *desires* the flesh and blood woman. And a woman, does she not experience the same division in counter fashion? Love has a hard time of it, however, as long as dream and desire live a separate existence.

THE DOMAIN OF DESIRE

The chapters focusing specifically on the sexuality of love delve further into the question of desire and how, for the man in particular, love and desire are often confused. While Lusseyran does not go into what the situation might be for a woman, isn't it that the dream and love are often more confused for her? We certainly have to be careful not to slice up the problems of love so neatly into two piles, one belonging to men and the other to women. But, Lusseyran's experiences are those of a man; he is clear that this is his given perspective, the one he knows by virtue of his own being. His stories of experiences with fellow prisoners at Buchenwald, where he became the confidant of men who wanted to speak of their wives or their lovers, further emphasize that we are presented with a man's point of view concerning love. That point of view does not stop us from understanding some dimensions of love itself. These days, with the men's movement and the upsurge of feminism, it is altogether too easy to forget that it is really possible, and actually a necessity, for the sexes to come to deeper understandings of love by deeply listening to each other. Of course, what is spoken, on either side, must go beyond surfaces, beyond mere opinions and haggle. Lusseyran avoids these traps by keeping his focus completely on love.

We are bound to be totally refreshed by seeing someone take on the problem of desire in order to keep questions of love between a man and a woman located in the actual arena where they are lived, our bodies.

So much hinges on desire that seems as though it should not; it verifies the actual physical presence of love, assures that we are not just living an abstract idea—ours, or those of the philosophers, the theologians, or the educators. How something so lofty as love chooses to announce itself as an urge, an impulse, an attraction—that forever remains a mystery. But, this enigma is the given with which we must struggle and come to terms. You may be shocked to see in print what Lusseyran says concerning sexual desire. He takes what others often present as disparaging about the way in which men live desire and verifies that it is all quite true. It becomes problematic only if lived without sensitivity and reflection. It is quite true that men have a tendency to take desire to be love; when desire goes, love seems to have disappeared. Men are given the task of working through this confusion, not avoiding it or pretending it does not exist. It is also quite true that for men, the sense of self, of identity as a man, is tied into feeling the potency of their sex organ. The tremendous challenge presented in love's announcing itself in this way in the body of man is how to cross the boundary between desire, which is not about loving another but about loving oneself, to, through desire, discovering love for another.

Lusseyran does not say that the only way for man to come to love is through desire. We must remain clear about the terrain he has chosen to consider so that we will not feel scandalized. He chooses to speak of sexual love, and he is doing so spiritually and with intense depth of soul. He is no spiritual prude, thinking that it is possible to confine love to the planes where the messiness of bodily life does not interfere. No, he chooses to seek love, in its body, soul, and spirit dimensions right in the midst of the sights and smells and touches and sounds of sensory life. He spent his whole life here, developing the capacity to experience soul and spirit through the senses. He gives us all hope in something that we all know—that spirit is not somewhere where body is not; but he is also aware that not only can spirit be found there, it can also be overwhelmed in the presence of bodily desire.

The way through this dilemma of love and desire that is lived and struggled with by so very many of us can only be found in developing acute capacities of observing our own engagement with desire, carefully noting its every turn, its every nuance, its every flicker and glow. Not an easy task, and in fact it may be far more difficult to develop this kind of observation than it is to learn the highest and most subtle kind of meditative practice. However, to develop such capacities belongs to the true spiritual work of the age of the consciousness soul. This is the time in the evolution of consciousness when we are given the strongest experience of the physical and thus the sensory realms. Our spiritual work consists of finding, through these realms, the experience of soul and of spirit.

SEXUAL LOVE

Lusseyran's concern with sexual love, I believe, needs to be understood in the context of his meditative achievement; otherwise his writing will be gravely misunderstood, taken only as interesting musings, or impressionistic images, or, when it comes to the question of desire, exclusively male fantasies. Quite to the contrary, we have instead the most disciplined description of lived sexuality along with astoundingly astute clues to finding the way to the creative source of the love that announces itself in such pressing ways in the body. To have moments in which the true spiritual love breaks through, however, takes a meditative reading of this work, going over it again and again.

Often, with this work, sentences are themselves worthy of meditation, I hardly need to point them out, though I am remembering some:

In love we are seeking; that's all we are doing.
    At the moment of orgasm, a man has never been so great. Nor so alone.... It would be so good for you to know this. But you should also know that he does not want this solitude, that he came to you in order to get rid of it.

While we are often taken aback, astounded by such sentences, more important than our admiration for things so well said is that we experience a feeling for entering into the creating source which engenders such expressions. Only by getting a glimpse, a little flicker of this source, will the potential criticisms of what is being said be deflated. To acquire this glimpse, one must take this book in hand as a work that asks for full and active engagement.

Of all the significant insights in this work, it is in the sixth chapter that I believe we come to the most astounding achievement. Try to imagine what purity of soul would be required to be able to so closely describe the actual experience of the love act between a man and a woman in such a manner that the true wonder of it breaks forth in all its splendor. Imagine how difficult it would be to search for the splendor of love right in the midst of the sexual act and not fall either into the titillation of it or to recoil in horror that one was approaching the pornographic. The reader, following the example of the writer, must approach this reality with purity of intent.

A most astounding flowering of the careful discipline of observing the course of sexual desire the way it is actually lived comes in this work with the discovery that, in the love act, it is the moment after the act itself that bears the most significance. Through the act of making sexual love, both the man and the woman intensify the sense of who they each are as man and as woman. What looks like an act of union, up to a certain point, is actually a deepening of separation. Because of this intrinsic component, sexual love can easily turn into a kind of struggle for power, each individual attempting to verify his or her own existence; that happens when making love is not experienced in its spiritual dimensions. One side of desire seeks this enhancement of the lower ego. Another side, however, seeks to break through to the higher self, one's ultimate, true identity. This possibility occurs because even while the enhancement of self goes on, it is at the same time the self's own dissolution. It is perhaps not the ecstasy of orgasm that counts as a quasi spiritual experience, but that the moment of ecstasy announces the possibility of something more. To take sexual ecstasy in itself as something spiritual only falsely elevates the ego. The penetration of the woman by the man and the enfolding of the man in the woman already crosses the border that divides one from the other—and, in fact, for a few moments, each becomes the other. One does not just intimately experience the other, but a kind of exchange occurs, an exchange that can be experienced to the extent that love is not an assault. Lusseyran says:

> If a man were always a man from the beginning to the end of love-making and if he were only that, and if the woman would remain woman eternally, there would be no love.... Instead there would be this irritable, impoverished substitute: desire.
>
> It is when desire is completed that the moment of union occurs, for then there is a true resting with each other without any longer a seeking, without the element of want. Desire then hovers around the couple in its true spiritual nature, blessing this unutterable moment of engagement.

KNOWING LOVE

This book not only takes us into entirely new considerations of love but it also lights up the difficulties of living in the age of the consciousness soul and shows the possibility of living within this kind of consciousness in a healthy way. Consciousness has so evolved that it can now look at love, desire love, imagine it, think about it as if it were a reality existing completely on its own. Love, however, can only be known through loving. It is not an object existing as others exist. Living the illusion that it is an object also means that it is possible to engage in love in a completely detached manner, thus using it for purposes other than love—for mere pleasure, power, as an addiction, self-verification, abuse, pornography. Or, another kind of detachment is also possible: one that arises when others tell us of love that is beyond our grasp, love of the cosmic variety. A corollary of this distancing which makes of love something to look at is that we enter into the illusion of love, whatever it may be, is essentially the same for everybody, and if it is not, then it should be. If love is an object, something to go looking for and to find, then it must be the same kind of object for everyone.

At the same time that we might hold to a belief in love existing as an object, there is another, paradoxical side to living in the consciousness soul. In this age, we are increasingly freed from the constraints of external authority and left more and more to wrestle with our individual experience. Certainly we are now freed from the external constraint of trying to love the way someone, some institution, or society itself tells us to love. So, here is the paradox—love seems to be something objective, and simultaneously love is completely ours, to be created out of our own inner solitude; and no one can tell us what it is or means, for it will be and mean something quite different for different people.

Lusseyran's answer to this terribly difficult dilemma needs a good deal of contemplation:

> Love has not been made for the community. And to look at it doesn't mean looking at others doing it, but to look at oneself doing it.

He is saying that society, organized religion, education, family, tradition—these forms can no longer tell us how to live the reality of love. In this sense, love does not belong to the community. And, if we are in this position of consciousness that looks, then the way through it is to stop looking at others and begin looking at ourselves. Brilliant! We cannot sidestep the consciousness soul without inadvertently stepping into atavistic versions of love from the past. We have to go through this kind of consciousness. Our desire to love is now more like a kind of empty intention; we do not and cannot know what love is except by doing it. By doing what we do not know we are doing, but have the intention to do—that is the course love must now take, the course of adventure, filled with doubt, apprehension, very little happiness, a great deal of emptiness, but the joy that comes with reinvention. The condition under which this new approach to love opens up a new horizon for humanity is that both soul and body have equal value. One is never, not for an instant, lived as having more worth than the other. We must become observers of our body and of our soul life, both together. Lusseyran's observations here form the basis for a true spiritual psychology of body, soul, and spirit, one which does not divide and separate and which nevertheless dearly understands their differences and mutual relationship. Even the sexual organs are taken into this understanding, which must be the case if one is to avoid speaking of body, soul, and spirit abstractly.

Once one has stepped, in a fully conscious way, into the consciousness soul, not only love but everything surrounding love between a man and a woman has to be considered anew. Everything concerning love has to be reinvented, which does not mean made up, but rather, revisioned in light of this kind of consciousness. The question of faithfulness in love arises. As with love itself, one must tread the perilous line—faithfulness is not like a thing that can be possessed. One can no longer really say, "I will be forever faithful." At best, one can say, "I want that to happen." And marriage no longer takes care of the problem, seeming to insure that faithfulness will take place and that if it does not the marriage is broken. Indeed, in a certain way, marriage no longer exists, at least not in the way that it used to; it, too, has to be reinvented by each individual, each couple, daily. Please understand: there is not an option. The alternative is to love without living love, to enact patterns that no longer give life and, more importantly, do not bring anything creative into the world. For love to try to exist as it did in the past turns it now into a commodity, a commodity filled with emptiness that only drains the world and does not renew it.

When Claude Julien, the director of Rudolf Steiner College Press, wrote me, giving me the assignment of writing an introduction to this book, he lightly suggested that a warning ought to be written for the cover of the book. It would say: Do not read this unless you are determined to confront the true nature of your own being. He is quite right.

13

A Psychology of Body, Soul, and Spirit

Anthroposophy, Psychosophy, Pneumatosophy

Rudolf Steiner

On the Focus of this Introductory Guide

This series of twelve lectures by Rudolf Steiner provides a basis for an entirely new psychology. The first four lectures (on "Anthroposophy") provide a precise, dynamic understanding of the human soul in relation to the activity of sensing and to the subtle processes that structure and form the human body.

The next four lectures (on "Psychosophy") focus on what we can know of the human soul on the basis of direct observation alone. No theorizing takes place; no special faculties are employed. Steiner was a disciplined clairvoyant but here he seeks to show what can be known of soul life through the immediacy of engaged observation of oneself and others. Therefore he refrains here from using his higher capacities, relying only on unmediated observation to form a picture of the activity of soul life. The particular nature of this kind of unmediated observation is important and will be addressed in this introduction.

Finally, the concluding lectures (on "Pneumatosophy") portray the relationship of soul life to spirit life, particularly with regard to how to awaken individual spirit life and how to distinguish between illusory and genuine spiritual experiences.

Although the content of these lectures ranges far beyond the usual subject matter of ordinary psychology, it is here perhaps more than anywhere else in Rudolf Steiner's work that the foundations of a psychology rooted in Anthroposophy may be found. This is especially true of the middle set of lectures on "Psychosophy." These not only exemplify the content that any true psychology must encounter and struggle with when it tries to understand the life of the soul, but also illustrate a specifically *psychological* mode of thinking. Deep study of these lectures will result in ways of understanding soul life that one will not find expressed anywhere else in the whole discipline of psychology. More than that, anyone who works carefully with these lectures will find that the beginning of an increasingly conscious soul life becomes possible.

I suggest that readers start by reading the four "Psychosophy" lectures. This allows one to begin by concentrating on what is most important for psychology—a psychological point of view. One can then move on to the four "Pneumatosophy" lectures to see what might, from this point of view, constitute "a psychology of spirit." Finally, turning to the opening four "Anthroposophy" lectures, one can then read those with a view to discovering what might constitute "a psychology of body." This introductory guide follows that order.

(If you choose to read the text straight through, a different and perhaps equally important imagination develops. First, in the "Anthroposophy" lectures, a picture of the whole human being unfolds from an inner standpoint. This leads into a deep consideration of the life of the soul: "psychosophy."And then in the last section, we see how soul life can be employed to perceive specifically spiritual realms: "pneumatosophy." My attempt here, however, will be to try to free the psychology implicit in the text and thereby begin to make explicit at least the foundations of a spiritual psychology. For this purpose, I shall follow the order suggested above.)

The lectures took place over a period of three years, from 1909 to 1911, almost a century ago. One might be tempted to think that whatever they have to say about psychology must be dated, and that if it is relevant to the field of psychology at all, it must be only to its history or early development. It is also tempting to think that, since Rudolf Steiner is not usually regarded as one of the founders of modern psychology, his efforts in this direction must be considered, at most, an interesting aside. But a very good argument can be made that these lectures are, in fact, a wellspring for the true stream of psychology, and that all that presently passes as psychology are but wandering tributaries.

I repeat: these lectures form a new foundation for psychology. I say this because the view of the soul presented here has a wider, fuller, deeper, and higher context than is present in any existing psychology. Steiner presents a context for considering individual soul life that includes the forces that actively form the human body and extends to the interplay of the living body with the surrounding world. These relationships are in turn embraced by the ongoing creative and dynamic activity of the cosmos, which is not here considered in the abstract but as consisting of regions of spirit beings. Furthermore, these realms and their interrelationships are considered in terms of their inner form and activity. This context itself forms the field, the enterprise, of Anthroposophy, begun by Rudolf Steiner. Something of the nature and perspective of this context, that is, of "Anthroposophy," is presented in the first lecture.

My introduction will not compare what Steiner presents with all or even with several other schools of psychology. To do so would lead us far away from the text instead of into it. I mention Steiner's relation to the field of psychology only to alert readers who approach this work from a background of the psychological disciplines to its contemporary importance. This book is not just another psychology to be put alongside all the others. Rather, it presents a possible future for the discipline as a whole.

ANTHROPOSOPHY AND PSYCHOLOGY

A Psychology of Body, Soul, and Spirit may be read not only by those with an interest in psychology but also by those with an interest in further developing the practice of Anthroposophy. If the text is really worked with, the way one reads and studies any of Steiner's other works will be radically transformed. At the same time, the very practice of any aspect of Anthroposophy will also develop in new ways. Whether one's field is education, medicine, art, drama, eurythmy, economy, or business—no matter what practical form one's spiritual work assumes— the perspective this book offers has the potential to restore the often missing soul element. Because this element is often lacking in anthroposophic work, much of the good that anthroposophic enterprises could bring into the world is unfortunately undermined by the dysfunctional soul life of those involved. The horror stories of those who have been subjected to the "help" of less than healthy anthroposophists could fill several volumes, and probably should be documented.

The soul element in anthroposophic work is often said to reside in artistic endeavors—painting, music, eurythmy, and so on. This point of view is true, however, only insofar as the artistic work is done from a real, conscious presence to the actual processes involved in soul life and does not merely follow formulas for what a particular color, movement, or tone does in the soul. Soul life is certainly not limited only to artistic work, and formalized soul must be understood as something quite different from living soul.

Attempts to develop a spiritual life without developing a consciousness of the fullness, depth, and *particularity* of soul life—which must be entered into not just as preliminary to something else, but as an ongoing task—typically result in living the abstract ideas of spirituality, not its actuality. The instances of abuse wrought by such ignorance, regardless of the spiritual or religious practices involved, are well known. What makes Anthroposophy unique, however, is that Steiner *did not* bypass the soul realm and shoot directly for the spirit. The decided lack of soul knowledge and soul work within Anthroposophy cannot be attributed to an oversight by its founder. From this point of view, even though this particular series of lectures occurred fairly early in the corpus of Anthroposophy, it may well be the most central work, not only to read, but to take seriously as the foundation for a true renewal of the anthroposophic movement.

When this book is read—deeply read—it is impossible to come away from that encounter without realizing that the modern initiatory path of

Anthroposophy is a *spiritual-psychological* endeavor. This realization means that the whole of Anthroposophy must be studied and practiced in a spiritual-psychological manner. By coupling the terms *spiritual* and *psychological*, I mean to convey the possibility of a spirituality practiced out of a deep, abiding, and very particular, rather than general, awareness of one's soul life.

Spiritual practice carried out without the accompanying presence of soul life results in a spirituality that has no "inside" and no depth. Such a spirituality lacks the mark of having encountered, struggled with, gone through, and deeply loved the qualities of soul life as described by Steiner: mindfulness, deep memory, emotion, feeling, beauty, joy, pleasure, inner conflict and tension, vulnerability, loss of control, and even all the more difficult sidetracks these qualities can lead one into. Such qualities, of course, must also be addressed when speaking of spirituality. Experience shows, however, that if these qualities are approached without a deep sense of soul interiority, the ensuing spiritual practices become manic, carry a huge shadow, tend toward dogmatism, and tend to exclude precisely those who might dare to bring this vital, interior dimension to their spiritual work.

SOUL LIFE AS THE SUBJECT MATTER OF PSYCHOLOGY

Soul life, as Steiner shows vividly in the four lectures entitled "Psychosophy" (the "wisdom of the soul"), humbles us, because we do not, and cannot, control it. Could anything restrain us more from controlling others than the realization that our own soul life largely controls us and that we have plenty to do to learn to submit to the wisdom of the soul? And what greater deviation from soul life could there be than to think that, from some imagined superior spiritual position, it is our duty to control others?

Steiner indicates why we are unable to control our own soul life and why, instead of trying to control it, we must come to know and follow its ways. The reasons have to do with the origin of soul life itself, and as well with the ongoing content of soul experience. Steiner describes the origin of soul experience as the life of desire. Wisely, he does not define desire, just as he does not define soul. Rather, he points out that desire does not originate within the soul but within the world. Elsewhere, he refers in passing to a second origin of desire: "Boredom causes desire in the soul. It gives birth to a longing for impressions, and the soul life is surrendered to it, yet there is nothing to satisfy that desire." In another place, he speaks of yet another way of considering desire—as the astral, future-time current flowing into the soul. More will be said of this current.

The flow of desire shows up as the most basic polar continuum of forces within the soul—the dramatic, conflicting forces of love and hate. Desire, we could say, expresses itself as the urge toward unity, sought either through the bridging of differences through love or the annihilation of differences through hate. Such differences exist both within ourselves and in our relationships with others. Desire, which may be understood as the deepest unsatisfied longing imaginable—a longing with no object—and its bifurcation into a tension of the opposites of love and hate, gives the soul its dramatic character, and constitutes a built-in urgency toward development—provided, of course, that one remains present to the tensions of inner life.

Because we are so steeped in the pop culture of psychology, which maintains that anyone at all can understand psychology without undergoing a rigorous inner training, such key words may easily be misunderstood. These key words—*desire, love,* and *hate*—do not have the sense and meaning for psychology that they do for ordinary experience. First, they must be understood within the context of the whole life of the soul as described by Steiner. They have little to do with the subjective senses of desire, love, or hate. The desire, the love, and the hate spoken of here are autonomous, inner, dynamic qualities; they do not refer directly to what our habitual "ego" might desire, love, or hate. Even the word *inner* has to be qualified, for it does not mean "subjective," nor does it mean "personal." *Inner* must be understood in a much more metaphorical way, as the dimension that gives life experiences the quality of intimate engagement rather than of a mere string of events.

A constant confusion, present in the very heart of the discipline of psychology, has to do with the assumption that psychology is concerned with the personality and that when we do psychology we are concerned with what goes on "inside" a person. Before psychology even starts, therefore, "interiority," the necessary *standpoint* for the discipline of psychology, is converted into the idea of literal things going on inside people. In other words, we consider a person's "psychology" without ever having developed a truly psychological mode of thinking about soul life itself. Psychology is usually practiced out of the same mode of consciousness we live in everyday life. However, when Steiner speaks of the soul, of desire, of love and hate, he is not speaking of something going on subjectively in some imaginary "everyone." He is speaking of the soul *from the place of soul*—which is the only true and valid subject matter of psychology. In order to understand this book as a whole, then, it is necessary to realize—and to realize deeply—that what is being discussed as "soul" is not an entity of any type, not even an invisible entity. Nor does what is being discussed have to do with some literal content of a supposed invisible entity. When Steiner speaks of "soul" he is speaking a language of *form*. Let me try to express more fully what I mean by "form."

When Steiner describes the inner quality of soul life as a "love-hate tension," this cannot be understood positivistically, as though, somewhere within us, a subjective experience of a tension occurs, or a constant conflict between wanting to love and wanting to hate someone or something. Such an understanding turns the language of form or process into a language of content or stuff. In the language of form, words are used, in order, through words, *to go beyond words*. The polarity serves to awaken the thought-quality that soul is not some kind of container but rather an inner, dynamic, mobile, developing, regressing, conflictual, flowing, relationship. A relationship with what? The soul is "in relation" with desire, with the body, with the spirit—none of which, incidentally, can themselves be considered to utilize the language of content without degrading what they are about.

A reader might well ask why this text is so difficult to read. It is difficult because it is not presented out of ordinary consciousness. But neither is it presented out of clairvoyant consciousness. Instead, it arises out of *soul-consciousness*. The lectures on soul life are certainly given to us from soul-consciousness, and to do psychology we must be able to enter soul-consciousness. Otherwise, we are really not doing psychology at all, but only talking about psychology from the safety of ordinary consciousness. The text is not presented from the viewpoint of Steiner's ego-personality. In fact, it is impossible to do psychology from the viewpoint of ego-personality, although most psychology tries to do just that. Therefore, nearly all psychology is in fact pathological. It is pathological because its very language prohibits entry to the life of the soul.

A Psychology of Body, Soul, and Spirit does not operate within the popular deception that makes many people go looking for the "archetypes within," their "inner child," their "true self," and all the rest. You must understand that the work you are about to read, in being true to soul, puts a deterrent before us: it cannot be understood simplistically or easily. This deterrent, however, is at the same time a doorway through which we may awaken to soul life. Psychology, as practiced in this text, forms an integral part of the work of initiation. All psychology ought to do the same, but it has sold its soul.

Something else brings home my point about the way to approach this work. This has to do with the second intrinsic aspect of soul life described by Steiner. Steiner calls this quality of soul life "judgment." He also says that his meaning of this term must be understood in a "verb" rather than a "noun" sense—*judging* rather than *judgment*. He then further qualifies the term by saying that he is referring to something like "reflection," "mirroring," "pondering," or "mulling over." Thus, what initially seems to be a kind of content, or cognitive act in its concluding stages, is in fact much more subtle. Here the word *judgment* refers, really, to the momentary, provisional end-points of a qualitative, always, at every moment, ongoing soul process. Only in this latter sense does judgment belong to soul life. The word *judgment* generally carries the notion of something that has already happened, a conclusion that has been reached, but in the context of describing the most basic qualities of ongoing soul life, it would be quite incorrect to understand "judgement" in this sense. Even if we add the qualifiers (reflection, mirroring, pondering, mulling over) we still risk making the error of understanding these terms in the everyday sense as something we do. We think about things, ponder them, mull them over. The soul's engagement in such activity connotes something different.

You will notice—at specific places in the text, but really in the book as a whole—that words are used to describe soul life, while at the same time these very words seem to have to be erased. For example, *judgment* connotes one thing: an attempt to reach a final conclusion. But, as soon as you think you understand that concept, the term is reintroduced, but is now said to mean "mulling over." "Mulling over" doesn't really go anywhere, except over the same territory again and again. So, what kind of soul quality is being described? It is a quality that can be imagined as a kind of intensive experiencing—living experience, not having experience. Soul experience is something like the reintensifying of what we encounter in inner and outer ways. Such reintensification never comes to a conclusion, not in soul life. There are provisional conclusions, and these are what we experience as mental images. The soul quality described as "judging" can be understood to mean that we relive our life at the same time as we are living it. And this reliving, which happens simultaneously with living, consists of the upsurge of personal and even collective past, of waves of emotion, feeling, attention, memory, desire, even past lives, and many other qualities that qualify any moment as not something just gone through, but gone through with multileveled meaning.

Once we understand the term *judging* in this way, it becomes clear why Steiner says that not all experience is soul experience. We may, for example, perceive a rose, but that experience is not necessarily a soul experience. Only when it is relived—not necessarily after the fact, but at the moment it occurs—is the experience a soul experience. Such reliving, contemporaneous with living, describes a basic function of soul life. *Soul life gives interiority to experience.*

PSYCHOLOGY AS PSYCHOLOGICAL THINKING

What is the nature, or method, of observation employed by Steiner to come to this understanding of soul life? This is an important question to carry with us while reading and studying this book, particularly the section concerned specifically with soul life. Steiner does not give any direct indication of his method. He says only that "*psychosophy* is to be a deliberation on the human soul." He then goes on to tell us what will be considered. Or, he says, "What is soul life when we contemplate it as such, within the limits just spoken of?" Not much to go on; we must consider the text as a whole.

Steiner's presentation of soul life is not just his opinions about the soul. The language of the text is not didactic or dogmatic. It does not conform to the style of pronouncements. We may conclude that he derived a great deal from the work of Franz Brentano, since he considers Brentano's views and limitations in some detail (lecture one of "Pneumatosophy"). But he surely does not merely repeat Brentano's findings, though Brentano's phenomenological method certainly forms one aspect of Steiner's style of observation. Steiner's method attempts to describe faithfully *the essential qualities* of any experience. The method is not introspection, which is a peculiar kind of observation that "looks" inward. In other words, introspection turns an inner experience into naturalistic observation, converting the "inner" into the "outer." We may also be sure that Steiner's method is not empirical in the usual sense. What he has to say does not derive from conducting a series of inquiries about certain matters and then arriving at conclusions.

How does one observe the life of the soul? If we meditate on this question and consider it in light of Steiner's text, we come to an understanding of the nature of the field of psychology: *before you can do psychology, you must already be able to stand within soul life in a conscious way.* The question of method cannot be approached from the outside, searching through all the possible, known methods to see which one fits. It may therefore be more helpful to rephrase the question by asking not what method is used to do genuine psychology but, "What aspect of me is allowed to do psychology?" We may be sure that it is not the ego-personality or the ordinary self that does psychology. The ego-personality could not produce the text you are about to read; that would be impossible. The ordinary ego-personality could, at best, only preach about the values of soul, or about the values of spirit, or even the values of Anthroposophy. There is not a trace of preaching in this text, because it is not about soul as viewed from some external perspective. If the text were *about* soul rather than a speaking *within* soul, we would be presented not with a psychology but with a belief system about psychology.

This question of method is so important, because our answer to it determines how we read this book; and it also determines how, beyond the work of reading and study, we go about doing psychology. The requirement for reading this book is to read or hear the text *as the soul* that is spoken of. The text is spoken from the viewpoint of the soul and is addressed to the soul. There is no other possible way to do psychology. Entering this text requires a complete change, and there is no way to do it but to just do it—to plunge in. There is really no way to prepare; it is not a matter of simple transition or gradually growing toward it by developing and harmoniously expanding the habitual self. The method is really quite simple. Steiner does not talk *about* soul; he speaks *from* soul. That is the entire method. There is, however, an entrance fee for doing psychology. The fee is that you need to leave behind your well-known-to-you self-identity. You must suffer the experience of leaving behind not only what you know, but also what you *think* you know of yourself. This requirement qualifies psychology as integral to the work of initiation.

Another aspect of method seems worth mentioning. Reading this book, you will necessarily experience a rupture from your ordinary ego-personality, which would like to understand the text by the logical means of everyday thinking. This brings you into a new way of thinking. It takes a different frame of mind to cross the waters and engage in the psychological work of reading this writing. Thus, just as this book cannot be approached from within our usual self-identity, neither can it be approached out of our usual structures of thought. To do so would completely miss another basic requirement of doing psychology. An intellectual training is required, one not necessarily acquired prior to reading and studying this work, but acquired *through* the intellectual effort required to read, study, contemplate, and meditate on it.

This intellectual training, it must be emphasized, is not specialized nor acquired through specialist training. In fact, this training takes the opposite direction. This does not, however, mean sinking more deeply into everyday intellectuality. Specialist intellectuality hones the ability to observe the objects of interest, albeit more closely and finely than in daily life, utilizing what we might call "spectator consciousness." If psychology goes in that direction the only conceivable outcome is either trivial nonsense or technologies of behavior control based on technical modes of thought. Assuredly, such a misuse of psychology does occur, even in the work of those who purport to be doing soul psychology; it is not exclusive to behaviorism. On the other hand, working from a non-specialist intellectual stance that can be immediately understood, psychology often becomes negligible, inconsequential.

The third alternative presented in this series of lectures is that one conceives of a *psychological mode of thought*—a psychological intellectuality, as it were. The "Psychosophy" lectures most exemplify that mode of intellectuality in this book. Psychological thinking extends outward—on one side toward the body and sensing, and on the other toward the life of spirit. Notice the extreme difference between the psychological mode of thinking exemplified by Steiner and the kinds of intellectual categories usually associated with psychology. I mean categories such as myths, symbols, empathy, confessional reporting, biography work, dream interpretation, case histories, theories of the self, trauma, abuse, analysis, visualization. For the present-day soul, such categories are passé, because they have been usurped by ego-personality and, rather than serving the soul, serve narcissism. They are categories that belong to dead thinking: one can no longer catch sight of the soul through them. When used by psychology, these categories, unless they are used *to say what cannot be spoken* and not as literal content, become manipulative tools. Sadly, this is all too often the case because almost no psychologist today understands this art of psychological thinking.

By calling into question the present categories of psychology, I am not saying that abuse is invented or that there is no psychological trauma, or that dream interpretation is not helpful, and so on. But when the therapeutic endeavor lacks the capacity to address soul life, remaining instead on the surface, it can, at best, merely make adjustment and adaptation somewhat easier. Yet in so doing, the soul becomes even further walled in and incapable of the transformations it needs to meet and develop the challenges that karma and destiny set for it. The fact is that when the lazy mind takes the phenomena psychology addresses to be some positive content, the soul is left out of psychological categories. When, for example, the events of a person's life are organized in a well-ordered biography—fixed into time periods that make it look as if the events of life are pat and nailed down—then the soul is abandoned by the very endeavor whose work is to care for soul. The soul cannot shine through these categories of time periods, primarily because the principle mode through which soul can shine through in our time is *thinking.* Not just any kind of thinking, but living, psychological thinking! In other words, lazy thought approaches psychological phenomena with the same attitude of consciousness with which it approaches the phenomena of the sense world, unaware that such naturalistic thinking does not apply. *The soul cannot be perceived.* However, in thinking, and only in thinking, it may be apperceived.

I have tried to demonstrate that Steiner demonstrates a psychological mode of thinking. The literalist, approaching this work from outmoded categories of psychological thought, will argue that if this text is a model of psychological thinking, then psychology is really in trouble.

The text is so difficult, so elusive, so hard to get hold of, that this mode of thinking could not possibly be brought to bear in actual situations with other people. Of course, that is literally so. The aim while doing therapy would not be to think *what* Steiner presents here, but to think *as* he thinks here. We need a psychological thinking that evokes rather than nails down. We need ways of thinking that, at any given time, address one aspect of the soul's life, and do so in a way that conveys that the reality being addressed is inexhaustible. We need thinking that surrounds and protects the inner life of soul. At the same time, we need this thinking to be clear and precise, not inflated, emotional, sentimental, and full of mystifications. This text, it is easy to see, serves as a model of psychological thinking.

SOUL TIME

A Psychology of Body, Soul, and Spirit serves not only as a deep source for the renewal and total reimagining of the field of psychology; it also proposes including within such re-visioning a dimension of psychology that, as far as I know, has *never* been addressed before. This dimension is brought forth in the "Psychosophy" lectures. It has to do with time and the soul. Steiner carefully describes how the soul lives within an actual current of time, which comes to the soul not only from the past but from the future as well. A consideration of this quality changes the way we view the whole of psychology! Certainly, the whole of therapeutic psychology is changed by this astute observation.

There is a huge bias in psychology which advocates understanding the reasons for our present behavior in terms of what happened to us in the past. The bias takes many different forms. For Freud, it was the personal traumas of the past; for Jung, it was both the personal and the collective past. Each psychology has its own version of the past as determinant. Steiner, too, recognizes this factor of the past as important, but he approaches it in a very different manner. For Steiner, certain aspects of the past exist within soul life as autonomous desires, longings, urges, and memories—aspects that were never satisfied, may not be conscious, have no world to relate to, and, most significantly, have no future. It is not a matter of giving such autonomous factors a future, since they can never have that. Rather, his approach is twofold. First, some way is found to give these factors a world. He suggests, for example the procedure of eliciting associations, which can be healing for all such factors of the past—*except for sexual matters*. More important by far, however, is the strengthening of our sensitization to the time current from the future. But what does this mean?

The time current from the future, which is real and actual, moves in the reverse direction of the time current that moves from the past toward the future. Jung's psychology as well as the existential psychology of Maslow and others all focus on the importance of what we can become rather than what we are due to past circumstances. These theories, however, utilize a teleological imagination of the future. There is an understanding that we are moving *toward* something and not merely being pushed from behind. Steiner has a very different sense of the time current from the future, which he hesitatingly calls the "astral body" of the soul. It is the "not-yet" and it plays an enormous role in our soul life. This future time current has nothing to do with literal clock time—it is not in linear time. One can begin to actually experience such a current by imagining, at the end of each day, the events of the day in reverse order. One could also write one's biography in reverse order or simply perform a certain task in reverse every day. After a while, a new sensibility will dawn. It involves living a sense of possibility, as though we are drawn toward something, or the sense of the "not-yet" as a powerful force. This aspect of soul life reverberates into life as openness, as a constantly creative factor, and as real life movement.

The soul has no means of registering the content of its future time current except as it overlaps the time current from the past. Nonetheless, the effort to make this current conscious is experienced as an expansion of soul life. It is experienced as a capacity to live consciously in "not-knowing." This is the capacity to experience the activity of creating our responses to each moment. Becoming aware of this current radically alters the soul qualities of past events as these continue to influence the life of the soul. The two time currents, past and future, overlap; and feeling the not-yet quality (that sense of "not-knowing"), a conscious and creative "not-knowing," also brings the substantial feeling of the possibilities present within the past that affects us. This is the past not only as determiner but as "possibilizer."

Imagine, for example, rewriting your biography. Usually, we consider our biography to be our life story, a life review. We look at our past in order to see how at each moment that past enters the present. Something very different would result, however, if you wrote your biography while paying attention to the open possibilities that attend each past event. Your biography then is not only what has already happened; it also intimates the coming-to-be that accompanies each event you have lived through. Learning to listen for this aspect of the past creates an imaginal biography, a past that is truly worth paying attention to, because at each place along the way one could get a feeling for the future. Not the literal future, but the ongoing "not-yet" that one is in each of life's events. Neglecting this dimension of soul life, a whole half of psychology and of our understanding of the life of the soul has been neglected.

Toward a Psychology of Spirit

The sections of this book are arranged so that each set of lectures—those on the body and sensing, those on soul life, and those on spirit life—can be read more or less independently. Nevertheless, I wish to present a view of the book that emphasizes soul and the inherent foundation for a new psychology. Thus far, I have touched upon the qualities inherent within soul life. Many other extremely valuable considerations concerning the phenomena that derive from these qualities may also be found in the text. Phenomena such as attention, boredom, emotion, aesthetic feeling, and the dramatic character of soul life are all addressed. These phenomena, too, must not be considered with the understanding of ordinary consciousness. Rather than understood through the static ideas of our habitual intellect, they must be worked with in such a way that the continuous, dynamic quality of soul is *felt*.

In addition to the qualities inherent in soul life, Steiner gives detailed pictures of the relationship of the boundaries of soul life with the body, as well as with the spirit. Body and spirit are both intimately bound up with soul life. Yet, at the same time, they must also be considered on their own terms. The lectures on the senses and the body, and the lectures on spirit, express these dual concerns. In his book *Anthroposophy (A Fragment)*, based on the first set of lectures printed here, Steiner considers in detail the life of sensing and how the currents involved in sensing constitute the formative forces of the human body.[1] The autonomous nature of spirit and the healthy way of developing the soul as an organ for perceiving the spiritual worlds is basic to the work of Steiner. It is the subject of his central book, *How to Know Higher Worlds*. To some extent, these two works, *Anthroposophy (A Fragment)* and *How to Know Higher Worlds*, go into the matters of body and spirit in greater detail than the present work which, however, is most valuable for understanding the soul's relationship to body and to spirit. It is this aspect that I wish to emphasize as a ground for re-visioning psychology.

The psychology of spirit inherent in *A Psychology of Body, Soul, and Spirit* may be seen as proceeding in two directions. First, there are the considerations of the spirit as it lives in the life of the soul. These considerations have to do with the quality of soul life that we experience as the sense of the "I." Our capacity to arrive at the realization *"I am"* is not, however, inherent in soul life. And yet, paradoxically, once installed in the soul, experiencing and living "I am" (the judging quality, described above) does belong to soul life in an ongoing way. But originally it must come from *elsewhere*—it is not given. The "I" experience does not enter the soul through our sensory relation with the world. There is nothing

---

1   *Anthroposophy (A Fragment)* was the result of Rudolf Steiner's attempt in 1910 to write out what he had tried to convey in "Anthroposophy," the first course of the present lectures. See "Further Reading" for this and other books mentioned.

in the outer world that could lead to the inner capacity of a first experiencing of the "I." The "I" is not of a sensory nature; we do not learn it from experiencing the world. It is an element that differs equally from the current of mental images from the past and from the current of desires from the future. Rather, it is the element that makes it possible to receive the past in an individual way and face the future in an individual way. The sense of the "I" enters soul life from the spiritual world. Within soul life as such, once "I"-being has awakened, we experience a definite "I"-consciousness.

From the point of view of psychology, the experience of the "I" makes certain soul experiences possible. It makes possible, for instance, the free remembering of something from the past. Memory is also evoked by the presence of something in the physical world that touches off remembrances of past occurrences. Here, we have a soul-body relationship. To remember something from the past freely, however, is different. Yet the capacity to do so is crucial for a healthy soul life. This capacity can be developed by the practice of doing some task in the opposite order than we usually do. In fact, this is the same kind of practice we need to do to become aware of the time current from the future. The two capacities are related. As we tap into the reversed time current, we strengthen the capacity of the "I" to freely remember events of the past.

"I"-consciousness is not a familiar term in psychology. "I"-consciousness is not the same as *ego-personality,* though a relationship exists between them. However, the possibility of developing a more fully conscious soul life depends on "I"-consciousness within soul life, that is, on the spiritual aspect of soul life. When the "I," in effect, reflects only the past—as happens when there is no feeling for the time (or future) current—then we have what psychology generally speaks of as ego-consciousness, and its attendant egotism. As Steiner says: "I"-image, or "I"-awareness, has a certain characteristic. It is taken hold of powerfully by all interests and desires, for they anchor themselves firmly in the "I." Despite the egoism represented by such interests and desires, there is certainly something very unique about this self-perceiving of the "I."

Steiner adds that the "I" does not belong to the soul current flowing from the future.

So, whereas ego-consciousness is really the accumulation of past experiences reflected by the "I," and such consciousness is (in more usual psychological terms) the *ego*, the "I" is more than this. The "more" consists of "I"-consciousness reflecting, within soul life, the individual spirit nature.

This individual spirit nature is what Steiner means when he says that there is something unique to the "I." Now the term *"I"* is used throughout Steiner's texts, and the specific manner in which he uses the term has to be determined by its context. Anthroposophists often fail to make the fine but extremely important distinction between "ego" and "I." Consequently, they often do not differentiate between egotism and individual spirit. Even more often, psychologists fail to make such a distinction, and in depth psychology, for example, there is a bias against the "ego," which is, unwittingly, a bias against spirit (the "I").

Steiner recognizes the unique qualities of the "I" and gives detailed descriptions of the interplay between "I"-consciousness and soul life as a whole. If these factors are taken into account, *all psychology must, in fact, be spiritual psychology. Furthermore, when these factors are taken into account, spiritual psychology assumes a clear, definite, and precise meaning—it becomes a discipline concerned with the whole of soul life, which includes the dimension of spirit.*

I have said that the psychology of spirit, as developed by Steiner in this book, proceeds in two directions. The second direction is developed in the series of four lectures entitled "Pneumatosophy," a term meaning the "wisdom of spirit." If, when reading and studying the "Psychosophy" lectures, there are persistent questions about what is meant by "spirit" and what the basis might be for saying that the "I" relates to the spirit aspect of our being, these concerns can be clarified by studying the "Pneumatosophy" lectures.

The "Pneumatosophy" lectures develop the aspect of the psychology of spirit that deals with developing the soul as the perceiving organ for spiritual realities. This path of soul development is well known in Anthroposophy, but not enough attention is usually given to exactly what is meant by it. Let us start at the beginning. The reality of spiritual worlds cannot become known to us in a healthy way unless we work toward those worlds *through the soul*. The method requires the repeated and regular formation of an inner, symbolic image that, as far as the physical world is concerned, is an incorrect—an erroneous—picture. A well-known example involves developing an image-based meditation of the Rose Cross. Steiner gives the details of this particular meditation in *An Outline of Esoteric Science*. There is nothing in the perceptual world that has the nature of a black wooden cross with a circle of roses. In *A Psychology of Body, Soul, and Spirit*, Steiner indicates repeatedly that an absolute requirement for this meditative exercise has to do with certain *moral qualities* of soul. This is the second, crucial aspect of a psychology of spirit. The principle may be stated thus: *The psychological foundation of conscious spiritual experience is the contemplation of images without in any way basing such contemplation on self-interest, curiosity, or a desire to achieve something for oneself—not even a higher state of consciousness.*

An even deeper aspect of the psychology of spirit is contained in the method of concentration and meditation that is necessary for the soul to develop into an organ of spiritual perception. We must ask: What in us allows us to consciously make and concentrate on a symbolic image? And there is another question related to the first: Why does Steiner emphasize the erroneous nature of the images to be contemplated? Indeed, why does he not recommend contemplating a "real" spiritual image, such as the image of an angel?

Steiner's response to these questions is quite startling: error originates in the spiritual world, and our stepping stone to this realm is through this aspect of the spiritual world itself! Thus, our first access to the spiritual world is through error. But we must recognize this error consciously. And, in addition to recognizing it, we must have the inner moral force not to be taken into the error: we must be able to utilize the inherent spiritual forces to bootstrap, as it were—or per-haps better said, "soulstrap"—ourselves into the spiritual world. If one were to contemplate, say, an inner image of an angel, the difficulty would be that it is unlikely we would recognize this image, too, as an error. No inner image of an angel accurately portrays in any way the nature of an angel.

The precise nature of the *moral quality* of soul must also be made clear, for only through this moral quality is it possible to use the soul to perceive into the spiritual worlds without coming to any harm. The moral quality, as described by Steiner and worth much contemplation, can be discovered by imagining first that human beings are presently unable to affirm their true and full nature, and then imagining human beings in the future who have the capacity to attain a higher nature. By carefully practicing such an imagination—not just once, but repeatedly—it becomes possible to use the error of inner images to overcome that error and develop toward new capacities. The implication of this procedure is that the psychology of spirit is a practical tool that is concerned not with the present but with the highest possibilities of human reality in the future. *The psychology of spirit is the psychology of the future human being.*

Certain kinds of psychology and so-called spiritual psychology make use of techniques of imagination. The psychology of spirit devel-oped by Steiner, however, throws a whole new light on the use of such techniques. Visualization practices, active imagination practices, sha-manic practices adapted for weekend use by spiritual seekers, the use of altered states of consciousness for healing, guided imagery prac-tices—none of these can be accepted at face value as being helpful. In Steiner's terms, such practices all come under the rubric of spiritually illusory practices. They might take one into spiritual realms, but with-out exception these would be, in Steiner's terms, "Luciferic" spiritual realms. No judgment is made against these realms by Steiner; in fact, his whole method of the psychology of spirit makes use of these very same realms. Nevertheless, what is brought to bear in the methods he suggests is a clear cognizance of the error involved and the attendant moral soul force that can cancel out the destructive effects of making use of spiritual error.

What kind of harm and destructiveness could Steiner have in mind when he speaks of the dire effects of using soul life to develop spiritual capacities without moral balance? He presents those effects in some detail in *How to Know Higher Worlds* and in other writings and lectures. At the very least, it leads to increased egotism—or increased self-absorption—now placed under the mantle of spirituality. The more dire effects include inflation and depression, even psychosis.

It needs to be strongly emphasized that the possibility of taking up the practices offered by Steiner for becoming present to true imagination rather than illusory fantasy depends completely on an ongoing presence, as consciously as possible, to soul life as I have previously described it. Since the soul becomes the medium through which spiritual experience becomes possible, it becomes imperative to be able to face even the darkest, most shadow sides of our soul life, over and over again, and more and more deeply. We are never finished with the soul. Any attempts to engage in spiritual practices, such as those described here by Steiner—*while bypassing the soul or feeling that one has, after all, already done all that*—can result only in destructive spiritual practices.

A third aspect of the psychology of spirit developed by Steiner, which is really a kind of subset of the second aspect—the development of healthy spirit imagination—concerns the creative imagination. The creative imagination belongs to the domain of phenomena considered by a psychology of spirit. It is important to emphasize this aspect of the psychology of spirit, because creative imagination is often considered a function of soul life alone. In Jung's psychology as currently practiced, for example, creativity is considered in this way. As described by Steiner, however, the creative imagination consists of currents intruding from the spiritual worlds into soul life and experienced as autonomous images. Steiner speaks of such images as genuine creative fantasy, occurring midway between mental picturing and fully conscious spiritual imagination.[2] Creative imagination, then, is a central phenomenon of the psychology of spirit. In spite of all of its richness, complexity, and depth, creativity in itself does not belong to the realm of the soul.

Strictly speaking, the psychology of spirit must be differentiated from the investigations of spiritual worlds that become possible when we use the life of the soul to develop spiritual perception. In order to remain true to the discipline of psychology, true psychology of spirit will always stay close to the soul realm. Such a psychology is interested above all in the kinds of border phenomena that occur when spiritual worlds touch the soul realms. It is interested especially in how these border phenomena occur in daily life—how they are a healthy part of soul life, and how they give indications of movement toward or away from a healthy spiritual life. In the lectures on "Pneumatosophy," Steiner goes beyond these considerations, but in this introduction we are concerned only with spiritual psychology as such.

Let us consider *imagination* more closely. When working with soul qualities to move toward perception of the spiritual worlds, images are used to enter the world of imagination. *Imagination*, for Steiner, is characterized by a particular quality of experience—the presence of inner images that have a distinctly autonomous life of their own. Psychologically considered, when such images occur in life (and indeed they can occur without the specific practices outlined by Steiner), the spiritual worlds have intruded into soul life. Whether such intrusions are helpful or harmful depends on two factors: the moral sensibility of the person experiencing such images and the degree to which that person has in some manner come to a living understanding of soul life. Often such an understanding can occur without having psychological training.

If autonomous images intrude in forceful ways when moral sensibility of the kind mentioned above is absent or weak, then images that

---

2   Rudolf Steiner uses the terms *imagination, inspiration,* and *intuition* in an extraordinary sense. Thus, throughout this book, these words are italicized when used in that way. What we ordinarily call "imagination," might be referred to as "mental picturing" or "fantasy." See lecture three of "Pneumatosophy."

seem intense and significant are really no more than imaginal presentations of one's own deficient moral qualities. If, on the other hand, no
real sense of soul life is present, the experience of true *imagination* can
become overwhelming. Here, we have one basis for developing therapeutic measures that can help people who are experiencing the presence of the spiritual worlds. In present-day psychology, such awakening
of *imagination* is often assumed to belong strictly to the soul realm.
Autonomous images are said to be soul experiences, with no recognition of the involvement of spirit. There are also many practices that
encourage the awakening of autonomous imagery, either taking it to be
a way to stimulate individual creativity or taking all such imagery to be
spiritually helpful, without any moral consideration. When this kind of
imagination occurs in a spontaneous and disturbing way, psychology,
as currently practiced, usually assumes that such occurrences indicate
psychological imbalance. A psychology of spirit can be of the greatest assistance in understanding what is actually happening and how to
work with these experiences in healthy ways. Careful work with this
text will give very direct indications about the most helpful ways to
work with such experiences.

A second way that the spiritual worlds enter soul life concerns the
relationship between emotion and action. Emotions belong to the realm
of the soul. Understanding the mysterious way that an emotion, impulse,
desire, urge, or feeling transmutes from emotion into action—understanding that transition—also belongs to the psychology of spirit. In this
transition, soul gets beyond itself. Steiner's consideration of the relationship between emotion and will reveals the nature of this transition. First
of all, emotion touches into the body. This is the only way, in fact, that
emotion can act in the world. Saying that the body is involved, however, does not clarify any of the process involved. But, if we could be
aware of that process, Steiner indicates that we would, in a soul manner,
be aware of *intuition*. We can begin to be aware of *intuition* when we
begin to realize that what lives in our consciousness—deeply felt and
experienced not only as knowledge but also as bodily feeling—is the

activity of something that goes beyond our own soul life. Our will is not completely our own; it is the cooperation of soul life, through embodied emotion, with actual spiritual forces.

In addition to imagination and *intuition*, the psychology of spirit also concerns a third element, *inspiration*. *Inspiration* is closer in content to spiritual *imagination* than it is to spiritual *intuition*. Whereas spiritual *intuition* is related to the soul activity of emotion working into the body as forces of will, spiritual *inspiration* for Steiner has to do with the soul's experience of the autonomous images of spiritual *imagination* as more-than-autonomous inner pictures. Spiritual *inspiration* perceives that these autonomous images are the spiritual deeds of beings of the spiritual worlds. Spiritual inspiration consists of forming the thought that the images are indeed the acts of beings. It is difficult for language to describe precisely the nature of this realm. We might, however, express it thus: *inspiration* is the actively-coming-to-form thought of the reality of spiritual beings revealing themselves through autonomous imagery.

In spiritual work, it is important to recognize the qualities of *inspiration*. Without such recognition, we may be captivated by the play of all sorts of images. These may fascinate us so that we lack a deep respect and reverence for the realms that have opened. One can easily miss the possibility of giving those worlds their proper meaning. Considered in a more psychological way, on the other hand, when one has no understanding of the nature of the spiritual worlds—and has not gone through the kind of careful movement of soul toward those worlds as described by Steiner—then, when *inspirations* enter, sensing the reality of spiritual beings can be extremely frightening. The usual sense of the word *inspiration* must therefore be put aside. As developed by Steiner, *inspiration* does not necessarily mean that one is able to utilize these experiences in an act of creating something in the world. That may happen, but *inspiration* can just as well be a terribly frightening feeling of being invaded.

In the lectures on Pneumatosophy, Steiner focuses on the necessary procedures for using soul experience to develop the capacities for experiencing the spiritual worlds. I have tried to emphasize the psychology of spirit implicit in the practices described by Steiner. In order to remain psychological, a psychology of spirit must stay strongly on the side of the soul. The boundary where soul and spirit touch must be described from that point of view. Thus, as I have indicated, a psychology of spirit also involves the careful work of understanding how what occurs at this border may or may not be healthy. This allows one to begin to recognize that there are enormous differences between soul pathologies and soul/spirit pathologies. Ordinary psychology does not recognize these differences, and I have barely touched on them here. However, the sufferings of soul and the sufferings that may accompany arrival at the soul/spirit boundary must be differentiated. Each must be worked with in a different way. A therapeutic psychology based on a clear sense of soul does not proceed in the same way as a therapeutic psychology of soul/spirit. Such concerns go beyond the scope of this text, though hopefully it can open up these differences for research.

SOUL AND EMBODIMENT

The most difficult lectures in this book are the ones that come first, the four lectures that are entitled "Anthroposophy." These deal primarily with sensing and the body. My reflections on these lecturers will focus on the kinds of experiences and phenomena characteristic of the soul-body boundary. Thus they will begin to outline a "psychology of the body." The four lectures do more, however, than merely develop a "psychology of the body." They differentiate "anthropology" from "Anthroposophy" and "Anthroposophy" from "theosophy." Steiner alludes in a sketchy outline to the long evolution of the human body. This is done to help us understand that the human physical body is intimately interwoven with the whole cosmos. He then presents a way of understanding the human senses—first in an enumerative way, and then more deeply from the perspective of spiritual science. At the time of these lectures, Steiner described ten senses. Later, he spoke of twelve distinct senses.[3]

Steiner first considers sensing through careful attention and observation of ordinary consciousness. Anyone can repeat his observations. As we do so, we come to realize the complexity of sensing. By the way Steiner arranges his presentation, we realize that each different sense provides a *particular* form of knowledge without the intervention of thought. The first description of the senses, however, does not touch on the soul–body relation, and is thus only a preparation for such a consideration.

The second description of the senses goes deeply into the spiritual question: *What makes sensing possible?* Here, sensing is considered by way of clairvoyant consciousness. Steiner develops dynamic pictures of the interplay between spiritual forces and the etheric and astral bodies, which is different for each of the senses. We take a very large leap from the first to this second description of sensing. By carefully following through this spiritual understanding of sensing, we begin to dissolve our notion of the human body as a physical organism that happens to be formed in such a way that it contains a number of sense organs. Even if we do not fully understand the meaning of *Atma, Buddhi,* and *Manas* or the meaning of the etheric and astral bodies, we are nonetheless alerted to the fact that the human body, *the living human body,* must be understood as the confluence of the activity of high spiritual beings—subtle life-forming and soul-forming forces—with physical matter.[4] The second and third lectures in the section on "Anthroposophy" develop this spiritual understanding of each of the senses. Indeed, these lectures offer what amounts to a short course in the whole of Anthroposophy. Fortunately, the editors have provided footnotes throughout, indicating where many of the concepts presented here can be followed up in greater detail in Steiner's other writings and lectures.

3   See *The Foundations of Human Experience*, lecture 8, August 29, 1919 and *Toward Imagination*, lecture 3, June 20, 1916.

4   *Atma* (spirit body, or spirit human being), *Buddhi* (life spirit), and *Manas* (spirit self) as well as the other aspects of the human being are discussed in detail by Steiner in the first chapter of both *Theosophy* and *An Outline of Esoteric Science*.

Let me now present keys that might be helpful in understanding the importance of Steiner's view of sensing and show how, on this basis, he develops a radically new approach to the human body. It is this new view that I believe to be of the utmost importance for the "psychology of the body."

Steiner describes the human body from an inner perspective. This inner standpoint indicates the capacity to observe and describe the senses and the body from the perspective of consciously developed *imagination, inspiration,* and *intuition.* He states, for example, that a true understanding of the human organism "requires the development of a spiritual-scientific ability to observe and grasp the whole human being from within." We are used to conceiving of the body as viewed from spectator consciousness. This ordinary conception of the body—as currently understood by science and medicine, for example—views the human organism as a closed system. The body that we are, however, is not a closed system as such. The living body is an open field, a locus for the convergence of relationships with the physical world and for more complex relationships with the spiritual worlds.

An example of the human body as an open, dynamic, and interactive field may be seen in Steiner's description of one of the senses—the life sense. In the first lecture, which lists and describes the senses, we learn that the life sense is experienced as a feeling for the body's well-being. In fact, we experience the life sense only when there is some disharmony among the inner organs of the body. We experience hunger, thirst, tiredness, or a feeling of energy. The life sense is one of four senses through which we become aware of ourselves as bodily beings. The other physical senses are touch, movement, and balance (though touch is not considered as a separate sense in these lectures). The life sense gives the particular experience of the wholeness of the body.

The second of the four lectures on "Anthroposophy" presents a second description of this life sense from the point of view of clairvoyant perception. This description uses the more specialized language of Anthroposophy. There is, for example, a high spiritual being, *Atma.* At some time in the future, human beings will have this spirit being as part of their makeup. But for now it is lent to us. Atma suffuses the etheric body and brings a kind of cramping or a frozen quality to it. This contraction of the etheric body causes the astral body to be "squeezed out." The astral body is the source of experiences such as pleasure, conflict, and tension. This "squeezing out" of the astral body is the process that is lived as our experience of the life sense.

The first description, given from ordinary consciousness, can be comprehended quite easily. The second description, on the other hand, has real meaning only for those who have clairvoyant capacities and—to some extent—for those who accept what Steiner says as true, while others, of course, may take it as equivalent to an abstract theory of the action of the life sense. But there is a third way of working with this description. The description can become the focus of sustained image meditations, from an inner perspective, of a particular functioning of the body. Approached in this way, we can begin to develop an entirely new imagination of the body. We then proceed similarly through all the senses. With regard to the life sense, for example, we can gradually come to a most interesting conclusion. The body itself feels qualities such as pleasure, aversion, pain, joy. But these qualities are not feelings I have; they are the body's ongoing relationship with a spiritual being, the being that provides for us the sense we have of being a body. This is the body as a whole experience, not as a conglomeration of anatomical parts, organs, and physiology. Physiology does not give us an experience of the body at all; it gives us only concepts *about* the body.

We can get to the point of experiencing a strong sense of this quality of bodily life without having developed clairvoyant capacities. As the first step toward developing a "psychology of the body," I would suggest working through each of the senses in image meditations drawn from Steiner's descriptions. Even anthroposophists who work with the senses do not really practice the kind of imaginative procedure that will result in a new imagination of the body—a true spiritual "psychology of the body." Albert Soesman, for example, has written, from other standpoints, a fine book on the twelve senses (*Our Twelve Senses: Wellsprings of the Soul*). But he never mentions the fact that the body is not a product, or something completed, but a dynamic, open relationship with the spiritual worlds.

A set of meditations could be developed in relation to each of the twelve senses. For movement, it would be necessary to develop an imagination of the interplay between *Buddhi*, or life spirit, and the etheric and astral bodies. The specific ways these forces work are described in the text, and it is crucial to develop the meditations based on the specific forms of interaction. For balance, one might meditate on the specific relationship between the spirit being *Manas* and the etheric and astral bodies. These first three senses—the life sense, the sense of movement, and the sense of balance—all give us different qualities of experiencing ourselves as embodied.

The second series of four senses provides experiences of the body's interactions with the surrounding world. These take place through the senses of smell, taste, sight, and warmth. With these four senses, we are more on our own, since they do not involve a higher being, though they do involve the astral body. It may help to think of the astral body as the "soul body," which means here that through these senses we have some bodily experience of the inner qualities of the outer world. As we work meditatively with these four senses, we gradually develop a "psychology of the body." To do so, however, requires that we have a feeling for analogy. Smell, for example, is *like* the body interacting with outer substances through the will. Smell is *like* a struggle, or conflict, between a substance in gaseous form trying to enter the body and a counterforce of will that struggles to penetrate the interior of that substance. Taste is *like* the interaction of the feeling body with the feeling nature of substances. This means that taste is the body's way of experiencing the interaction of feelings. Sight, on the other hand, is analogous to thinking. It is the body's way of thinking that penetrates things of the world. For the sense of temperature, coldness is *like* the uninhibited flow of the soul within the body into the things of the world; warmth is *like* the uninhibited soul within the substance of things, flowing into the body.

With the three higher senses considered in this text—the senses of hearing, speech, and thought—something new enters. Reading, studying, and then meditating what Steiner says concerning these senses and the interactions involved can lead to profound experiences. For here again we are not alone but constantly cared for and helped by very specific spiritual beings. With the sense of hearing we are given the help of angels, who lend their own soul substance so that we can hear. Hearing is thus a truly spiritual sense. In the case of the speech sense, we are given the help of archangels, who lend their own soul substance to help us understand human speech. And with the thought sense, it is the Christ Being, whom Steiner also calls the "Universal Human," who makes possible our access to the thoughts of others in an immediate and sensory way.

In working toward a "psychology of the body" (which is only incipient in this text), it is necessary to understand such terms as *etheric body, astral body, sentient soul, comprehension soul, consciousness soul,* and *sentient body,* none of which are explained in the text. These terms are explained in many of Steiner's other works, and will not be explained here.[5] In keeping with the earlier sections of this introduction, however, it is important to refrain from a static understanding of these concepts.

Most importantly, however, it should have become apparent through these descriptive ways of speaking about the body that the body in its fullness is not something visible. The etheric body is invisible to ordinary perception, as is the astral body. These "bodies" should not be considered separate from the body we are, but as the more-than-physical aspects of embodiment. This is also true of the other terms. Furthermore, the body is not just the completed product that we see. In fact, the body-as-completed, finished organism is an illusion. The body, as considered from an inner perspective by Steiner, is at every moment in the process

---

5   See the chapters on the makeup of the human being in *Theosophy* and *An Outline of Esoteric Science.*

of coming into being and moving out of being. The same forces that form each of the sense processes at the same time form what we might term the "extended" or true body.

We have come to live in our bodies according to the medical-scientific concept of the body. The medical view of the body is based on the anatomy of a corpse and on the physiology of a dismembered human body. Consequently, we must imagine soul and spirit back into our own living being. In this way, we can regain a soul-sense of embodiment. If we approach the lectures on sensing and the body with this need in mind, they can help to awaken the long-forgotten reality of our embodiment. Soul and spirit are not some kind of invisible entities lurking around as ghosts in a machine; the body is ensouled and inspirited through and through. But, to properly understand such a statement, we must keep in mind the body as more invisible than visible.

Our living body is not self-enclosed. The body opens to the surrounding world and is in a constant interchange with it. We take in the world at every moment—not only through the sense processes but also through the life processes. At every moment we return ourselves to the world—not only, for example, through breathing, but also through the activity of sensing. This activity of sensing moves from the exterior nearest the soul (i.e., the immediate body), through an increasing penetration into the world, and finally to a bodily sensing of the soul/spirit being of others. Thus, the living body is more like an open field of forces. However, we must understand such forces in terms of the soul and spirit, and not merely in terms of the physical.

Not only is the body open as a field to the earthly realm, but it is also open to the cosmic world. The body is sensible; it can be sensed in very subtle ways by others. It also senses; it is capable of great knowledge without the use of concepts. The dynamic, full soul/spirit body described by Steiner cannot be conceived of as an object in the world—for example, the way a rock exists as an object in the world. The body, in the mobility of its ongoing soul and spirit processes—its animation, its sensing, its relationship to formative forces and the spiritual worlds—is through and through a *time body*. We do not just exist in time; we are a part of the very fabric of time, and a part of the very fabric of pure spirit activity.

The body, in its relationship to the sentient body, sentient soul, consciousness soul, and astral body, is always and in every moment thoroughly an expressive body. It is not true that we have a body that can also have certain kinds of expressions, such as sadness, joy, anger, and so on. Expression is body; it is body in its emotional and soul aspect.

CONCLUDING QUESTIONS

You might consider *A Psychology of Body, Soul, and Spirit* to be too high, too steep for you. It may not seem to answer your immediate and pressing questions. You may ask, does this book, in fact, present any therapeutic application for understanding the body, soul, and spirit? What does any of this have to do with real people, with people who are suffering? True, this book does not suggest any technical tricks. But therapeutic psychology should not consist of concepts to be used as a bag of tools that a practitioner applies. A perceived need for such "practical" tools is simply a sign of psychological immaturity. Therapy does not, or should not, consist of doing anything. Rather, it is an act of remembering the fullness of soul life and the soul's involvement with spirit, and *remembering* the fullness of the soul and spirit fabric of embodiment.

The concepts in this book cannot perhaps be brought directly into the therapeutic situation. But the real therapist in the consulting room must always be able to engage in the art of improvisation—soul in the moment. To improvise, one must really know, understand, and live soul life—one must be able to live it consciously and from within. For this, a true soul education is needed. Unfortunately, however, that kind of education has gone out of psychology. Nevertheless, this book can serve as an extremely valuable starting point for this much needed self-education.

A final question, based on the radically new insights of this book, asks: Shouldn't we abandon the term and field of *psychology* altogether and start something new? We might call it "psychosophy." Indeed, there might be a great temptation to do exactly this in some quarters of Anthroposophy. I think this would be a great mistake. Anthroposophy has the opportunity, especially in the field of psychology, to engage a much wider world. It has an opportunity to bring something new and valuable to the field of psychology. I cannot imagine that anyone would wish to confine the considerations of soul life as developed in this book to the small sector of people interested only in Anthroposophy. It is more likely, on the other hand, that the understanding of soul life as presented here—if made available to all serious students of psychology— would result in a much wider interest in Anthroposophy.

14

GIVE US THIS DAY
THE STORY OF PRAYER

RUFUS GOODWIN

THE SOUL IN PRAYER: PSYCHOLOGICAL REFLECTIONS ON THE VOCATIVE RELATION

Praying seems to be something that we do in much the same way as we converse with another person. But there is a difference. Instead of establishing a relationship with another person, as we do in ordinary conversation, in prayer we establish a relationship with a spiritual being—an angel, a saint, Christ, Mary, or God. Hence, when we consider the prayers that have been formulated throughout history, as Rufus Goodwin does in this book, they all seem to have the characteristic of being addressed to another. They are "vocative." They seem to be a recitation—out loud or in silence—of words addressed to a spiritual being. Similarly, when we make up our own prayers, we seem to be addressing some invisible being, whom we believe to be present and able to hear what we are saying.

Yet the context of prayer is not really ordinary conversation but conversation that takes place explicitly *through the depth of the soul*. This introduction, therefore, explores the concerns of soulful conversation, how it takes place, and what actually happens.

I am not a theologian or a historian of religion. I approach this subject—so well treated by Rufus Goodwin—not as an "expert in the field," but as a researcher, a phenomenologist, of soul life with a particular interest in the ways we reach out from the depths of the soul to embrace all that awaits us in the spiritual worlds. Thus, I shall try not to say anything about praying that cannot be verified by careful observation of what actually occurs in an interior way when we pray. My purpose here is simply to encourage conscious engagement with the soul life while praying. One would think that such encouragement would be unnecessary and that surely the soul is engaged when we pray. But I suspect that the soul is usually no more engaged in prayer than in any other aspect of modern life. What is more, we can fool ourselves more easily in this area than any other. Piety, intensity of emotion, a stance of devotion, belief—all these would seem to be qualities of soul. These qualities are certainly good and beneficial. But they do not necessarily indicate *presence* of soul. Prayer can easily be soulless. This is the possibility I want to work against.

Why do I say that prayer is an act of the soul rather than an act of the spirit? Consider the difference between praying and meditating. Meditation may begin with the soul, but it moves toward, or into, the spirit. For example, suppose I begin to meditate on Sophia—divine feminine Wisdom—by concentrating on the inner image of Sophia described in the Apocalypse of St. John: a woman, standing on the crescent of the Moon, clothed in the rays of the Sun, and wearing a crown of twelve stars. To meditate this image means focusing on it so intensely that I no longer feel my own body or my emotional state or other thoughts. All that is present is a kind of inner presence of the reality I am meditating.

On the other hand, I might *pray* to Sophia by saying something like: "O, Sophia, Holy Soul of the World, give us the blessing of your almighty Wisdom; may Your presence guide us toward the unity of Heaven and Earth." When I pray in this way, I do not have the same kind of experience as I do when meditating.

I do not lose the sense of my body's presence, and a certain kind of emotion may become very intense. The one similarity with meditation is that, if other thoughts intrude while I pray, then prayer does not go well, just as my meditation suffers when extraneous thoughts intrude.

Prayer as an act of the soul requires that we refrain from quickly rattling off a string of words. Each word, when savored, relished, and spoken as a treasure evokes an image, or perhaps several images. We always know that we are in the domain of soul when we experience the presence of an image. Thought also belongs to the realm of the soul, as does feeling. Nonetheless, it is image that reveals soul activity most clearly. From the soul's perspective, the art of prayer consists of making ourselves available to the images present in the words spoken. We learn how to do this by understanding how images work, and how prayer is the perfect interweaving—within the word—of thought, image, and feeling.

Prayer, then, speaks the language of soul in images. But these images are not simply present, waiting only to be completed by our words. Were this the case, praying would be mechanical, as it is when we thought-lessly repeat the words of our prayer. When we are more present to what we are saying in an interior way, the images and the words form a kind of to-and-fro relationship in which the words give birth to images that *change the quality of the words we speak*. The words and the images go together. The images are not arbitrary, nor are the words and the images external to each other. Therefore, in thinking of prayer, it is better to try to conceive of a "word-image" field—a *gestalt*, or whole—with two different aspects, rather than thinking of word and image as separate. The words do not merely touch off unrelated fantasies of images; rather, a reverberation occurs between the words and the images.

Image might imply that, as you pray, some kind of vivid picture should arise with each word. Sometimes, in fact, there may be images of this sort. More often, however, the image is not pictorial but a "word-image," an inner echo of the words, as they are spoken outwardly. If we pay attention, we can feel in this echo an incredible seemingly unending depth in what we are saying. This depth can extend to the point that the words seem no longer to come from me as I know myself to be. It is as if a being within me were speaking. The literal words may feel quite flat in comparison, but not when praying, since a reverberation occurs in prayer that changes the quality of the literal words.

Praying is not just something that we do; praying is something we enter. One aspect of entering is hearing the resonant quality of the words that we speak. This reverberation has to do with image. Another aspect of prayer as the language of the soul has to do with repetition. Why do we repeat the same prayer over and over—the rosary, the Jesus prayer, even our own private prayers? Repetition, too, is related to soul speaking the language of image. In ordinary conversation, we say something once and expect the hearer to hear and understand what was said. From this point of view, it might seem strange that prayers are repeated. God certainly hears the first time and, in fact, hears before anything is said, hears from eternity. So the repetition of a prayer is not needed to get our point across.

One might be tempted to think that repetition makes praying into a kind of ritual or that repetition places the person praying into a kind of trance state. But, if we stay with simply trying to describe the soul nature of praying, we find another aspect of the logic of image. An image, for instance, is not flat like a picture painted on a canvas. An image is simultaneously the canvas, the painting, *and* the painter. When we repeat a prayer, much more is involved than a repetition of the image. In the first place, there is the world from which we pray—the ordinary world of speaking the prayer; then there is the soul world into which our speaking reverberates and from which it reverberates back into the language we speak. These worlds operate according to different laws, and it is a function of prayer to bring these two worlds into a particular relationship to each other.

If you give close attention to the act of praying and acquire the ability to experience the reverberation to and from the soul world then, while repeating a prayer, you will begin to notice another aspect of the resonance of the image. The prayer will not be the same each time it is spoken. Very subtle differences occur. If you pay attention to these you will notice something like a "thinning" of the image. Finding the right words to describe this quality is not easy. The process seems to be something like making a painting first with acrylic and then, perhaps, with pastels, and then again with watercolors, and then with even lighter watercolors—and so on. This refining process continues to unfold as we pray. One cannot put a number to how many times a prayer must be said before such a refining can occur, or say how long one would have to pray for it to become fully evident. It certainly seems possible that, as long as we are saying a prayer and repeating it, a further refining of image occurs. It is important to develop the capacity to experience this kind of subtlety when we pray.

At the same time, we must also begin to acquire a feeling for the presence of a different reality. This "different reality" is unimaginably deep. From the perspective of ordinary consciousness, the act of repeating words can be boring and frustrating and seem to go in circles—in fact, to go around the same circle. But from the point of view of the soul, the soul's very nature is *depth*. When you are in soul, you step into depth only to find more depth, and more depth, and more depth. How do you know you are going into depth? You recognize it because of the subtle variations. There is no separate, "ordinary" world, with a boundary between it and the image (the soul world), so that when you cross that boundary, you are in the soul world. Entering the soul world is not like crossing the border between two countries. Crossing the boundary between the ordinary world and the soul world is more like going from a place where things are sharp and clear to a place that is more like mist. As you gradually find your way into the mist, however, you discover that it is not just one homogenous blank cloud. There are subtle variations, which you begin to notice because to do so is the only way to find your way in this new, unfamiliar world. Repetition of a prayer acknowledges that we are attempting to give ourselves over to a different reality. It educates us into the unfamiliar reality of the soul world.

Another aspect of repetition is that through such repetitions we begin to dissolve our habitual, analytic mode of consciousness. We work against everything within us that demands explanations and wants to know what is going on and be in control. We bring a life problem or difficulty into prayer not in order to get a literal answer or a solution, but to take this hard-edged, impenetrable difficulty and put it into a medium where it will *dissolve*. Much of our difficulty is related to the way we approach life's circumstances, a way that is probably analytical. Or perhaps we have come up against something that defies an analytic attitude. Under such circumstances, it is perhaps best to simply sit and pray, over and over. This takes our linear consciousness and bends it into a spiral. When we question prayer—for example, by asking whether our prayers are really answered—we have fallen back into our ordinary, analytic mentality.

In the act of praying, we move from a world that is direct and seemingly evident to one that operates according to laws of *indirection*. Repeated entry to a world of indirection gradually educates us to perceive more of the qualities of indirection in everyday life. Therefore, it is unnecessary to know whether our prayers are being answered. Life itself begins to be the answer. As long as we approach prayer as though we were sending a message to God and were then waiting for a specific, direct response, we subjugate the soul in prayer to the laws of the ordinary world. Praying depends on developing a taste for the soul world. We begin to savor life's subtle nuances and begin to rid ourselves of the illusion of solutions.

To be relieved of the ego's desire for a solution to every problem does not mean that prayer changes nothing in life. Quite the contrary. It changes us. It does not bring a literal solution to our problem but develops new capacities in us. Above all, it develops the capacity to see a problem in more than one way, and to see that we were stuck because we were set on one way of looking—one without imagination.

Image-reverberation and repetition—these two qualities considered together deepen and take us more fully into the spiritual worlds and help provide a sense of the emotion of prayer. When we pray we do not move away from emotion as we do when we meditate. But our experience of the emotion of prayer is not the same as our experience of emotions such as grief, gratitude, love, and so on. Life's emotions tend to be more sudden, more violent, more overpowering than emotion in prayer. Certainly, while we pray, the emotions behind our reasons for praying may arise, but these emotions are not the same as those involved in praying itself.

Life's emotion comes from experiences brought from the past. When we bring emotion to the moment of prayer, it meets with the current of soul-image and, as these encounter each other, they form a kind of whirlpool. Any emotion we may have brought to the moment of prayer thereby takes on a quality of deep reverence. When we begin praying, we may experience an overwhelming feeling—for instance, we may feel grief or joy resulting from something that has happened in our life. These emotions do not go away but are held in a new kind of space, one that gives them room to breathe.

Of course, we do not have to be in an emotional state to pray. Prayer creates its own emotional realm by bringing us to a recollection of ourselves. For a while, we are not spread out and torn in all directions by the outer world. When we put aside intellectual cleverness, willfulness, and even our ideals and aspirations, we begin to experience an inner feeling-tone, a kind of abiding warmth. This quality of warmth belongs to the soul realm. It is not something that we do or bring about.

The emotion of prayer thus has its own particular quality that transforms any emotions we bring to the moment of praying. This particular quality of emotion in prayer can also be described. Ordinarily, when we suffer an emotion in life, we are quite alone in our experience. But when an emotion takes hold of a group of people, then the individuality of the experience is completely lost and the whole group is taken over by something more than themselves. In praying, although we are "alone," there is the special and extraordinary circumstance in which we suffer a particular emotion, but the pressure of it, the way it can overwhelm us is lifted up and we feel our emotion being held by an invisible presence. This presence does not take our emotion from us, does not resolve it, but helps us to carry it. This experience is different from empathy or compassion or the experience of someone simply listening to us; *our emotion is held but not taken away, which transforms it.* As long as it remains untransformed, what we feel just sits there—like a shapeless lump. It may be a heavy lump, as in sorrow, or a light lump, as in joy. In prayer, however, it is illuminated. There is light in it, a light that we do not put there but feel as an actual, living presence.

We may describe this experience as a kind of listening or hearing. In ordinary conversation, when I talk to someone, I speak, and then I listen to hear the other person's response. Likewise, in prayer, the soul speaks its own language of reverberation, repetition, and affection. At the same time, it listens. But in the image-space of prayer, the binary, two-way relationship of speaking and listening does not exist. If I say the "Our Father," it is not as if I were saying something and then had to wait to hear a response. As we pray, the reverberation, repetition, and warmth of feeling take us into a world where the kind of separations we live in ordinary life do not exist. When we step into prayer we are with another presence, but in a way different from the one we are in when, for example, we are in the presence of another person. The presence in prayer is not "over there." The implication is not, however, that this presence is necessarily within me or that, in prayer, there is a divine presence within me.

To speak of this presence thus takes us to the most mysterious aspect of prayer.

It is important to note that in praying we do not move out of ourselves. If anything, we go deeper into ourselves. But then an odd thing happens. In going deeper within ourselves, we lose our subjectivity. The inner space of the praying is one in which the presence I address encompasses my own subjectivity, without in any way taking away my freedom or making me feel invaded.

Once I can feel this presence while praying, the whole question of whether or not my prayers are answered completely disappears. This question arises only when we have not sufficiently stepped out of our stance of egotism that still wants something in a purely personal way.

The presence of the spiritual beings to whom we address our prayers do not, I think, make an inner appearance because we summon them. Prayer is not a magical act of conjuring. "Oh, Lord," "Our Father," "Hail Mary," or "Dear God" may seem like summoning a presence, a divine being, but they are not commands. They are words of *praise*. Every prayer begins with praise, and every prayer is an act of praise. If we take the language of prayer, and look at it as human language on the one hand, and as the language of the soul on the other, the words with which we begin praying do two things. On the side of ordinary speaking, we begin every prayer by announcing our humbleness—with an act of humility that, so to speak, puts us in our proper place. But these same words, from the soul point of view, are words of praise, words that speak the glory of the spiritual presence we address. *Praise is what the soul does in prayer.* Whether we pray in supplication, thanksgiving, sorrow, joy, in all instances the archetypal gesture of the soul is praise.

Seen from the side of the soul, praise is not the same as when, for example, I tell someone how wonderful she is. Ordinary praise is but a shadowy reflection of the soul's praise in prayer. The soul's praise is not found in the meaning of the words, but in the gesture of the soul that recollects us, without at the same time becoming self-enclosed. As we come to ourselves, our soul turns outward, which forms the basic tone of every prayer as the tone of praise.

Praise. What a wonderful word! To praise is to ascribe glory. Typically, this is done through song. In prayer, all souls sing. Indeed, from the viewpoint of the soul, all prayer is in the image of song. You can feel this tonal quality of song every time you pray. Even though you may be saying words, at the deeper level of soul, the reverberating that I spoke of occurs as a kind of song—with rhythm, melody, and, when we pray well, harmony.

Everything said thus far concerning the soul in prayer leads to the conclusion that any speaking, carried out in the way I have described, would count as prayer of some sort. At the same time, it is not hard to imagine that, if this is prayer, then there can be some kinds of praying that are very dangerous and detrimental. One can, of course, pray to detrimental spiritual presences without knowing it. Thus, it is not a question of the words, but of our relationship to them. It is not what we pray, or whom we address through the content of our prayer that determines whether our praying leads us to a relationship with helpful spiritual presences or with beings that are not helpful at all (even when they seem to be). The prayer by itself does not insure the right connection.

Every modern person wishing to develop a prayer life must face this dilemma, which never existed before. Two new circumstances exist today—the simultaneous strengthening of the psychological ego and the radical decline of soul life. These psychic circumstances of our time make the art of praying different from what it ever was before. We now have to confront the question. Do the words we speak in prayer in fact form a relation with those to whom they are addressed? In the past, this question was irrelevant because soul life was intact and human beings were not as egotistical as they are now. One did not have to be aware of the soul's place in prayer. It was there quite naturally. During prayer, one might have had to battle other beings who would come to insert themselves into the soul, but the soul was naturally oriented toward the spiritual worlds.

If there is no awareness, no actual experience of the soul and its activity during prayer, then, when we pray, our words can be usurped by any spiritual presence at all. Why? Because we are not fully present in what we are doing. We may think that we are, but without a direct and immediate sense of the soul, our praying will inevitably become egotistical, even though we may think it is not. Without some sense of soul, we are most likely speaking only to ourselves when we pray. Certainly we have no assurance that our words address who we think they do. You may ask: Does not the content of the words assure that the intended relationship is formed? Perhaps; but only under one condition—that we engage in a particular kind of *thinking*.

That is, to pray we need more than image, repetition, and emotion in prayer. We also need a particular way of thinking. This way of thinking does not think about what I am saying when I pray, but rather thinks within the words I say. If I pray, for example, that someone be brought to health, I would be distracted if I started thinking about that person and all he or she is going through while I was praying. I can do that between prayers, but not during prayer itself. Nor, while praying, do I need to consider the meaning of the words I am saying. If I say the "Our Father," I do not think about what it means to address God as "Father" while I am saying it. That would be an attempt to be analytical while I pray. But there is another kind of thinking. We can think *within* the words themselves as we pray. The best way I can describe this thinking is that it is as if each word is created the moment it is spoken. A different, more conscious relation to language then occurs. Ordinarily, we are not very conscious at all in our speech. We just speak words, and alongside our words there are thoughts or emotions. And if our emotions are reverent and our thoughts are holy, we think that we are praying.

It is a blessing that we are not conscious in our speech in ordinary life. Trying to be conscious there would be like trying to be conscious of every movement we make—we would stumble and fall. For example, when I say the word *Lord* in ordinary conversation, I cannot be aware of forming the *L*, the *O*, the *R*, the *D*. In prayer, however, we must begin to develop a kind of word-consciousness in which our words and thoughts do not exist side by side, with words acting only as instruments through which we convey our intentions, thoughts, and feelings.

We should become poets when we pray. The ideal of praying is that during the time of prayer everything within us becomes "word." Our thinking, our emotions, our imagination all become centered in the word, so much so that we become word. When we recollect ourselves in prayer, it takes place through the word, and exists in the word, the fully embodied word.

The importance of the word in prayer—the word as prayer—is not a matter of theory. When we experience the life of the soul in prayer, a new attention, a new light begins to shine on language, on the words we speak. In the word-image field—as the image side of the field becomes more conscious—the word aspect of the polarity also changes. The words we speak in prayer begin to be more sensuous, even erotic. As we pray, even silently, the words no longer come, so to speak, out of the head; the whole body speaks, our body becomes a sonorous instrument. In this moment, soul embraces body and we are lifted, but not separated, from the materiality of our being into the body of love.

When language can be felt resonating through the body rather than being only a kind of instrument—a means for expressing our intentions, thoughts, and desires—then we are in the body of love. In praying, this deepening sense of language occurs as a presence to the tonal quality of the words we are saying. This presences moves into the foreground as the semantic element of the words, while not yet disappearing, moves more into the background.

When we experience our own body in its sonorous quality, we discover ourselves as a musical instrument. Through prayer, we discover that we are musical instruments. The words that we pray are the music of this instrument. But there is more. When we pray, if we listen closely to the music of the words playing through our body, we have the distinct feeling that we are not alone as we pray. It is as if we have joined a chorus of singing. Because it is so unified, one must be fairly astute to detect this chorus: it is almost like a single voice. Then, too, one must be able to place the content of the words one is saying in the background and pay more attention to the tones that resonate through the body. When one can do this, a quality can be heard that shows that we are joined by an invisible chorus when we pray.

We can tell that we are in connection with the one we address in our prayers by the presence of a multiplicity of voices praying with us. This quality demonstrates in a most convincing way that, when I truly pray, I am joined with something beyond myself.

This experience is one of beauty. When we pray we do not pray alone but we join a community of prayer. This should not be taken literally. When I pray in this way, however, the community of the praying that I join is not somewhere else reciting these same words. It sings the same song with me.

I think that the community of praying we join is the community of the angels. It is never just God and me, or Mary and me, or Sophia and me. It is our egotism that imagines a direct e-mail connection with the spirits. The only corrective for such vanities is that prayer works through the medium of the angels, and in order to join them we must search for and find the singing nature of our own angelic aspect.

We cannot, however, go directly to the angelic aspect of our being. We must come first into the soul aspect. As we have seen, this is not so easy. Then, from the soul aspect, we must rediscover the body—the mysterious, powerful wisdom of the body which is far more than our physiology. Finally, through the body, we discover the musical dimensions of language and the word that play through us.

But why pray at all? The usual answer to this, given by theologians, is that we pray to praise God, to ask for something we need, to give thanks, or to repent. When we ask this same question from the viewpoint of the soul, however, the answer is different. *What the soul seeks in prayer is prayer.* This is not a circular argument but good spiritual psychology. Prayer seeks a relationship with prayer, and finds this by gradually opening to the chorus of prayer. At the moment this happens and we move from a sense of being solitary to finding that our praying belongs to a much larger context—which itself is prayer, the constant prayer of the cosmos—our prayers are answered.

If through prayer we can gradually move out of our isolation and begin to have moments when we enter the larger reality of prayer, then these moments begin to change the way we live. Where, exactly, is the dividing line that separates the earthly, physical world from the soul world and the soul world from the spiritual world? Where are these beings who are singing, singing, singing praise every moment?

Well, if we could truly live in a conscious way in the soul, we would perceive that everything, up to the human being and the fabrications made by human beings are, in their very existence, acts of prayer, prayer in action. Look at the natural world; look at it through the eyes of the soul. Is there anything there that is not a song of praise? In order to see that all of the natural world is a prayer, however, we must look at it, not from the outside, as spectators, but from the inside, as manifold gestures of the soul of the world. The birds chirping at the crack of dawn; the ant scurrying across the kitchen table; the deer visiting our yard at the close of the day; the soft breeze playing through the birch trees; the blue of the sky; the flow of the streams: All of the world is a prayer because all of the world is of soul. In the world, you will find all of the qualities spoken of earlier—repetition, image, feelings—and a kind of thinking, the wisdom of the world. The world, seen and spoken of in this way, is none other than the prayer of the World.

We have the capacity to refuse to pray, as well as the capacity to make a world of things that refuse to pray. This refusal occurs first when we turn away from and lose the actual experience of soul. Then, we may seem to pray, but in fact it is no longer possible to pray. For prayer is the fundamental gesture of the soul. It is what the soul does, the ground and principle of all its other activities such as imaging, feeling, thinking, willing. Thus, one cannot help but pray as long as there is a sense of soul. Recovering prayer is the same as recovering soul, and recovering soul is the same as recovering prayer. But, soul is narrowed and misunderstood when confined to individual human beings and excluded from the surrounding world.

In this book, Rufus Goodwin has begun the work of returning prayer to the soul. Hence, speaking on behalf of soul, I welcome it as a valuable contribution to the return of soul and spirit to the world.

15

THE BOOK OF STONES:
WHO THEY ARE AND WHAT THEY TEACH

ROBERT SIMMONS AND NAISHA AHSIAN
WITH CONTRIBUTIONS BY HAZEL RAVEN

This extraordinarily beautiful book, by its title, *The Book of Stones,* softly and without fanfare, but with immense truth, announces that this writing comes directly from the stones themselves, is of them, not an imposed, conceptual theory about stones written from a non-soul-engaged perspective. Of the myriad books now available about gems and minerals and their metaphysical properties, this work is both the base and the crown. There is something different, very different about the book you hold in your lap. (It may be a little too heavy to hold for very long in your hands; but, after all, stones are supposed to be heavy.) The love, care, precision, beauty, embrace, depth and height that characterize this writing and the very design of the book itself resounds a new, emerging form of spiritual metaphysics; an engaged metaphysics, one that dissolves the separation between the properties of the stones and a passiveness of the stone-holder; a radical departure from the usual kind of spiritual metaphysics that expects to get something without giving very much.

This book, by the very way it is written and presented, boldly declares that working with stones beckons us to an I/Thou meeting rather than expecting the goodies to come pouring in the moment a purchase is made. The spiritual-metaphysical properties of stones as listed in the book are more "the promise," spoken by the stones, of what could happen if we approach them as living beings. We can obscure and severely limit this most basic dimension of stonework if we take the many attempts to put the intimacy of a soul connection with stones into scientific terms and then proceed to take those terms naively and literally.

To take what is promised by the stones literally would trap us in a terrible kind of materialism. It is their promise and has to be heard and felt on their terms, not in terms of our personality needs. For example, if a stone promises prosperity, to take that offering literally is to abuse the speaking of the stone, for "prosperity" spoken in an intimate relationship cannot possibly mean, "you are going to make me materially rich." If I say to a dear friend, lovingly, with all my heart, "I wish you prosperity," I am not saying, you will become materially wealthy because we are related. I am saying that because of our intimacy, your soul prospers and the world shines brighter.

The new work proposed in this writing begins, at last, to go beyond needing backing by science on the one hand and practices from the past on the other hand. Just as the human being emanates an electromagnetic field, so too do stones. However, I never relate with another person as soul-being in terms of an electromagnetic field, and the attempt to be scientific can obscure the mystery of our meeting in an effort to make it more acceptable to those who cannot understand loving a stone. It is time to roll the stone out of the closet! There is the unmistakable presence, a Who, that accompanies every stone with which we establish a relationship. And the connection is spiritual while being completely within matter. Here, by working in depth with stones, the age-old and false division between spirit and matter is demonstrated as wrong each moment we really take the time to notice what is happening while holding a stone. Matter's spirit and soul reveals itself to us in utmost particularity. Sometimes we are shocked and are thrown into tears with the overwhelming recognition of the soul of matter. Sometimes we simply feel that it is going to take time for the relating to develop.

Just as the scientific understanding of what happens when we hold, carry, meditate with a stone is not to be taken literally, neither are the references to spiritual/occult systems such as shamanism, alchemy, or occult lore to be taken as fact. The two, when de-literalized, are saying that the range of the felt-sense of a relationship with a stone simultaneously spans the whole of the outer cosmos and the whole of the inner worlds, which are, after all, one. Stones, in other words, are the most perfect tool in the entire universe for simultaneous world and self-understanding. Scientific explanations are a metaphor for the outer dimension of the relationship, and magical explanations are a metaphor for the inner dimensions. The science metaphors impress upon us that matter matters, and the occult metaphors impress upon us that all matter is ensouled. It is time, though, if work with stones is to move to the next level of what can happen, to move away from dualistic mentality and move toward more adequate imaginations such as "resonances," "fields," "currents," "emerging," "interactive unfolding, "wholeness," and a host of other, more descriptive and thus truer senses of what is happening. The philosopher Martin Heidegger said that any explanation can only go so far as the explication of the phenomenon. A wonderful notion. In the case of stones, the explanations tend to be way, way ahead of the explications. To explicate, means simply to fully be present with, to listen inwardly and intently, and describe the phenomenon from within the phenomenon itself. Here lies the precise manner in which this book is both base and crown of all books on the mineral worlds. More, much more time is spent with explication than with explanation. That is, you have the chance to meet the stones, intimately, closely, soul-fully, before trying to explain how they do what they do.

Each stone works simultaneously in three ways, at three levels—a physical level, a soul level, and a spirit level. There is nothing theoretical or speculative with this suggestion; it is wholly a matter of noticing. In order to meet at the physical level, empathy of openness is required. We have to suspend judgment, see what is here before us without preconceptions, and be able to be perceptually present with a simultaneous focused and diffused attention, to see the stone in its particularity, with focus, and to see also its relations with its world-surroundings, with diffuse attention. To meet at the soul level requires more; we have to be present to how a stone goes on exerting its presence when it is no longer physically present. I remember, for example, working with Azeztulite. It took a long time really to see this stone. I thought it at first just a member of the category "quartz," that was supposed to have extraordinary properties. Then, one day, I really looked and saw the sparkling, multifaceted light gleaming from the white depth of this stone. What I previously perceived through known categories disappeared and I saw this stone for the first time, even though it had been in my house for several months. The next morning, when I awoke, there was the inner presence of multitudinous gleaming, glowing lights, and a felt sense of felt-connection with the stone. I knew then, we had moved to a soul level of relating. Then, later, in meditation with the stone, a conscious blending with the inner qualities of the stone took place, such that I could not tell where I ended and the being of the stone began. And, there were endless soft white currents, infinite in depth. At the moment that happened, everything I ever knew about religion and spirit was suddenly gone as I was faced with a spiritual presence that was inexplicable and yet soft. Its presence was nonetheless so powerful that all previous religious categories fell away. I did not know what to expect, nor do I now, as the work seems to be to allow what it wants to unfold.

Stones are not simply commodities to be bought and sold, used and put aside. Just as the alchemists knew there was a relationship between the seven metals and the spiritual beings of the seven planets, and our bodily health, there seems to me to be an intimate relationship between the millions of stones and the spiritual beings of the millions of stars. And, I suspect this relationship has to do with the health of the Earth, that we who find ourselves drawn to stones are called to be servants of the Soul of the World. Our teachers showing us the ways to do this are the stones, and what they have to teach is far, far beyond anything we can possibly imagine. This book is the portal to working with spirit-beings, who through millions of years of development, are embodied Wisdom.

16

Cooking for the Love of the World

Awakening Our Spirituality through Cooking

Anne-Marie Fryer Wiboltt

This highly unusual and oh, so significant writing takes something we all do every day, several times—eating—and helps infuse this act with a deeply reverent and spiritual consciousness. The book accomplishes this intention by brilliantly and beautifully placing food within an understanding of the earthly and cosmic forces of plant life as well as providing exquisite recipes that transform nature into the art of cooking.

It might be helpful to forewarn you just a bit by urging you to work with the whole of the book. Because of our tendency to compartmentalize our actions, there may be a temptation to look upon this book as two books rather than one—a book on the spirituality of food and a practical cookbook. But Anne-Marie is very clear in what she is doing with this writing. She helps us perceive our bodies, our lives, the world around us, and the larger universe as a whole form of multiple, related activities that come together in miraculous ways through the act of eating. Until we can consciously enter into the miracle of food, we are lost in one popular speculation after another concerning how to eat.

Miraculous is a good word, one I want to introduce as describing the experience you enter as you read this book. The wealth of information that is now available concerning nutrition, calories, carbohydrates, and the thousands of diets available to help us achieve some notion of health and ideal figure, goes beyond anyone's capacity to comprehend. What has been lacking until now is an entirely new way of understanding food and eating. And gosh, no, not another theory that takes on the status of a trend that will change in a year or two!

This writing is far more radical than that. It invites us into the joy of paying attention to the magnificent beauty of nature, not as some brief ecstatic moment of experience, but carefully, lovingly, and continually. As we do so, over time, we develop an entirely new relation to food because we have overcome the spectator perspective and become engaged with being intimately interwoven with the world and, indeed, with the cosmos.

By far the most significant aspect of paying this kind of new attention to the natural world in relation to food and eating is to begin, slowly, to live into the element of rhythm that characterizes the movements of the cosmos, the Earth, and the human body. The rhythms of the days, the seasons, the years, of morning, noon, evening, of waking and sleeping, and of expansion and contraction, intertwine with the rhythms of plant life. These natural rhythms and their relationships one to another are severely disrupted, so it is hardly surprising that pathologies of eating are rampant, ranging from the obvious epidemic of obesity to the more secret epidemics of anorexia and bulimia. Neither psychological answers nor fewer carbs nor fast-food lettuce and tomatoes, rather than fast-food hamburgers, are likely to do much, because all of these ways of trying to address eating pathologies neglect the necessary element of *rhythm*. More than anything else, this book is about refinding our place in the great natural motions of the cosmos as manifested in the growth of the foods we eat. Eating can be a way of coming home to our place within the cosmos.

The kind of language I am using to open the door to your reading is quite different than the mode of speaking you will find within these pages. Anne-Marie is a gifted writer because she is a gifted observer. There is a term for this kind of engaged, loving, participant observation. It is called phenomenology. The intent of this kind of observing is to allow the phenomenon to reveal itself rather than imposing our constructs and theories in order to understand. This book is full of this kind of observing, and as you read, you will find yourself taken back into the world as it appeared when you were a child—except then you perhaps did not have the words to describe the wonders and mysteries of the unfolding of the plant world.

There is a kind of second innocence to this writing, and for that reason you can trust it without reservation. There is no attempt to convince you of the merits of this way of looking at the world, at food, and at eating. The phenomenon itself convinces, once you can see.

This holistic approach to food is why you must read the book as a whole. If you simply go to the recipes and try them, it is likely that you will soon move on to others in other places. If, however, you study the writing, you will feel the wonders of the world, and the recipes will be flavored by the devoted attention that you now give to the world.

You are about to be refreshingly astounded by a writing on food that concentrates on qualities rather than quantities. There is no mention anywhere in this book about how many calories you should take in or how many carbohydrates. The living world is a world of exquisite and particular qualities. The world of the dead is the world of quantities. Thus, we cannot be nourished by theories of eating that are founded on the imagination of dead things. When we do embrace such views about food and find some results for a while, we are equally astounded to find that the pounds eventually come back. Materialistic approaches to nutrition, food, and dieting can only yield concern for quantities, to the point of obsession. These approaches to food are part of the problem of commodification that they try to address and cannot solve, because the theories of these approaches, which concentrate on food as commodity, exist at the same level as the problem.

When we think of spirituality or "being spiritual," we tend to think of how to be less of this world and more part of a nonmaterial realm. That kind of spirituality does not characterize this book. And, it is true, when you do find nutritional interests among spiritually oriented folk, there is something that tends to be just a little bit wispy about those interests. Often the notion is that it is necessary to purify the body in order to be spiritual. Or it is necessary to refrain from eating meat and meat products in order to be fully spiritual.

The notion of the spiritual realms that you will find in this writing is much more embracing of the world. While the pollution and contamination of foods is certainly something that this book tries to get us to move away from, that has to do with the way in which food has been deadened before it gets to the table, deadened by chemical fertilizers, genetically engineered seeds, and chemical preservatives. But the fullness of the world and all that is offered by nature as gift is embraced. What we are given here is food and eating as everyday festival.

A very important transition is made in this writing as Anne-Marie moves carefully from descriptions of plants and the natural world to the art of cooking. The core of this art is to consciously work with the rhythms of the natural world, to intensify them into smell, touch, and taste in such a manner that we are taken even further into being a part of world-rhythm. There is a radical secret here—namely, that if we cook and eat reverently, not with false piety, but genuinely experiencing the cosmic processes of expansion and contraction in the preparation of food, then we are serving the world in our eating. Imagine that! Eating can be renewing for the Earth, not just for ourselves! It makes perfect sense. If we are bodily deadened by what and how we eat, then we will perceive the world as mere objects to be used to keep the engine running. If, on the other hand, we see the world in its living activity, feel the connection of this life to the life of the body, and prepare food and eat in relation to these living qualities, we will perceive the Earth as a living being: embodied ecology.

While I may seem to pit the artistic qualities of this book against the harsh, quantitative approach of scientific nutrition, I do not intend to oppose art and science. In fact, the kind of observations that fill this book, in many ways, satisfy the most basic aspect of science: to observe carefully and clearly without prejudice. The observations of the plant world described herein satisfy this basic tenet of science.

While this writing is without question also artistic, it might be helpful to clarify how I am using the term *artistic*. I use it in two senses with respect to this book. By *artistic*, I first mean that the kind of observation of the natural world, of food, and of eating that characterizes this writing takes place in the realm of feeling. My second use of the term *artistic*, more in keeping with its usual usage, is the way in which the realm of feeling can be taken up in an act of making, which in this book refers primarily to cooking.

The artistic realm is the realm of feeling. Not emotion and not personal feeling as "I feel this way or that way." Feeling is a way of knowing, a kind of cognition, not like the energetic reaction of emotion. We know things through feeling that cannot be known in any other way. Think of any of the arts—painting, music, dance, and all the rest. We know the world through these art forms in ways that cannot be known by intellect alone.

Artistic sensibility, however, is not confined to the well-known and structured arts. It can be applied to anything, especially the world of living beings. The living world is inherently feeling-filled. Feelings first belong to the living world, not to us personally. The feeling of the golden wheat in a field, the feeling of the rolling water over rocks, the feeling of the approach of spring, the feeling of the leafing of the plants, of the deep mystery of the root—these are the ways the world is described in this book.

The Earth, nature, the cosmos is feeling-filled. And if we can attune our feeling life to the feeling qualities of the world, we become, or can become, scientists in the realm of feeling. We have thus combined art and science.

This book does exactly that. Doing so is inherently life-giving and life-supporting. And then, given this new science, we can imagine even more fully the extraordinary art of cooking. Cooking requires an imagination that can inwardly see all of the feeling processes of the natural world, in detail and not just in some vague, sentimental way. Further, the art of cooking requires the capacity to take the feeling elements of the natural world and not only intensify them, but combine them in new ways, ways unheard of in the natural world—ways that enhance nature, renew the qualities of nature, and equally take us into the quite invisible spiritual qualities of nature. This book works in this manner, and when you carefully read it, you will perceive the natural world anew, and your experience of eating will be completely different, enhanced, elevated.

If we follow through the act of eating to what then occurs in the body, we are taken into the realm of metabolism. In spiritual terms, the metabolism of the body concerns the element of the will. While the connection of metabolism, will, and the body is most apparent in the metabolism of the muscles—how we actually move and get around and do things in the world—it holds equally true for the processes of digestion, and also of reproduction. Not only are we nourished by food, but also food determines the quality of our acts of will in the world.

We are not very aware of this connection until the body becomes once again more sensitive. Taking up the practices within this book does result in an increased bodily sensitivity, where it becomes possible to feel the relation between what and how we eat and the ways we relate with others.

While it might first sound somewhat incomprehensible, eating has moral ramifications. The spiritual approach to food taken in this book inevitably takes us in that direction and toward an understanding of planting, growing, cooking, and eating as an essential aspect of a spiritual path.

17

THE UNKNOWN HIERONYMUS BOSCH

KURT FALK

In contrast to every form of art criticism and art history, this writing
teaches us how to enter into the living activity of painting, painting
not as something that we look at, displayed before us, but rather as living spiritual activity that is before and within us at one and the same
time. Even more, this remarkable book you are holding provides a new
and astounding way of spiritual practice—meditation with paintings.
This new form of meditative practice is developed in the most careful
way imaginable. You will find this book an invaluable guide in learning
how to develop picture-attentiveness, a form of perceiving that focuses
awareness with the whole while also noticing particular details. It is not
an analytic form of consciousness; it is something more than mental; it
is a high form of intuition.

The form of the book is somewhat unusual. It consists of a very
detailed text, but somewhat of an outline format. When we received
the text for publication and heard of the story and work of Kurt Falk
from his wife Anne Stockton, we strongly felt that the text should not
be severely edited. Kurt Falk had left this writing where it is at his death.
No one would really be capable of taking up the writing; the mark of
Kurt Falk's inner spirit pervades the work completely. In addition, the
text reads so clearly as it is, and in this form it can be most easily utilized
as a practice manual for meditating with the paintings of Hieronymus
Bosch, as Kurt Falk intended.

Bosch's paintings become a whole new way of questioning—*of
questing*—not in order to find an answer or solve a problem, but rather
as a way of developing the inner capacity of letting things speak for

themselves. That is, working with this book develops the spiritual quest of **listening**. Listening is fundamental to any spiritual practice, but it is even more so to the spiritual path depicted in so many different ways by Hieronymus Bosch.

We are given a very specific inventory of spiritual practices in this writing. The paintings of Hieronymus Bosch are not to be approached as if we were spectators at a gallery, or would-be intellectuals in an art history class, but rather as supplicants entering a holy place, crossing into the space of contemplation. That is, it is the paintings themselves that are the meditative "device," rather than any interpretation of the paintings. The commentaries provided by the author are meditations and are best worked with in that manner. The descriptions of each painting help us to stay with the images, and to let them enter into our soul-being.

Working with painting as a spiritual practice requires something very different than other forms of spiritual practices. This work takes place in the realm of **feeling**. That is, it is necessary to enter into the feeling of the paintings, not what the paintings make us feel. Feeling is an objective realm, perceivable through the region of the heart. All art embodies feeling, but few authors, critics, or historians know how to speak of it, and fewer realize that feeling can be a path of spiritual initiatory practice. As you read this work, try to read it from the stance of feeling. Place your attention in the region of your heart when you look at the pictures of the paintings. Kurt Falk speaks the language of feeling and has found a way to convey this in a cognitively understandable manner. But it is beneficial to take what is spoken in this book into the realm of the heart rather than take the book only as a new and interesting approach to understanding the paintings of Hieronymus Bosch. It is that, of course, and you are completely free to stay at that level with the work, where a great deal can be learned. However, there is much, much more available in what Kurt Falk has given. This "much more" is nothing less than an initiatory path of the feeling life.

From the very first words of this book, it is apparent that Bosch's paintings are instruments of contemplation. Not any contemplation, but the contemplation of Christ. Bosch's paintings are all religious, but they have nothing to do with religion; in fact, many of them are direct criticisms of the corruption of religion that was rampant during his time, and in spite of the fact that many of them were commissioned by churches, the priests never realized that the paintings they received were protests against the degraded state of the church. The Christ that Bosch was concerned with is the imagination of what every human being can become, as well as all that has to be gone through on the way toward becoming a spiritual human being. His concern is the future human being.

This is the sense of Christ that we take into contemplation through the paintings of Bosch. Contemplation here is not as we usually imagine it—an experience of solemnity—but rather contemplation that takes place in such a way that our very bodily constitution alters over time. It is possible, with the help of this book, to go through a body-soul-purifying process.

The word *pure* is certainly fraught with dangers, and I don't mean it in the sense of "untarnished" or some religious notion of that sort. I mean "purification" in the way that Dante understood purification. The word itself refers to the desire regions of the soul.

Dante's *Divine Comedy* exemplifies the path of purification of desire. And I think that Bosch's paintings are in this same genre. In Dante's imagination, *all* desire is good. Desire is like a big net thrown out by God to draw us back to the Divine. The trouble is, we take one desire as the whole of desire at any given time. Dante gives a wonderful picture of desire as a diamond through which a ray of light shines. Desire is the whole of the diamond and all of the rays. We go wrong when we take one facet and one ray as the whole of desire. Bosch's paintings are very much within this kind of imagination of the purification of desire as being present, with intensity, to the fullness of every moment of experience, whatever that might be. He shows us the folly of singularly focused desire; and he shows the fullness of the desire for the Divine.

The outline in the first part of this book of Hieronymus Bosch's paintings is an extraordinarily important contemplative listing. Take it as a spiritual listing, a guide to contemplative practice. If you want to work on purification of the desires, go to one of the paintings concerned with that domain and work with it; if you want to work on the development of the sense of the spiritual "I," go to another painting. And, if you want to enter into spiritual development with care rather than trying out this and that, moving from one thing to another, then work with these paintings, which also show the folly of following those who do not know what they are doing. Or begin to develop the awareness of how much of what seems oriented toward helping our spiritual growth may be removing from us the very possibilities of growth. In fact, working with the paintings can help us awaken to the fact that deception is rampant in the spiritual growth industry. Unless we take our inner awakening into our own hands, we may find ourselves trying one thing after another without any developed critical capacity. The central image for inner spiritual development out of our own forces is the Tree man image visible in several of Bosch's paintings and the central image in the Cairo painting that inspired this writing.

It is completely unnecessary to have all the paintings in front of us as we read this spiritual inventory of spiritual practices, and of those things that can interfere with clear consciousness but which look as if they are providing spiritual service. We may want to look at the paintings, but it is actually good to hold the word descriptions of the paintings given here for a long while. When you do look at the paintings, you will discover that you see them completely differently than if you had gone to the images first. The words are not dictating how we see but are rather a preparation for true seeing.

The paintings of Bosch also teach us how to see spiritual events on their own terms rather than in terms that have been sanctioned by the church and often obscure the more esoteric dimensions of religious practices. There are, of course, many more forms of spirituality than are found within religion, but Bosch even goes beyond any of those. The true secret of Bosch's art is that he depicts the future development of the human capacity to produce spiritual experiences out of one's own inner soul forces. By "one's own inner forces" I am not referring to ordinary ego consciousness but rather to a completely conscious spiritual individuality.

The soul of the author is obviously deeply engaged with the artistic work, and thus our soul also resonates with this engagement and we begin to notice details while never losing a sense of the whole of each painting, and indeed of the complete oeuvre of Bosch. It is not even necessary to have the paintings alongside the descriptions of the paintings; we are still affected by feeling a sense of the unfolding of particularity within wholeness. The words of the text emerge out of the meditative silence of the author rather than appearing as already present words, that secondary kind of writing that speaks about something rather than from within it. And we see the paintings through feeling, not through intellect. That is, one gives oneself over to the images, enters into them, lets them wash over oneself completely, such that one becomes the image itself. It is apparent that Falk has followed this procedure himself, that this writing is a product of direct experience rather than intellectual curiosity.

We also have the hint in the spiritual inventory of Bosch's paintings that one can work contemplatively with the paintings in a specific series in order to allow spiritual capacities to unfold in a kind of order. It seems important not to place too much emphasis here because, in spiritual work in these times, there may not be a prescribed order. Nonetheless, it can be helpful to consider the paintings in the sequence spoken of by Kurt Falk.

There is a kind, a type, a prototype of spiritual progression that is hinted at by virtue of the description of Bosch's paintings occurring in the order that they do. This progression should not be understood as processional, as linear, as if one had to proceed inwardly in development from what is felt from the first painting all the way through what is felt in the last. The sense of progression conveys that everything that one has to go through and develop interiorly does not all occur at once to the point of conclusion. On the other hand, when one is working inwardly with one felt sense expressed in a painting, then everything else, that is, the whole world of feeling is also affected. We perhaps find it difficult to understand this mentally, but the heart does not have this same trouble. The heart, that great center of the feeling life, lives in contradictions, paradoxes, and multiple simultaneous happenings. This kind of sensibility is needed in working with paintings as an instrument of spiritual development.

It is extremely important not to take this spiritual inventory of the paintings of Bosch as sectarian. That is, the scope of the spiritual initiatory practices here does not belong exclusively within, say, the tradition of the Catholic religion. The initiatory practices depicted here are the **New Mysteries.** They have to do with the future of humanity, not a specific religion. They have to do with the process of entering into the spiritual "I," a call made to all human beings. Even more, the diversions and illusion of the individual process of spiritual development are shown over and over; notice in particular the forces of ossified thinking, perverted feeling, and will that is taken over by other forces than the purified soul; these are chief among the misdirections we have to face and overcome.

There are two ways of reading this book. It is a work that, on the one hand seems intended for those who are engaged in some form of spiritual practice, and in particular to those who are in one way or another involved in what might best be termed "esoteric Christianity." That term alone covers an awful lot these days, so it might be better to specify it even further by saying that the book intends to be helpful for those on the path of a Rosicrucian/Anthroposophic work. For such individuals, this work offers a remarkably new and exciting way to have a sense of where they are in their inner life. Kurt Falk has done nothing less than discover that the paintings of Bosch are a mirror of the soul on this spiritual path. Thus, those who are engaged in this spiritual work will immediately have a sense of recognition in the descriptions of the paintings.

At the same time, however, there is another way of reading this book. It can be a true awakening to a desire to engage one's soul and spirit life in a disciplined way. That is, it also addresses the seeker who may not even know that he or she is indeed seeking something different in art from the usual art history and art commentary. The writing recognizes that people have always looked to art for spiritual guidance in the feeling realm, and only modern art criticism and art history have steered us away from this noble purpose. For such people, however, it might be more necessary simply to read through the whole book, perhaps at first wondering a bit what is going on with this approach to art. Once having gone through the book, however, the reader will feel it begin to do its work as gradually one's whole inner life begins to be different, and one begins to be more aware that the feeling life is a mode of spiritual presence. It is that mode where all is interior, without a sense of there being any without at all. That is, Kurt Falk works with these paintings in such a manner that we are turned outside in, and the feeling realm is awakened.

A characteristic of esoteric Christianity as a path of spiritual initiation is that there is an emphasis on the development of individuality. For many people who are engaged in spiritual practices, individuality smacks of ego and the purpose of spiritual practice is to rid oneself of the illusion of individuality and certainly of that mark of individuality known as ego-consciousness. With the paintings of Bosch, it is as if each individual is called by his or her own peculiar path. Spiritual path thus means each individual has to find his or her own way by developing capacities of witnessing the interior landscape. As with Dante, so too with Bosch—the path upward is the path inward.

On this path, we are each the Prodigal Son, depicted on, for example, the outside of Bosch's triptych titled *The Haywain*. We stray and stumble, learning our imperfections, not with some goal of becoming perfect, but with the aim of facing them, getting to know them, stop projecting them onto others.

Bosch's paintings reveal that we are like the solitary figure of *The Haywain* traveling through the world of desire, learning, gradually, that desire is not to hold onto but is the indication that we are **being desired** by God.

Within such a view, which cannot be understood intellectually, but is given as a sensuous feeling, evil takes on very different possibilities than as something to be avoided or gotten rid of. The demons in Bosch's paintings exist right alongside the other spirit-beings. Trying to avoid evil inevitably results in projecting evil outward—as always belonging to someone else or some group. The path of desire carries with it a felt sense that it is through the individual confrontation of evil within each of us that we develop true capacities for spiritual freedom.

Confronting the sense of evil as within does not, however, make it something only personal. Whatever occurs within is decidedly real, and not merely something made up, a fantasy realm. And it is something far deeper and stronger than what psychology terms the "shadow." The true mystery of evil, however, is that it can only be confronted within and that it has to be faced without being opposed. The result of doing so, we are told in the description of the painting titled *The Temptation of St. Anthony* is that it is only through the demons that we can find the spiritual worlds. Not by opposing them or avoiding them, and certainly not by reacting in fear to their presence.

Often, the spiritual work of Bosch's paintings has to do with the colors more than the content of what is painted. Falk mentions this when working with *The Temptation of St. Anthony* painting:

> As far as the content is concerned, this triptych is second only to the *Hortus Deliciarum* in Hieronymus Bosch's known works. The two grisaille paintings on the reverse side of the panels are sparsely dramatic and the gray-greens stand in strong contrast to the world of color breaking out from inside the altarpiece. These colors are not for show, not used for their own sake, but their hues and qualities are meant to move and grip us.
>
> There is an absolute unity of form and color that makes the observer more than a mere observer. The colors of the painting release forces in him that lead him out of and beyond his habitual mundane world. Looking becomes contemplation that inspires our imaginative capabilities. Thus a purely aesthetic activity turns into a moral-spiritual affair because the realm of the conscience is affected.

This is quite an amazing statement! Through the colors we enter into a unity with the paintings and there is no longer a separation between looker and painting. The reason painting can be a very powerful medium of transformation lies in the way that color works. We are affected not emotionally, but feelingly—and the realm of desire then becomes an ethical-moral affair. That is, we are able to palpably feel where we are in our soul life, to feel where we are off the mark, and also become able to feel when we are on the mark. This inner direction all happens through color.

Yet another characteristic of the path of individual soul and spirit development shown through the paintings and the astute commentary by our author is that the way of feeling, the way of color, is the way through the thickness of the world. There is never an attempt to develop a spirituality that is separate from the things of the world. There is no absolute division set up between the earthly and the spiritual. They are two sides, two aspects of the same reality. To work spiritually in the realm of feeling is to completely accept being an Earth-being who is working to become, not a spiritual being, but *a spiritual human being*, which is something quite different than a human being who does spiritual things. The former is an advance in spiritual evolution, while the latter is where most of us are by nature and a modicum of goodwill. The object of this path of spiritual practice is not to have experiences of the spiritual worlds, to obtain enlightenment, and to leave the Earth, but rather to serve the Earth as fully bodied spirit-beings.

The way of feeling cannot work with absolute distinctions. The mind works that way. But feeling is all of the same fabric, so learning discernment in the realm of feeling is something very different than learning to make cognitive judgments in the realm of clear ideas. In our feeling life, we are more often confused than not. Here is where we most easily fool ourselves. It is incredible the way that Kurt Falk reads the paintings, helping us develop discernment in the realm of feeling. Notice how a painting depicts real and truthful feeling standing right next to illusion in the realm of feeling. Notice also how Bosch has made available to our feeling-awareness the difference between true feeling and the double of feeling; we see this difference vividly depicted in the ways in which institutional, dead religion contrasts with the sense of the living Church, which is not an institution, but rather a prototypal coming into being that constantly unfolds, metamorphoses, as the life of the "I"; "I" as in "Not I but Christ in me."

These introductory remarks barely touch on the first few of the twenty-nine paintings commented on by Kurt Falk. Indeed, this first part of the book can be a new meditation manual, a manual for initiation into the spiritual worlds through the life of feeling.

The second part of this writing casts yet another lens over the whole of the work of Bosch, bringing initiatory practice to an even higher level.

The inspiration for this book is the mysterious painting tided *The Last Judgment*, which Kurt Falk found in a museum in Cairo. You will read of this discovery at the beginning of the second part of this book. I only want to address the question of the authenticity of this painting. Is it a real Hieronymus Bosch painting? **It does not matter.** If you were trying to buy the painting or put it on exhibition, it would certainly matter. But, for the purposes of this writing, it has been a revelation for Kurt Falk and the key to all of the works of Bosch. If it is not authentic, it was certainly painted by someone who thoroughly understood Bosch and may in fact have wanted to provide a key to Bosch. The key image in the painting is the figure of the Tree man, the witness, the act of individual spiritual attention, the spiritual "I"-being, spirit-individuality, the inner presence of the individuated self.

The fact that Kurt Falk works with this one painting *in the context of the whole of the work of Bosch*, authenticates the painting as revelatory of the spiritual dimensions of the work of Hieronymus Bosch. This one painting fits within the whole context and makes clear what Bosch was doing. That is its primary importance, which may be something different and more significant than whether the painting is authentic. Falk, does, however, make a compelling case for the authenticity of the Cairo painting.

A different form of awareness is required to begin to perceive the significance of Bosch's paintings, and the nature of this awareness forms an important dimension of this second part of the book. It is, for example, necessary to be able to focus attention on the particularity of each painting while at the same time to be within a diffuse form of awareness. This kind of awareness can be part of the spiritual practice of working with the paintings and consists of looking at a picture of a Bosch painting, focusing on some particular element for a few moments and then shifting awareness to a diffuse awareness of the whole painting all at once. Shift between these two modes of attention while looking at one of the paintings. Then, after a few minutes, stop the shifting and be present to the painting and notice your experience. Not only your sensing/perceptual experience, but also, at the same time, what is felt inwardly. The sense of the paintings will begin to open up in decidedly new ways. You will gradually have an inner sense of the paintings, though it may be an experience beyond words. With this form of perceptual practice the articulations provided by Kurt Falk take on much more importance, for you will find these descriptions speak what you might not be able to say. He has worked to find just the right descriptive language, which is something akin to language that understands the qualities of dreams.

The dream qualities of the paintings of Bosch are, however, something quite different than night dreams. Bosch was not painting the imaginal landscapes of the so-called unconscious. Rather, he was painting the multiple spiritual worlds that are always here, all around and within us. Thus, Bosch's paintings, in some respects, mirror the surrounding landscape. It is as if the familiar world is layered with realm after realm of spiritual worlds. Bosch was not making up pictures of these worlds but rather pictures his seeing. He accurately pictures clairvoyant experience, but you have to be able to see through the content to the awareness out of which a content suitable to the awareness emerges.

It is crucial to understand that it is the qualities of the content of the paintings rather than the literal forms of the figures within the paintings that express the spiritual worlds. The genius of Bosch lies in his amazing capacity to create a content that vividly expresses the qualities and activities of spirit beings. Further, it is important to realize that the spiritual worlds are highly complex. All spiritual traditions and practices understand that the spiritual worlds are every bit as complex, indeed far more so, than the earthly world. The spiritual worlds are intermixed with beneficent and detrimental beings, with the dead who are helpful and those who are harmful, with levels that are helpful and levels that are not so helpful. Bosch beautifully pictures the wholeness and complexity of the spiritual realms, but it is how our attention is brought to their depiction by Kurt Falk that makes it possible to see much more of what is present in the paintings. The phenomenological description of the Cairo painting is nothing short of fantastic.

I also want to draw your attention to what may perhaps be the deepest aspect of the mysterious painting of Hieronymus Bosch and that no one besides Kurt Falk seems to be aware of except in the most superficial manner. Bosch's paintings are from the future! They come from the real, tangible stream of time from the future. Thus, the paintings are not really about the time of Bosch. They are not really about the decadence of the church, not at the deepest level of the paintings anyway. They are about what is coming to be. However, they are not predictive of the future. The future time stream is not predictive; it is not about what is going to happen the day after tomorrow. The esotericist and originator of Anthroposophy, Rudolf Steiner introduced this notion of the time stream from the future. It is not a theory, but something quite possible to experience, though not with the mind. It is the sense of everything of the world, of the cosmos, and of the spiritual worlds, and most of all, of the human being, as in the process of coming to be, and this coming to be is an aura of everything that is. The coming to be of the time stream of the future does not refer to the domain of possibility. It is not that the paintings of Bosch, for example, depict some possibility that will some day be actuality. The time stream from the future is a dimension of everything that exists, and is thus present now; it is the coming-to-be aspect of the now. We might also think of this dimension as the realm of prototypal imagination as distinct, for example, from the realm of archetypal imagination as discovered and worked with by Jung. The prototypal dimension is the realm of the not yet, of the coming to be. It also includes those forces that would attempt to diminish the sense of awareness of the prototypal realms, blocking an ongoing, subtle experience that as we live our earthly lives, we are also, at the same time, citizens of the cosmos.

There is a particular stream of spiritual initiation tradition in which the sense of the time current from the future is central. I came to understand this stream through the work we do at the School of Spiritual Psychology. The many practices of this spiritual work came first out of meditative work. Only later did it become apparent that these practices, completely of this time and not atavistic, were within this spiritual stream of the time current from the future. I will only mention the groups within that stream here, without going into the relation of the practices of spiritual psychology to them because the intention is only to locate Hieronymus Bosch as belonging to this spiritual unfolding and to show that Kurt Falk was deeply perceptive in intuiting this fact.

This spiritual stream runs from the ancient initiatory practices of Mani, which began in the region that is now Iraq in the third century AD. The religion of Mani had this future time current at its heart. Many of the spiritual groups within this orientation probably were not aware that they were working from the time stream of the future. Thus, they took what they were doing as something that needed to be in the world as actual practices at those times—which got each and everyone of these groups into the terribly difficult position of being labeled heretical.

I have also traced out an earlier branch of this spiritual stream that goes from Mani to Sufism. The Mani stream goes then to the Cathars, and from there to the Templars and then to the Troubadour poets. From there it goes to Dante and the *Divine Comedy*. It is quite explicit that this great literary work is an initiation document and directly connected with the Templars. Then the stream goes to the development of the Tarot in northern Italy, and it is at this point that there is a connection with Bosch.

What happens after Bosch? Where does the stream go? Falk locates Bosch within the Rosicrucian tradition and then to Anthroposophy. That is certainly not a straight-line evolution. What seems to me to be most important is the continuing sense within each of these spiritual groups of being pulled by the not yet of the future rather than being pushed from behind by the past. There is this same future sense, the coming to be: the unfolding of the spiritual human being within Anthroposophy.

18

An Unknown Destiny
Terror, Psychotherapy and Modern Initiation
Readings in Nietzsche, Heidegger, and Steiner

MICHAEL GRUBER

New psychologies spring up nearly as fast as new model cars. Each of them bears pretty much the same assumptions. There is something from the past, not fully conscious, that must be dissolved, eliminated, eradicated, and maybe forgiven, if one is to feel comfortable within the world. Other forms of therapy—concern for the soul, connecting with archetypal realities, awakening a sense of Self—exist only at the outer margins of culture. The more common and more universal view of therapeutic psychology degrades the "Queen of Disciplines" into a primarily pragmatic technology oriented toward restoring individuals to being servants of the collective realm, the masses, the State. Radically put, Michael Gruber convincingly shows us that psychology has become the servant of terrorist structures of consciousness.

We are primarily aware of the physical dimensions of terrorism and are wholly oriented toward strategies of war against it: terrorism fighting terrorism. We remain totally unaware of how the dominant mode of spectator consciousness—in which we become onlookers not only on the world, but also on ourselves—turns destructive at a certain point in the evolution of consciousness because of the inevitable unfolding of the primacy of power and control. That point has forcefully arrived. We have become free and independent (or act as if we are) of the spiritual forces of nature and of the cosmos and seemingly become the creators of our own human destiny.

254

The formation of the egoic structure of consciousness is responsible for this illusion, an illusion that substitutes self-centeredness for individuality of being. By this I mean the notion of having the right to be an independent entity rather than feeling the mysterious individuality of human life in its ongoing currents within the undisclosed mystery of Being. This illusion is upheld through all-pervasive intrinsic fear, which results in the construction both of a world of distractions to veil the fear and defenses that keep it from being exposed. As a consequence, a doubling of egoic consciousness has come about that has made it possible to manipulate fear as the instrument to perpetuate control within the system of this dominant structure of consciousness. The control comes about by turning everything—even intangible realities—into something to be commodified, placing it within an imagination of need and of scarcity that keeps attention occupied with the "outside" and the fantasy that inner peace is attained through outer satisfaction.

Michael Gruber shows us, in magnificent ways, that the only way through the age of terror is through taking up forms of modern initiatory practices. This path of knowledge is led, surprisingly, not by spiritual leaders and initiates, but is undertaken through self-initiation founded in the felt sense that soul and spirit must always be entered simultaneously and without detaching from the world. Spiritual practices alone lead to various sorts of mania, while soul practices alone lead to self-absorption. In our time, spirituality and psychology must merge into a creative synthesis of spiritual psychology if we are to break through into new structures of consciousness.

Spiritually oriented psychology frees us from an obsessive, singular view toward the past, which can serve only to keep the focus on what is done, completed, and perpetuates a closed system, unable to find the truly new. Such spiritual psychology is a creative rather than a destructive explosion, opening the closed system of consciousness into the emergence, within ongoing life, of the practical workings of divine forces that compose both the world and the human being, both intrinsically one and expressed in a world-individual polarity. What we find in the world is always ourselves, spiritually displayed, and what we find individually is always the world in its signification.

Psychotherapy, understood in its most radical sense as the practice of the "Queen of Disciplines" concerns initiation, an insight that leads this book into extraordinary places. Psychotherapy, as intimated by Michael Gruber, may be the only contemporary venue available for initiation. It is primarily a prototypal action between people, in which the vertical imagination that has characterized spiritual practices of the past is now found in the "between." This implies a revolution in the initiatory process, one in which the "gods" are no longer situated in the vertical "above" or "below." The gods have not completely disappeared, but now persist in the soul/spirit field between people. As long as this shift goes unrecognized, however, people still rely on dead religions for the shell of spiritual experience or on outmoded, atavistic kinds of spiritual practices that, at best, can take one only into a memory of the spiritual worlds; not its living presence all around us.

The trouble, of course, is that psychology is completely contaminated and can only impotently touch the outer surface of what is now available as soul/spirit experience. Indeed, psychology does not even recognize the autonomy of spirit experience and, at best, in a few of the depth psychologies, classifies spirit experience as a variety of soul or psychic experience, depriving it of the reality of imaginal realms and presences that are autonomous from human-being, but only disclosed and opened through human heart-presence. That is to say, psychology can, when it stretches real hard, understand human beings as having spiritual experiences, but it does not have the proper tools to understand what it is to be a spiritual human being and not simply a human being doing spiritual things.

In *An Unknown Destiny,* Michael Gruber has written the prototypal book that gives us the basic new tools to undergo and recognize that humanity is passing through an as-yet unrecognized initiatory shift of being. It is extremely important to notice—well, one cannot help but notice—that this book is written in such a way that the whole of it is in every part; it all occurs simultaneously and it is only due to the limitations of having to put it into standard linear language, that it unfolds page by page. When reading this book it is important to feel that we have been invited into the intensity of meditative consciousness. While the form of the writing takes us through essentials of the work of Nietzsche, Steiner, and Heidegger, it is no mere exposition of or commentary on what these individuals thought and did. The writing is already within a new mode or octave of consciousness. Having to struggle within this new form brings about at least the beginning of the formation of new capacities. It is a book to undergo rather than simply to read. It is a book to bear, as in bearing a new child.

I have never been particularly fond of Nietzsche, probably because I saw many of my fellow students, years ago, taken, fascinated, even entranced, with his passion, but with no way to let that passion open into something creative. At last that view changes here. A central effect of Gruber's creative approach to Nietzsche is to demonstrate, not simply talk about, the fact that it is necessary to throw oneself across the threshold into initiatory realms, into the completely unknown. Initiatory experience cannot be planned; one cannot, in advance, know where one is going or what will happen. Even more, this chopping off of one's purposive, calculating head must be done with the greatest enthusiasm possible. Still, why choose Nietzsche to exemplify this necessity? Part of the answer lies in suggesting that Nietzsche's program for abandoning of our mental structures is exactly what is needed to enter the unknown and to develop the capacity of letting life unfold from the unknown, unknowingly, and with the fullest attention.

A further response lies in Zarathustra, Nietzsche's Zarathustra. Living intimately within the soul-being of Nietzsche was—no, *is*—the paradigm of fully bodied imaginal consciousness. And Zarathustra is additionally paradigmatic of present-day initiate consciousness, which includes an awareness of the massive tendency always to reduce the human being and world-being to the reductive "nothing-but" category of material processes, wholly subject to the intense cleverness of sub- and unconscious presences that seem deep and mysterious—even the realm of the gods—but are in fact hell-bent on making hell seem as if it were paradise.

The entry point and wholeness of the initiation of humanity is to be found in developing the capacity of imaginal consciousness. This book is written wholly from within imaginal consciousness. Michael Gruber tells us from the outset that a different and wholly unfamiliar structure of thinking is needed to enter into the next stage of consciousness and that this structure is "heart-thinking," which gives access to the imaginal realms. Here, then, is the key to the whole of what this book is about and the reason why it is not possible to read this work without undergoing inner change.

Heart-thinking consists of taking in, in a completely receptive manner, what is before one—sensory experience, or ideas, or images and even dreams—not mentally, but through reaching out through the heart to feel their presence as the interiority of Being, and even as the traces of spirit presences. Feeling is something active. It is not simply the inner reaction to something. We feel—as in "to reach out and touch." The interior heart region is the only bodily region capable of this reaching out to touch that is accompanied with a particular kind of consciousness—the consciousness of the inner presence of the inner qualities of what we attend to. What we attend to in this manner echoes within us. Then it fades gradually, like the after-image of a candle. The fading, however, is not the disappearance of what was received; rather, what was received now finds its way into the larger cosmos; it finds its connection with spiritual presences. Then, the Whole is felt as inner resonance and can be expressed as intuitive insights. This way of knowing is a new yoga; it is what Rudolf Steiner called "the new yoga of Light." It is our access to imaginal consciousness; it is the way through dualistic, separative consciousness.

The complete sense of what imaginal consciousness consists of has many dimensions. The dimension that is most clearly demonstrated in this writing is that this new form is a new orientation—one that is "situative" rather than "situated." Rather than speaking of something as if it is already formed and completed, as we do when stringing thoughts together, this mode of consciousness enters the unknown in the deepest of Silence, and waits with full attention until something wants to be said. It is a thinking-together with spiritual presences. We feel, then, something coming-into-being, situating, rather than as already here to be described as a dead corpse. We always feel such situative thinking as inspired, brilliant, new, creative. And true. Such is the way of this book.

Central to imaginal consciousness, and thus to Zarathustra—and through him, Nietzsche—is the complete engagement of the gods, of God, with the human. God seeks to be known, longs to be known by human beings, for this is the way God knows God. The engagement between the gods and humans is a kind of play in which one becomes the other, and the un-manifest continually becomes manifest. None of this vast complex unity is available to usual consciousness. Entry is gained through attending to the longing of the heart, gradually recognizing that this longing is not ours, not our wanting to fulfill some need or desire, but is the presence of God's longing for us. Developing the capacity to follow the presence of longing into new forms of consciousness requires becoming present to the creative capacity of attention. Attention is not just noticing something, letting something get hold of our attention; rather it is the creative, generative spiritual organ through which the presence of the workings of forces beyond us can be felt as intimately engaged with us. Through developing attentive presence, transformations of the heart ensue, reconfiguring the whole we are and are within.

Equally central to being present to the imaginal is that we run into the opposing forces of darkness, those necessary beings that are impediments to smooth sailing in imaginal realms when that sailing is also world-oriented. One would think that having discovered heart-thinking, where even thinking itself is felt as a cooperative endeavor with spiritual presences, would open a new and beautiful world. It does, but that does not rid either us or the world of the impulses of revenge, violence, cleverness, and forgetfulness that now dominate earthly materialistic consciousness. Now, however, the context is quite different. At least potentially, a modicum of freedom is present in which it becomes possible to attain a creative presence with these delicious darknesses. Nietzsche, in the end, however, may well have been swallowed by them though the fatal wound of his own hubris or "amor fati." Thus, something more is needed that the leap into engagement.

Although Nietzsche participated deeply in the felt realization that consciousness itself is formed of and by love—and in the living of "amor fati"—he still manifests a certain thrashing about. There is still present in him a blending of love and passion, and felt-sense of presences without the capacity of truly allowing and perceiving their autonomy within a unity of consciousness. Rudolf Steiner, the second presiding genius engaged by Michael Gruber, had enormous respect for Nietzsche and even wrote a book about him, *Nietzsche: Fighter for Freedom*. Steiner recognized in Nietzsche the beginnings of heart-thinking. Thus, it is not surprising to find these two, Nietzsche and Steiner, side by side in this book. The chapters on Steiner are a remarkable synthesis of Steiner's enormous gifts to the world; while the sections on psychotherapy are of particular importance in recognizing psychotherapy as a modern initiation practice.

The kind of therapy suggested in the Steiner section of this writing is an excursion across the border into the land of the unknown. What a therapist needs to develop far more than any theoretical knowledge or techniques is the capacity of complete surrender. Surrender does not just happen. It is not just a kind of giving up, or letting go. Rather, it is an active process, a conscious process of yielding into an unknown that is something more than an absence, a void, but is an opening to a resonating presence of a field that encompasses both therapist and patient. Some depth psychologists are familiar with this field and have written and theorized about it as the "interactive field." Michael Gruber adds significantly to our knowledge of this realm, first by noting that being within this field of the "third" requires a pouring of all of attention into the field so that nothing is left as observer of even as witness. Further, this yielding into the field that has captured the patient in overwhelming ways—that simultaneously threaten and announce freedom of being—is nothing less than an excursion into the land of death without a map. It is entirely reminiscent of descriptions of spiritual awakening and its attending dangers.

A brilliant sketch of the new territory of therapeutic initiation is given which, in its detail shows that initiatory experiences, which are now happening spontaneously by many people, are typically put under the old classification of psychological illnesses. They are not psychological illness at all. They are spiritual rumblings that can happen within the emotional body, or the life body, or in the realms of character, wishes, desires, longing. Most significantly they are something that at once announces and thwarts the awaking possibility of developing the capacity of creative generation of oneself as world-relation at each moment. That is, what is now increasingly coming about in the world is the possibility to apprehend every moment as our coming-into-being rather than as "having" an identity, which may be threatened by the press of past difficulties.

The pathologies of new consciousness, a consciousness sensitive to and capable of receiving impressions from creating spiritual presences as well as destructive ones, are pathologies or sufferings of becoming rather than of having-been. Scratching around to locate the origin of such suffering in the past—and even in the archetypal rather than the prototypal imagination—serves only to feed the darkness. Obsessions with death and dying, chronic fatigue, attention deficit "disorders," terror of fragmentation, dissociating, certain kinds of delusion, and most significantly because it is now epidemic, bi-polar disorder, are illnesses that have to do with the real, substantial time stream from the future; illnesses of *potentia*, of coming-to be. Simply to be removed from the soul's becoming due to living within a culture of the past, which is now "egotized," is already an illness. In addition, because there exists absolutely nothing in the culture that prepares and strengthens the heart forces for the influx of the coming-to-be, the shatterings of the soul that occur due to the overwhelming experiences of this initiatory threshold that is now upon humanity. This book is utterly groundbreaking, and courageous beyond belief, in bringing these new pathologies to light. Furthermore, these new sufferings require completely new senses of the practice of psychotherapy and the training of therapists. As long as therapists are educated in old ways, the revelations of these sufferings remain closed.

An additional factor enters when experiences of suffering related to being overwhelmed in the dimension of coming-to-be occur within a culture dominated by technicity and materialism. Under these conditions, these experiences often do not show up as sufferings at all, but rather as the capacity to inflict suffering, especially terrorizing trauma, on others without any feeling or comprehension of the moral depravity involved. This tricky situation is due to the process of doubling. Doubling was first recognized as a pathology by Robert Jay Lifton, though there are many precedents of the phenomenon in literature, such as the writing of Guy de Maupassant. I have traced out this heritage in my book, *Freeing the Soul from Fear*. Nowadays, however, what was an unusual phenomenon of seeing oneself before oneself—doing things that one would never do (Jekyll and Hyde, is an example of this phenomenon)—has taken a further step in development.

The individual spirit being of a person can be doubled by a force that looks, acts like, and seems to be one's spirit being. But it is taken over by cleverness and power. We see the phenomenon everywhere in corporate culture and in politics. It is a spiritual pathology, intensely difficult to break through because those bearing it are, within this culture, the highly successful. This book provides a first step in working with this illness in an extremely clear picturing of the various forms of doubling. This first step is thus to become aware of the phenomenon, to realize that there is an inherent incredible cleverness to doubling that cannot be countered, and then to be able to enter into a heart field with one who is experiencing the malady. Being within the field of the heart allows the phenomenon to open up in an attitude of wonder, and also involves including others who are connected with the individual be a part of the therapeutic work, and letting the field go into the laconic presence of death.

Modern therapeutic initiate consciousness does not take place inwardly, separated from the world. One way to grasp the overall structure of this book and why it is written the way it is—as a creative synthesis of the three figures of Nietzsche, Steiner, and Heidegger—is to see that, by entering their spiritual imaginations, we come to Wholeness. With Nietzsche, as presented here, we have the dimension of individual initiation as it can take place in the midst of a dead culture that refuses to recognize that it is dead and thus perpetuates destruction. The other polarity of individual initiation is world initiation. The Earth, in its union with the human, has to be understood, felt, and experienced as not only living, but as conscious. The human being in this sense of the unity of Earth-human is something entirely different than consciousness of Earth. This unity is the dimension of being most clearly spoken by Heidegger; it is the aspect of the human world he was most concerned with. And in this context, it is Rudolf Steiner who seems to hold the polarity together in one unity, the unity of I-World.

As a way of helping to clarify the bridging capacity of Rudolf Steiner, we may note that his detailed esoteric description of the evolution of the world never separates the evolution of the Earth from the evolution of the human being. It is not the usual picture of evolution, which acts as if the Earth were finished and completed before the ape-to-become human mysteriously emerges from the protein soup—a fiction of science that does not recognize its fictionalizing.

Rudolf Steiner had capacities of clairvoyantly thinking with evolution, of reliving the entire process of evolution. To give one example of the polarity of person–world evolution, consider how Steiner speaks of the relation of gemstones to the human being. Gemstones came into being on the Earth at the time when the human was evolving into a sensory being. An intimate connection thus exists between gemstones and the human senses. According to Steiner, gems, when they were still fluid in form, were the presences of angelic beings, who participated in

Earth evolution to assure that as the human senses formed they would not become so completely Earth-bound that humans would completely lose the capacity to experience something of the spiritual field though the senses. They represent a sacrifice of angelic beings, who now, in a way, remain here, as frozen memories of spirit activity. This may sound far-fetched, unless entered into as an imaginal picture, something like a myth—not myth as fiction, but myth as something that never really happened, but is always happening.

There is still a great inability to see and to feel the intimate ongoing connection between the Earth and humans. Certainly, there is now the recognition that we can and are harming the Earth, but we still live in a dualistic imagination, thinking and living as if the Earth were other than us, rather than a human–world polarity. Heidegger, I think it would be accurate to say, expresses at least part of this polarity-of-unity with the term *Being,* though Being of course is even more than this. Heidegger, throughout his philosophy, decries the forgetfulness of Being. Michael Gruber, I think, intuitively sees that going to Heidegger brings out what may be more difficult to understand in Steiner; just as he goes to Nietzsche to bring out and emphasize and reawaken the pull-to-freedom, which is the center of Steiner's work, but exists in a more pressing sense in Nietzsche.

Any spiritual psychology focusing on the human being without being able to develop a comprehensive imagination that includes the Earth, is doomed not only to failure, but operates out of the old consciousness that will be swallowed by darkness. Ekhart Tolle, for example, operates out of this kind of dualistic consciousness while trying to put forth a concern for the Earth. As a consequence, what he says results in a kind of new age egotism. This evaluation does not intend any judgment of Tolle per se, but rather as indicates the necessity of finding the way through terrorist structure of consciousness, no matter how appealing and "life-renewing" they might appear on the surface. Sadly, one of the great harbingers of terrorist structures of consciousness is to be found in much spiritual work and writing—that is, in spirituality of the type that

has not found the way through dualistic consciousness and sees spirituality as something essentially private, inward, self-developmental, and,
with world difficulties now so pressing, tries to add on to an egoistic
mode of operation a concern for the world.

The chapter in this book on Heidegger is thus pivotal. The healing
of the world cannot, as Gruber clearly states, be a matter of old consciousness with new content. We must develop the capacity to "think
Being." "Being" sounds like a terribly abstract, philosophical term,
not connected with experience. In fact, like true thinking it is an experience unavailable to anyone unable to get beyond the "me"—or even
the "we." Thinking being is an experience available meditatively, and
is a "thinkingly" clear felt sense of the animated unity and complexity
of all that is, directly apprehended. It is the return of the living sense of
Mystery, something to behold, rather than something to be utilized. It
is something to be listened to from within as a formative force. Doing
so brings about a form of consciousness characterized by a different
structure of thinking—meditative rather than calculative thinking.
It is a structure of thinking that thinks along with the things of the
world, rather than about them, allowing them to disclose their own
meaning and purpose. This meaning and purpose is conveyed within
a field of unity with the individual, as a felt imaginal presence. It is
not something that can be apprehended through usual knowing, nor
spoken in usual language, and it does not follow the laws of our logic.
Thus, Heidegger devotes much of his writing on Being to the mystery
of the poetic language that simultaneously reveals and conceals, and is
essential to the primary creative act of dwelling.

The new initiatory therapy lives and breathes within this context of Mystery. It makes possible being completely and lovingly with
someone within a field of un-knowing and wonder—not waiting for
something to happen that will "solve" the mystery, uncover the hidden background from the past, but becoming available for disclosures
that do not make logical sense, and are, rather, felt presences of the
unfolding of an individual life in moments of harmony with that of

others and the Earth. In these moments, individual healing cannot be separated from the healing of Earth.

Because there is an aura of mystery and discovery that surrounds even present forms of therapy, most therapists are more than likely unaware that they function within a kind of calculative thinking. Working with feelings or dreams or images does not move one away from this disposition of thinking. Images, for example, are treated as "things" to be looked at, as ways in which the psyche reveals itself rather than as worlds to be entered together by therapist and patient—worlds that cannot be known cognitively, and worlds that are far from personal and even far from the presence of archetypal worlds. The challenge of this book is to radicalize therapy, to see that all of psychology to this point has been nothing more than a preparatory and transitional discipline, a training of consciousness for modern initiation, which now takes place with others, rather than through one's solitary meditative practices. I hope that at least a few therapists will feel the truth of what Michael Gruber has written and take up the magnificent work that he proposes.

19

I Connecting: The Soul's Quest

Kristina Kaine

This is a radical and remarkable book in many respects. Kristina Kaine, in a clear, straightforward, and simple but sophisticated manner, provides a very new and different view of the life of the soul; that is one aspect. Then, on that basis, she develops an even more clear understanding of the individual human spirit; that is a second aspect. Then, she also proceeds to show us how each of these dimensions intertwine in actual daily living. This is certainly a substantial writing, but it is not for the academic or for the intellectual effete. We find ourselves on every page of what she says. It is a strong book, a strong writing, which, if you take the needed time to study, issues into a different way of living, one that is full of inner excitement that surely expresses itself in behavior and will be readily noticed. You will become more calm, more centered, more able, more heart-oriented, and, most of all, more selfless and interested in others.

Suggesting these qualities result from developing a sense of "I" may sound like a string of new age promises, but there is a difference, an enormous difference. New age material is typically conveyed in a way that makes us believe that we already have the capacities to achieve the kinds of qualities stated above, and if we just do one kind of simple practice or another, wear an amulet, hold a crystal, learn the latest approach to the Tarot or some other divination device, the desire will be achieved. The book you hold is not this kind of self-help manual. Rather, you are invited into the riches of becoming a participant/observer in soul and spirit life. It is work, but a very different and new kind of work that can perhaps be characterized as play-work. That is, it is fun, the imagination gets engaged, and you begin to notice things in your daily relationships that make favorable differences.

Because this is a book about soul and spirit life, it seems to me that it might be helpful to clear the ground a bit for readers, as I tried to do above by indicating that this is not another of the more typical self-help books. A second distinction is also necessary. In our time, when the term *soul* is used, we think of depth psychology—not only the contributions of C. G. Jung, but also James Hillman, Thomas Moore, and the revival of depth psychology in archetypal psychology. This book is also not within that genre. Depth psychology's approach to soul is situated within a Platonic cosmology. I don't want to become lofty here and go into ancient philosophy. However, if we do not know what cosmology we stand within, then we are simply lost and wandering around, homeless. Platonic cosmology is only one aspect of depth psychology, there are other aspects such as Gnosticism, but it is the former that is important here in relation to the writing in this book. For Platonists, soul is a reflection within the human being of archetypal realities existing in the soul realm. These archetypal patterns are the patterning for our actions, our behavior, our emotions and thinking, as well as our pathologies. The standard dictum of depth psychology is "who is the god behind what I am thinking, feeling, or doing."

I made the argument in the introduction to Rudolf Steiner's work, *A Psychology of Body, Soul, and Spirit*, and also in my introduction to Gerhard Wehr's book, *Jung and Steiner: Toward a New Psychology*, that the Platonic background of soul work in psychology needs to be complemented with a more Aristotelian understanding of the soul. Aristotle was more earthly-oriented than Plato, and understood that soul life is formed not only by archetypal realities, but also through the senses, through how we take in the world and how the world lives on within us. It seems obvious, but no one has developed a soul psychology on this basis. The foundation of such a psychology is found in this writing. It is not that what we sense is taken into the soul in any literal way; not, for example as storage of memory images. Rather, how the world around us enters soul life expresses as a contraction or expansion of the soul. And, as our author so well explains it, as a rhythmical dynamic between aversion and attraction, a moving toward those things liked, an expansiveness, and away from those things that are disliked, a contraction. There is much more to it, of course, and it is all beautifully explained in this writing. But, since there are many books now available on the soul, it is always necessary to prepare the reader for the approach to soul being taken. Current writing on soul ranges from the excellent work of many depth psychologists, to a host of writers who use the term without any real understanding. This book expresses a highly developed understanding of soul, but from quite a new perspective.

One dimension of such an understanding of soul that seems to go well beyond what can be found in depth psychology is that there are levels of soul being. Soul is not just one big bowl of soup. And, in addition, soul is not some thing or quasi-thing, nor is it a theoretical concept. Soul refers to the activity of innerness. And such activity takes a variety of forms that are described as levels, interpenetrating levels of awareness. This book describes all of the levels of soul activity, how they interpenetrate, and how we can begin to notice differences in soul dimensions.

You will not find references in this book to archetypal realities because the background is, as I said, more Aristotelian. Others too, have shaped the background of what Kristina Kaine works out, and she is surely indebted to her mentor, Mario Schoenmaker, a gifted spiritual teacher who lived and worked in Australia. And, there are also resonances of the work of Rudolf Steiner. It is not necessary to have a background in the work of these individuals, but it is right to honor them as Kristina Kaine has done by bringing into practical form what was contained in their vision.

One of the most important descriptions in this writing concerns characterizing soul activity, the innerness of soul, not as something that goes on inside us, but rather the picturing of soul activity as both within us and all around us. We are within soul. Soul thus has the character of a subtle field of forces of a purely non-material kind, not of a bounded entity. This, as you will discover, helps give an account of many different kinds of experience in which we feel the presence of soul "all around us."

The field phenomenology of soul life that is such an important dimension of Kristina Kaine's writing teaches us to think differently—with more inherent mobility, less literally, less verbally, more with presence than with abstraction. Thus, by the time you finish this book, you will find you are not the same person who opened the first page. You have to be actively engaged in developing new capacities as you read the book. It is not a book of information but one of formation, of an awakening of soul into consciousness. Once you have the sense of the actuality of soul, it is really impossible for life to proceed as previously. For one thing, you will want to experiment with this new-found consciousness, become familiar with different levels of soul activity, learn to experience inwardly the difference between the sentient level of soul and the awareness level, for example. Inwardly sensing such differences makes living richer, deeper, and provides ways of working with difficulties, conflicts, and emotions, in ways that therapy never got to because of the lack of soul consciousness in the discipline and profession of psychology.

The chapters on soul life alone make this book exceptional and worth not only reading, but rereading again and again. But, in a way, the work with soul in this writing is but a prelude to a new and incredibly exciting psychology of spirit that forms the central creative effort of Kristina Kaine.

Individual spirit life expresses itself as the essence of our being and lives as our "I." Kristina works through the many senses of the "I." In a way, it feels like an awkward term, partly because we are so close to this region of the temple of our being that it is a bit of a shock to see it taken out, so to speak, and examined. Equally, however, we think we are so familiar with our "I," for after all it is us, it is who we imagine ourselves to be, that there does not seem to be anything that can be said. The time has come, however, the evolution of consciousness-time, to begin working in an inward way with the "I." If we do not, then there will be individuals who will work with the "I" in highly manipulative ways. This has already happened, for example, with the founding of Scientology. L. Ron Hubbard quite clearly and explicitly developed Scientology and used it as a way of manipulating the individual human spirit. In his foundational book, *The Fundamentals of Thought*, he says:

> The individual man is divisible (separable) into three parts (divisions). The first of this is the spirit, called in Scientology, the Thetan. The second of these parts is the Mind. The third of these parts is the Body.
>
> Probably the greatest discovery of Scientology and its most forceful contribution to the knowledge of mankind has been the isolation, description and handling of the human spirit, accomplished in July, 1951, in Phoenix, Arizona. I established along scientific rather than religious or humanitarian lines that the thing which is the person, the personality, is separable from the body and mind at will and without causing bodily death or mental derangement.
>
> In ages past there has been considerable controversy concerning the human spirit or soul, and various attempts to control man have been effective in view of his almost complete ignorance of his own identity. Latterly spiritualists isolated from the person what they called the astral body, and with this they were able to work for various purposes of their own. In Scientology, the spirit itself was separated from what the spiritualists called the astral body and there should be no confusion between these two things. (page 54)

If you peruse this book by Hubbard, you will find that he is very well aware of the tradition of soul that is also the background of Kristina Kaine's work. I bring this to the fore, not out of any interest in inspiring desire to look into Scientology. I want to make clear what is at stake in the development of a true sense of our "I"-being. And I want to make clear, that whereas in 1951, Scientology discovered how to manipulate the "I"-being of persons, with the publication of the book you hold in your hand, Kristina Kaine has restored the *sacredness* of the "I"-being to its rightful place. She has given us back our individual spirit, not only knowledge of it, but how to care for our "I"-being, develop it, and become, through this new consciousness, oriented toward being a healing presence in the world.

What is not yet recognized is that most of our sense of our "I" still remains unconscious. The aspect of our "I"-being within our consciousness is our ego, though ego also is in intimate connection with our soul, and when the soul lives in contraction rather than expansion, or in an unhealthy rhythm between the two soul motions, the "I" will express itself in one form or another of negativity—either a sense of inability to face the world or an inflated sense of our abilities, for example.

That Kristina Kaine also sees the critical importance of the harmonious relation between soul and spirit adds a significant dimension to all spiritual work. Even those spiritual traditions that do understand the spiritual Significance of the "I," such as Anthroposophy, tend to neglect the soul, with the result that the "I" will always be confused with egotism without the realization that one's spiritual work is egocentric.

You will find something quite amazing happens when you read the chapters on "I"-connecting, after having developed a sense of the levels of the soul and their activity. You will, at least momentarily, undergo an actual experience of the deepest and highest sense of the "I." And you will be quite astounded! It is like entering a vast, unending loving resource that makes it known to you through immediacy and intimacy of contact. You will feel confident that there is nothing in the world that you cannot meet without a sense of challenge and joy. The experience, of course, quickly slips away, but it is unmistakable, and is the greatest impulse for taking up the exercises described in the writing, which will strengthen this sense of "I"-being.

Then, there is the further exciting work of learning to place attention within soul and spirit and to begin to recognize how these dimensions of our being can be out of harmony. Many habits you have lived with for years and perhaps have been keeping you out of harmony can begin to be addressed from the place of spirit-"I"-being. We begin to understand that the activities of soul are autonomous and tend to go their own way until brought into right relation with our "I." It is not that the "I" controls the soul; it does not. It is rather that the relation is like music. That is what is meant by sensing whether soul and spirit are in harmony. When we are in harmony there is a bodily feeling of being in resonance with both soul and spirit; we feel the sense of being within our destiny, a sense of unfolding and changing and, most of all, a sense of being, at the very core of ourselves, creative beings who are called to live every moment within the stance of the creative sense of the "I," for that is what the "I" does—it creates. In the absence of feeling this creative core, we feel pushed into the comfortableness of habit and conformity.

The sense of the creative being of the "I" has great significance for what goes on in the world beyond ourselves. Not only do we find ourselves other-oriented when we experience the creative presence of the "I," we are able to stand against the usurping of the "I" that is now taking place everywhere in the world. I tried to speak of this usurping of the "I" in *Freeing the Soul from Fear* as doubling which is a pathology of the unconscious "I." I mean by doubling that our spirit-being, our "I," our spirit-individuality, when it remains unconscious can be taken over and controlled in a radical ways on a mass scale. I did not really have the tools to say what I was trying to say in that writing, and it is only now, with this work of Kristina Kaine's that the predicament and dangers we face in this time of the evolution of consciousness become fully apparent.

It is imperative to recognize the consequences of failing to come to an experience of the "I." Doubling is now a rampant pathology in our culture, and consists of cleverness taking the place of creativity, incredible cruelty taking the place of selflessness, complete self-centeredness taking the place of community, and force taking the place of true inner power and authority. We have to ask how it is possible for the cleverness and cruelty that we see with many corporate leaders, politicians, heads of state to exist. When we look at these people, it is easy to see that the person is "not there," that something has usurped the very core of their being. This pathology cannot be accounted for nor understood by any current psychology because it is not about psychology; it is about the spirit. We have not had a full understanding of the individual spirit and its operation in daily living, until this writing by Kristina Kaine.

Nor have we had any sense whatsoever that we now face a whole host of new pathologies that look like psychopathologies, but they are not. We have yet to recognize that there are pathologies of spirit. Many of them look exactly like psychological difficulties and are being treated as if they were. There is, for example, a kind of anxiety that concerns spirit, not soul. But, many illness such as anorexia, attention deficit disorder, and autism, I think have to do with the spirit. And, in many cases have to do with an awakening of spirit around others and in a culture that does not know how to recognize spirit. In other words, the pathologies of these difficulties lie more on the side of failure to recognize spirit and how to work with spirit in right and healthy ways. One result of this book will be, I hope, new ways of looking at the inner sufferings of individuals.

The indications, though, are clear. The world will continue falling into chaos without the sense of the "I" as a central light. On the one hand, soul without spirit leads to self-absorption. But the "I" that goes unconscious leads to cultural chaos. And the "I" that becomes conscious without working toward the harmony of spirit and soul activity within us is removed, detached, objectively cold. An amazing quality of this writing is that the way to harmony is clearly articulated.

The replacement of the "I" does not occur only in the drastic manner indicated. A ground has to be well prepared for that to happen. There first has to be a culture that brings about the complete exteriorization of the "I," that is, of the qualities that are inwardly experienced as personality, talents, creativity, goals, and the peculiarities that mark each of us as "I." When culture falls to the level where all such qualities are seen to be available "out there," then all that is left of the human being is an easily manipulated unconscious soul life, and an equally vulnerable egotistic sense of the "I." Since this condition leaves the soul so vulnerable, there is much inner pain, anxiety, and depression. The pharmaceutical companies feel they can handle those problems, but the real problem with pharmaceuticals is that they dull the sense of the "I." And, therapy of the soul, while it can help develop soul consciousness, if it cannot address the sense of the "I," results in living in more conscious painfulness without the dimension of joy and enthusiasm that are both exclusively spiritual qualities.

As this writing makes clear, coming into the sense of the "I" is an evolving process. That is because the kind of consciousness involved is, for each of us, entirely new and thus there are no concepts that can adequately express the experience. This book is perhaps the closest you will find to expressing what happens. The inner sense, however, is still something quite different, lying in the realm of the wordless. If there begins to be an awakening of the "I," our author indicates that it may be experienced as anxiety. You may not realize what is happening. This is an exceedingly important moment and it is crucial that it not be interpreted as being primarily a psychological difficulty. It is the moment when we get the first glimpse of the fact that the "I" is me and not me at the same time. It is certainly not the small "me," but it is not even "me" in a larger sense, because it is both personal and transpersonal at the same time. If it were merely personal and individual, its awakening would not be frightening because there would be a strong sense of familiarity. But, the awakening involves an equally strong sense of unfamiliarity. One so strong and so central that absolutely everything in your life is thrown into question, but also into a new light. The work is to let the questioning be present without acting on that questioning and develop the capacity of living within this new light of the "I." This book is a manual for doing precisely this kind of spiritual work. It is new spiritual work in the world, new because the spiritual being is not "out there" somewhere to be venerated or addressed, but right here, the central heart of every human being. This book is a guide to coming to be a spiritual human being—something quite different from just being a human being. And it is something very different than a human being doing spiritual things. This book, this writing, marks a most significant turn in inner work, in spiritual work, and in our very way of being in the world.

20

HEALING PANDORA
THE RESTORATION OF HOPE AND ABUNDANCE

GAIL THOMAS

Creative ideas populate this book as living beings. They entice us to imagine the whole of the Earth, as well as the built world, as fecund, offering unending abundance when approached with reverence. Starting with a myth of abundance—since it is a myth, an ever-permanent truth and not a theory—requires that we think completely differently. Do not, for example, place a notion of abundance in polarity with a notion of scarcity. Within this myth, there is only abundance. Of course, there are conditions under which abundance reveals itself, and the primary conditions are that we think differently and that we live a more intimate bodily life.

Gail Thomas radically rearranges how we think and proposes a very different bodily life. She teaches us how to think and live *with* the things of the world rather than *about* them. Thinking and living with the things of the world requires developing the mythic imagination, the capacity of approaching Earth and world as a *who* rather than an *it*. Our author models mythic thinking from page one to the end. Mythic thinking touches, rubs up against, and enters the soul. Thus it is impossible to read this book without undergoing change—deep change—and assuming new kinds of responsibility toward the Earth and her creatures.

We are used to being spectators of the world, always looking to what can be gained for our advantage. This terribly destructive way of living and of treating our earthly home is not only challenged here, it is broken through forever by the forcefulness of the sensuous imagination. The unfolding of the sensuous imagination occurs through the telling of stories of the evolution of Gaia, Ge, Earth, Mother, into the stories of Pandora, the All-Giver.

Pandora the All-Giver? We expect to hear of her as the dispenser of evil into the world. Such a characterization, one that has gone unquestioned for centuries, turns out to be a completely male imagining of Pandora, enacted first by the ancient mythographer and misogynist Hesiod. Hearing the full story of Hesiod alone makes this book worth reading. Dr. Thomas turns the deprecation of the feminine that lies at the very foundations of the Western imaginings of the world upside-down and inside-out.

It is simple, really; when you imagine the Earth as a *who,* you have to get the *who* right. The Earth is a she. And then it is a matter of following through with that image, being true to it at all costs, not deviating, not unconsciously falling back into the mode of thinking that characterizes the Earth as an *it.* When the Earth is characterized as an *it,* the most that can come from such a restrictive image is civilization. Civilization concerns all the outer built things, the structure and institutions needed for collective life, and an overriding idea of progress at all costs. But when we get it right, that Earth is a she, then we receive culture. Culture concerns the inner life of the Earth and her relationship with all creatures, humans, and the active and harmonious connection of Earth with the built world and its creative forms. The story of these two intersecting images, as given in this writing, brings only what Pandora can bring: hope.

The ways in which Pandora works deeply in the human imagination are not what we might think. That is, the very truncated story of Pandora that we have all heard barely scratches the surface. From there, we must go down if we are to find riches. The first region in that downward direction concerns imagining abundance. Abundance must be reimagined. If abundance simply meant that anything we wanted is available, we would quickly turn destructive, like children who are given everything they desire. What Pandora gives to psychic life is obstacles, in order that we humans can build the inner capacities to withstand any and all difficulties and still adhere to unquestioning reverence toward the Earth. That is one message of this book—powerful, creative, new, and with stupendous implications. This message shifts the notion of abundance from a fantasy of literal goods to the real imagination of what constitutes culture: culture as psychic abundance, culture as acts of the psyche rather than completed institutions in the world such as the symphony, the art museum, and other artifacts of civilization.

Culture becomes mere artifacts of civilization because of human hubris. We cut ourselves off from the gods and goddesses, and in turning ourselves into deities, forget the most central aspect of being human: the fact that we die. Pandora brings the realization of mortality into the soul. This keeps us in our rightful place—and it keeps culture lush, fruitful, and luxuriant.

How can it be that holding death in the psyche brings the abundance of culture? Thomas brilliantly works with this question, which involves the mysterious ways of Pandora. Her answer runs something like this, though only reading the text will take you through the actual experience: the gods and goddesses have vanished. Pandora works at a deep level as the reflection, desire, longing, and unconscious memory of the gods and goddesses. This is her primary task.

This writing, though, is not of the "goddess within" genre. We are not being asked to look for our inner Pandora. We are being asked to reside deeply within the activities of the world. There we will experience desire and longing. We typically interpret our experiences of desire and longing as having to do with something we are missing in the personal dimension. Out of these intolerable feelings of something missing, individual depth psychology was born. Now we can begin to see that there is something more to intolerable feelings of something missing. The gods and goddesses are missing in the world, and we miss them terribly. Gail Thomas originates cultural depth psychology as the way to invite them back through their primary representative, she who mirrors all the gods and goddesses: Pandora.

Cultural depth psychology as outlined in this writing does not work through the imagination of the Olympian gods and goddesses as so much of depth psychology does. Even when depth psychology tries to give due to the darker and more shadowy side of the soul, it does so through imaginings of figures such as Persephone, dark Aphrodite, Hermes, Hestia, and all the rest of the Olympians. Pandora does not belong to this bunch. She does not come from on high.

Some of the great research in this book draws on the work of Jane Harrison's interpretations of vase paintings of Pandora and the relation of those paintings to the Eleusinian Mysteries. Dr. Thomas points out that Harrison was doing this pioneering grounding of cultural psychology at the very same time that Sigmund Freud originated his brand of depth psychology, of which Carl Jung's psychology is a later metamorphosis. Harrison's explorations were primarily of the mythic regions of the chthonic rather than the Olympic imagination, and those realms are followed through in every aspect of this book. Thomas shows us, mythically, that culture only happens when there is an imagination of the chthonic realm, which includes the memory of the dead, the ancestors, and the ways in which they are psychically active right now in the world.

The emphasis on the chthonic realm means that the imagination of culture has to be able to hold things that, from the viewpoint of civilized consciousness, seem destructive. That is, if we are to have real culture, we must learn to hold in imagination, in the psyche, all of the spilled contents of the vessel of Pandora: death, disease, fate, destruction, corruption, pollution, lying, cheating, fatedness, cunning, and these kinds of things. They all have to be deliteralized and reimagined as the fertilizing of the world into the making of culture. Dr. Thomas carries out this reimagining in skillful ways that continue to astound more and more from chapter to chapter.

As the spilled contents of the vessel of Pandora have to be culturally reimagined, so, too, does the one quality left in the vessel, Hope. You will find the way this author reimagines hope very surprising. Once one becomes accustomed to this new form of cultural imagination in the light/dark of Pandora, it then becomes possible to see the operation of doubles of archetypal cultural patterns in the things of the present world. The example given by Dr. Thomas is the computer, which, in its own way, is a mysterious box that promises to give us whatever we want and need. But Thomas stuns us by showing that the computer is itself a mythic double of the vessel of Pandora, a double that installs in our soul the replacement of a true sense of hope with the false notion of hope defined as expectation. While the example is certainly interesting, more importantly we find in this example, and in others in the book, a method. We can look at the things of the world as doubles of culture, not to negatively criticize how the world now functions, but rather as the symptomatology that can lead us to the particulars of true cultural imagination once we see through the doubling.

That Freud and Jung caught on while Harrison remained a rather obscure though certainly well-known cultural anthropologist is due to the inherent egotistical interest in our own inner psychic contents. The story of depth psychology, until recently, has been one of turning our backs to the world, hoping that by delving into the individual soul, somehow the world would benefit. Because of that background and the way in which depth psychology utilizes myth, we have to extricate ourselves from those methods that are now ingrained in order to understand and enter the method developed here by Gail Thomas.

Depth psychology primarily utilizes myth to amplify individual psychic contents. That is, its method is to take the dreams and symptoms of individuals and find patterns that are analogous to the patterns we find in myths, primarily Greek myths. The cultural depth psychology that Gail Thomas establishes here does not work that way. Her method is mythic reflection. As you read this book you will find Thomas moving from one myth to another, not willy-nilly but rather the inherent images of one myth reflected in another myth almost holographically. Thus, once you have the founding myth of Pandora as the basis of cultural depth psychology you can follow the mythic terrain of culture by letting aspects of one myth reflect into another, and then follow through with the implications of those reflections. It is a brilliant method, but it is one that has to be carried out with great care, as is done in this book. When it is not done carefully, always holding the central myth in imagination, as modeled in this writing, incoherent associations result. Individual depth psychology more or less goes back and forth between individual psychic manifestation and mythic amplification. The cultural depth psychology given in this writing takes us further and further into the mythic imagination, taking myth as the foundational language and gestural expression of the world.

While recovering the imagination of culture is the central theme of this book, the central manifestation of culture is the city, culture's local habitation. There are even remarkable mythic connections between the city and Pandora, pointed out in this book. There is a monument in Paris, a grand arch, with the figure of Pandora at the center. Dr. Thomas also indicates that in ancient Greece there was a statue of Athena in the Parthenon with an etched relief of Pandora on the pedestal. Thus, an investigation of the myth of culture leads directly to the city, and vice versa.

We are certainly not out of the Pandoran woods by going from the Earth to the city. In fact, we are taken into even deeper and darker places: darker from the viewpoint of masculine consciousness, but a luminous darkness from the viewpoint of the feminine consciousness espoused in this work. Along with Pandora, we are now introduced to the Medusa, to Pluto as a feminine deity, to Lilith, and to Clytemnestra, the murderous wife of Agamemnon. These deeper aspects of the mythological themes surrounding Pandora have to do with the relation between sacrifice and culture. The making of a city of culture, we are told, requires acts of sacrifice to the ancestors. Ever since the founding of the first city, such acts have ritually occurred, and when they are absent, as in the modern city, this absence of a right relationship with the dead shows up as the pathologies of the city. We no longer sacrifice, and our cities lack the element of the holy. Now with this work on cultural depth psychology we at last have ways of reimagining sacrifice. It cannot take place in the old forms of animal or human sacrifice.

The sacrifice now needed is giving homage to the frightening realms of the soul, which activates the inner powers of healing. In order to even entertain the possibility of enacting culture, we have to begin with the dire recognition that all we have is cultural pathology. Culture only shows in this time as culture in need of healing. In fact, at one place in the text, Thomas suggests that even individual illnesses are expressions of cultural pathologies. The illnesses of anorexia and bulimia are given as prime examples. Once the dire effects of banishing the darker realms from culture are faced, a remarkable healing begins. We become healers of culture by our bodily presence within the world, provided we have inwardly opened the regions of connection between soul and body, which are the primary regions through which Pandora links us to the world.

This book is foundational for new ways of working in the world. I recommend it for all developers, planners, architects, city officials, and indeed, all citizens. Nothing could be more practical. I know it is a practical guide because I have intimately observed Gail Thomas for over thirty years and have seen her bring the kinds of reflections exemplified in this book to practical work in the city. You might read this book and expect that the author teaches at a university. She does teach, at the Dallas Institute of Humanities and Culture, but in addition Gail Thomas's work focuses on the practical work of making the culture of the city.

Years ago, while at the University of Dallas, Gail formed a graduate program called the Center for Civic Leadership, which she directed. Students combined studies of myth and literature with a practical focus on the city. Later, at the Dallas Institute of Humanities and Culture, which Gail guided into being and directed for over eighteen years, yearly conferences on aspects of the city were held in the Dallas city hall. These conferences always brought together the mythic imagination and the practical work of the city. Poets, artists, writers, musicians, and great architects shared the stage with mayors, city managers, city planners, and department heads. The themes of these conferences always sparked the deep imagination and resulted in significant changes in the city. These changes happened very differently than most of what develops in large cities. After the conferences the ideas went into incubation. And then, usually quite subtly, differences appeared in the city. People began talking about making people places in the city. Sculpture began to appear. Artists' lofts sprang up. An understanding of the importance of the myth of the city entered nearly every new endeavor.

Dr. Thomas is also responsible for Pegasus Plaza in the middle of downtown Dallas. Pegasus is one of the formative myths of the city of Dallas, stemming from the time when the Mobile Oil Company topped its skyscraper with a flying horse. Right next to this building, Gail guided the imagination and building of a plaza that has a fountain flowing from a well deep within the basement of this skyscraper. This well and fountain are a remembrance of the creative spring of culture that arises when Pegasus's hoof touches the Earth. Around the meandering stream-flow of the fountain are large stones etched with the stories of each of the Muses. The Muses, in myth, spring from where the hoof of Pegasus touches the Earth. Thus, right in the center of the city, citizens and visitors are reminded of the myth of this city. The soul of Dallas concerns uniting the sensuous spirit with the creative soul. Being true to this myth constitutes the inner work of this place.

Gail is presently working with the city of Dallas to make the long-neglected Trinity River a focal point of the city. Plans were being made to straighten the river, place it in a concrete waterway, and run a major highway alongside the captured river. Due to the efforts of Dr. Thomas, the river will instead be returned to its natural meander, and the area around the river will become parkland. Three beautiful bridges will connect downtown Dallas with the neighboring community, perhaps the most psychically fertile region of the city.

You may be somewhat taken aback in reading this book and then realizing that the content is being put into practical application. If so, it is because you are reading this book imaginatively, but when you look out at the world you are shifting back into literal consciousness. We do that all the time, and for that reason, much of what we read of a truly imaginative nature can never find its way into the world. The very notion of "practical application" is being re-visioned in this book. Dr. Thomas is not a developer, a city planner, or an architect. She is an imaginer of the culture of the city. She observes cities in a fully engaged and partici-patory manner, gradually begins to see what is working within the inner dimensions of the city, and always, always asks: "What does this city want?" She has developed the imaginative capacity to listen to the soul of the city. When a city is listened to in this way, it responds. The inner soul of the city itself begins to bring to the surface long-neglected con-nections with the past, with the ancestors, and with the original intent of that place. As those stories are inwardly heard, a new future of hope can be imagined.

Gail Thomas works for Pandora. As you read this book, approach it as a practical manual for re-visioning culture. Reading in this way, you will find all the tools needed for making a new world of soul culture.

21

STONES OF THE NEW CONSCIOUSNESS
HEALING, AWAKENING, AND CO-CREATING
WITH CRYSTALS, MINERAL & GEMS

ROBERT SIMMONS

Dear readers, you are about to be amazed, moved, challenged and quite possibly radically transformed! The content of this book will do that if you allow it to. But, it is not the force of the content alone that will surge through you, prompting pleasurable inner upheaval and a rearrangement of who you are, placing you within the conscious possibility of experiencing much more vividly who you are intended to be as a spiritual human being. The internal fire of Robert Simmons warms this writing—or, I should say, fires it up, so that you can see your lives in a new light and feel a new kind of love ignited.

At last count, the number of books on what crystals can do for you was beyond count. They pretty much all follow the same format—a listing of minerals and crystals along with the characteristics they inspire. No one, NO ONE, until this book had developed a clear and persuasive framework for understanding why one would desire to work meditatively with crystals and minerals for other than what finally amounts to personal desire for improvement, healing or receiving qualities that one feels in need of. Spiritually seen, we have to say that a strong element of egotism follows the existing crystal path. Now, thanks to this writing, we are able to see that those many compendiums of stones and all the effort that so many people have put into working with stones has been a preparation for what is described in this writing—the potential for inner work with stones to be world-transformative! It is a matter of utilizing the ground we stand on to change the ground we stand on.

The title of this book carries two meanings. It promises that there is a grouping of stones that can be of assistance in initiating a different and advanced mode of consciousness. This promise means that working with the stones described cannot be seen as another "add-on" to who you are. Spiritual interests often carry the assumption that, after all, we are pretty good and effective and important the way we are, but it would be nice to be able to be even more that way, and crystals can help fill in the gaps. Working that way with stones will not produce a new consciousness.

A second way of hearing the title is that the writing itself is exemplary of the new consciousness. This book could not have the title *Stones of the New Consciousness* while the writing is itself an example of old consciousness; that is, if the very tenor of the writing of this book were typical and usual, that would be a cause for some degree of suspicion on the part of the reader. The form of this writing does not disappoint, and thus it requires a degree of openness to enter fully into the flow, a willingness to release any concern of wondering where it might be going and, most importantly, the capacity to notice what is occurring inwardly as you read.

Of course, the title immediately brings up the question of what counts as "old" and what counts as "new." The terms here are not about time per se. It is not so much a matter of what came earlier and what came later; in fact, one is urged to be cautious of that way of reading, for consciousness is always whole, and thus "old" and "new" cannot primarily be thought of linearly. If something is promised to be new as a consciousness, that means that the Whole has reconfigured. Thus, the writing itself is within this reconfiguration and is not merely a "journalistic" report about it. When you complete this book you will notice an ongoing reverberation, as if your consciousness, down to your toes, "hums" a "new tune" one never heard or felt before, but one that has been longed for without knowing what the longing was about.

The way into this book is to keep in mind that the author has been through everything that he speaks of within the writing. The authoritative voice herein comes from someone who has undergone radical transfiguration of being through work with stones. This transfiguration occurred without a road map. He did not know where he was in the process, for how can one foresee where the road is to come to at least a provisional stopping place if the road is not even there until being made, step by step by the inner practices described in this writing? Still, something of the nature of "new consciousness" did come to our author when he woke one morning to a voice that said that the new consciousness is "blessing." This active word "blessing," which is both a doing and a way of being as well as the very most intimate gesture of the world toward us, constitutes the path of this book.

Does "blessing" mean that we are blessed by stones? Does it mean that we approach stones within a blessing mode of consciousness and being? Neither of these alternatives would be "new consciousness." In our more usual consciousness, those who are intrigued and interested in stones typically carry the notion that somehow the stones themselves have special, maybe magical properties that are available to us merely by being in proximity to a stone with given attributes. That is "blessing" in the old sense. Similarly, if one thinks that it takes someone with a particular gift to convey the power of stones, that understanding of "blessing" is also old. What is new and transformative here is the very experience of "blessing" as the "between," the overlap between our consciousness and the stone's consciousness. This is the transfigurational "space" where we can, at last, be relieved of our intrepid egotism, get out of ourselves and dwell within qualities so large and vast and deep and unending and so active and all-encompassing that not only are we changed, but currents of change then reverberate into the world.

Robert Simmons was not content with the appearance of "blessing" as a "message" heard upon waking one morning. To stop there would be incommunicable—it would not help others in the quest, and stopping with inward satisfaction would have the result of taking the new consciousness as something merely personal, not for the whole of humanity and the Earth. The comparison might be exaggerated, but I am reminded of the great mystic Jacob Boehme. He was polishing a pewter dish one day when he suddenly saw into the light on the dish, and the whole of creation opened to him. This vision lasted a very short time. He then spent the rest of his life writing huge volumes trying to convey the vision. Boehme was willing to engage in this life work because he knew he saw something for the whole of the world. This story is a helpful analogy in reading the present book. There is a moment of a real vision, the words spoken by an unknown presence: "The New Consciousness is Blessing." The whole of this book is an unfolding of what those words really say.

You have before you the writing of a stone initiate. Do not, then, take this writing as another popular book on stones, and maybe wonder why it seems considerably more complex than the others. This writing contains perhaps the deepest mysteries of the Earth—and of the Cosmos (as we know them so far). Thus, the chapters form a complex interweaving of myths, stories, biography, alchemy, science, description, experiences, dreams, meditations and practices—all oriented toward providing an invitation for us to enter into this new spiritual path that has as yet been singularly tread by this author. Imagine what it is like to set out where consciousness has never turned its light, and imagine the great gifts offered in this book—gifts of understanding, ideas, descriptions and tools to set us on that path.

Robert Simmons establishes a reasonable theory that adequately accounts for his initiatory experiences with stones. I am using the term *theory* here in its original sense rather than in its more restricted scientific sense. The term originally meant a "seeing," as when, for example, Greek heroes left the community to explore the unknown, going through innumerable trials to finally come to a "vision" or a theory, which is then brought back to spiritually advance the community. What Simmons sees is brought back in multiple forms. Science is one of the forms.

Why the science in this book on entering a new consciousness? Science is first of all a mode of consciousness rather than a body of knowledge gained by means of a certain method, as we typically understand it. It is a way of knowing, primarily of knowing the material world. While there are "social sciences," they follow the lead and methods of the physical sciences. The key here, though, is the interest in the physical world, in matter. The new consciousness resolves the false and illusory split between matter and consciousness. The whole of this writing is based on the dissolution of that split. It is thus possible, and is brilliantly done here, to read the findings of scientific research of a physical sort for its contribution to understanding not only consciousness but also future-consciousness. Indeed, one of the great spiritual tasks of our time is to work with the findings of science to hear them resound metaphorically, imagistically and symbolically within the soul. Such a practice, beautifully exemplified in this writing, saves us from the deadly literalism and materialism of the findings of science that sit there waiting for their completion within us as soul realities.

The science part of this book consists of Simmons's careful reading of research that he interprets as showing integral relationships between the human body and the realms of crystals and minerals. The intriguing research on the liquid crystal within the body, the research showing the emission of light by DNA, the now-large body of research on the thinking, feeling and capacity of consciousness exhibited by the heart, and the coherence of this body of research with some of the stones described in this book all make an important bridge between science, body, consciousness and world. The key dimension is the connection made between the research and the properties of stones such as the various forms of Azeztulite (with their relation to the "Nameless Light") and Moldavite and Rosophia (with their intimate connections to the heart and the imagination of a world-of-the-future, which is here now).

The most significant aspect of scientific discoveries reported by our author is his interpretation of the research that provides a feeling for how it is possible for the human body to perceive emanations of power from crystals and minerals. Simmons intuits an age-old truth concerning any kind or form of knowing: we cannot know anything of the outer world except through the existence of the known, in some form, as it exists within us. For example, we can see because the eye not only receives the light, but because a subtle form of light, etheric light, is emitted by the eye itself. We see not only because light comes into the eye, but because light goes out to meet the light. Something of this same sort applies to being able to sense the currents of stones. We feel the substantial qualities of stones, Simmons shows, because of the liquid crystal dimension of the human body. This research is significant in the context of this writing because Simmons has entered into a dimension of non-duality with the spiritual quality of "blessing." That same region of overlap, the process that exists between ourselves and the stone—not coming from here alone, not coming from there alone—Simmons is convinced should show up in the findings of science; and he found it with what is being called the "Liquid Crystal Body Matrix." The crystal within resonates with the crystal without, in the overlap of vibrations. Thus, we enter an entirely different kind of spirituality—one that does not separate spirit and matter. It is a spirituality that matches the very essence of stones as simultaneously spirit and matter, and of the human body partaking of that same unity.

In the research into scientific "evidence" for how crystals could possibly affect the human being, we have more than a search for verification from the present-day arbiter of what counts as real. One more link is provided that prevents such a hasty conclusion. That link is Simmons' report of research showing that meditative practices induce long-term changes in the body. This research provides the needed vision that allows us the insight that crystals do not only affect the body; working meditatively with crystals can elevate the vibratory qualities of the body to a higher state of coherence matching that of certain stones.

"To what end?" you may be asking. And you may be thinking, "I want to get something from crystals; I don't want to become a crystal." This is the point at which you are challenged to inwardly separate using crystals for your purposes only and crossing a threshold to enter into dimensions that are beyond our personal selves and are our deep soul and spirit participation with the Earth and the Cosmos and its intentions. Work with stones, though, is not quite such an either/or proposition; it is a matter of seeing and feeling that even when we utilize stones for our own purposes, the currents—because they occur "between"— are also world-shaping.

It is perfectly possible to read and derive much from this book without entering these very deep dimensions. An invitation, not a demand, is issued. There is plenty, heaps, loads in this book for those who have and are quite satisfied with a bit less serious relationship with stones. In fact, some may need to stay with simply experiencing the stones for a good long while. The time to enter these deeper dimensions will be felt as an inner pull. This is not a book designed for a one-time reading, but rather one of those rare writings that changes each time you read it, encompassing a great deal and existing simultaneously on different levels.

A number of sections in this book refer to and describe meditative practices that center in the region of the heart, while emphasizing the centrality of the heart rather than the mind in working with many of the stones of the new consciousness. The qualities occurring "between" the one working with stones and the stones themselves—the region of overlap—can only be recognized from within heart-consciousness. This locus also provides further clarity concerning exactly what is meant by "new consciousness." Simmons' heart approach is congruent with the research of Joseph Chilton Pearce, as well as the meditative heart practices of the School of Spiritual Psychology and the Heartmath organization. Working with stones, particularly those listed in the Stones section of this volume not only assist one in developing capacities of heart-consciousness but also strongly suggest that the new consciousness is heart-consciousness.

Heart-consciousness first entails feeling. Feeling, not emotion. Feeling belongs to the heart and is the heart's capacity to, in effect, go beyond itself and come into connection—with anything, anywhere— and it is a form of knowing unlike any other kind of knowing. Thus, the word *feeling* is understood in exactly the way it functions as a word: a reaching-out to touch another, to feel the immediate presence of another, even when the other may be at a far distance or may be a spiritual being. Feeling is an act, just as when I reach out my hand and feel/touch the presence of another person. It is not an emotional reaction. The outer boundaries of the feeling heart are unknown. The new consciousness is not space- and time-bound. In addition, heart-consciousness is inherently creative consciousness. In the overlap that exists between the one working with a stone and the stone itself—a region that exists for the heart prior to the separation between the person and the stone—a particular and new mode of consciousness can be experienced, a mode of consciousness with its own laws. For example, the laws of cause-effect are suspended and we enter the lawfulness of simultaneity, instantaneity and synchronicity.

While this kind of creative consciousness is new to most if not all of us, it has its precedents. The Grail myth is one such precedent, and the integral practices of Sri Aurobindo and the Mother are another. Our author delves into both of these sources to amplify the creative nature of the new consciousness. How heart creates is somewhat different from how we typically understand creativity. We generally take "creativity" to mean that we produce something out of our imagination, something not pre-thought but more spontaneous and unknown. Heart-consciousness works like this too—with one great and wonderful addition: we are completely conscious within the process of the creating. Working with stones, Simmons shows, can enhance and further develop this new kind of creativity, not only for us individually but as something that can be brought into the world.

In this book the word *heart* most often refers to the organ of the heart. When "heart chakra" is intended, that term is always specified. Something exquisitely interesting happens when the capacity to enter into heart-consciousness is developed. We are fully conscious, and fully ourselves—in fact, we are ourselves in the way we are spiritually intended to be. We are our true "I." In ordinary and usual consciousness, our sense of "I" is that of a "me"—a me that is distinct and separate from others and from the world, and is completely oriented toward its own interests and survival. When we are within the heart, we are uniquely "us," and we also recognize from within, as a kind of moment of oscillation, that others are (like us) completely unique, and yet we are not separated from them but rather in intimate union with them. Others are as intimately with us as our jugular vein. And the world, too, as well as the Earth and the spiritual worlds, from within the heart, are uniquely themselves while at the same time a perfect unity of ourselves and these others exists. Both are coming into existence at each moment. This is the new consciousness. The Grail stories tell us the path of Parsifal toward this new way of being. Sri Aurobindo, the Mother and the creative telling of their story and furthering of it by Satprem give us a picture of a mighty exploration of this creative domain. Robert Simmons shows how working with stones can help develop and intensify the creative capacities of the new consciousness of the heart.

The heart that is the center of heart-consciousness is and is not the physiological organ of the heart: a conundrum for the mind, for sure. An analogy may help. Imagine a being whose lower part lives and is immersed in the water, and whose upper part lives within the air and earth environment. Further, imagine that the part living below the water is solid, substance, physical, while the part that lives above, in the air, is also of substance but diaphanous, subtle and visible only to those who have undergone a practice to see in new ways. This unity is a kind of picture of the heart and of heart-consciousness described in this book. The heart spoken of in this writing is the physical heart, which is also simultaneously a spiritual organ of perception that can, in its own ways, feelingly think and feelingly will.

This kind of soul, spirit and matter unity also characterizes the Light Body that working with stones can assist in building up. Heart-consciousness reconfigures the body into the Light Body. A human potential begins to be an actuality through stone assistance. With the Light Body, it becomes possible to perceive the Light Body of the Earth and to see that Earth herself is in a process of evolution, of spiritual evolution that is intimately interwoven with the spiritual evolution of the human being. One cannot occur without the other, as this writing confirms.

Simmons gives a very detailed meditative stone practice for experiencing the Light Body, a practice consisting of a stone layout on the body. It is an amazing practice utilizing the most important stones of the new consciousness. Such stone layouts are often utilized for healing; here it is used for body transfiguration. When done, no intellectual questions concerning the nature of the Light Body will remain. Experience resolves the inevitable doubting of the mind. It also resolves the doubting of the cells of the body themselves.

One of the most fascinating sections of this book, a point of intensification of the whole of the book, concerns the new consciousness and immortality. The word is terribly confusing and makes us think either of angels or Frankenstein. The thought that working with stones might result in immortality could well bring you to a heavy pause in reading. Immortality should not be approached as a mental question. Our mentality is not up to it. Experience the stone layout for the Light Body. Within the consciousness of that layout there is simply the absence of being a transient organism. Something bodily occurs, and this occurrence is not the result of a dimming of consciousness into a trance state or a suggestive state, or a delirious state of ecstasy. The change occurs in the opposite direction. We find ourselves more intensely as well as more widely conscious, more vividly present, more here than ever, and it is immediately inwardly given that being a Light Body is our true nature.

Why does this state not persist? Is it due to the habit-nature of the cells, as Simmons suggests based upon the research of the Mother? Perhaps. Habit is our way of inhabiting the past every moment instead of living within the coming-to-be. Habit is the abode of security, one that we cannot simply discard, as it is deeply inscribed into every dimension of our being. It would seem, then, that with every movement into the unknown we are condemned to meet only a version of what we have already been. The way through this enclosure formed the central research of the Mother in India (with somewhat mixed results). Now, with this new work with stones, the question has been reopened.

In order to enter the question of immortality from the point of view framed by Robert Simmons, and in order to enter it not cautiously but rightly, it is important to notice and inwardly work with the sections of this writing having to do with the Soul of the World, She who in the esoteric tradition is called Sophia. Simmons has done an amazing job of interweaving science and spiritual practice. In addition, he skillfully incorporates the necessary dimension of soul. Soul concerns interiority as it exists individually but also as the interior animating dimension of everything. The reason why it is not yet possible to enter into the Body of Light and for it to persist is that the cosmic and personal dimensions of soul can and do separate from its (better said, Her) unity with spirit. It is a necessary and nonetheless tragic separation, one that theologies of the spirit have pondered endlessly. Through soul separating from its unity with spirit (for example, the Gnostic myth of the fall of Sophia tells this story), longing for spirit becomes unfilled desire that holds fast to past experiences, either to avoid future difficult and painful experiences or to try to endlessly savor the pleasurable ones. At the same time, soul gives the gift of experiencing interiority, along with the dimension of freedom. If we were only spirit, our spiritual practices would make us into automatons of the good. Much existing work with crystals would in fact unwittingly make us into such automatons who, having this or that crystal, are magically transformed into our higher selves. The pinnacle of the innumerable contributions of Robert Simmons in these pages is to be found in his artful inclusion of the soul dimensions and stories of the World Soul and Sophia in a work of spiritual meditation with stones.

Working with stones by way of the many practices detailed in this book, particularly always starting such practices with the one titled "Heart Alignment," will ensure that a reorientation of the soul toward the spirit occurs with every occasion of working with stones. Such work changes desire that is only personal and often disguised as selfless (when it is actually self-centered) into longing. The shift from desire into longing alleviates the press of feeling that we have to get something for ourselves, for the "me" in this work with crystals and minerals. As long as spiritual work with stones is "me"-centered, it can be of no real assistance to the needs of the world, though it may assist our conceptions of what we might think the world needs. Spirit is always impulsive. It explodes out, tries to get to the goal without going through the thickness of the world. The Grail story tells of the dangers of the manic spirit and the necessary detour through the world's interiority in order to arrive at the goal, the Grail, which is immortality properly understood. By "properly understood" I mean that it is not literalized immortality as spirit without soul would conceive of it, and neither is it bound to the desire for immortality as soul would conceive of it without spirit. Parsifal, the main character of the Grail story, is a name that means "through the middle"; the "middle" resonates with the place of the heart as the middle between mind and will, thinking and doing, and it also resonates as the path through the thickness of the interiority of the world, between the mania of the heights and the depression of the depths. Following the trail of what a true sense of immortality might mean and the role of stones in coming to such an experience is one of the most exiting aspects of what Robert has given us.

If you begin to find an inner feeling of mania while you read, then slow down—the soul quality of the writing is being missed. The soul quality occurs between the words, and in the gulps and pauses, and in the seemingly irresolvable questions, and in the holding of the whole of this writing in its unity. In the many practices described, a very special soul dimension is to be discovered; when you enter into it you enter into the nameless, so it is mostly without words and close to impossible to describe.

Sophia is certainly mentioned, many times, in this writing and in relation to this concrete experience of intimations of immortality. It is not so easy, though, to have a real sense of the Sophia, and even more difficult to enter into relationship with her. There is a tendency to place her among the goddesses, to make a cult of her. Such inclinations are radical misdirections, for she is the source of all the goddesses without herself being a goddess alongside them. It is as much of a mistake to think of her as a Goddess as it is to think of God as a old man with a beard; that is, she cannot be personified, though she is the source of all personifications of spiritual and soul beings. Perhaps a brief picture will help. This picture comes from the visionary spirituality of Jacob Boehme, whom I mentioned before.

A central aspect of Boehme's visionary state concerned the moment of creation. It is a moment that is happening all the time, not some time in the distant past. He first describes God as the Simultaneity of pure interiority and all-concentration and as pure expansiveness: concentration inward and expansion outward, simultaneously. This simultaneity, however, creates nothing. It becomes only a vortex of motion, for a vortex is precisely this same simultaneity, now in a form approaching creating but not in itself able to create anything. And, within this vortex of concentration and expansion exists desire and imagination. It is not an empty void. Boehme includes nature within the deity. An incredible move. But, God is only potential, there is no created, only creating, which by itself is only potential. There is another element present. It is described by Boehme as a kind of Mirroring—a vast Mirroring, as vast and without end as the creating vortex itself. This Mirroring is Pure Receptivity; it is Sophia, Wisdom, who by Her active radical receptivity brings about the patterning of all of the created. Upon "seeing" the presence of Sophia, She who is present from the beginning, a lightning flash of untold proportions happens (today we call this the Big Bang), and creation takes place. As creation takes place, however, the Soul of the World, Sophia, becomes detached from its original unity with the One. This process of increasing detachment is called the Aeons by the Gnostic tradition. It is, in the words of the Russian Sophiologist, Bulgagov, the task of the divine humanity to reorient individual and World Soul toward the spirit. When we are within the heart we are within our divine humanity.

Robert Simmons intuits—that is, inhabits—the very essence of this myth, this truth that never happened but is always happening. His devotion to Soul, and to the Soul of the World, will not allow him to put forth a theory of crystals, of stones, that manically flies off to a projected goal, leaving the whole of the world behind and unrecognized in its soul being. His devotion to Soul, further, will not allow him to bypass the meaning of his night dreams, soul's language, as informative of the way of stones, nor does he bypass the details of what he experiences, felt interiorly. It is this devotion to Soul that leads him to the heart and makes the heart the leader of this new discipline, this new path, this new consciousness.

Large portions of this book are dedicated to describing practices with stones, various "tools" for working with stones, how stones heal, and the vital compendium of stones of the new consciousness. These chapters are integral with the whole of the book, and letting this writing live deeply within the soul means being able to integrate these sections within the fullness of the context of the book. They are as much a part of the thinking of the whole as the thinking chapters are aspects of the doing. It is helpful, for example, to do some of the practices and then go back and read sections of the book that might have at first seemed abstract. Those sections change considerably once experience with the stones takes place.

The compendium of stones of the new consciousness, the descriptions of what the stones facilitate and the descriptions by Simmons of his experiences with the stones are invaluable. For example, the descriptions are written in such a manner that we are led into being able to notice things beyond what strikes us in our usual consciousness as important—that is, beyond our personal desires. He speaks very specifically of the flow of felt-currents through the body. These felt-currents differ in quality and form of movement for different stones. Noticing these currents gradually awakens body-awareness.

Development of the new consciousness demands awakening to body-awareness. Body awareness is something very different than awareness of our body. The latter takes our body to be the material, physical, physiological, anatomical thing—perhaps with meridians and chakras inserted which we can, through practice, become aware of. That is old consciousness. It is our ingrained thoughts and ideas about the body that are then filled in, mostly in illusory ways, by what we might experience with stone meditations. We find the way out of that constructed view of the body into immediate body-awareness, first by being able to notice body sensations in conjunction with stone meditations. More importantly, transformations of body are occurring with the stone practices, and the "trails" of those invisible transformations are what can be experienced in body-awareness. The various currents do not "mean" anything; that is, they are really not intended to be interpreted as meaning something other than what they are—the flow of forces through the body that are loosening, transforming, subtlizing body, changing body from an abstract noun we live and have no real connection with except through sympathizing with our desires and having antipathy for what we don't like, into the continual creative act of bodying. Instead of carrying around something like an anatomical corpse, filling it with either abstractions or lofty ideals, we begin to feel the complete unity of body, soul, and spirit. The differences of our trinity of being are differences of function, not differences of being. We are one, unified, unfinished, always bodily unfolding, feeling interiority within the folds of our flesh; and we are living substance on the way to becoming consciously spiritualized, but never disembodied.

A further and crucial dimension of working with the particular stones listed in the compendium concerns the loosening of the habits of the cells of the body and the reorientation of soul from the desire to satisfy the "me" to the longing for the divine characterizing the creative "I"—a longing that includes world-longing and Earth-longing to be, once again, included within the Whole of creation rather than separated off for utilitarian use and pleasure. Working with the stones, feeling their working on you bodily, is a process of catharsis. Catharsis means purification, the purification of the soul, the shifting of soul from darkness to luminous darkness. There is no opposition here between the Light and the Dark. Rather, there is the realization that there are two kinds of darkness. There is the abysmal darkness, darkness without the eternal Light, where we know who we are only in the smallest sense of ourselves, given through the turbulence of our desires and their satisfaction and the fleeing from unpleasantness. That is living in the dark. Then, there is another kind of dark, the kind we enter through working with the stones of the new consciousness. This is illuminated or luminous darkness—the Light beyond the Light is the way the esoteric Sufi tradition described this lighted darkness.

The purpose of this writing is to invite us into a process without end. A new way of living. There are other ways to enter into this process, but they are often tortuously difficult or filled even more with personal intentions than we have to confront when working with stones. For, with stones, we have the Silence of the stones that meets and beckons us—something that, by its very nature, removes us some from our own inner chatter and takes us out and beyond our usual selves. We need give only the slightest attention to a stone and we find the Silence, the deepest Silence imaginable, which is the entry into a new world. If we had to achieve this Silence on our own, we would almost immediately convert it into something that we want for ourselves, blessed solitude. But the stones, well, they are everywhere, and they are in and of the world, the Silent spiritual world of matter, the very matrix of our being. This matter is not the same matter known by physics. The last time such holy matter was known was during the time of the Vedas. Now, it is being rediscovered with this work with stones.

Just quietly holding one of the stones of the new consciousness puts us into resonance with the Truth. The Truth, though, is not something that one has and can possess. For example, in experiencing the Body of Light through the assistance of stones, if one takes the experience of the Light Body as an illumined body, there was not sufficient and careful enough attention and one might feel that, at last, one has the Truth of the Light Body. One has not actually become the Light Body but has instead identified with one's thought of the Light Body. The actual Light Body concerns the much more invisible experience of the source of the Lighting, physically embodied, rather than what is lit up—a vast difference, and one that the stones themselves direct us toward if we but attend to them.

There are many and multiple ways of working with stones. A list of those ways is given in one of the chapters—wearing them, meditation, shamanic journeying, receiving messages, body layouts, healing grids, crystal acupuncture, and many other practices. It is crucial, however, to know that working with crystals not only provides information but shapes the information provided. These methods may or may not result in an entry into the new consciousness, because the methods themselves shape what one is able to experience. For example, the shamanic world, real and powerful in its own right, is something very different than the world one enters through the heart. It is not a matter of excluding one in favor of another. Simmons displays a wonderfully open eclecticism at the very same time that he tries with all his might to orient us toward the magnificence of a particular direction. Active engagement, though, is first, and anything that will bring that about opens the possibility of finding this path that is particularly suited to this stage of the evolution of consciousness, the stage Rudolf Steiner spoke of as the age of the spiritual soul. And this path is suited to the mighty challenges and tasks of this time.

Robert Simmons's journey, remember, begins with Moldavite and then continues with Azeztulite. Rosophia is a stone of particular heart significance These are perhaps the prototypal stones of the new consciousness, with the rest serving as necessary reflectors, aspects of development, cleansing, healing, clearing and purification, in the particular ways needed for what is coming into being in the world—the entry of humanity into the guidance of the Feminine. The chapter on Azeztulite and its connection with the Great Central Sun points to this very significance. The Great Central Sun is a reference to the center of our galaxy. On December, 21, 2012, the Earth will line up with the Sun and the center of the galaxy. In ancient Egypt the center of the galaxy was called Isis, the one who is also called Sophia. The Sun is the son of Isis and Osiris, Horus. A temple inscription has her saying: *"I, Isis, am all that has been, that is, or shall be. The fruit that I have brought forth is the Sun."* And the Earth is us.

The Great Central Sun has been occluded for centuries and is thus esoterically known as the Black Sun, the Sun behind the Sun; or Sophia is known as the Black Madonna. The center of our galaxy shines a thousand times brighter than any other part of the galactic body, yet this presence lies hidden to our view. It is not likely that on December, 21,

2012, the center of the galaxy will suddenly become visible. The moment marks the entry into the new time of the Feminine. Robert Simmons says that in a microcosmic way, Azeztulite is the stone of the Great Central Sun. The alignment begins the process of Her continual giving birth to a new consciousness, a new body and a new Earth. She may have prepared the way by installing this new stone, Azeztulite, into the Earth.

By being in alignment inwardly with our perfect nature (the Sun of the heart), and by surrendering our usual earthly ego to the heart, we come into connection with the purified spiritual Soul (the purified individual soul and the Soul of the World). The alignment of 2012 will be a new resonance of the human being, the resonance of the spiritual human being, who is humanity in a new form, something entirely different than human beings who do spiritual things. We begin our working partnership with the gods, or we could begin it at that time. The latter part of this book with its essays on the stones—their qualities and properties when worked with inwardly—is a training manual for learning the ways of this new, conscious partnership in the work of creating.

It is utterly amazing how Robert Simmons has been working these many years, intuitively and yet with great knowledge and even greater persistence, to prepare us for this moment. True originality and genius operates like that. It is not a matter of pre-knowledge and then working out the details. It is working totally from the pull of the heart, each trial, each practice discovered, revealing a little more. Proceeding in this manner is certainly something more than trial and error. Only a true friend of Sophia would be able to follow such a path so tirelessly. Robert Simmons, we are filled with gratitude that you have so honored this friendship!

AN INTERSTITIAL WORD

Lee Nichol

In the two introductions that follow, for Joseph Chilton Pearce's Strange Loops and Gestures of Creation *and for Jake Tan's* Healing Ourselves from Medicine, *Robert Sardello teases out primary threads from each of these works and reweaves them in ways that shed new, sometimes startling light on the primary works themselves. Like the best literary criticism—though this is not his design—Sardello surfaces meanings that the original authors themselves may have only peripherally intended, but which are clearly implicit in the original writings.*

There is one word for the tone Sardello expresses toward the Pearce material—exuberance. It is clear that he is thrilled by what Joe Pearce has written. This excitement very likely arises from the sense of constant possibility that is marbled throughout Pearce's book. While Pearce's gaze is unflinching with regard to the density of the socio-spiritual malaise that currently besets post-industrial Western culture, it is his vision of human spiritual freedom, of what we can become, of the future-as-possibility, that defines Strange Loops. *Sardello points to "the mirroring activity of fact and possibility, the given and the potentia, the mind and the heart, the pre-frontal cortex of creativity and the foundation of mid- and hind-brain, limits and evolution," as the polar dynamisms that animate Pearce's vision. Here Sardello hints at the terrain in which "strange loops," with their acausal, nonlinear transformations of mind/ matter, arise and unfold. Heady territory, indeed.*

And yet, it is in the "thick of the world," at the kitchen-sink level, that we must seek out our spiritual nature. To do so, we must "hold to the small act of the freedom of noticing," our innate capacity for spiritual attention to the inward and outward flow of experience, including attunement to the heart's mode of knowing. Science itself seems to be confirming the unexpected role the heart plays in our apprehension of and participation in the living world. Fine, says Sardello, by all means proceed with such science, wherever and whenever possible. But beware the "anything is possible" variety of science, the one that implicitly tells us that because we can do something, we therefore should do it. And beware as well the science in which data stands in for, then replaces, our capacity for living knowledge.

Inwardly then, as readers, we find a complementarity, the general levity of Sardello's writing being counterposed with a certain measure of caution, of gravity.

This sense of gravity, or, perhaps more precisely, sobriety, infuses Sardello's engagement with Jake Tan's remarkable Healing Ourselves from Medicine: How Anthroposophy Can Save Your Life. Here, we are very much in that "thick of the world," face to face with disease and malaise, both spiritual and physical. Sardello takes up this challenge directly, eschewing any easy way out. We are these diseases, and the sooner we come to terms with this, the sooner we have real prospects of sustainable healing, outside the fragmented paradigm of modern medicine.

The urgency with which Sardello addresses Jake Tan's concerns arises in part from immediate, non-theoretical circumstances; twice, during the period of this writing, he was taken into illnesses of his own. Illness, recovery, illness again. So, when he speaks of the necessity for transforming through illness, for allowing it to fundamentally change you—and when you feel this viscerally as you read—you can be sure that this is a view from within. It is just this transformative possibility that Sardello means when he speaks of "open-system medicine," in which "all of life reveals itself," health and illness are not enemies, and we have the very real prospect of once again knowing healing as an art, "with the incredibly exciting prospect that we can become the artists!" Here then, yet another inversion, in which the genuine seriousness of *facing our illnesses is balanced by enthusiasm for what can happen when we do so.*

Indeed it is these very inversions, this dancing to and fro with apparent opposites—gravity and levity, exhuberence and sobriety, sky and earth, sacred and profane—that characterize much of Robert Sardello's work, as writer, as teacher, as friend

22

Strange Loops and Gestures of Creation

Joseph Chilton Pearce

This book is a many-leveled, polysymphonic writing on the human spirit that can be heard on one level, or many intertwining levels simultaneously. I hope to alert you to a reading style that allows the sentences to resonate within your bodily being, wherein the book has the power to heal our disturbed brains. When Joe Pearce writes that the child's most important inner directive is to maintain contact with his or her caretaker or nurturing one, and explore the world out there, he speaks to deep and forgotten recesses of the soul. We can hear a resonance going beyond those who nurtured us initially, and open again to a full soul contact with an all-nurturing Source.

The first half of this book shows how imbued we all are with the pathologies of our present day, and just noticing and becoming aware of these pathologies can be a marked advance for us. To notice, for example, how we are continually beset with subtle contradictions in social directives, such as, "Good job, hope you can keep it up." Such everyday happenings are usually passed by, but one begins to sense the contradictory opening up and cramping in of the body that ensues. Or becoming aware that our attention is constantly split in dozens of different directions through habits so ingrained they seem part of the inbuilt wiring of the brain, pathologies that are given top value in our "multitasking" world. Or to become aware of and notice our constant anxiety, defensiveness, and underlying fears amid the equal offerings of ways to medicate or drug them away.

A small dimension of freedom and creativity still exists for us, seated in the prefrontal cortex of our brain, but unnoticed in the ever-present pull toward the fear- and survival-centered lower brain. Just noticing, becoming aware of our capacity for noticing itself, we find such capacity within us existing in perfect calm, a center that can reestablish coherence, an inner body harmony with the widest spiritual reaches, though typically overpowered by the negative commands of a culture of fear. Just holding to the small act of the freedom to notice, to become aware, will show, as your reading proceeds, not only what is at stake in doing so, but how this awareness can intensify and increase in resonance.

Such noticing is quite different from a self-therapeutic psychology. This noticing is of a spiritual nature based in the capacity of attention, an intention that can be very focused and yet diffused at the same time— we might say "here within" and "wide open" simultaneously.

This book addresses not just the severely critical concerns of our culture and time, but points toward our capacity and wisdom to go through the "thick of the world" and discover that right here, in the midst of chaos, is where Spirit is to be recovered. This thankfully spares us the wispy sort of spirituality that abandons the world for some supposed heights of the ecstatic. Indeed, most spirituality is not only other-world oriented, it is anti-"this world"—an escapist spirituality that opens the door for the very abuses that validate our destructive culture.

So to really see what is going on in the chaotic conglomerate of culture, one has to swim in it with acute awareness and be able to recover, by deep searching and sifting for the spiritual elements present, those which provide a reorientation from within. This project, it seems to me, is the essence of the tactic taken by this book. It comes, perhaps, from the wisdom of a life that never made the false split of spirit and world in the first place.

This may sound heavy, but no self-sacrifice or heaviness is involved in the spiritual endeavor this author has followed for decades. Rather, it comes with the insight of the spiritual nature of play—awareness that when one truly plays, one is also being played with in loving care by the spiritual Source. Free of the cultural pressures of competition with its winners and losers, here is the invitation to enter into that true play always at hand, on every level.

The whole sense of this writing originates in and expresses the intelligence of the heart, so different than a book out of the intellect in our head. *Strange Loops and Gestures of Creation* is in no way written sterilely from the spectator point of view, even as the research drawn on often is. As you read, you will feel taken into a world where everything resonates within your body, your consciousness, your soul and spiritual awareness.

The central insight of this book—developed in many and varied ways—is the "looping" activity of fact and possibility, the given and the *potentia*. This looping-mirroring is a living ontological activity that, once noticed and attended, begins to awaken us from our typical hypnotic state of survival awareness and its fearful compulsions.

Although this book is essentially a spiritual writing, it does, in a certain clear sense, incorporate aspects of a materialistic science. But it turns such science inside out in a reversal of consciousness, one that can take place while reading. Sensing that almost anything seems possible to mind's creativity, technological science assumes anything it imagines can be brought about with impunity, without regard to ethics or consideration of consequence. Becoming aware of the intelligence of heart, we are compelled to operate within a new form of science that asks not just what is possible, but what is appropriate—*appropriate* to the well-being of self and Earth. Such a question does not originate in the mental realm but the spiritual, and is felt bodily, once our senses and heart are attuned. So the central part of our being that simply must be allowed to function and be attended is the heart. Once you enter into the part of this writing concerning the mysteries of the physical heart, and let that text resonate bodily, engagement with the healing of brain and mind ensues. Most writing on the heart tends toward sentimental mush having little to do with the heart, but all to do with our culturally conditioned mind using emotion to render heart as a pool of froth that cannot do anything. There is, however, on the fringes, a science that works with and for the Whole, and found here are astounding findings concerning an intelligence of the Whole as it emanates from the heart.

These findings can and are easily usurped by the cultural counterfeit of a true science, one which mirrors the actual while leaving the Spirit out, allowing science to be used as servant of the technology of the "do whatever is possible" variety, without regard for consequence. There is great subtlety in the ways our author negotiates these findings, bringing out the implications fully—that the heart is the center of true intelligence, and thinking that operates without this center (the binary, exclusionary, digital intellect) can neither apprehend, understand, or develop technologies of the Whole.

The discoveries of field-effects, such as the radiances of the heart, have been detected on a materialistic level by a counterfeit science. Blinded by our cultural trance, we miss the implication of non-local fields actually being involved with their localized expressions, as found in materialistic science. A prime example concerns the scientific findings detailed in this writing, which show the connection between the radiating field of the heart in its conjunction and resonance with the radiating resonant fields of the Earth and Sun. These findings are sound, but are based on being able to measure the electromagnetic activities of heart, Sun, and Earth. Taken for granted is that the totality of field phenomena are electromagnetic, that is, completely material. This mistaking the messenger for the message brings the blind assumption that the heart is "only physical," in spite of ages of cultures that have understood the heart as spiritual and physical simultaneously. It is an instance, found throughout present science, of taking the footprint in the snow as being its own cause, rather than the result of something unseen.

We can see the electromagnetic messenger through electromagnetic instruments, but not the message conveyed, which is of the non-material Spirit. Intellectual materialism, because it cannot see the source, discounts anything that cannot be measured. Taken into researches of the heart, this kind of thinking results in the formation of a "double" of the human—the self caught in the illusion of controlling inner, invisible processes.

This book, in tracking such findings through a bumbling science, brings a restoration of such to their true Wholeness. How the author does this is an example of "remaining connected to the source of nurturing while exploring the world." The result of such humble "method" is that the widest regions then begin to open.

Science's inability to follow this "spiritual science" may not be due to just the politics of science, but more to the conditioning we all undergo by our enculturation itself. As a culture we are caught in the throes of a massive imbalance between the dictates of our sympathetic nervous system (that automatic and natural danger-alert response of the "old brain," with its large array of attendant negative hormones and disturbances), and being unable to bathe in the restorative powers of the parasympathetic system and its balancing wholeness. Science is itself part of this culture of fear. How could it be otherwise? Scientists are not exempt from our cultural imbalances and the absence of true nurturing. They too live in the bombardment of a counter-active electromagnetic force; they too are subject to the heart-numbing force of a truncated development of self, the ultra-blind then leading the blind.

Admittedly, I have slanted this foreword by the introduction of the slippery word "spiritual." It sounds like starting with a conclusion, but is not. I would not have introduced the word if it did not appear as a phenomenon within the interstices everywhere within this book. It is, for example, not falling into materialism when the author points out that the "self" comes into physical embodiment in the "neural tube" of earliest embryonic life, which is the matrix of the developing brain, while at the same time is the source of the morphologically unfolding heart. If one is caught by a science without a Source, the true importance of such a finding slips by us and remains within the dusty annals of other scientific findings (unless someone comes along with a technology to use such findings to further the scientific illusion of control over all natural process). This brings our life into a double of itself, a split system. But by paying attention to these findings with all one's wisdom rather than intellect alone, one will hear what these findings are saying: there is an indivisible connection between heart and mind.

Hearing in this way, we can follow such findings out into the farthest reaches—not by "jumping" out there as though without a clue, but by full inner listening. We do not have to jump into hypothetical regions, but rather witness and begin to resonate with a capacity to see/feel/know the presence of the spiritual realms as integrally in resonance with the physical realms. This allows the author to say, with conviction and precision, that the self expresses the universal through the heart, and the individual aspect of things through the mind. Wow! The strange loop-mirroring phenomenon is taken to the outermost reaches. We have a way, built into our very nature, of being "here" (in this flesh) and "there" (in the spirit) at the same time—and this is the way toward restoration of the true sense of culture as an expression of creation.

Pearce keeps listening, ever deeper. If we are to find the way through the paralyzing activity of living without a nourishing presence, it is finally death that must be confronted. Not theologically or spiritually in the old sense of spiritual—that is, detached from the rich thickness and substance of the tangible world that resonates with the presence of spiritual activity. For our survival mentality and its false culture is merely trying to protect itself from the threat of death.

This work addresses just this deepest of all human questions—the unknown of death—in a most creative way by addressing the phenomenon of evolution. This phenomenon also starts the book and is an inner presence throughout the central chapters. In the final chapters the issue returns in its full significance. Bye-bye, false opposition between "creationists" and "evolutionists." Here in this book you will find a truly creative understanding of evolution, as an urge within all creation to overcome constraint and limitation as they arise. In humans, this includes death, and our crippling fear of it. The clues to this new vision of evolution are to be found in the mysteries of DNA as the bridging of matter and spirit, body and soul.

Once moving from a material to a holy science, we see how connection with the intangible can set up a powerful resonance that can bring the fulfillment of our evolution. This kind of resonance that can move matter from the invisible to the manifest, Pearce terms "crossovers." He tells numerous stories of how such crossover between the physical and non-physical has occurred with particular individuals, which leads to what might be felt as our having worked the issue to a neat and tidy point. But not so!

The real bombshell of the book is found in the manner in which the reality of Spirit is directly addressed. Though related to the phenomena of "crossovers" (as between potential and actualization), the living reality of Spirit is in a realm to itself. The living presence of Spirit in an individual, and certainly within cultures (which is in no way connected with religion or being religious), is not an issue of "wisdom-thinking" as worked through before. Resonance cannot account for the incidents of people being "infused" by Spirit. The author gives profound instances of such "Spirit-infusion," which, though moving beyond the mirroring of the strange loop category, once having occurred enter into that mirroring effect itself by intensifying the resonance of the creative within it.

So I have slightly modified my opening paragraph of this foreword by saying that much of what is talked about in the book, as the mirroring of the physical by the non-physical, still falls short of full Spirit as itself. For Spirit is not a field at all, and cannot be encompassed by the "laws" of fields and field effects. And everything that is said here concerning the strange loop-mirroring effect, as well as resonance, leads right to this door of Spirit—and I doubt that there is any other pathway that leads so clearly through the world to this door.

The question arising at this doorway is: how can we be completely, bodily open to Spirit, that we might ourselves be infused by it, yet still tend to the everyday world? No mental answers are spelled out here, but the implied koan is given throughout these pages.

23

HEALING OURSELVES FROM MEDICINE
HOW ANTHROPOSOPHY CAN SAVE YOUR LIFE

JOAQUIN G. TAN

Medicine has become one of a vast number of cultural forms that operate from the fiat assumption that all of life is a closed system. The human body is taken to be a complex relation of genetics, anatomy, neurology, and physiology, woven into a view of illness and disease as an interference in the smooth operation of an efficient civilization. This theory of the human body is now accepted as fact, carried into prominence by the support of technologies that perfectly mirror the view of body as a complex object. Centuries and centuries of understanding the body as an open system—that is, the view that body is soul is spirit, in manifold relations, and the medicine supporting that viewpoint—is, alas, strangely now called "alternative" medicine.

In a very short span of time, one that most readers have seen occur, a profession of great honor, respect, intelligence, and wisdom, combined with compassion and care, has lost its soul. We have seen medicine change into television and billboard advertising that promotes itself as belonging to the tradition of care, while also somehow successfully promoting treatments and drugs that carry with them the hugely multiplying phenomena of iatrogenesis—that is, illness caused by medicine. Still, the vast majority of people have been taken in by the persona which medical practice uses in order to maintain a false image of itself, since the very notion of health as it is currently conceived interweaves with a culture equally manipulated into being a closed system.

Those who belong to the "healing" professions inevitably begin the road to their career guided by the inspiration of a spiritual calling. They are filled with the idealism of helping and healing, and want to work with people, not with people-as-objects. Their education, however, is an initiation into viewing the body as a thing or process, as if the body, which does the viewing of the bodies of others, were not part of the circuit. This mode of consciousness is inherently oriented toward having "power-over" whatever it surveys. Such power is insatiable. When such power promotes itself as being for the "good," we are in a circuit from which it is most difficult to extricate ourselves.

A closed system is based on a mode of consciousness that looks upon a phenomenon as a mere *thing*, something "separate" and "over there"—closed in on itself, perhaps hugely complex, but not inherently in its very structure and operation anything beyond what can potentially be discovered by sensory observation and its extension through instruments. Perhaps the chief characteristic of a closed system, however, is that it views the subject of that system as a "nonrenewable resource," one that can only be fixed (when "broken") by those who have the sanctioned power and authority to do so. The moment that one walks into a medical doctor's office, the body that one lives—the body that is open to the creating currents of the cosmos—no longer belongs to that person, and one relinquishes the spiritual right to engage in any treatment that further opens body presence to the currents of wholeness. This central dimension of closed systems turns the body into an economic commodity.

Jake Tan brings a vastly larger view—a wider, broader, deeper tradition—and ways of practicing medicine in the original sense of the very meaning of the term *the art of healing*. This is the only true medicine; the rest is at best a subset of being in a healing relation with the body as inherently a structural and functional ongoing dynamic openness beyond itself, irreducible to the "only-physical." We belong, not to ourselves considered as objects, but to the mighty rhythms of the cosmos—to the movement of the Sun and the Moon through the sky, the rotation of the constellations, the motion of the planets, the rhythms of day and night, the seasons, the year, the interweaving of the elements of earth, air, fire, and water, the very motion of the Earth, and most of all, the continuing unfolding of body in time, as time.

To know the body as Jake Tan knows the body is a spiritual gift and a spiritual discipline, and requires inner development as well as external knowledge. If we want to know the body deeply, we must take it into our soul first with a feeling of humbleness, respect, and veneration; of wonder, with a mental silence. It requires that we are able to "touch" the bodily being and that we let it "touch" us. This "touch" is what produces the imaginations, inspirations, and intuitions through which the body reveals itself to us as a spiritual gift. Achieving such a mode of consciousness is impossible if we are not "transparent," if we do it with desire, with lust for knowledge, if we don't vibrate with the being of the others, if we don't empty ourselves first. Jake Tan is a model for this form of knowing as "being together with."

The central and essential gift of this book, coming from this kind of heart-relation with the body, is the gift of returning us to our bodies. Jake does this in ways that can be felt. That is, what we are given is something so deeply more than an "alternative" medicine. He takes us through the thick and difficult questions of what is actually going on in medicine, gained through years and years of concentrated research. The intention of this aspect of his writing concerns much more than trying to convince the reader that something is terribly wrong with medicine as currently practiced. When you carefully read what he has written, the body itself responds and begins to be able to feel more of its own inherent vital forces. Jake Tan fully understands the value of thinking—of real, vital, alive thinking—for thinking is central to medicine. It is medicine itself.

I want to emphasize this central dimension of "thinking as healing" with a story, one told hundreds of times a day, I am sure. I, like so many, have a dear, dear friend who was told by a doctor that he has cancer, and that he will ultimately die of this cancer. This alone stifles a most central dimension of the character of one who is supposed to be involved in the healing of others: *the will to heal*. When my friend went a different route altogether, this doctor went totally ballistic, pulling out every fear tactic to keep my friend from taking this path—in spite of the fact that my friend came to the quite natural strategy of continuing both forms of treatment. Having been inculcated with fear, there is an unavoidable confusion of thinking, which results in a very huge risk that one of the most important dimensions of healing for this person—thinking—is in danger. Knowing this person well, however, what seems to be happening is a change in the modes of his thinking—from thinking already completed thoughts to coming to the presence of the spiritual gift of thinking as it originates within his very being. In this instance, my friend seems to have the inner strength to avoid the tactic of fear put in his way so that the medical authority remains in power, and indeed, insulated from seeing his own narrowness. This inner strength came from the fact that the kind of treatment he elected to pursue does not view illness as an attack by an enemy, so fear was removed right at the outset of treatment.

Jake Tan's writing frees thinking from fear. It makes it possible to approach our own bodily being, and any illness that might beset us, without falling into fear. Unless fear is diminished, it is not possible to choose between one form of medicine and another with any inner clarity.

It is always better to develop the capacity of thinking before one has been given an annunciation by an "other" that one is going to die. And, one of the very best ways to be introduced into the art of thinking is by watching it happen, following one who is doing it, getting into that rhythm oneself. If one were to do no more than carefully read Part 1 of this book, a significant healing would take place. On the one hand, being held so skillfully by this writing brings about a significant "deprogramming," one that helps us return to ourselves. At the same time, there is the introduction to returning to the Art of Healing, with the incredibly exciting prospect that we can become the artists!

We can, through coming into conscious connection with the spiritual center of our being, heal ourselves. Many people try to do just this and simply do not have the tools to do so, and thus, when something gets hold of them—called an illness—and they have suspicions about "standard" treatment, they end up in a cauldron of possibilities with nothing to do but try one after the other in the hope of chancing upon one that will miraculously work. Thinking, of the sort that goes on in this book, is a first and terribly necessary step in returning ourselves to ourselves! Then, of course, it is necessary to try on this kind of thinking for oneself. We could never do that if we did not see it happen and if we were not invited to engage in the dance of thinking with someone as generous as Jake Tan.

A breakthrough of consciousness concerning health and illness occurs by taking in and really digesting one of the central imaginations of medicine as an open system: that illness and disease are not enemies. We now think of health and illness as opposites, and hold to the notion that, at all costs, illness is to be eradicated so that we can live in health without opposition. Open-system medicine does not so much have an alternate theory as it does the capacity to carefully observe the way the body, and indeed, all of life reveals itself—as a dynamic polarity that is always between health and illness. There is no health without illness and no illness without health. Further, the polarity sides toward the dimension of illness, for very, very important purposes.

We are not static beings, machinery to be kept in perfect order. Rather, we are, in our very being, ever changing, developing into new "selves." Often, when we wake in the morning and do not feel well, we say, "I do not feel myself this morning." Ah, that is the sign of a shift in the polarity, one that signals that we are changing, becoming someone new. That often does not feel good, and it is terribly important to have the right kind of support as we undergo such changes of body, soul, and spirit. It is terribly important that there is medicine available, that there is the art of healing, the art of "making wholeness" from this ever-shifting dynamic. Here is the very center of the "art" of healing that Jake Tan so closely adheres to: healing supports the evolving of the human being, rather than seeking to repair what is conceived as broken to a previous condition. If medicine is an "art," then there is, as with all art, a making involved. "Making" someone well concerns the skill and the genius of helping one become more, so that when the symptoms of the illness subside, the person sees the world differently, lives differently—more essentially, more truthfully, more wholly, more completely.

Medicine as a closed system simply does not have the conceptual tools to consider the human being in this way. Jake gives us such an open-system picture of the human being based in the Anthroposophy of Rudolf Steiner. Be sure and read the short biography of our author at the end of the book. You will find that he came to this view of the human being only after searching, carefully, for many years, through many approaches to human reality. He found that Anthroposophy matched what he was experiencing directly, with people with illnesses. He found that Anthroposophy is not culturally bound, and that it is exactly the kind of open system that he "knew," from practice, characterized the human body. He did not first study Anthroposophy and then apply that knowledge to the human being. Such abstraction was avoided, and for this reason, his approach to medicine is considerably more grounded than often found in anthroposophic medicine.

Open-system and closed-system ways of knowing remain separate as long as the value of each remains unrecognized by the other. While the first part of this book demonstrates the severe limits of a strictly closed-system of knowing, direct contact with the outside world is essential too for the "art of healing." Knowing within an open system requires that an elaboration of the impressions received be worked on inwardly, and that intuitive knowledge be developed from that elaboration. A fluid relation between the logic-field based in sensory impressions and the non-logic field based on inner presence, and the harmonic synthesis between these two fields, can lead to the comprehension of the living human body and its illnesses. The real aid in bringing these two modes of knowing together comes from looking at the rhythmic conception of life in harmony with the harmonies of the universe. Such a comprehensive system of knowing founds the second part of this book—how to make homeopathic remedies for ourselves.

The essential principle of homeopathic medicine is "like cures like." A substance which produces the symptoms of a given illness, when sufficiently diluted through a rhythmical process, has the power of healing the given illness—in spite of the fact that not one molecule of the substance remains after the systematic, rhythmic dilution. This way of healing was discovered by Samuel Hahnemann. Anthroposophic medicine uses this principle in formulating its medicines. Until 1910, homeopathy was the primary way of medicine in the United States. There were homeopathic medical schools, and the system was respected and accepted and acknowledged as valid. The American Medical Association turned against this way of medicine, declaring its own methodology as the only valid medicine, for it could not understand how something that has no measurable chemical in it could possibly heal even the most serious of illnesses.

It may be helpful to state an imagination of how homeopathic remedies work, complementing the description given in this writing. When we feel ill, we have the sense that something that is felt at first as a strange and intruding part of us, is taking over. It is as if a part tries to take the place of the whole. We do not feel "ourselves." This experience is the source of the fear that comes with illness, a fear that is then literalized by medicine as a closed system that sees no value in illness. If something has inculcated fear and is therefore a threat to the body, then that threat has to be removed—that is the attitude of medicine as a closed system. However, when a substance is allowed to resonate its rhythmic pattern by sensitizing a medium to the vibratory action of the substance, it does so also in relation with the wholeness of myriads of other resonances, in harmony. When a part—trying to act like the whole, and thus throwing us out of harmony—is brought into relation with the resonating whole of which it is but a part, the part again finds its rhythm within wholeness, and symptoms disappear. It is not a matter of "getting rid" of an illness. We already have all illnesses within us. As long as these potential illnesses have not lost harmony with the whole, we do not feel ill. It is not, however, the case that being out of harmony is meaningless, and it is the task of medicine to keep us in harmonic resonance with the universe. In the polarity of health-illness, it is necessary for imbalances to occur in order that the dynamic wholeness that we potentially are can continue to develop and unfold.

In working with the various homeopathic remedies listed in section 2 of this writing, it is important to refrain from taking a typical diagnostic medical attitude. Because medicalization of the body is now so complete, it often happens that other approaches to healing are placed within the view of the body as a closed system, and one takes herbs or homeopathic remedies as if they were simply another kind of drug. Taking remedies in this way is not very effective; indeed, if it works, it is really no different from a kinder standard medicine.

The descriptions of the mineral, plant, and animal remedies in this book begin with "symptom pictures." The symptom picture should be read through carefully. Not every symptom listed will be experienced, so the question arises how one should respond when there are only a few of the symptoms listed. The list is not a "checklist." One is not trying to determine how many of the symptoms one has. The symptom picture is simply read, carefully, slowly, taking it as if it were something more akin to a dream-picture. In fact, it is very good to be making an inner picture of a person, even of oneself, with all the symptoms, allowing that picture to live within one, much like waking with a very peculiar dream-image. The intent is to let the symptom picture, bodily felt, come into resonance with the "spirit" of the healing substance, the vibratory qualities of the substance.

When one takes a homeopathic remedy, it does not act like a drug. Symptoms are not covered over, and there may well not be the immediate cessation of the illness. Taking more of the remedy does not increase the dosage; more is not better. The symptoms may actually increase for a time. But, they begin to differ from simply experiencing the symptom without the remedy. It begins to be possible to notice and to track a sense of your own spiritual being beneath the symptom. It is as if something invisible and beautiful is developing within you, and you sense that the symptom is in some manner responsible for this emerging sense of a self that is new, vulnerable, waiting to become integral with the whole of your being. It is not as if you will ever reflectively know what this new sense of self "is," because it is not of the nature of something to be known. It is to be lived. Gradually, you have the sense that this particular illness was necessary to the unfolding of your destiny and your future, your true individuality.

Something more can be said concerning this felt-sense of the emerging and unfolding of the self. It is felt in the region of the heart; it is felt as intimate warmth, as if the illness was a necessary purifying of the body. As the illness works its way through, one realizes how much emotional and thought illusion one has carried concerning who one thought one was. And, one realizes that there is no direct way to get at these illusions, of which there are undoubtedly more. And, one begins to deeply appreciate the gift of illness and disease as perhaps one of the few ways to clear illusory feeling and thinking concerning oneself.

There is purity to illness. It means business, and simply sweeps through doing its work. It cares nothing of our personality, which simply gets in the way, and the stronger its resistance the stronger the illness seems to be.

There is also the other side of going through homeopathic healing, the actual bodily healing process. An astounding increase in bodily sensitivity occurs, and one experiences the actual sensation of a healing going on. It is as if the cells of the body resonate, sing, vibrate, and one recognizes the opportunity to live a different, more acute, and lively bodily existence. This new bodily life can be very hard to protect and to sustain. We now realize how harsh the present sensory world is—how much noise, absence of care, absence of a sense of nurturing goes on. To avoid being thrown right back into the sensory, emotional, cognitive chaos of stress, it becomes clear that one has to take up some kind of cultivation of the inner life. The "art of healing" is also the initiation into the inner life, or can be. The title of this book could have well been: "Medicine as a Spiritual Path."

Jake Tan has written a very multifaceted book, something like a symphony with many movements, each of incredible beauty, and if you follow the book through, step by step, more than once, you have entered medicine as a spiritual path. First, it is a book that introduces new thinking about the body, and how to think critically about current medicine. Second, it is a book with innumerable references. The references can be read on their own. You will be taken into a sense of the world of standard medicine, be able to have some sense of what lies behind it, and be introduced into the critical spirit that is always inviting us to look closely at things, and, particularly with medicine, to refrain from taking what is said without question. Then, there is the third symphonic movement of the book—the presentation, with great clarity, of a view of the human being that sees the human body as holy—not in a mystical way, but with all the precision of science, of spiritual science. The fourth movement of the book is the practical work with making remedies for healing. This part of the book can be read over and over again, slowly, as it is really something more than information; it forms the soul into coming into inner relation with the spirit, so that the true nature of medicine as the art of healing begins to dawn. A further movement of the book are the appendices to Section 1, in which the rhythmic unfolding of the development of the individual is presented. Not only does this picture help us to see that how we treat the health of our children from an early age will, in large measure, determine their future health and well-being, but the picture, as well, develops within us a living sense of the wisdom of the human being.

This is a rare and valuable book—a work of reflection, a handbook, a work of spiritual direction—and, most significantly, a book that can save your life!

24

THE MYSTERIOUS STORY OF X7
EXPLORING THE SPIRITUAL NATURE OF MATTER

ANONYMOUS

Transcribed by Anne K. Edwards

The contents of this book have been published several times, first as
an article in *Light*, the journal of the College of Psychic Studies
in London, and subsequently in two editions, one by Neville Spearman
Press in 1981 and a second by Findhorn Press in 1996. There is compelling interest in this document for several reasons. The material was
received telepathically by Anne K. Edwards, a gifted American psychic
who worked in close collaboration with Peter Caddy at Findhorn in
Scotland. Some members of the editorial board of *Light* were skeptical
about the book, while others were adamant that it was an extremely
important document for the future of humanity. The story of its origina-
tion—from a group of Russian men imprisoned for years in underground
caverns, with almost no food, no light, and the most dire and bare circumstances imaginable—inspires a deep faith in the life of the spirit.

While these factors make for a most fascinating book, the controversy
surrounding its publication has centered on the mysterious way in which
the document was given to Peter Caddy and whether or not the content
is really from people incarcerated in this manner. No one suggested that
the document is false; only that it could have come from some other
source. Kathleen Raine, for example, felt that it was a transmission from
those who had died and did not realize that indeed they were dead. All
the prevailing views are given in this present volume. A very striking
omission is that none of those who examined the document provide

help in understanding the content itself. The content has been left all these years to float "out there" without serious commentary. This introduction intends not only to right that neglect, but also to suggest that what these people experienced is indeed of critical value for the future of humanity, and even more, for the future of the Earth. Perhaps in these edgy times we are able to be more open and to listen to what these incredibly courageous people have done from a place of the heart, holding in abeyance doubt, skepticism, or need for "scientific" verification.

A Short History

I was helped a great deal in my research of Anne K. Edwards by Paul Fletcher, who is a central figure in the reorganization of the Network of Light group in England, of which Anne K. Edwards was a member. In the 1930s, the Alice Bailey writings included information on a Network of Light and Goodwill. In 1945, Anne K. Edwards met Peter Caddy in the Philippines and told him about a Network of Light meditation of about 370 groups worldwide with which she was connected. Peter began to collect her writings on the Network for a future publication that never materialized. Network of Light meditations were held at Findhorn and concentrated on connecting with "space brothers" and on preparation for an expected nuclear war. Later, in the 1960s, connections were made with Sir George Trevelyan and David Spangler, and the nature of Findhorn began to change. The central interest in extraterrestrial phenomena and telepathic connection yielded to nurturing community, including farming and creation of the renowned gardens presently cultivated there.

In the late 1970s Paul Fletcher, Sir George Trevelyan, and Eileen Caddy set up Friends of Findhorn Wales Onearth Network. This was part of an outreach effort by Findhorn, which made contact with the Northumbria Seekers and the Wessex Research Network, groups inspired by Sir George Trevelyan and not outwardly connected to Findhorn. During the 1980s there were annual Onearth Gatherings in Wales as other networks continued to grow. Decades earlier, Wellesley Tudor Pole had already founded the Silent Minute and the Chalice Well

Trust, a Glastonbury-Iona-Ireland meditation. The Lucis Trust, the organization founded by Alice Bailey, continued to develop the Triangles Meditation Network in which people in England began to meditate on a Glastonbury-Findhorn-Iona triangle.

After 1995, momentum waned, but it was rekindled in 2001 when Nigel Blair, who ran Wessex Research and Network of Light in southern England, developed a connection with Paul Fletcher in Glastonbury and helped relaunch the British network with worldwide connections in 2002. Paul corresponded with Dorothy Maclean in 2002 to 2003 to check with her, and she indicated that the forming of a purely meditative network rather than an organization with gatherings and meetings was the right thing to do. In a letter to Peter, she said: "You may have heard that in the 1960s, some years before the Findhorn Foundation came into being, Peter and Eileen Caddy, Lena Lamont and myself were in daily inward touch with what we called the Network of Light. This worldwide network had been telepathically contacted by Naomi (Anne K. Edwards), a sensitive American medium who later visited us. For a long time we contacted these groups on the inner, without any outward verification, our purpose being to send love and light to strengthen people who were "working for the Light." Peter Fletcher told me that Dorothy was also in telepathic contact with the prisoners of conscience (the group of seven Russians who had been incarcerated underground).

In 2005, Nigel Blair died, and the Wessex Research Group continued on the path of giving talks and workshops, while Paul Fletcher and five others from around England continued the Network of Light work, the basis of which is a meditation on the first of each month at 9 p.m., informed by the work of Ronald Heaver and Wellesley Tudor Pole. The Web sites for these two groups are: www.networkoflight.org and www.wessexresearchgroup.net.

Reflection on the Text

Our usual consciousness is highly mental, consisting of a fairly narrow range of vibrational activity centered in the region of the head. This range of consciousness limits us to experiencing the world as one of highly defined, separate things, seemingly of a purely material nature. This form of consciousness works reflexively in such a manner that we human beings developed the habit, now completely ingrained, of imagining, sensing, and feeling ourselves within this same limited range. Thus what we call "reality" is in fact the result of habitually imposed constrictions that have operated now for at least six centuries.

Right at the outset, we are informed in this writing that what we are about to read comes from extending this range of vibrational activity. When we are able to do so, then we experience much, much more of reality. All spiritual traditions are very aware of this fact and provide numerous contemplative and meditative means of broadening, heightening, and deepening awareness beyond mental awareness. Central to any and all of these traditions is the necessity of entering into the Silence. To do so requires stilling the mind. Imagine, now, being in an environment in which the surroundings themselves fulfilled completely the conditions that usually come about only through arduous practices—silence, darkness, the absence of sensory input, fasting—and that these are the conditions under which you live for years and years. Add, then, the factor of Grace, huge, to be sure, and something impossible to account for rationally, and we can begin to understand what happened to this group of Russians who were imprisoned underground.

What is of particular interest, though, is that their account of what spiritually happened to them is immediate, direct, descriptive, and without the framework of any one of a vast number of spiritual traditions that speak of subtle bodies, auras, psychic organization, soul, spirit, karma, destiny, or spiritual hierarchies. In this sense, we are given detailed descriptions of an initiation into being a *Contemporary*; that is, this is an initiation for the present and for the future, not out of the past. For this reason, this document is a sacred document of our time, for everyone, and it indicates what could become of the human being, how we could develop, and indeed, the utter necessity of doing so. In a profound way, these prisoners are us. We are imprisoned within the binary, digital, mental, intellectual consciousness, culminating in being tightly bound within a now completely simulated world with no way out. All previous spiritualities, given this condition, become escapist spiritualities, oriented toward becoming free of an impossible world. The result of not being able to see what is directly affecting every fiber of our being is unending ache, existential anxiety, longing, distraction, numbness, boredom, fear, rationalizations, living from the past without inspiration—all of such a magnitude that, as the guru of the contemporary situation Jean Baudrillard points out, the only breaking through available is terrorism. He presents us with the unthinkable—the only reality is terrorism. The rest is simulation.

There is another breakthrough. It is given in the contents of this book! If you are a spiritual practitioner of one sort or another, you may be tempted to place what is said in this writing within a practice you are familiar with. It takes close reading and intimate feeling to come to realize that a new form of spirituality is being described—a spirituality of radical receptivity. A spirituality of "Yes"—no matter what the conditions. This "Yes" does not signify resignation but rather begins with a receiving of what is given, taking it all into the Silence, making inner contact with an unknown dimension that has not been spoken of before, entering into the very substance of this dimension and finding it to be, when we are one with it, the creating substance for the New Human Being—and the New Earth.

The narrowness of the actual has cut off the infinity of the real. The writing speaks of making contact with the "potential Power," the *Power of Potentia*. The simulated world has reduced this irreducible Power to "energy." Energy is now a completely confused term, carrying with it a perverted understanding of Aristotle that anything actual has to come from something actual. Spiritual and metaphysical work that places "energy" at the center of all its explanations does not realize that it has fallen into line with the corporate conglomerate who, long ago, met in a congress and decided to appropriate the term *energy* as indicative of the unending movement of material progress. Thus, the true meaning of the term *energy, energia,* which means "formative force," has been appropriated by materialism to mean unending progress through material forces. The sense of the *Power of Potentia,* much more prevalent in Plato, has been lost altogether. Thus, when I hear the term *energy* showing up time and time again in classes, I don't know if people are talking about spiritual reality or gas.

The basis of this writing is contact with the *Power of Potentia.* It is the ever-present, real presence of what could be that is in union with every particle of what is. It is the presence of the "coming-into-being," of "possibility" within the actual. When these two dimensions are seen and inwardly felt as one, we have entered into the power of Love. Love is the united activity of the Power of Potentia in conjunction with the actual. If this fullness of reality is contemplated for even a short time, a new, flexible, ever-changing, dynamic framework for understanding this text will arise within. For example, within this understanding it is hardly surprising that this group of prisoners encounters the presence of Christ. Christ is the perfect union of the potentia of the human being—what the human being could become—with the actual person of Jesus. Here we have the union of Potentia-Actual, and thus a being of pure Love.

There is a foundational reality to be experienced that leads to everything that is spoken of in this writing. It is the reality of Wisdom. She is a Presence, not the capacity of our being wise. Wisdom is the spiritual Being of the interconnectedness of the Whole. When these prisoners were trapped there in the darkness, what they finally came to experience surrounding them was Wisdom. They were not separated from the nexus of the Whole, and they came to realize that their separation was only physical. The dark surrounds constituted the mental picture of where they were. In these conditions, turned inward, they contacted another reality than the mental picturing: the simultaneity of being surrounded outwardly by Wisdom, the activity of the Whole, which, when taken in, becomes Love, the simultaneity of which becomes the substance of what they speak of as sound (that is, tone) and color. Tone-color becomes the new substance, the radiance, for creating the New Human Being and the New Earth.

From within the context of Wisdom and Love, neither tone nor color can be understood to be the same thing that we mean by tone and color from within our binary mental consciousness (whereby we take them as something sensed "out there," which then affects us inwardly). Tone-color as the substance encountered by these prisoners is to be understood from within a completely non-dualistic consciousness. It is an inner, subtle quality that is simultaneously encountered in the world, but in such a way that one is completely conscious of the unity of "in here" and "out there" as a spiritual reality. Further, rather than simply registering sense qualities as we do from within our form of consciousness, the perception of these qualities by these people transformed their very bodily being.

The spirituality of receptivity is thus based in Wisdom, contacted by these prisoners through the presence of Grace, and developing such active receptivity is one of the ways to seek the new Feminine spirituality needed for this time. This spirituality proceeds completely within the realm of feeling—feeling, not emotion. "Feeling," rather than being reactive (as is emotion), is the act of the heart reaching out to touch the intangible real. This is where Grace entered and graced this group of prisoners. The reality of Feeling is exactly as the word says it is—to feel is to touch, as when we reach out and feel someone or something. To feel with the heart is the active occurrence of radical receptivity. As you read the text, be aware of the language of receptivity. The prisoners say, for example, that instead of using the usual senses of speech, hearing, and sight, they used radiance. Radiance is the activity of radical receptivity.

Within this different way of apprehending the writing, we can quite readily begin to enter into the realities that this writing addresses. These realities can be sensed only with a broadening of consciousness. We first have to silence the mind. To do so requires giving the mind something to attend to—just trying to be mentally silent, you will find, is impossible. If, however, you make an inner image of something like...floating on a clear, calm lake...within a few moments you will bodily feel as if you are in fact floating on a lake. Keep returning to that image. As you do, you will notice a remarkable relaxing not only of the body but of the brain itself, which will begin to "tingle" in relaxation. Then, enter into the Silence by feeling the presence all around your body of a quality, the quality of being lightly touched all over. This is the Presence of Wisdom. Then place your attention in the center of the heart. Don't think about being in the heart; place your attention there. Done repeatedly and regularly, this little set of practices places you in the kind of inner place that the prisoners were within. You may wonder how it is possible to do so readily and easily what took them years and years to find. They were a group of initiates. They underwent an initiation into the new spirituality of receptivity. Like all initiates—those who do something spiritually for humanity for this first time—their action enters the world and makes it possible for everyone to now do what previously was unimaginable.

The spirituality of radical receptivity based in Wisdom shifts completely the direction of the will. These initiates point out that due to the presence and centrality of self-will, we have lost the power to come into connection with Wisdom and Love. This self-centeredness now has invaded spiritual practices so that we pursue spiritual work in order to achieve something for ourselves, or we indulge the more subtle egotism of trying to achieve something for the world—a reverse of the true spiritual presence of the Will. These initiates found the way out of self-will into World-Will; not what do we want and how do we do it, but what is Wisdom unfolding within the wider world?

Within this primordial meaning of "Will," spiritual practices lead us into the unknown. We offer something, our very being, to the spiritual worlds, but we do not and cannot directly know the result. Any direct result, based on trying to get something to happen or asking for this or that, would be merely the revelation of our own egotism. Notice in the writing that wondrous things happen to these prisoners, but nowhere in the text do we see them asking for specific things or utilizing old forms of religious consciousness to try and get something to happen. In addition, they repeatedly note how all that is developing for them is for service to the world, not for self-service. This is a basic characteristic

of the spirituality of receptivity. While there are strong elements of service in many spiritual traditions, serving comes to the center of this
spirituality and radiates everywhere from within it. We come to identify
ourselves as beings-of-service, rather than human beings who serve now
and then. Serving is what identifies us as spiritual human beings rather
than human beings who do spiritual things.

The great difference between the spirituality offered here and what
we have become used to is that much, perhaps all, of what one is led
to expect from engaging in spiritual practices is released. What occurs
then is unending nourishment. While a great deal of spiritual practice is
now oriented toward "having an experience," full spiritual nourishment
makes new forms of action possible, radically new forms that may be
hard for us to accept. It may be hard to accept that spiritual currents
from the heart, released into the world as a shaping of the radiance of
tone-color, can actually do something in the world. We cannot look with
the habit of cause-effect consciousness, for through those eyes nothing
of this work can be seen. Wisdom is the Life of the Whole. Thus, when
Wisdom acts through these individuals, there are subtle reconfigura-
tions of the Whole. In addition, this reconfiguration can only be known
inwardly and bodily through a transfigurational knowing rather than an
intellectual knowing. Within this way of being, we know because we are
different. So the Whole is different. Thus, the result of this new way of
action is not easy to perceive. It unfolds rather than being intellectually
known.

How about the particular colors described by these prisoners? Deep,
deep blue is what they first sensed in their dark surrounds, and they came
to feel its presence as the quality through which all of creation is held in
form. The early editors of this document argued whether these individuals were in-body or out-of-body when describing various tone-colors,
coming down on the side of being out-of-body. That terminology itself
may come from previous kinds of spirituality. Within the spirituality of
radical receptivity, the "in" versus "out" distinction no longer makes
any sense. The revelation of the phenomena itself is what is important

because it is living and active. The "blue" as well as all the other colors are active qualities and probably should not be related to what we know as colors with our mental way of perceiving. Further, the colors such as "blue" should not be heard as nouns when you read them in the text but as verbs—the bluing, not the blue; the yellowing, not the yellow; and so on. They are qualities, active and powerful, that are simultaneously inner and outer, as is the case whenever there is the union of the Power of Potentia with the actual.

Within the Silence and the heart, contemplate the descriptions of these active/receptive qualities by inwardly naming the colors. When these colors are named within this pure-body awareness, they are no longer concepts but can be felt as powers. Each of these powers has a great range of possibility. The text, for example, points out that bluing ranges from the quality of summer expansion to that of depression (feeling blue). Thus it is not a matter of looking around inwardly—or outwardly—for something blue, not even blue "light," but of coming to be within and to feel, that is, touch, the many ongoing rhythms of "bluing, yellowing, greening."

You may feel confused when the prisoners speak of the centrality of thinking, as for example when they say that their bringing forth new substance out of the radiance of colorings is realized by the power of thought. This brings a kind of dissonance just as one is beginning to have a sense of a new form altogether—a bodily, heart, feeling, transfigurational form of knowing. "Thought" here cannot be imagined in the usual sense in which we understand thinking or thought. What we call thinking, in any case, is not really thinking at all, but rather "thoughting." It is the utilization of past thoughts, both our own and that of culture, to at best invent something that seems new but is in actuality an inventive reconfiguring of the past. Intuition and genius go beyond this, but when the prisoners say that they shape through thought, they mean, I am sure, a completely new mode of thinking that is not intellectual, not rational, not "thoughting," but a full-body force. They are thus speaking of thought as a particular patterning of the Power of Potentia as it enters into its union with the actual, resulting in the Power of possibility.

The great power and problem of language need to be noticed as we work our way through this text. What these individuals experienced has no words. They perhaps could have tried to convey their experiences poetically, a language that is itself a making. However, they had a different intention—they explicitly say that they wanted to convey what they were experiencing in ways that mental consciousness could absorb in order to communicate the findings to mass consciousness. In this manner, this new spirituality would enter into and become a part of natural existence on Earth. Once this intention is absorbed, many possible argumentative issues simply disappear. There is an inherent possibility of misunderstanding the whole text since the prisoners took upon themselves the task of speaking to mental consciousness. At the same time, there is great power in their way of working, for the language of the text is quite familiar and non-specialized. Yet, it is not possible to read this work without feeling an inner transformational power operating. That is the dilemma they chose to accept.

To stand in the truth of this document we cannot bypass the fact that it is speaking from within esoteric Christianity. They clearly said that Christ spoke with them. This fact should not be off-putting to those who read this work but are themselves centered in a different stream. The prisoners' connection with Christ is not one of religion, nor is it a connection with esoteric Christianity as it is outwardly portrayed. The connection is found in the acts involved. The overlap of the acts of these prisoners with those of Christ concerns sacrifice. It is action wholly for the sake of others. It does not mean giving up something or undergoing some kind of brutal torture. The essence of sacrifice, of making holy, is the projection of the substance of oneself for the sake of others. Here, in this document, it is clear that this is the way the prisoners creatively utilize the color-tone substance. The substance is not used to bring some specific result. It is a gifting, completely without end, a way of being which inherently lacks any sense of wanting, needing, expecting anything in return. This gift-action constitutes healing understood as the restoration of Wholeness, not an act done to take away or clear up some injured part. Something does "come back" as a response to giving creative substance to the world, and what returns is felt as a gift rather than, for example, what someone is owed. Because of this felt quality of the gift, new capacities and wonders continue to unfold. It is not a matter of accumulative knowledge and getting better at a technique. It is a matter of being able to stay within the not-knowing.

The radical nature of the spirituality entered into by these prisoners of the underground becomes most clear with their descriptions of the transformations of the Earth that occur through their projection of the tone-color substance. It is as if they have found the way into what alchemy has always known, but now they are themselves the alchemical retorts and the interior substances of those retorts, simultaneously. We also realize that alchemy was not interested in the transformation of the human being for the sake of the human being, but for the spiritual evolution of the Earth into what Henry Corbin calls the "*Terra Lucida*," the Light Earth. Just as we live in a narrowness of mental consciousness, so too the Earth lives in a narrowness of hard substance. But it too contains the seed of its own transformation when brought into conjunction with the purified human who is able to work wholly for the evolution of the Whole.

In their spiritual work with the Earth, our beloved prisoners intuitively realized that the spiritual evolution of the human being is in union with the spiritual evolution of the Earth. It is an insight that was, for example, clairvoyantly observed by Rudolf Steiner. The evolution of the Earth did not already occur, and when that was "finished," along came the human being, perhaps crawling out of the slime. Human-Earth is a single reality, and they both evolve simultaneously. It would be a misreading of the text, I think, if one feels that, well, these prisoners worked on themselves for a good long while and then decided to try out what they learned on the Earth. The action of Love does not segment itself in such a manner, either. We are of the same substance as Earth, not only physically, but in all dimensions. It is true that because the text is written in the form of usual consciousness, it may indeed seem as if these prisoners developed inwardly first and then turned their efforts to the Earth. But, feeling the text in its wholeness, we discern that the transformation of both is there from the start. The condensed state of human consciousness coincides with the condensed state of Earth consciousness, they say.

It is particularly interesting to note that in order to work with the transformation of Earth, these individuals had to work at refining their own bodies even further by refraining from coarse food. Only then did Earth open herself to them. Thus, we cannot carelessly say that the human being and the Earth are one. Rather, there is a remarkable inner coordination of development and evolution—and from this particular practice that the individuals had to undergo, we can only conclude that Earth is in fact more spiritually advanced in its natural state than the human being. It is for this reason that the prisoners had to refrain from coarse food, allowing their bodies to absorb and become more of the Light, in order to match their being with that of the Earth. It took entering into the human Light Body to enter into transformation of the Earth.

The sections of this book containing descriptions of spiritual work with the Earth are worth a lifetime of contemplation. Here, in fact, is where the spiritual work done by these prisoners offers something truly new for the future, and it is as if everything they underwent in their own transformation was a preparation for this spiritual work with the Earth. They discovered, through utilizing projections of the color-tone now directed toward the Earth, that they could "see" through the Earth, which became transparent. Rocks, minerals, crystals became fluid and transformed into new forms. The mineral content itself changed into new content. Vegetation also became fluid and transformed into instantaneous fluid growth, which could be taken in liquid form that sustained life for a long period of time. New, extraordinary crystal forms were seen to develop. It was as if the Light vibrations of the humans were combined with the Light vibrations of Earth to make Earth joyous in a newfound unity of creating consciousness.

While blueing is the tone-color that is the basis of form, yellowing is the tone-color for entering into the substance for the Earth. Those of us who do not have the capacities that these people developed can still work toward the same things they were seeing and experiencing. They were connecting with the Divine, first through Wisdom, then through Wisdom becoming Love, and tone-color as the real and actual presence of Love as transforming action. Through entering into the Silence, then into the interior of the heart, we can feel the same kind of substance as these individuals did, though at a much more subtle level. We can also work spiritually with the Earth. These prisoners discovered a yoga of the Light. Here is one practice I can suggest: By being present in a purely sensory way with the things of the world, hold the activity of mind in abeyance, and enter into consciously "gazing" at the sky or a tree or a mountain, a lake, rocks. Pick a central point on which to focus the activity of sensing. Keep your focus there, while at the same time allowing your vision to also move out toward the periphery; then gaze at the whole (center and periphery). Looking in such a way engages the heart. Following some minutes of such concentrated sensorial gazing, it's possible to close the eyes and experience the after-image; upon letting the after-image fade away, we then, in the void, feel something very similar to the tone-color substance these prisoners utilized in entering into the fluid and transparent Earth.

Our beloved prisoners entered into an advanced stage of spiritual development in which creation was put in their hands. What they lived will eventually have to be lived by everyone. For this reason, they speak of their initiation as deeply connected and oriented toward the collective realm rather than, for example, individuals who are specifically spiritually oriented. It is, of course, most likely that our collective consciousness cannot comprehend what these people went through since we are still caught in cause-effect mentality. That does not imply that the way of working described in this writing has been barred from entering the world. It is now here, now present and available. Their work has entered and mingled with the etheric currents of the human body and with the etheric currents of the Earth. When the present commodification of the world has reached its limits, we will enter into a deep experience of helplessness. After we have thrashed around, complained, blamed, and found that none of these reactions do anything at all, it will then be possible to make the turn toward inwardness. These prisoners discovered that inwardness was all around them; it is not a matter of turning away from our surroundings and going inward. It is a matter of developing the capacity to experience the inwardness of everything.

The inward interconnection of everything is the experience of Wisdom, and from there we can be on our way to the recreation of the human being and the Earth. The picture given to us by these individuals is real. Its completion is very far off, but its inception has already begun. There is always the danger of reading spiritual documents as if they are describing literal fact when they are describing real facts—that is, they are describing the real possibilities, not the literal completeness of something. The two are not the same. With the first, one expects to look around tomorrow and see clear signs of the transformations described, and if one does not see or does not have the capacities to see that indeed such transformations are going on, then there is disappointment, skepticism, and rejection. If one can "see through subtle eyes" instead of "looking-at" with literal eyes, the truth of transformation is present.

It is of the essence of being a contemporary, spiritually considered, that initiates are unnamed. Initiation, these days, can occur on the subway—and does. That these heroic individuals will never be known by name is hardly a deficit. Rather, we are able to identify immediately with them. They are us.

WAYS OF THE HEART:
ESSAYS TOWARD AN IMAGINAL PSYCHOLOGY

ROBERT D. ROMANYSHYN

There is much to praise in this book, this truly extraordinary writing. Psychology is able to breathe again because Robert Romanyshyn restores the cosmological soul dimension. That dimension can be situated within a tradition of soul best exemplified by Dante's *Divine Comedy*. There, in that greatest of all comedies, we find ourselves interpreted by the cosmos. Rather than trying to interpret our lives, actions and motives, we best understand human reality when it is placed within the harmonies, tensions and dramas of the cosmos; we find ourselves by discovering our place within these larger dimensions. We find out who we are, learn what it is to be human, enter into the soul's path of desire; we take our proper place within the dramatic action of the whole of the universe, from the depths of hell where egotism reigns supreme, to the mid-realm of purgatory where the imagination gains ascendancy, to the heights of heaven-bound consciousness, where soul lives in inspiration. While I want to be careful not to embarrass my friend by comparing him to Dante, the inspiration of these essays lies in that direction. For example, in Dante's *La Vita Nuova,* there are numerous images of *tears of the heart.* The deep and abiding loss of Beatrice motivated Dante to relinquish a long excursion into philosophy and politics to return to the poetry of desire. Robert Romanyshyn belongs to this long, honored, and mostly forgotten tradition of the weeping soul. He gives us a psychology of desire and wisely remembers the full range of desire, from longing to loss, from joy to sorrow and mourning, always locating these experiences in connection with a desiring cosmos.

Each of the essays of this book explores the intricacies of the currents of the heart, developing the vocabulary for soul's own voice rather than the speaking for soul that characterizes most psychology. Psychology always fares better and approaches its true destiny of perpetual subtlety and elusiveness when its adherents do not approach soul head on, but rather work in the interstices of several disciplines. The life of the soul in this book shines through the intersecting labyrinths of phenomenology, depth psychology, and poetry. Perhaps the most important of disciplines for this work is phenomenology because it assures that our author never falls into theorizing about the soul but is committed to letting the inner qualities of the things of the world speak for themselves. The fundamental tenant of this book is that we are here to learn to listen.

The discipline of adhering to being present to what is present also guarantees that the speaking of the heart never falls into sentimentality or poetic flourish. Like Dante, Romanyshyn is constantly concerned that the speaking of the heart never obscures the search for the truth of soul. Such adherence to the truth of soul becomes particularly important in the development of a depth psychology emphasizing embodiment. The most creative aspects of this book come together in locating soul at the meeting point of body and world. Situating psychology here requires a capacity to shape language from the substance of desire, an ability to freely feel desire without it turning into imaginative fantasy. It requires a perfect balance between the will of making, working in conjunction with a completely receptive waiting.

Romanyshyn reluctantly describes himself as a psychologist. The title of this book utilizes the term "imaginal psychology." He likes the term "metaphorician" better and the term "failed poet" perhaps the best. These terms indicate that this writing is stretching toward a new discipline for which there is still no name. While, on the one hand, it may be unsettling for a reader who comes to this book expecting direct answers to questions concerning soul life to find that immediate answers blunt the capacity to receive what one is looking for. Once the intellectual dimension of the searching settles down, great internal joy awakens as we are privileged to participate as readers with someone who has developed the capacity to be a witness to soul life. We experience a quieting of the kind of speculative knowing through distance that our author characterizes as the way of knowing that belongs to the critic.

These essays take a form conforming to the metaphoric nature of soul life. One essay nests within another and that one within yet another, each resonating with the rest. Because we are taken into the domain of desire, longing, reverie, and dream, what is being conveyed cannot be understood in the way we understand the language of abstract thought and information. You will find repetition from one essay to another, a spiral-like movement from one essay to the next. Soul loves repetition. It perceives little, subtle differences from one way of saying something to the next. Where the mind can only construe that the same thing has been said again, the soul enjoys the little difference in nuance, the different way that something is said. For example, when you have a dream that moves you, you feel a desire to tell and re-tell it. Part of the delight of soul consists in the re-telling. Notice in the essays how there are subtle but distinctive differences when a description shows up more than once, a story told again, a point reiterated. This going over things more than once is essential to the language of desire. Repetition invites daydreaming, a way for the night-dreaming soul to enter into the day world; if you find yourself drawn more toward daydreaming as a result of this book, it is indeed a successful writing.

Now that a plethora of books concerned with soul are available, it has become necessary for readers to become much more discriminating concerning what belongs and does not belong to the terrain of the soul. There are but a handful, maybe less, of writers who have developed the capacity to witness soul from within and do so consciously. Robert Romanyshyn ranks high on that short list. Mostly, books about soul are actually speculative thoughts that stand outside what is being spoken about. Very few writers are able to navigate that in-between language that speaks of the ever-present domain between spirit and matter. Most works that claim to be about soul approach the subtle without subtlety—head-on, directly, ascending to the heights with a project to get better, have more hope, more faith, do better, be better. The imaginal realms project no such goals. Their aims, as shown so well herein, have more to do with maintaining and deepening the erotic field and pushing us toward individuating within the arduous process of desire.

While Freud rightly called the dream the royal road to the soul, Robert Romanyshyn proposes reverie as the royal road to the soul of the world. Of that small handful of soul psychologists now writing, there exists a common intention to get soul out of the consulting room and into the world. Many times, even within this group, the actual doing of a world-oriented soul psychology is more of a hope, a possibility, rather than an actuality. It takes a radical departure from the soul psychology of Jung and the post-Jungians to engage the soul of the world because the methodologies were not yet worked out in that tradition. Reverie is one of the key methods that can be truly fruitful in this endeavor. It is a way of being with the actual presence of the things of the world while letting soul shine through them. The standard methods of depth psychology—dream interpretation, myth, amplification, interpretation, tend to leave what is present and seek for the soul "behind" what is present rather than within it. Reverie is a dual mode of consciousness—it is a way of being phenomenologically present to whatever reality is of interest—art, buildings, mountains, the glance between people, the endless variety of the world—while also being present to the autonomous image-character that speaks through that reality. No interpretation is involved; only the capacity to let the language of soul speak through what is at hand by developing the capacity of the witness, that ability to be present without seeking after answers, an ability also characteristic of the poet.

Reverie is completely different from fantasy. The ego is always the center of fantasy images, seeking to get some personal pleasure out of what it concocts or seeking to transcend the arduous reality of the present. Reverie dwells in the interior of the moment; it lies on the border of the subjective and the objective, letting each complete the other in order to have a glimpse of the whole and of the context of the whole as nothing short of the universe itself. Romanyshyn demonstrates over and over how in reverie we are in communion with the depth of our own existence, the existence of the world, and in communion with the dead, the angels, the spirits, and with the gods—all at once. Such multiple experiences that are nonetheless unified are possible because he has discovered that the imaginal grounds the whole of our being and that of the world and shows us how to practice the kind of inner hospitality needed to receive such a large gift.

The capacities to be developed for becoming adept at reverie are given in detail. We have to find our way into stillness and silence as objective qualities. We are asked to find and value the melancholic side of ourselves, a necessary quality needed for the humility characterizing this way of the soul. We are taught how to seek the truth at a slant and how to encounter the radical otherness of angels, angels who are far more than messengers, friends, or companions, angels who bring us into the fearful void and darkness where we can be quiet enough to hear the quiet speaking of the soul. We are shown how some streams of poetry—Rilke, certainly, but also T. S. Eliot, e. e. cummings, Keats, Yates, Kathleen Raine, to name but a few, have known and quietly promoted these ways of the soul in their poetry and thus are our best instructors.

The methods we use in investigating soul determine what we are able to find as belonging to the essence of soul. Because the method of reverie, brought by Gaston Bachelard into a legitimate mode of philosophic investigation, had not been applied to psychology, an essential element of soul life remained unspoken. Grief, mourning, loss, longing, are ways of speaking of this element. We, according to standard psychology, are supposed to get through our sorrows and return to productive life as soon as possible. For Romanyshyn these are the most valuable experiences of life because they can take us into deep memory, reverie, and hope. Do not think this is a psychology for depressives! It is a psychology that recognizes hope as the capacity to live in possibility without rushing to seek its fulfillment.

The soul, when felt through the kinds of experiences developed in this book, is like the slight undulation of air left in the wake of the movement of the wings of a bird. It takes an attunement to what can almost but not quite be seen to enter soul's domain consciously. Romanyshyn quotes Jung as saying that such a realm is like "a subtle perceptible smoke." Such stuff is imaginal psychology made of. And because it is so light—I do not mean the opposite of heavy, but rather so inwardly brilliant—the tendency is to claim this domain as the nonutterable. Maybe soul is to be experienced in silence, in ever-deepening silence.

Ah, but there is only one kind of courage that dares step from this silence and speak it into the world, and that is the therapeutic courage shown everywhere in this book. It is not a book about psychotherapy but a therapeutic way of life that allows silence to dwell in the word and thus a soul-speech. It turns out that there is not a specialized language of psychology, and when it pretends to have one the soul thankfully escapes it. The soul rests in the how of language, not in the what. This writing demonstrates that how. It is not essentially a book of information. It is one of those rarest of writings that lives as a gestural field that invites the reader to come in and rest, and in that rest find the solace of soul, fleeting though it may be.

Unfortunately, soul is a noun while its reality has no such substantiality. This psychological fact—that soul is not an entity of any kind or sort—accounts for why Romanyshyn concentrates so much on poetry as a better language model for psychology than science. Not only does poetry have the power to speak the beauty of soul, it is nearly the only way available to speak the act of making rather than the already made. Soul can be better understood as a making in its inception, in which soul is the maker, the making, and the made all at once and inseparable. Imagine the kind of discipline, then, needed to speak such an ephemeral reality. If you read this work slowly, savoring each word, not trying to read it as you would read other books, something of the wonder of this creative psychologist will begin to dawn on you. It is discipline backed by years of study, surely. And then, it is a discipline able to completely let go of those years and instead of flaunting knowledge, holds it all back. That is the discipline—one of having a lot—given through study, experience, sorrow, wanting—and then holding it all back and waiting and listening and speaking out of that inner silence.

Is imaginal psychology transferable? Can it be studied, learned, placed into textbooks and applied in the world? Yes, of course. Robert Romanyshyn has been doing exactly this, in varied forms, for the past thirty years. To be a student of such psychology requires, however, that one be more like an apprentice than a consumer of information. In order to get the meaning of this book, to really get it, the reader also has to approach it realizing that all the knowledge and prior learning one brings to this book also has to be held back and one has to apprentice oneself, not to the author, but to the reality that finds voice through this author. The reader is asked to feel the words, sentences, paragraphs, chapters, in a bodily way, as if you are engaged in a beautifully choreographed dance. Let yourself dance with this book and then you will get it.

There are two essays in this collection that at first reading may not seem to fit into the themes I have thus far mentioned. These essays, one on media and one on virtual reality, are, I think, the gems of this book. We get a glimpse of another side of Romanyshyn. He is able to see through the technological world and what it does to soul life without reacting against it. For someone so engaged with the imaginal realms, with poetry and reverie, it might seem odd that technology is seen as helping re-discover soul in the modern world. Television is presented as image-consciousness that, through bypassing literacy, invokes the sensuous, embodied, non-rational, dream-making capacities characteristic of soul. That is, television is presented as an ally to the kind of soul psychology presented here.

Virtual reality is seen as disembodying us. This technology, Romanyshyn argues, certainly takes us into an imaginal world, but a disincarnate one. At the same time, this disincarnate imaginal world is analogous to a dream world in which one is not quite sure who is in control—the dreamer or the dream. Thus, in spite of its disembodying potential, virtual reality is seen as holding the power to teach us how to be awake while dreaming.

These two essays can be seen as depicting a frame within which imaginal psychology takes place. Imaginal psychology as presented by Romanyshyn is not a nostalgic attempt to go back to what soul used to be. It is a postmodern psychology, made possible by the technological world. If television and virtual reality teach us to inhabit dream consciousness in the waking world, we do so unconsciously. That is, we now live in a dream world but do not know that is so. It is, however, only in such a world that it now becomes possible to develop the discipline of waking dream consciousness that knows imaginally what it is doing. Imaginal psychology was not possible at the time of Freud or Jung because television and virtual reality had not yet taken hold in the culture. This realization is, I think, an amazing insight. It prevents a lurking opposition between soul and technology. In addition, Romanyshyn shows us that psychology is always historical and contextual. When true to soul, this strangest of all disciplines does not make any claims to permanent knowledge. We cannot say: "this is what soul is all about, forever." We can only say that this is the kind of psychology needed to reflect how soul can live and thrive in this present world.

Coda: Love and the World, part 2

Green Man, Earth Angel

The Prophetic Tradition
and the Battle for the Soul of the World

Tom Cheetham

Tom Cheetham has written a remarkable book that has the power of shifting our way of imagining the world. This power stems from his insight into a core longing felt within the heart of human beings, a longing for wholeness that feels as if it were a memory. We imagine that there was a time, long ago, when human beings lived reverently in relation to the earth and the cosmos. We felt, so the story says, whole, in our place, with God at the center and the periphery. Then the Great Disjunction happened. Matter and Spirit were split into two isolated realms. God was removed from the world and placed in His heaven and the earth, gradually at first, and then more and more rapidly, became the great supplier of commodities, mere material substance. Different thinkers locate this disjunction at different times and due to different factors, but it is always depicted as occurring sometime in actual history, and the story says we have been on a downward course ever since. This way of imagining the unfolding of evolution always looks to the past as the better time, and all our efforts need to be focused on retrieving the sensibility of the past. The more sophisticated tellers of this story do not imagine we can return to the past, but they do feel we can return to the values of the past, or find ways of living those past values, primarily by living in relative isolation from the present world dynamics, encompassed in a shield of fear.

Cheetham's first creative contribution lies in pointing out the obvious, but it is obvious only to one who has a living inner life. The longing for wholeness is an archetypal longing. It belongs to the essence of the soul to feel such longing. It will always be there. This longing motivates us to search for the ultimate inner meaning of our existence and to at least find ways to assure we do not go off on collective tangents that depart from world destiny. When we understand that the longing originates in the soul, new ways of imagining the world have to be sought, and these new ways have to be conscious soul ways. Here lies the second and truly great contribution of this book. Cheetham recognizes that a longing of the soul has to be responded to in kind. That is, only soul can respond to soul. Only soul understands soul. If we are to ever get anywhere with this archetypal longing, we have to approach it on its own terms. A metaphysics that excludes imagination, the hallmark of soul, as a world force, is fated to painful longing without the slightest possibility of resolution. Metaphysics that has no place for the category of imaginal being splits spirit from matter with no way for them to ever be linked. Longing becomes replaced by abstract thought that turns into systems of science and technology. Materialism characterizes the other side of the split. Materialism is the outlook that says that everything in the universe can be understood in terms of the arrangement and action of purely physical forces. And, more subversively, materialism offers the notion that all longings can be quieted through material means of every sort.

Cheetham develops a method of proceeding from longing to questions of metaphysics. His method consists of making us feel deeply all that we have lost with the way reality has been split up; the loss of the imagination, the loss of living speech, words as angels, the loss of reading that speaks from within reality rather than about it, and most of all, the loss of the sense of place. He throws us into the depth of loss, the depth of despair, really. We cannot recover what we cannot feel. Cheetham's method involves a descent into hell, a necessary descent, but one that distinguishes the hell we live—the literal, surface-bound, consuming, manic world, with the fructifying descent into the darkness where we await the voices and visions of the archetypal worlds.

Cheetham progresses in his method by seeing through the split of spirit and matter, seeking to establish what a metaphysics with imagination as the forming force of the world would mean. As long as we think only in terms of spirit and matter, and its two primary manifestations in the world, religion and science, we contribute to the loss of the subtle, participative sense. An archetypal metaphysics views creation as happening every moment. All is alive. And soul is not in us; in this metaphysics, we are in soul. The implications of such a view are enormous. However, it takes more than the idea of such a metaphysics to begin discovering the ways to live such a proposed reality. And here is the third great contribution of this book. Such a metaphysics exists. The outlines of it can be found by interpreting the work of C. G. Jung in a radical way, and the further outlines of it are found in the work of Henry Corbin, the primary emphasis of this book.

Cheetham makes a long and fruitful excursion into the work of C. G. Jung as a preparation for introducing the reader into imaginal metaphysics. We have come to think of Jung as the phenomenologist of the soul. When we come to Jung's work on alchemy, however, we find that the alchemists were seeking to make spirit conscious. They were working out an imaginal metaphysics of transformation in their theorizing-visioning, and they demonstrated the practicality of this metaphysics in the practice of alchemy. Jung did not quite see them this way, but, in truth, the alchemists were attempting to free spirit from matter and were not just projecting their fantasies onto matter. Alchemy was simultaneously a transformation of self and of world into completeness. Jung reads this completeness, this wholeness, as involving the incorporation of contradictories, the light and the shadow of soul reality. Cheetham's understanding of Jung's project and the limitations of that project are brilliant. Once those limitations are clear, he is able to establish an all important bridge from Jung to the astounding work of Henry Corbin, from depth psychology that never quite made the metaphysical leap, to Islamic mysticism's fully developed imaginal metaphysics.

Central to the movement from Jung to Corbin's creative interpretation of Islamic mysticism is the difference between the darkness of the Shadow in Jung and the luminous darkness of the divine Night. In Jung there exists a throwing together of soul experience and spirit experience without really seeing that there is a decided difference. Jung's adamant commitment to soul made it impossible for him to conceive of anything outside of soul, or to plead ignorance when it came to saying what was behind archetypes. Even spirit, for Jung, is the soul's perception of spirit. One result of this limitation of Jung, a limitation that still exists in present depth psychology and even in Archetypal Psychology as put forth by James Hillman, is that spirit experiences are not recognized as such. For example, there is no recognition that there are these two darknesses—the Shadow and the luminous darkness of the divine Night. The former is a soul experience, to be integrated into consciousness for completeness, the latter a spirit experience necessary to wholeness, not only of experience, but also of the world. And without that recognition, it is really not possible to tell when one is conscious in soul and when one is conscious in spirit, and certainly, it is not possible to have any sense of the relation between the two. Hillman solves this dilemma by taking an adamant stance against spirit, as if that opposition would cancel the reality. At the same time, Hillman acknowledges a debt to Corbin for bringing forth the notion of the *Mundus Imaginalis*. Hillman interprets this as the imaginal world of the soul, saving depth psychology from sophisticated subjectivity. However, in Corbin, and even more importantly, in the Islamic sources of this term, the *Mundus Imaginalis* is the imaginal world of the spirit. The confusion wrought by interpreting spirit phenomena as soul phenomena has meant that depth psychology tends to honor the darkness of the descent into hell as if it were the realm of the holy. Depth psychology is unable to distinguish the realm of the unconscious and the realm of the superconscious. Hillman's interpretation of the *Mundus Imaginalis* is a misinterpretation. Cheetham's teasing out of all the exact quotations from Corbin that establish the clear difference between Shadow and Luminous Darkness constitutes one of the scholarly delights of this book that frees us enough from Jung to be appreciative of his efforts while reorienting the search that archetypal longing pulls us into.

While the soul realm is perceived through soul, it is more appropriate, says Cheetham, to say that the superconscious realm is perceived through the "supersensory senses." While soul is certainly an imaginal realm, the luminous darkness takes us into the imaginal world. These supersensory senses have to be prepared for through meditative disciplines that gradually bring about an alteration of our physiology, one of the effects of the meditation practices in the Islamic mystical tradition. The difference between soul sensing and supersensory sensing distinguishes the darkness of the lower soul from the Black Light, which is the Light that itself cannot be seen but which makes everything else visible. What are first visible upon entry to the imaginal world are colors, but colors without matter. These colors are the mark of entering into the realm of the *Mundus Imaginalis*. They also mark entering into the non-knowing of the heart, the perceptual organ for sensing the spiritual worlds. One of the most beautiful sections of this book describes the seven prophetic colors and their functions.

In this imaginal metaphysics, all beings and things and places are mirrors of the spiritual worlds, illuminated by the Light that makes everything else visible. We are, in effect, then, composed of the artistic play of spiritual beings. The imaginal metaphysics of Ibn 'Arabi, as interpreted by Corbin, is a fruitful gnosis that accounts for the divine worlds and for the earthly world, but does not confuse them, nor does it separate them the way we do in the Western tradition. It is a fruitful gnosticism. I say fruitful in contrast to Jung's gnosticism, which confusedly mixes soul and spirit, and never resolves the intense archetypal longing.

The gnosis outlined by Corbin is in opposition to any kind of incarnational Christianity. For the metaphysics of Ibn 'Arabi and other Islamic mystics, the incarnation of Christ is an impossibility, for it historicizes

God. Cheetham indicates that in this cosmology, to say that Christ *is* God incarnate is equivalent to saying that God is dead. The entry of God materially, wholly, and substantially into historical, material, and public time and space is the archetypal act of secularization. In the gnosis of Islamic mysticism Christ is an ever-present reality of the soul. And Christ did live but, in this gnostic imagination, he did not die on the cross. One of the most interesting sentences in this book describes an intriguing imagination of what happened to Christ. Indeed, the chapter comparing Corbin's view of Christ with the view of Christianity is a pivotal chapter in this book. Corbin speaks of Christ as a man, but also as a figure of Light—both. Christ is also the Soul of the World. This theological chapter gives a basis for approaching the world as spiritual image, populated with Presences.

The doctrine of the Incarnation in the exoteric version of Christianity collapses any sensibility of the angelic hierarchies. The angelic realms no longer have the power they once did, and that can still be found in esoteric Christianity, which is far more compatible with the view put forth by Corbin. We find this collapse evident in religion these days, which no longer has a conception of the creating power of the angelic realms. So, there is an imaginal theology accompanying, even preceding, imaginal metaphysics. This theology is founded on Beauty rather than on Salvation. Cheetham puts his finger on the key element for responding rightly to archetypal longing, and his uncovering of the senses of Beauty in the work of Corbin is stunning.

Beauty is the strength of imaginal theology, and its hope-that which holds the possibility of guiding our longing to its destination. And Beauty is the core imagination for any culture seeking this destination. Beauty is not something given but strived for through purification of soul. Beauty here is completely objective, "subjectively objective." By this term I mean that in imaginal metaphysics all dualism is resolved so that there is no longer a subject-object distinction; rather, subject and object are one. Further, Beauty is not an abstract concept but rather the theophany of Sophia. And, while Beauty is a sort of destination, She is a destination that takes us always farther into the unknowing.

The path of Beauty is epistemologically complex because it is based in non-dualism of knowing. In imaginal knowing, you know only through the aspect of the known within you. But, it must also follow that an object known, knows when it is known. Beauty is understood completely interiorly but not subjectively.

The difference between a world based in Beauty and one based in a theology of Salvation is more than an interesting comparison of two cosmologies. Cheetham shows how destructive technology is tied to Christian theology of Salvation. Drawing on the philosopher Gianni Vattimo, Cheetham shows that radical freedom is the destiny of the Christian tradition, and that such freedom makes the earth a playground of destruction. There are no longer any boundaries. The section of this book concerned with technology is fascinating in that the view of freedom coming from Vattimo's understanding of Christianity is based upon the notion that with freedom there is always the risk that a choice to make a world in harmony with the spiritual worlds does not seem to be an option. The difference between freedom and nihilism collapses. Such a view commands a great deal of reflection, for powerful elements of this view can certainly be seen in the present world in which we find wars being fought pitting these two—freedom and nihilism—against each other, which may in fact, then, be wars of self-destruction. This country's battle cry is freedom and strikes out at the apparent nihilism of terrorism. But, what if freedom, as presently politically understood, is no more than a form of nihilism?

This view of freedom without limits as nihilism is not completely accurate. Freedom is nihilism only when it is not filled, completely, with the content of love. So, to read technology as the fulfillment of the Christian tradition, and the Christian tradition as finally nihilistic in its total freedom, leaves something out. It leaves out the option of the choice of love. The difference, then, between the Christian tradition and the kind of technological world it ultimately creates, and Islamic mysticism and the kind of world it imagines, hinges on the detailed process of metamorphosis and initiation into the source of love, the Beloved, described in such detail in Islamic mysticism. Exoteric Christianity lacks a necessary angelology as a way of proceeding to the Beloved, and without such an angelology it almost certainly does lead to nihilistic freedom. The intricate and careful way Cheetham works out these concerns is truly wondrous. In particular, his section on the radical work of Archetypal psychologist Wolfgang Giegerich is invaluable.

While James Hillman takes Jung toward the direction of Corbin but never reaches the autonomy of spirit, Giegerich takes Jung toward the direction of Jung's alchemical view of spirit freed from matter, which leaves matter, and indeed the world, open to the kind of nihilism suggested by Vattimo. We have rid the world of things from their status of being the appearance of the shining of the gods and the angels, says Giegerich. And we are left with only one god, the one we have created: technology, best exemplified by the bomb. It is not, however, particular technologies Giegerich is talking about, but rather the world-creating/destroying idea of technology as how we save ourselves. The description of the intricacies of this view and how Giegerich arrives at it are worth the price of admission to this book. Giegerich's view of the incarnation, however, is based on an incapacity to imagine that God became fully human in Christ. Fully human. For Giegerich, the incarnation of God is incarnation into a different kind of flesh than the rest of humans. Flesh from above, is, in Giegerich's view, not the same as natural flesh. It is, in effect, technological flesh. The event of this "technological" flesh has ultimately meant that abstract technology is our god.

Cheetham wants to make the most difficult case possible for valuing the world and then finding how it is possible to find meaning and avenues of responding to the longing for wholeness that will not go away. It is easy and rather cheap to begin with an abstract notion of wholeness. That approach, characteristic of the New Age movement and those captured by nostalgia for a past that never was, is abstract and begins by turning away from the world as it is now. Cheetham is one of the most courageous thinkers I have ever read. He shows the very basis of the now dominant worldview, and he shows how this basis is indeed nihilistic, and as he is doing so, he also shows us the way out, which is by going through the labyrinth, not ascending to thoughts that ignore our situation of being lost in the labyrinth. The way through the nihilistic, technological world, is twofold: love, described as an initiatory process with definite and clear steps of purification and perception, and the resanctification of the world And this twofold path has, in addition, to be founded in a priority of the imaginal in order to avoid making a false dichotomy between spirit and matter.

The last section of the book concerns the word as the way out of nihilism and the way to rightly respond to archetypal longing for wholeness. The living, breathing word, not those collections of words found in the dictionary and strung together into dead sentences. Cheetham begins a reflection on the word based upon Ibn 'Arabi's view of language as the unique articulation 'of the divine Breath. Our breath, articulated, nondualistically, belonging both to us and to world, speaks human and cosmic reality simultaneously. This is poetic, creative speech, speaking without knowing in advance what one is going to say. Speaking that lives in the region of holy Silence. The excursion into spirit must always return to soul in order to be connected with sensuous reality, and it is with speech that this return continually occurs, embodying spirit without collapsing it into matter. We come, then, to a new understanding of soul, soul as the embodying process of spirit, and as the spiritualizing process of matter. These intertwining processes live together in word-breath. The world speaks and the symbols of its speaking are the breath of God. The discipline needed to hold technological destruction at bay is the capacity to read the world. This discipline requires, says Cheetham, an imaginal asceticism, an ongoing purification process that works to keep us from falling into the false desires of the present worldview and inspires courage to be fully present to what is present.

These few indications of what you will find in this book will, I hope, entice you to enter into a study of a work that certainly does not belong to the world of throwaway books. This book requires slow reading, for as you read these living words you are undergoing a transformation. At the end of reading, the world will not be the same.

SOURCES

1. *Educating with Soul*, Robert J. Sardello (Dallas: The Center for Civic Leadership, The University of Dallas, 1979).

2. *Dragonflies, Studies in Imaginal Psychology*, Robert Sardello editor (Dallas: Department of Psychology, University of Dallas, 1980).

3. *Stirrings of Culture* (1986) Robert J. Sardello, Gail Thomas, Editors, (Dallas: The Dallas Institute Publications, The Dallas Institute of Humanities and Culture, 1986).

4. *Psychoanalysis and Spiritual Psychology*, Rudolf Steiner, introduction by Robert Sardello (Hudson, NY: Anthroposophic Press, 1990). Reissued: *Freud, Jung, and Spiritual Psychology* (Hudson, NY: Anthroposophic Press, Great Barrington, MA: SteinerBooks, 2001).

5. *Jung and Steiner: The Birth of a New Psychology*, Gerhard Wehr, Foreword by Robert Sardello, translated Magda Jaekel (Hudson, NY: Anthroposophic Press, 1990).

6. *The Angels*, Robert J. Sardello, Gail Thomas, editors (Dallas: Dallas Institute of Humanities and Culture, first edition 1990).

7. *The Speech of the Grail: A Journey Toward Speaking That Heals and Transforms*, Linda Sussman, introduction by Robert Sardello (Hudson, NY: Lindisfarne Press, 1995).

8. *Sing me the Creation*, Paul Matthews, introduction Robert Sardello (Stroud, UK: Hawthorne Press 1995).

9. *Anthroposophy (A Fragment): A New Foundation for the Study of Human Nature*, Rudolf Steiner, introduction Dr. James A. Dyson, Foreword Robert Sardello (Hudson, N.Y.: Anthroposophic Press, 1996).

10. *So that You May Be One: From The Visions of Joa Bolendas*, with Essays by Robert Sardello, John Hill, and Therese Schroeder-Sheker (Hudson, NY: Lindisfarne Books, 1997).

11. *Seeking Spirit Vision: Essays on Developing Imagination*, Dennis Klocek (Fair Oaks, CA: Rudolf Steiner College Press, 1998).

12. *Conversation Amoureuse*, Jacques Lusseyran (Fair Oaks, CA: Rudolf Steiner College Press, 1998)

13. *A Psychology of Body Soul, and Spirit: Anthroposophy, Psychosophy, Pneumatosophy*, Rudolf Steiner, introduction Robert Sardello (Hudson, NY: Anthroposophic Press, 1999).

14. *Give us This Day: The Story of Prayer*, Rufus Goodwin, introduction Robert Sardello (Hudson, NY: Lindisfarne Books, 1999).

15. *The Book of Stones: Who They Are and What They Teach*, Robert Simmons and Naisha Ahsia, with contributions by Hazel Raven (Berkeley, CA: North Atlantic Books, Berkeley, California (revised edition 2007).

16. *Cooking for the Love of the World: Awakening Our Spirituality through Cooking*, Anne-Marie Fryer Wiboltt, with pencil illustrations by the author, (Benson, NC: Golden Stone Press, 2008).

17. *The Unknown Hieronymus Bosch*, Kurt Falk (Benson, NC: Goldstone Press Press, 2008).

18. *An Unknown Destiny: Terror, Psychotherapy and Modern Initiation: Readings in Nietzsche, Heidegger, and Steiner*, Michael Gruber, introduction Robert Sardello (Great Barrington, MA: Lindisfarne Books, 2008).

19. *I Connecting: The Soul's Quest*, Kristina Kaine, foreword by Robert Sardello (Benson, NC: Goldenstone Press, 2008).

20. *Healing Pandora: The Restoration of Hope and Abundance*, Gail Thomas, Benson, NC: Goldenstone Press, 2009).

21. *Stones of the new Consciousness: Healing, Awakening & Co-creating with Crystals, Mineral & Gems*, Robert Simmons, introduction Robert Sardello (East Montpelier, VT: Heaven and Earth Publishing L.L.C., 2009).

22. *Strange Loops and Gestures of Creation*, Joseph Chilton Pearce (Benson, NC: Goldenstone Press, 2010).

23. *Healing Ourselves from Medicine: How Anthroposophy Can Save Your Life* Joaquin G. Tan (Benson, NC: Goldenstone Press, 2011).

24. *The Mysterious Story of X7: Exploring the Spiritual Nature of Matter*, Anonymous, transcribed by Anne K. Edwards (Berkeley, CA: North Atlantic Books, 2011).

Coda 1: *Ways of the Heart: Essays Toward an Imaginal Psychology*, Robert D. Romanyshyn (Pittsburgh: Trivium, 2002).

Coda 2: *Green Man, Earth Angel: The Prophetic Tradition and the Battle for the Soul of the World*, Tom Cheetham (Albany, NY: SUNY, 2005).

COPYRIGHT INFORMATION

CPSIA information can be obtained at www.ICGtesting.com
Printed in the USA
BVOW071959230712

295971BV00001B/8/P